MAIN ST.
$MARTS

**Who got us into this economic mess
and how we get through it…**

Grace Ross

Printed in the United States of America

First Printing, 2010

ISBN 978-0-9834185-6-6

Grace C Ross
www.GraceRoss.net
10 Oxford St.
Worcester, MA 01609

More information on Main Street $marts is available at:
www.MainStreetSmarts.com

Cover Illustration/Design Copyright © 2010 by Joseph Bastardo
Author photograph by Robert Spencer

Contents

List of Figures

Acknowledgments

I have always wondered how people write acknowledgements. The most immediate people who helped with the many concrete aspects of a project are relatively easy to name. And mentioning those who encouraged and egged you on when you were feeling overwhelmed and ready to give up are harder to remember all of but certainly possible.

But how do you thank those whose feet you have sat at learning the meaning of your life work? And what about all who opened the door for you to a field they were experts in but you knew little about? Or those who did the more personal and vulnerable act of opening a window in on their experience, shared with you what was painful, challenging and they knew was ignored or devalued by our larger society? And even those who may have challenged you, had fights and sharp disagreements with you, may even have treated you badly, unfairly or discriminated against you, but you learned a valuable lesson in the experience?

If I acknowledge the incredible wisdom and challenges that others have shared with me to make me able to write this book, then I also have to acknowledge that I cannot thank you all. And I would risk serious dishonor of key figures I might pass over or forget.

For those who had a direct hand in the project, it is my experience that no large task happens alone — and so this could not have happened without you! Thanks to Cara Lisa Berg Powers, Sharron Tetrault, Mike Prokosch, Chris Patterson, Roxanne Reddington-Wilde, Sara Kilroy, Sandy Eaton, Amaad Rivera, Keleigh Waldner, Jason LaMountain, Kevin Ksen, Betsy Leondar-Wright, Chris Horton, Elizabeth Comparetto, Tiffiniy Cheng, Linnea Paton, Amy Grassette, Jared Cowing, Christeen Friend.

My deep gratitude to those who did the technical aspects of the book: Tony Schinella and Amy Rothstein. My tech team which gets me through so many projects (and provides much more than just technical help!): James O'Keefe, Hugh Esco, Jason King, Ida Hakim, Bruce Dixon.

Thanks to those whose special guidance was foundational to certain chapters (again I mention just a few): Elaine Bernard, Scott Harshbarger, Susan Mortimer, Martina Robinson, Felice Yeskel, Pat Baker, Noah Berger, Claire Sullivan, Russ Cohen, Aaron Tanaka, and Steve D'Agostino.

Those who encouraged me when I might otherwise have given up and are therefore of immeasurable value: Jim Henderson, Jennifer Solin, Luz Gonzalez, Gary Hicks, ChaCha Connor.

My amazing spiritual support and sister travelers: Sarai Rivera, Lucas Glenn, Ebony Barkley.

I cannot write anything without thanking those who were my mentors over the years: Richard Katz, Faith Evans, Grayland Hagler, Melvin King. Some of those whose writing informed my imagination: Audre Lorde, Kate Rushin, Alice Walker, Maya Angelou, Starhawk, Minnie Bruce Pratt. Or some of those whose lives led me to see how creating change is possible: Ella Baker, Jay Naidoo, Bayard Rustin, Harriet Tubman, Mary Ovington, Steven Biko, Mahatma Gandhi, Barbara Deming.

Those who have influenced me by loving and supporting me are surely too many to name but I have to thank just a truly tiny example of those who engaged with me most deeply to help me overcome some of my own greatest personal limitations: Jerry Koch-Gonzalez, Roberta Praeger, Janet Meyer, Vicki Woodard.

And those who sustain me through it all always and put up with all my emotional ups and downs– my chosen family: George Friday, Kelly Bates, Jim Hammerman, Estelle Coleman, Frances Brookner, Grove Harris, Robin Scott-Manna, Robin Souza and those who have slipped out of my world these days, Paula Hooper and Kathy Hager.

And while it is my mother who appears periodically through the book, it is my father's love of the world that informs why I wrote this book, ran for office and have always reached for the best I believe we can be.

And there are those, hundreds or thousands who have shared with me their personal stories — some of which show up in the book, numerous of whom I will never know your name and all of whom in little and big ways have taught me what is true in our world.

One Perspective

For me, what is practical and realistic ends up trumping ideology; I know this sometimes gets me accused of being boring.

Deeply rooted in community values and hopefully the best in American traditions, my perspective tends not to fit easy categories. On the one hand, I am uncomfortable with big government tax and spend solutions. I can be very conservative with my expectations of integrity and local being better. I believe that government has an obligation to use whatever resources it requires as efficiently as possible to the greatest benefit of all.

On the other hand, I am driven by a fundamental commitment to real democracy. The more informed people are, the more they can participate in government, the better. Full democratic participation — government by and for the people — increases how much all of our skills and perspectives are put at the service of social good; thus, we create more realistic and deeper solutions and we expand our capacity for success as a society. As a goal, representative government should be a vehicle for us, the people, to accomplish a just and peaceful society, and not be an end in and of itself.

Ignoring a deeply mangled economy is not an option. Whether it is boarded up buildings down the street and tens of thousands displaced, or friends running out of unemployment before the next job comes, statistics underscore the wide spread, collective and unacceptable nature of this economic depression. And however the pundits want to try to spin it, it is our lives being destroyed. We have a right to be angry, to demand an accurate and truthful economic picture, to respect for our ability to understand and a right to participate in the policy decisions to turn this around for our future, the future of We-The-People.

Whether you are driven by a sense of urgency about global warming or simply recognize the life-quality costs of ever increasing pollution and the near end of fossil fuel reserves, clearly, our economy must transform; we are challenged to move from an unconscious assumption of infinite growth and consumption to a sustainable, much more locally focused and controlled set of interlocking economies.

Expensive solutions — possibly increasingly costly — simply must be off the table. Single issue "solutions" will fail in the face of our ever more interdependent society. As we bump up against the real limits of our earth's ecosystem, our belief in unfettered individual choice will be forcibly unraveled by reality and systemic push-backs beyond our control. We will open our minds and struggle to understand a reality of multiple systems interacting with each other; we will come to enjoy the challenge and beauty of comprehending worldwide ocean currents, the health and air quality impact of a giant rainforest tree, and the effect of butterflies flapping their wings. And what it means to try to understand these as part of the system we also live within. Or we will be painfully jarred as our linear understanding of life fails to address that interactive reality.

I rarely figure any of this out alone. When I ran for governor of our Commonwealth of Massachusetts in 2006, people told me repeatedly how smart I was. I reminded them that few of the ideas I ever shared were my own. These ideas came from years of listening to the people of Massachusetts; it was the best of our ideas that just made me seem smart. Now, if they ever just left us in charge...

Given that experience and my commitment to the usefulness of multiple perspectives, in this book I try to share the best thinking about our economy that I have been able to gather. It reaches for the most practical solutions while trying to bushwhack a path through a veritable jungle of overgrown ideological traps. I hope this exploration will leave you feeling better able to grasp the realities behind the rhetoric — with a practical sense of what is possible: how we really can, together, guide our Commonwealth to the far end of this economic depression with the least damage. Possibly we can be better and more realistically positioned than most for the future economy we are moving into...

Introduction
Massachusetts and the
Failing Economy

The Chinese symbol for crisis is the combined symbols for danger and opportunity. In this crisis, I have learned that the greater the danger, the greater the opportunity.

No one can argue that we are not living through a crisis fraught with dangers. This book is about pointing out that it is also fraught with opportunities *if* we can work together to grasp them.

> *On November 15, 1929, seventeen days into the Great Depression ushered in by the Market Crash of October 29, 1929, President Herbert Hoover said, "Any lack of confidence in the economic future of the United States is foolish."*[1]

That was 1929 ... and the Great Depression. From the stories of my childhood, I imagined the Depression lasted a few years, but the U.S. economy did not re-stabilize until 12 years later in 1941. That was when the government declared an overwhelming government jobs effort — which put aside all other financial considerations — known as the Second World War effort.

While we continue to hear from economists and some top financial pundits who say that this crisis may only last months, it will not. It will last years. It will be difficult and harsh. Many people are angry and are scared and we have a right to be. But how long it lasts and how hard it is will depend on what policy decisions are made now, and how quickly and decisively.

This book charts one realistic path with a focus on Massachusetts policies. These policy choices will either maneuver our Commonwealth through safe enough waters or actually continue to steer us directly for the rocks. We have to dig deep and understand some of the forces that got us here. Many forces were actually predictable even though all the most visible economists these days say they were not. Out of that, we can grasp some principles or criteria to keep our eyes on to assess what will guide us most safely through the storm. We have to recognize the policies that try to dodge or skim over those deeper fissures; political expediency will not get us out of this mess.

Reflecting on the choices of present Massachusetts leaders and whether they will show the decisive, incisive leadership we will need, I offer some broad brush strokes of policy; why in a crisis where everything seems to be going wrong, smart policy choices have the opportunity to address and begin to resolve numerous and even fundamental problems simultaneously.

A lot of people I talk to find the bleakness of our present situation depressing. They seem to want to change the topic before we get to highlight the life-changing opportunities before us. Similarly, you may find this book a challenging read. The depth of the mess we find ourselves in can be hard to comprehend and daunting. Even though voluntarily steeped in the fundamental issues of our times, I often also struggle to conceive and face the magnitude of the numbers and the reach of the problems.

I also find myself telling stories to remind us that if humans got us into this mess, then working together, I have every reason to believe we can get ourselves out of the mess.

But we cannot get out of it if we fall into the incredible human capacity for denial. We cannot fix a problem until we can name it. Ideology at times can help people sort of close their eyes and dive into what might otherwise be too scary. These days, however, ideology has been driving our political and economic choices to the point of becoming a source of denial itself.

> *As former Federal Reserve Chairman Alan Greenspan himself said in Congressional testimony after the October 2008 crash, when asked if he had "found that your view of the world, your ideology, was not right, it was not working." "Absolutely, precisely," Mr. Greenspan replied. "... I was shocked..." And he admitted that he had missed the subprime housing bubble.[2]*

So while I know that my deepest values keep me motivated to face and work on our greatest challenges — commitment to the love and survival of all of us, for instance — I want to invite you to join me in this exploration; I encourage you to commit to trying to put aside as many of your assumptions as you can. Join me in seeing if we can understand as many of these dynamics as possible so we can work to solve them together.

Massachusetts and the failing economy

How we got in this hole and how together we can begin to climb out of it.

As our mother-ship, the Commonwealth of Massachusetts, enters dangerous waters, it does not need to crash into the rocks or even get trapped in stagnant waters as the tsunami bears down on it. Instead, as a state we must begin steering away from the rocks and shallows into deeper waters, hopefully skirting the worst of the storm.

I was struck by how sailing images no longer hold meaning for many of us even though our coastal state is steeped in the history of whaling and fishing trades. We have over-fished those stocks. But like many other things in our lives, we are going to have to find a new balance with these natural food sources, especially as our economies turn more local again in the face of global warming and climate change.

Old houses on our Massachusetts' shores still sport widows' walks, those balconies up near the roof where women would anxiously pace watching and awaiting the return of their fisher folk especially as storms gathered. Our surrounding structures still remind us that even as we shutter windows and prepare food to weather the storm, we need to access the most far-seeing vistas and keep watch for the well-being of all of us.

The storm is upon us in its early stages. We are in the ship together, our state. It is not enough to see how well the ship (the state budget alone) is put together. We cannot sail the ship as if the weather remains the same. The bigger the storm, the more important it is to pay attention to the impacts of waters and winds around us. *If it is going to be really big, the more important that we act preventatively and quickly.* How we position ourselves right now will make the biggest difference in how much the storm batters us.

While it seems safest to perhaps hole up near the coast or even try to outrun it, those actions actually endanger us the most. A ship is built to be out in deep waters, where it cannot run aground or be smashed up against rocks. If the captains guiding our ship have never experienced a major storm, they may expect to control the situation or avoid bold action and stick by the shore as worked with gentler weather. Those are ***very*** dangerous choices for those of us stuck riding out the storm on this ship. Sticking near the shore, thinking that the familiar outline will shelter us somehow, is most dangerous; heading out to the deep waters is the only possible safety.

If these elected leaders believe large storms no longer happen or belittle the warning signs that others have been pointing out because their ideological assumptions block the way, we are in danger. If they are too isolated or arrogant to hear the voices of the least prestigious workers — the firemen in the boiler room or the look-outs at the top of the ship's masts — closer to the early pertinent warnings, we are all endangered.

Some deep assumptions have come from business-as-usual in recent decades: years of prosperity for the very wealthy not only who head large corporations but who we have also placed more and more of in the top leadership of our government. Regular people (the majority of us, the bottom 60 percent of income earners) have been in a worsening recession, losing actual spending power for at least a decade. Closer to the water, we have seen the change in the weather, wind and water patterns.

Those who were supposed to be paying attention and guiding our ship have too often told us from their hang-out in the captain's quarters that we were wrong and not to worry. We need in this time, if ever, to come to believe not only in our right, but our ability, to be part of the "We, the people" who are supposed to run this government and steer this ship.

Instead of a campaign slogan of "Yes, we can," we need an actual belief in ourselves as an electorate, in our ability to understand our society and body politic, to grasp complexity and become partners in creating the larger destiny of our society. Herein lies the potential greatness of our society. But it is a source of greatness we have all allowed to atrophy and be poisoned by anti-democratic beliefs. As if voting once in a while was enough to be a full participant in our self-governance.

A misplaced faith in the messages of those in power has benefited a smaller and smaller number of those at the very top. In their rush to increase their wealth and power, they have ignored the reality that we are all on one ship economically and therefore politically. The

story they have filled the airwaves with has undermined our lived
awareness that in fact, we are each other's keeper.

The proverb that a rising tide lifts all boats does not become true
because it is a social mantra; a rising tide can just as easily sink lots
of boats and may actually be the forewarning of a massive storm
approaching....

If we turn this ship, instead of the headlines of today, imagine
these possible headlines:

*During the Depression, Massachusetts makes itself a safe haven for
businesses and residents*

*After a decade of losing population and business, Massachusetts
becomes a magnet during economic crisis*

*Massachusetts changes the bottom line for business, workers,
municipalities and the economic recovery....*

Part I

The Storm Brews, the Seas Roughen

Once upon a time, value was based on what people traded their time and goods for. In a small village or area, some highly valued materials became the basis for barter. Early economists could make sense of simple buying and selling as the value of an hour of time or a simple material. Value became more complicated as higher level skills of workers demanded different pay. As businesses traded farther and farther away, and hired workers for pay and needed investments of capital, pricing became complicated. In more modern times, value was originally directly tied to valuables like silver and gold. Images of large paper sheets in huge printing presses and gold bars stockpiled in Fort Knox inform our assumptions about money and wealth. Federal Deposit Insurance Corporation (FDIC) signs in banks inform us that our deposits and savings are insured.

We know banks use our money for loans and investing. We know there are some kinds of government regulations that protect us. We know that economists and financial leaders have created complex theories beyond our simple village economics. We also know that U.S. banking regulations have evolved based on lessons going back through the Great Depression. They affect everything from the amount of interest we are charged, to our credit rating system and how bankers have traditionally written mortgages.

But some thing or things went deeply wrong in ways economists and financial experts did not foresee...

Assumptions

To begin to turn around the ship that we are all on that is heading toward the rocks — this Commonwealth of Massachusetts has entered the same economic Depression as the rest of the country — we first need to acknowledge that *our circumstances have changed.* In a huge economic downturn it becomes very clear that our choices need to be made together, to make the best of our limited resources. If not, we will get in deeper and deeper trouble. This challenging economy is teaching us this right now as will our worsening environmental situation. My choices do impact your choices. This will be the lesson of the current age.

We need to keep our eye on some key economic facts. In normal times, 70 percent of the economic engine is consumer spending. About 20 percent is corporate spending, and another 10 percent is government spending.[1] This means when regular people do not have money to spend the economy cannot grow; all choices, all policy decisions have to be made with that fact front and center.

Discussion without understanding the logic of policy can go awry fairly easily. We need to grasp what is necessary to turn our economy around. If we the people are not keeping our eyes on that prize, we will be washed into the stormy seas when our storm-battered ship breeches its hull. The powers-that-be have actually been shortsightedly steering in that direction for a while. Their direction has been based on ideological assumptions or desires for further wealth and power, as opposed to the long term consequences of those actions not only for us but for them and their children.

To even discuss sensible economic decisions we must get through our ideological blinders. We have gotten used to allowing ideology to decide policy as opposed to being driven by reality. Political discourse has gotten so partisan that we cannot discuss economic choices without getting called names and pigeonholed in some corner. I am interested in helping us fix our problems. I am not interested in figuring out who gets points for the right idea or who gets slapped down because they said things that have become socially unpopular among the powers that be. To reverse this dynamic we can draw on our deeply shared positive American values. We need to be able to look each other in the eye and honestly tell each other the truth and rely on each other in this time of crisis. That cannot be done while we are divided among happy little ideological camps, self-righteously throwing mud at each other.

One fact: *this is a real crisis*. Plenty of economists are still trying to sell their wares by claiming the economy is doing badly because people are being too negative. We hear again and again that the market is struggling because *people are afraid of* investing or taking risks. Actual market realities have scared investors. We are scared too when we look at our pocketbooks, the future of our jobs and of government revenue streams for necessary services. This crisis is not just in our heads.

I have been to numerous presentations by different economists in positions of power. Pretty much all of them said that this economic crisis came out of nowhere. For instance, University of Chicago economist and Nobel Laureate, Robert Lucas, is quoted frequently on the airwaves these days. He *"doesn't see much fundamental change coming out of the crisis, either. What it has reminded us of,"* he argues, *"is simply the impossibility of seeing these events in advance."*[2]

Contrary to these economists' comments, this crisis was predictable. In fact, we should be angry at the economists who try to guide our policy thinking but waited until December 2008 to admit that the recession started in November 2007. Newspapers editorial writers still claimed that the people predicting a serious economic downturn were just naysayers trying to make everybody feel bad.

In reality the signs of recession at the end of 2007 were clear. One of the early indicators economists usually highlight is housing starts — that is, how many new houses are being built. Housing starts had been down for ten quarters (of a year) by the time economists admitted the recession.[3] I remember hearing that figure and thinking, "Oh my god, for two and a half years housing starts have been down." (In Fig. 1.1, you can see both the increased production created by the housing bubble and the dramatic impact of the burst).

The second obvious indicator was the pinch most of us regular folks on the ground had been experiencing for years. Add the impact of the subprime lending scandal and the foreclosure crisis; the economic meltdown was already front and center in most of our lives. *As regular people, we realized we were headed for a major downturn.*

Figure 1.1   Single unit housing starts 1969–2010[4]

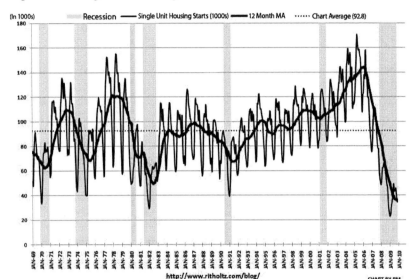

Just as major economists were unable to predict this serious economic downturn, many of them are now trying to tell us that it will be over soon. There is no economic basis for predicting a short recession or that it is not going to get much worse.

One relatively recent engine driving this economic crisis is the foreclosure crisis. That particular economic sector pulled down the entire banking industry and threw credit card and other parts of the credit industry into trouble. The foreclosure crisis cannot magically turn itself around. It is pulling down property values and tax income for municipalities whose costs are skyrocketing for boarding up vacant houses, dealing with vandalism and trying to stop fires and water floods from broken pipes, etc.

In addition, future trouble brews for mortgage holders. The subprime mortgages that tipped off this crisis included a delayed interest payment spike of 25 or 30 percent per month; those resets are mostly complete. A whole other set — two sets in fact — of "creative" (industry terminology) mortgage instruments start hitting their resets sometime in 2010 or so. They are called Alt-A and Option ARM mortgages with even larger, up to 70 percent, interest rate jumps. That additional round of mortgage resets (out of reach for most of these home-owners) will continue until 2013 or so. There were home-owners in trouble at the end of 2009 because loss in property value meant they owed more than their house was worth. There are many who cannot afford their mortgage because of loss of jobs or work hours. Finally the commercial subprime market has begun its pre-dicted tank as of 2010.

Clearly the foreclosure crisis — even without all its collateral damage — shows that the larger economic crisis is going to continue for a long time.

We also simply cannot address a crisis until we can name and acknowledge the crisis. We have to insist on this fundamental honesty from everyone — from policy makers to the media outlets to the economists on television. If they are not telling you that this crisis is going to be heavy and difficult and longer term, do not even bother to listen to the rest of their analysis.

In addition, all of the ideological conversations about economics need to be put aside. Former Chairman Alan Greenspan himself, the economic guru who ran the Federal Reserve Bank, admitted to Congress as the market started to plunge that the economic models they used for decades were flawed. That means the ideology behind their arguments also does not work — at least as formulated.

Some people are going to argue with you that some policy is pro-free market or against free markets, pro-capitalist or anti-capitalist. That will not help us much. We really need to look at the steps needed to get out of the mess we are in; we have to start being honest about what it is going to take. With an economy in such serious trouble — knowing that 70 percent of the normal economic engine is consumer spending — we, the people without enough money to spend, are the real experts in turning this ship around.

When we talk to elected representatives, which we need to do more if we are to survive this, we need to stop letting them avoid real choices by throwing ideological mud at us or each other. Do not let them treat you like you are not smart enough; you know you need a decent paying job and your neighbor needs a decent paying job and that nobody can afford housing or health care prices that are through the roof; and no, it does not help any of us to have our neighbors go homeless while buildings are empty and falling apart. These are basic truths; you are more of an expert on them than any of the "experts" because they do not live our lives, the lives of regular people.

Figure 1.2   Share of family income by quintile: 1947–2004[5]

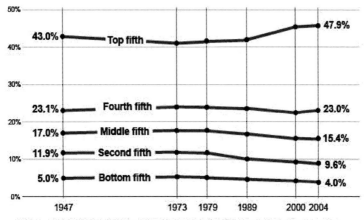

Source: From Table 1.9 in *The State of Working America 2006/2007* by Lawrence Mishel, Jared Bernstein, and Sylvia Allegretto, Economic Policy Institute.

For decades we have been told that regular people are not smart enough to understand what is going on economically. Our economic interests have consistently been put aside for some supposed greater good that is going to trickle down to us. What actually trickled down to us has been an economic disaster that has been getting worse for decades (with occasional small, bright spots). The folks at the top have been having an up and down cyclical economy, but you and me? We have been steadily losing ground. Most of us did not benefit from the recent recovery of 2002. Half the jobs lost in the last recession never came back.[6] The recession before that (1990s), the economic "recovery" just kept us where we were at its start. So we are at least three recessions from having benefited measurably from the supposed upturn that came afterwards.

Figure 1.2 takes all the families nationwide and breaks us into five equal parts, with the lowest income fifth at the bottom and the highest income at the top. You can see how our three-fifths, the bottom 60 percent, has fared for 55 years through 2004. Note that from 1979 onward our share of income has declined. Figure 1.3 looks at the income-earner who is right in the middle (the median income) — 50 percent of our society gets more income than this person and 50 percent makes less. It shows a line for the income of all households, and then just for those of working age. If you compare the decade between the last two straight lines through 2009, you can see most of us are not benefiting from any economic "recovery" of the last ten years unlike previous decades. For just those of working age, the loss of economic ground is even clearer.

Figure 1.3   Real median household incomes 1979–2008[7]

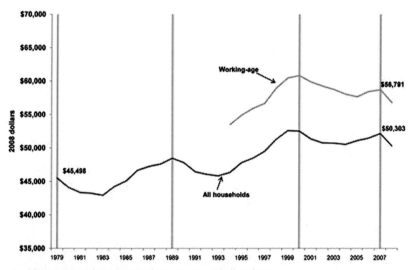

Note: Vertical lines indicate the start of recessions. Median income for workers age below 65 starts in 1994.
Source: Author's analysis of U.S. Census Bureau data.

The majority of people, you and I, and the others from the bottom of our economy through the 80 percent mark, are the engine that drives the economy.

Remember 70 percent of the economy is consumer spending. Without our spending, our economy's engine has been draining and draining and draining away. Some of that spending was made up by borrowing against our future wages through questionable credit we were extended. But now, normal spending to just keep our heads above water is beyond our reach. More and more of us are slipping into poverty. Pundits accuse us of frivolous spending beyond our means but even as we lost income our only increased spending has been for medical costs. (In Figure 1.4, the top line is all our spending as a nation. The bottom line shows our spending fairly constant if our ever-increasing medical costs are not included).

Figure 1.4   Consumption share of Gross Domestic Product (GDP)[8]

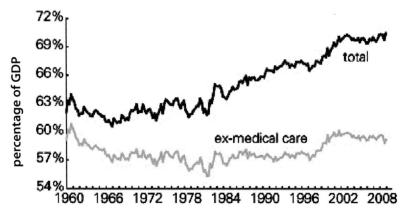

Importantly, we can be experts. In fact we have already shown our expertise. Look at the 2009 proposal to bail-out the big lenders and the huge banks, the Troubled Asset Relief Program (TARP). We voters called our Congressional representatives and told them not to bail out the banks. Two-thirds of callers said, "This is wrong." Congress did not listen. But we were right. Pumping in more than a trillion of our tax dollars did not change the banks' behavior or "fix" the credit market. The bankers gave the money to their executives, to their share-holders, paid off investors who had gambled away our economic future, and bought other banks. They paid even more to their lobbyists to stop re-regulation, like requirements that they fix these predatory "creative" mortgages.

Once again our Congress and other supposed experts are sitting there saying, "Well gee, we do not know how it went wrong." We, the people, knew it was going to go wrong from the beginning. We are going to have to fight not only with the experts who claim to know better than us but also with ourselves to believe in ourselves. For better or worse, too many in office do not believe in us. Clearly, we have to reclaim our government for and by the people if we are going to shift this situation.

We are also going to have to put aside this assumption that we are not all in this together. When I say this is an ideological assumption,

I mean every single commercial we have ever seen affects our thinking. The ads tell us to want to have a cleaner house than somebody else or a nicer car than somebody else. At work, we are not allowed to ask what somebody else gets paid because we are not supposed to know who is getting more money than whom. The underlying assumption here is that somehow I can do whatever I want to get ahead and it is not ever going to come back to haunt me or my children; that is a fallacy. Economic choices do impact each other. When a company takes its jobs across the ocean, that is not a separate act; it impacts all of us.

While financial leaders talked about deregulation and allowing the economy to right itself, they were pulling strings behind the scenes. They changed interest rates, for instance, to increase lending and borrowing so businesses could expand and make more money. They changed the rate of inflation that undermined the higher wages we organized and fought for. The idea that we have ever been in an economy "free of" larger forces has not been true for at least the last century. As our economy globalized, in addition to the Federal Reserve changing interest rates and our money supply every few months, we now have numerous international trade agreements defining business arrangements, stripping consumer protections and affecting labor and environmental laws.

Our expanding economies moved to globalization once we had used up all the "frontiers" (even the ones that had not really been unpopulated when we "discovered" them). Today, business anywhere in the world impacts business everywhere in the world. These business actions impact our environment and our health, population growth, the transmission of not just disease but things like beetles that kill trees or fruit flies that hurt fruit development. However distant, business choices about pesticides, chemicals and the weapons of war spread and affect people across the world. All of these have profound economic impacts. This will only become more obvious as global environmental changes hit closer to home.

The question is not: do all government policies affect the economy and our lives? It is: who is deciding these market policies and how are they changing the economy and our lives?

The New Deal Rescue
and Stimulus

What many of us think of as the New Deal was actually different policy "deals" built up over time. While the policy choices certainly put key changes in place, some may not have helped at all. There are those who will argue with some justification that it was actually the U.S. decision to enter World War II that finally turned the economy around for the long haul.

This last observation has led to some odd questions I have heard of late: Since we are already at war, what can we do this time to fundamentally turn around the economy? Do we need to enter yet another war? This is missing the point of a book because we have read only its cover.

Systems theorists can help us understand why human beings can so easily miss the underlying dynamics of a large system. One is that we mistake the apparent impact of a small pressure on a system as simply increasing without limit if we increase that same pressure.

Take a very familiar system (although a very complex one): the human body. If you put the human body in a cold place, it will shiver. Does it then follow that if you want it to continue to shiver you continue to increase the cold? Well, no, in fact, if you increase the cold a lot without other inputs to the human body, it will soon stop shivering, start experiencing hypothermia as the system starts shutting down, get frost bite in its extremities, and give up on trying to keep its extremities warm. Finally, the person will die.

So why do we get confused? Because we have assumed a direct cause and effect: cold leads to shivering in the human body. In fact, the human body is a system which will take whatever steps are necessary to try to keep its internal temperature within levels necessary for survival. A small amount of cooling can be fought off with a relatively small expenditure of energy by shivering. Once the cold becomes too energy-costly to fight off with shivering, our bodies give up on that strategy and go for more drastic measures.

It is not fighting a war that helps an economy. It should be clear to us that the United States government over-extended itself in recent years with massive war spending — part of what got our economy into so much trouble. So why did the World War II spending help the economy then? And bankrolling a war (two wars actually) now did not?

Not all government spending is stimulus spending, and not all stimulus spending is equally stimulating

When the Great Depression first hit, there were ideological arguments over what to do. Should the government intervene and how? If the government spent massive amounts of money and went into debt, might increasing the deficit make the economy worse and make the U.S. economy more vulnerable? And maybe it would not last that long anyway. Sound familiar?

Some actions had to be taken — like closing the banks when the wholesale run on the banks started. Deeper monetary policy changes were obviously going to have to be made (as had been made after the bank run of 1907 out of which the Federal Reserve was created); it was other stimulus policy that actually went in fits and starts and, some would say, slid backwards at times.

To reverse the economic Depression, first the government poured money into the financial sectors that had been speculating wildly and had made toxic investments. These investments tanking led to foreclosures of farms, then people's homes and businesses. Such propping up of banks might have worked in smaller, earlier financial crises. It was ineffective in a market rife with wild speculation by those with burgeoning fortunes in an economy ever more divided by inequalities of wealth. Those with the most had become accustomed to money begetting money, without any basis in work or the creation of actual goods or services.

The Depression-era government moved on to some temporary bank nationalization, direct government loans and safety net spending and then, a massive job stimulus program. These actually did begin to pull the economy out of the Depression although some argue they were too delayed and too small to have made a real difference. Unfortunately, as soon as there was some measurable success, conservative forces started yelling at the top of their lungs about the increased national debt. The government backed off some of its stimulus spending and the economy slumped again. That slump led to another spate of government spending in ways that did actually stimulate the economy again (job creation, etc.)

What about World War II made the real difference?

World War II was not only an unprecedentedly huge jobs and stimulus spending program but the call for patriotism finally overcame the ideological barriers to that level of government spending. In a time of war, conservative ideological barriers to government debt are trumped. The patriotic call moved everyone — including most of the very rich — from a "me" ideology to a "we" ideology.

When the war ended, the government enacted one more massive stimulus package: the G.I. Bill. This was a huge wealth transfer by the government into the hands of regular people, veterans, who had returned from the war. Regular people got money to purchase homes that created a long term wealth basis for wide segments of the population, including the creation of a middle class, as well as other stimulus of jobs, education spending, etc.

It was not war in general, or World War II specifically, that lifted our economy out of the Depression. It was the all-inclusive, nationwide patriotic call that swept away the opposition to massive government spending on jobs, economic supports for regular people and an infusion of money to support the expansion of wealth for regular people.

Compare that to today. The current wars are largely privatized efforts. Government resources are contracted out mostly to increase the profits of key military-industrial players — companies that have used the government spending to vastly increase the amount of money they can skim off in profits. The rest of the present war effort actually leads to disinvestment in regular people such as huge cuts in health care for returning military personnel, decreasing actual wages for soldiers, unfulfilled promises of educational advancement, even safety equipment at the front. Can you imagine deficiencies in military safety equipment being conscienced, seen as morally acceptable, in WWII United States of America?

World War II gave cover for huge stimulus spending by the government in ways that created jobs and actually improved the wages and wealth of regular people. The Afghanistan and Iraq wars were ushered in as part of a massive shift of global and economic policy by the U.S. government that opened up financial markets and put government spending directly in the hands of those already amassing huge income and, more importantly, worsening divisions in wealth among people in the U.S. — known as wealth disparities.

What government spending stimulates the whole economy?

I have to start by harkening back to where I started. We cannot really assess solutions until we can remove the ideological blinders that stopped us from accurately identifying the basis of the problem.

For some of you I am asking you to put aside, for now, your immediate reactions and read to the end of my argument.

Figure 1.5   Economic benefits of various stimulus provisions[9]

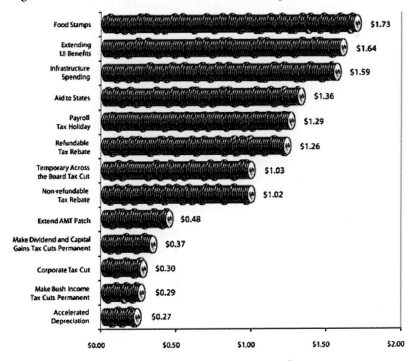

Economic Benefit for each dollar spent

Source: Mark Zandi from Moody's Economy.com

As stated earlier, normally 70 percent of our economy is made up of consumer spending. For decades, studies have shown that infusions of money at the bottom of the economy are actually the most reliable way to improve the functioning of the overall economy. No matter the party of the presidential administration, food stamps always prove the largest economic multiplier effect they measure; about $1.80 in economic activity is created per food stamp dollar spent. Extending unemployment benefits provide a very significant multiplier effect as you can see in Figure 1.5. Studies on welfare payments have found similar effects which are not surprising since they are essentially a type of unemployment insurance.

There is nothing counter-intuitive about the impact of survival spending at all. Those with the least money do not sock it away in savings accounts or buy Picassos or hide it in accounts in the Cayman Islands. They spend every cent just trying to survive. Money they receive is spent immediately to address ongoing financial commitments to meet daily needs.

A key factor in the impact of government money on the economy is how quickly it actually enters the regular economy. You may have heard the emphasis in Obama's Stimulus Package, for instance, on infrastructure projects being "spade ready," or, being completely ready to begin construction. A central advantage of food stamps and unemployment monies is that even budget deficit hawks do not have to worry about these disbursements being spent quickly enough to help turn our economy around.

Given that both minimum wage and welfare benefits were last above the poverty level in the early 1970s, this is an area of government stimulus spending where the deficits in household budgets have been significant and long term; lots of money could be usefully infused into these households without worries about delays or reductions in spending behavior.

Infusing money at the bottom has other benefits. Lower-income people spend more of their money locally. Money that is spent locally is likely to be spent at local businesses, paying local rents or property taxes, and buying local goods and services. Money spent locally tends to get re-spent locally, several times, before it disappears from the local economy into the global economy. Wealthier pockets are that much more likely to save money or spend it far away on financial instruments, not the production of real goods and services. This more commonly recognized positive impact of local spending nowadays has given momentum to the growing Buy Local First movement.

The market will fix it

The statement "the market will fix it" is one we hear a lot these days in opposition to government stimulus packages and more. Whether you believe the market fixes itself or not probably does not matter if we are getting away from rhetoric.

The concept of markets and how they function goes back to the beginnings of modern economic theory. Adam Smith sought to describe the workings of value and money; he put out the philosophical concept that left to itself, a market would always re-adjust toward real checks and balances based on real value of goods and services. In the relationship between money and value, when that relationship is local, feedback loops on pricing are immediate, direct and all labor had comparable amounts of education behind it, etc. It makes sense that when markets are local, simple enough systems they would correct themselves. When you add lots of intermediaries — time, distance and interactions with millions of other systems — money and the value of actual goods and labor become more and more distant from each other.

Lots of politicians these days argue that it is best for the market if the government just does not intervene. That left alone, even in a deep economic crisis like our present one, the "market will right itself" even if a fair amount of economic pain happens between now and then. They will tell you that this is what, in fact, the market does naturally.

How would proponents know this? Are they simply harkening back to Adam Smith and the beginning of economic theory when markets were much smaller and economic consequences still relatively uncomplicated?

Almost 100 years ago the Federal Reserve Bank was founded. Its mission is to supposedly ensure the smooth functioning of the "market" in the U.S. Its tools are to adjust interest rates and cash flow. Most years it does so several times. All other major economies have central banks as well; these similarly tweak their own market's functioning several times a year. The "market" has been neither "free" nor "left alone" for over a hundred years. The consensus of financial experts has been, for a long time, that the markets require intervention.

I welcome those who enjoy purely theoretical conversations to have them. We just need to remember that we have no empirical idea what the impact of "leaving the market alone" is. Those committed to a pure free market ideology should not be worried about the relatively minor impact of a stimulus package, dwarfed by the truly huge military spending packages and the bank bailout funding. Free market purists should have spent the last several decades dismantling the Federal Reserve — the most direct enemy of a free market. The almost constant interventions by the Fed are what derail any chance of the "market" to do anything by itself.

For now, even with approaching $23 trillion in banking interventions (investments, loans, guarantees, etc.) according to the Special Inspector General during the last few years[10], the Fed itself has admitted that its monetary tools are not up to the present challenge; the means of intervention at its disposal cannot reverse this negative market.[11]

The real issues are: Who intervenes? Using what monetary resources? For whose benefit?

Collectivized and government-run solutions

You will often hear on the airwaves ideological debates over collectivized solutions to large problems or even outright preemptory dismissal of solutions as "socialist."

The problem is that there are numerous examples in our society of collectivizing resources to address large scale problems more efficiently. Many of these we take so totally for granted that we do not even think about them as examples of collectivization or pooling and controlling resources as a group. The very ideologues who seek to dismiss some potentially powerful solutions to the present crises will at the same time trumpet the very market forces that created the collectivized solutions we practice and benefit from every day!

Every form of insurance is a collectivization of a problem so that we as individuals or households can pay less but access more coverage when needed than we could as separate entities. If we all had to save and put aside enough money to address all possible penalties for a car accident, for example, only the very wealthiest people could afford to drive cars. Likewise, few of us would be able to afford a house and save enough additional money to protect against potential major losses that become catastrophic in cost for home owners without insurance.

In one of my mother's less reasonable moments, she told me that she needed even more wealth than she had at the time. She thought she needed many hundreds of thousands of dollars in case she contracted a very long term, wasting disease that she lived with for decades. She told me, with absolute conviction, that if such a thing happened she might well run out of money and die destitute and homeless if she did not accumulate even more personal wealth.

In some theoretical reality, what she feared was a possibility. But most of us use collectivized solutions to protect against these outlying possibilities. Even with the vast wealth of our society redistributed evenly, I doubt we could each afford to sit on that kind of wealth "just in case." Instead, we completely buy into the logic of pooling resources to address these eventualities. We understand that a significant percentage of people will die before contracting lengthy diseases. My mother's wasting disease scenario is extremely rare. Instead, we put some percentage of our resources together, have a field of actuarial experts who look at all the data to predict the likelihoods of various risks, and we use that to determine risk pools — the amount of negative outcomes likely to happen and how much money would be needed to pay for the damages. Then each of us pays into the risk pool enough to cover if we are one of the unlucky ones.

This is the basis of the private insurance industry and public insurance systems which sometimes back those up. In addition, we have a number of public insurance systems — everything from Social Security and Medicare (which we all no doubt think of). The Federal Deposit Insurance Corporation (FDIC) collectivizes the risk to regular savings and checking accounts of bank failures through a schedule of bank contributions; the Federal Reserve is a collectivization of a risk pool to protect banks from "runs" and other economic instability. Policies where we use tax dollars to address public health hazards and product recalls represent a collectivization of solutions as does public paving of roads — none of which we could afford as individualized expenses.

And the one that tells us just how committed we are to collectivized solutions is that we still fight for public funds for firefighters — even with huge budget cuts and a probable Depression, not even the most diehard ideologues are proposing going back to individual payments to a private insurance pool for fire protection such as existed in the colonies. If nothing else, everyone figured out that if your uninsured neighbor meant a fire burned out of control, it was far too likely to engulf your house and property as well.

So do not let anyone drag you into some argument over the socialism of collectivized solutions — even ones run by the government. The FDIC and the Federal Reserve are the government-sponsored protectors of the pillars of our markets that are demanded by many of those most ideologically committed to a free market economy philosophy.

To address present problems, the question is not whether collectivized solutions work, they absolutely do; even government run ones are ideologically acceptable, clearly, to people across the political spectrum even if they refuse to recognize it.

The real question is: in what situations do collectivized solutions work and to what greater good or detriment? And who controls how they work and for whose benefits are those collectivized resources supposed to be used?

Money and Value

Real economists will have to forgive me for the simplified overview offered here and the loss of nuances that they may consider important. I am telling this story because it is important to know how value and valuation have worked in practice historically and the implications of how they work in the present.

Most of us think of money as a way of measuring the relative value of things, even if imperfectly.

Early economists saw the value of a commodity as the value of the materials that went into the product plus the value of the labor to create it. That definition was clearly too simple even in simple markets and so value got expanded to include, for instance, the time and labor to transport goods to market. The farther the market, the higher the costs of products became.

How do you value the labor? Labor might be valued differently in far off places. And what about labor that was more expensive to create? If it takes 15 years to become a heart specialist as opposed to six months to become a proficient weatherization worker, then should not a heart specialist's labor cost more? If only to pay for the years of labor of the various teachers who created the high productivity of that specialist's hour of labor?

In theory, one could quantify all of these elements and so estimate the cost of various products close to some common sense of value. In a local barter economy where most workers are independent and sell their own labor such valuation could be pretty close.

An additional layer to all of this, however, comes when workers are organized in a business. Not only is a boss purchasing their labor and selling the product without the workers having any real say in the price, but the boss's contribution to the product is harder to price. How valuable is their coordination and management? In addition, the boss is trying to accumulate capital to improve the machinery and techniques that workers use so that a better product is produced. To do this, the boss must either pay the workers less than the total value of their labor so he can start accumulating capital or he must inflate the product's price in the market so he can save enough profit.

All of these factors mean the price of work is not necessarily what the workers are getting paid. How much has the boss lowered their pay to slice more money off the top or how much has the price been inflated? Economists use equations to try to estimate this. As non-economists, you can see the relationship between a product's value and the money paid for it has gotten more tenuous.

As the relationships between the original product and all these complicated additions and subtractions continue to multiply, it has been argued that a better way to think about value is to start from the price actually charged in the market. After all, if the market price is below production cost, the folks producing the product will start losing money. Arguably, they will soon stop producing the product and it will vanish from the market. If it is priced higher than its value to the consumer, then presumably it will not get bought. If this is true, could we not assume that the market price must be in the right ballpark because the product is both still selling and still being produced? Then we could extrapolate backwards and figure out how much each component contributed to a price, right?

Effectiveness of working backward depends on relatively direct feedback between the market's price and those producing or buying. There are other examples of interruptions in that feedback loop besides simply distance or number of steps inbetween. Imagine a huge fad where reputation or excitement — like the supposed value of the Internet, then dot-coms — can boom even though most of them do not really produce much actual value.

Additionally, for the buyer to assess the value of what they are purchasing, the money they spend must also have value to them in terms of their effort or labor. How many times have we found ourselves as parents, or heard other parents, yell at a child, "Hey, I worked hard for that money, and you just went out and spent it on !??*!"? The child seems to have spent the money too easily, since they do not understand the effort that went into getting the money in the first place. On the other hand, if you could literally print money in your basement, why not just buy everything and anything?

For another example, once I am spending credit — money I do not even have yet — it is easier and easier to make purchases that may be beyond my actual future earning power. Once our economy becomes more about spending credit than money we have already earned, what the average buyer is willing to spend for market price is less and less tied to their sense of real value.

What happens if I am spending someone else's money and there are no real consequences to misspending that money at all? It starts feeling like play money; money and actual value likely part ways. Most of us assume that money — which feels real to us because we know how hard we worked to get what money we have — bears a close relationship to real value, but what if it does not?

Some of us have experienced directly or watched from afar what happens when the value of a currency quickly devalues and can no longer purchase what regular people need and expect. When inflation grows rapidly, the money people have been paid for their labor no longer has real meaning in the market. For a while, people may tighten their belts and go hungry. But just as likely, people start riots, call for government intervention, stop being productive at work or worrying about bringing in money. An entire country's economy can collapse. Governments that do not respond may be brought down or they may quickly institute police states to try to control angry people.

That is one way that a currency and the value of products in the market quickly and visibly part ways. But what happens when money and value start bearing little or no relationship to each other over longer periods of time? And how does this happen?

What is money anyway?

I have been asking around; it seems that other people must have the same images in their head that I do — of huge printing presses printing big, green-inked sheets of U.S. dollar bills that presumably make their way to big chopping machines. This is where money comes from.

Alas, that captivating image is more than 90 percent illusion. Nowadays, most money is created by banks. Every time they enter a new promissory note like a mortgage or credit card expenditure in their ledger, money comes into existence. When I say most money, we are talking about 90 or perhaps 95 percent of the money created these days.[12, 13] If you are like me, you are thinking, "How is that possible?" And surely it must be very carefully regulated? Well, not necessarily.

Where the story of money starts…

Money as part of barter systems, like wampum shells, stretches far back in human history. Those who could, built up hoards of these valuables. Banks came about when those who had such valuables sought storage where they would be better guarded.

In the Middle Ages, jewelry-makers, goldsmiths and others who worked with precious metals and stones as their trade had to pay for guards as part of their regular business.[14] So their shops became a logical place for others to ask to store their valuables and gold. By leaving it at the jewelers or similarly guarded business, they collectivized the cost of protection instead of each person having to pay for their own guards. The jeweler provided some kind of receipt for holding the valuables and charged a slight fee for the storage.

Instead of always going to the jeweler to retrieve the actual valuables for trade, the receipts eventually came to be used directly as a consistent measure of the value of those items in storage appraised by the jeweler or goldsmith. Those receipts could then become the basis of currency without constantly withdrawing the actual objects.

Some who held valuables eventually found that being a bank — protecting valuables which were rarely withdrawn — meant that they had value that could be lent out at interest. Initially, they may have only used their own valuables and any storage fees collected as a basis for loans. But with most valuables deposited long term, they began to loan against the value of others' valuables. Eventually, this aspect of their business — storage fees and interest earned on loans — became more profitable than their original trade and the first bankers were born.

Born along with the first banks were potential problems. Lending against any and all valuables in the bank was not originally part of the agreement by those who stored their valuables in these "banks." People who had agreed to store their valuables and pay a fee discovered that their value was essentially being loaned to others. Out of concern that their valuables might actually be lost in a loan that never got paid back, they might go demand their valuables returned. If loss of trust multiplied, the banker could end up with everyone coming and demanding their valuables back at the same time — essentially a "run" on the bank. If he could not quickly call in his loans, he might be in real trouble.

By the second half of the 1800s, periodic runs on banks, created by rumors or economic concerns, led to a series of "panics." At first, banks tried to protect themselves by withholding a portion of their assets to cover any immediate withdrawals and stop wholesale panics. However, once a run on one bank started, that bank might fail and fear would spread leading to runs on more banks. Restoring trust would become harder as panic spread and could pull down an entire local economy or more.

Banks started to create holding pools to which each bank contributed to. If a run started on one bank, the pool had sufficient assets to protect it and thereby stop the panic before it started. Banking standards were created that required that at least one third of a bank's assets remain unencumbered (no loans against their value). These banking commitments were publicly displayed. But even pools sometimes failed so regional "banks" or larger holding pools were created.

Even with these precautions, at the beginning of the 1900s, in the U.S. "thrifts" — not the banks participating in the regional pools — experienced a major panic. It was precipitated by a scam; people were enticed to put their money into local "boiler room" investments. Immediate returns were higher without the cost of overhead fees banks charged to pay into pools that provided "insurance" for your deposits. People put their money down to speculate on potential increases or losses on stocks which they did not own. The "bucket" companies as they became known, owned stocks. Periodically they could leverage their financial investments to raise or lower particular stock prices opposite to how their participating speculators had "bet" — thus making significant profits for the bucket companies themselves and shorting their regular "investors."[15]

After a particularly bad run in bucket companies in New York, panic ensued. It first focused on thrifts that failed quickly as they had not participated in the regional bank (the insurance pools) that regular banks had. Nor had they followed commitments to withhold assets from investing. As they failed, the panic moved towards regular banks. While these banks belonged to an insurance pool, it was not clear they could all sustain a run at the same time. J.P. Morgan and a number of other wealthy businessmen quickly lent the banks money, saving them from folding. At the same time, they insisted that a more robust system be organized.[16]

Thus the Federal Reserve was created to pool the regional pools and collectivize the risk nationwide; the amount of required bank reserves was standardized. The presence of the Federal Reserve (without its later authority as monetary caretaker and interventionist into our economy), however, was not enough to avert the Great Depression. Over time, as well, the percentage of reserves that banks are required to hold unencumbered has dropped. As of 2009, it stood at 17 percent.

Creating U.S. dollars

When the U.S. Treasury decides to print a bundle of more money—not just replacing worn-out or lost bills, they first assess the impact on the value of the dollar by such printing. But banks, through the extension of credit against their holdings, bring money into existence with no impact assessment.

How does this work in practice? Say you deposit $1,500 dollars in my bank. I then turn around and loan it. A credit card through my bank is used to buy an appliance for $1,500. My bank sends out the payment, as a loan with $300 in interest and is entered onto the bank's books. As long as the bank holds the required reserve percentage of each loan, that money can be re-loaned repeatedly, increasing the value on the bank's books many times over. The original $1,500 was actual cash. But all the value beyond that comes into existence because someone was loaned money and promised to pay it back with interest. That original $1,500 may lead to the creation of up to 90 times additional value on the books.[17]

Thus most modern money is created: cash value of 95 percent of cash in our banks; 17 percent in real reserves of the original money must be deposited.[18] The rest of the value can be loaned based on promised repayment and the market value of whatever the loan was for. So long as the credit extended can be expected to be repaid (borrower has enough money, etc.) and the value of the collateral for a loan is valued at realistic worth, the money created in this way has real value. The value of the loan for a washing machine was probably based on the price tag plus interest. But if the loan was for a home, how was its value appraised? What if the borrower promised but did not pay back the agreed upon money? What if the home appraised was overvalued, and the bank cannot make the money back by selling the house, the collateral?

First, I do not find it very comforting that these institutions — now "too big to fail" — already have lots of our money invested in them. In addition, they turn out to be responsible for the creation of most "dollars" in circulation these days. While their money creation is limited by the percentage of real cash they have to keep unencumbered, the value of the money they create depends on the accurate valuation of the collateral, of what they lend against. We as the public have a vested interest not just in the percentage of money they are required to keep on hand but also in the regulations over what kind of loans they are allowed to make. We need some say in what kind of assets underlie loans and according to what standards of value. Otherwise, because they are piling loans upon loans, a relatively small number of "toxic" loans can shake an entire bank.

The Gold Standard

Cash money, at least, is basically a paper receipt for something of real agreed upon value, right? It is where we get the term "the gold standard" — gold bars piled up at Fort Knox? Well, no, not anymore.

Coming out of the crash of 1929, with the sudden loss of hot air out of speculative bubbles and the runs on the banks, certain regulatory changes were made. First, if regular people's money were put in banks and banks were allowed to invest in risky investments that meant large sums would be available for extensive speculation on the open market; secondly, with such high levels of risk there was no real way to protect those assets. Because of the New Deal, as regular people our checking and savings were only allowed to be deposited in commercial banks *not investment or "private" banks*. Requirements for reserves and pooling were enforced for the Federal Reserve and commercial banks and our accounts were insured. Investments made by commercial banks were more closely regulated. Those regulations have been updated over the decades as new commercial activities were engaged in and better operating practices created. Too often, though, these regulatory changes had to be made because of some economic destruction by banks getting into trouble with how they used *our* assets (the Savings and Loan debacle, for instance).

But regulation has gotten more targeted and effective — until recent years, that is.

Another change came because economists searched for the patterns of behavior that led to recessions and up turns. Besides watching over banks and their reserves, the Federal Reserve was also charged with using its significant economic power to keep our economy on track. The sweeping mission defined "on track" as including striving for full employment, moderate long-term interest rates and to also keep the economic transactions from stalling out, deflating or growing so quickly that they lead to inflation; these goals can sometimes conflict with each other. The Federal Reserve can use their assets to increase or decrease the flow of money in the U.S. economy. It can adjust the "federal funds" rate, the preferred rate that banks use to lend to each other. The Federal Reserve intervenes several times a year to adjust the economy's functioning.

After the Great Depression, the U.S. dollar became arguably the strongest monetary system in the world. The U.S. agreed to continue to tie its dollar to a standard value of gold and the rest of the major world economies agreed to a set exchange rate for U.S. dollars — thereby creating a standard value for currencies.

As long as foreign investors did not try to make a killing by purchasing dollars in droves (a "run" on currencies, like on banks, is usually prompted by expected large valuation change), the Federal Reserve's manipulation of the flow of U.S. dollars could have a predictable impact on our national economy and exchange rates for international business transactions could be reasonably predictable as well.

From the mid-1940s through the 1960s, such stable monetary controls (called trade barriers these days) protected currencies worldwide from speculation by wealthy world forces. Economic troubles hit as we entered 1970 (you remember what was known as the world oil crisis, perhaps?); our federal government and the Federal Reserve tried economic interventions several times in the 1970s and we ended up with something economic theorists had not thought possible before: stagflation.

Up until this time, U.S. monetary goals and the Federal Reserve's mission, including striving for full employment and a predictable monetary system, had not seemed in conflict. But stagflation led to lots of economic theory soul-searching and reassessment of the impact of various monetary policies. The consequence of out of control inflation (that some say was created by trying to fuel job growth) was that job loss was defined as *part of the way out* of the stagflation trap. In the 1970s, the Federal Reserve's use of its market interventions with a partial eye toward maximizing employment and, therefore, much of our survival as regular people, was quietly whited-out of the equation.

With an apparently weak economy and an unheard of trade deficit in the early 1970s, the U.S. dollar was a sitting duck for speculation. Countries around the world asked the United States to guarantee that the dollar would not be devalued so that loans to cover the U.S. deficit would be repaid in full. Faced with a potential global run on gold, President Richard Nixon unilaterally ditched the gold standard. Since then, U.S. monetary policy focused on keeping economic activity within certain limits and has had a floating exchange rate with other currencies and loosened attempts at international monetary barriers.

Today, no set value anchors our currency — not goods, not labor, not the gold standard, nor even fixed exchange rates with other countries. Nor is the amount of U.S. monetary value in circulation determined by our government. Banking institutions create 95 percent of monetary value out of loans — historically based on deposits. In fact, institutions allowed to create loan value on any credit instrument create monetary value.

What was in place to protect the value of money in the 1970s after detaching value from gold?

- Regulations on banking reserves and requirements for the banking activities they could use their reserves for
- A set of guidelines for Federal Reserve Bank interventions
- A clear delineation between commercial and investment banks
- Oversight agencies
- Licensed agencies for rating the value of investments and independent appraisers

There was at least significant transparency and accountability, right? And as long as no one investor or bank got so large that they could throw the stock market through their behavior, this could not get too far off track, right?

Enter the ramp up to the present crisis…

When money is or is not money

Even though my family was relatively comfortable financially, it would never have occurred to my parents to give either my brother or me a car for our high-school graduation. I can remember how disgusted my mother was when other parents did, especially when the new cars were fancy and expensive. How, she would say, is that child ever going to learn the value of that car if they never had to work for it? I think both my brother and I did eventually get one of my mother's cars, when it otherwise would have gotten hauled off to the junkyard. If we learned how to repair it ourselves or paid for repairs from our own earnings for upkeep that was looked on with big smiles.

Economists, in trying to understand, research and then predict economic behavior, tend to think of money in terms of its value to acquire goods. In making economic equations, they try to quantify everything in purely economic terms. It is well recognized that personal engagement in an economic transaction depends upon how much people experience the money they spend as "theirs." Like my mother, economists recognize that the personal value attributed to a possession like an expensive car is likely to be less if the owner did not buy it with their own money. A 17-year-old will value that car very differently if given by wealthy parents, paid for by the savings from a huge childhood "allowance" or purchased from years of after-school, summer and weekend earnings at a hard labor job.

When you disregard the value of an expenditure or investment because you have little or no personal "skin" in the transaction, economists call this a ***"moral hazard."*** While economists tend to apply this strictly in monetary terms, I think it has much broader psychological and social parallels.

We have all heard stories of tenants who did not seem to feel invested in their homes and so did not necessarily keep the yards nice or even inform landlords of dangerous situations; there are social assumptions as to why this happens, which may or may not be true. It is well documented that people owning their own homes greatly increases the care taken in preserving the appearance and usually the upkeep of housing. And absentee landlords generally have the worst track record of up-keep, especially the farther away and so less engaged.

We tend to assume that it is the amount of money invested, the "skin" in the deal, especially in relationship to a household's overall income and assets, that impacts the strength of commitment to upkeeping a home. However, a recent study prompted by the foreclosure crisis found that it was the length of tenure of living in a home (more than five years) that was significant — not whether an individual or family owned their home or rented! Separating out a number of variables, this study shows investment comes from living somewhere for a while regardless of financial investment. Just as length of residence matters more than just ownership, so too we may misunderstand the value of an investment if we look at absolute dollars as opposed to relative cost to a household.

Losing the sometimes small financial investment even in a subprime mortgage can seem significant financially to those who have never had many assets. There is also usually a huge emotional investment in a family's first home. The vision of a future for children and the stability of living in a neighborhood long-term may create a much bigger emotional investment than can be measured by the financial down payment if lost. Most of us grasp this if we think about it in a society that creates such a mystique around attaining the "American Dream." Here, in addition to the value of money, is a greater personal emotional investment.

Most of us have a sense of working hard for money and have spent much of our lives concerned about spending wisely what we have. We are challenged, then, by trying to understand how money is valued by the wealthiest people in our society. Here, I think, is where economic equations truly fail.

Those who manage the larger sums of money in our society find it easier to conceptualize what vast sums can access or impact. While some financial experts think that fancy financial transactions like derivatives and credit default swaps are invaluable financial tools, many economists realized belatedly that such complex and huge financial transactions can be incredibly risky. Such transactions were often handled by bankers, brokers, servicers and insurers — all middlemen in institutions that no longer held any direct investment. Thus these transactions could be incredibly risky or even doomed to

long term failure without setting off any alarms for the vast majority
of managers of these transactions.

In short, there were many hands making short-term, sometimes
swift and vast profits that had no "skin" in the transactions. Our
entire economy fell victim to rampant ***moral hazard.***

When you must work to earn money which you then spend all or
almost all of on regular daily expenses, the meaning of the money
in your life is fairly clear-cut. It is all about purchasing capacity — an
understanding that fits with economic theories. But once you bring
in money beyond what you need to spend directly, beyond what your
children could spend or your children's children, money is no longer
about purchasing goods. I do not know when this reality sets in for
different people. But eventually acquiring money, the size of your
holdings, assets, becomes about social status, your sense of power,
the amount of social and political influence you can wield — *not purchasing capacity.*

We worry about gamblers who gamble away their families' home,
food, their own livelihood or money for their medications or old age.
These gamblers who have lots of noticeable "skin" in the transaction and lose and cannot seem to stop, are clear examples of addicts.
We worry about the damage to those around them even if we do not
muster compassion for the gambling addicts themselves.

In contrast, Americans have mixed emotional reactions to the
tales of Japanese executives who kill themselves when they fail the
economic trust placed in them as corporate leaders. The idea that
financial responsibility for other people's money should have such
personal meaning for economic leaders can be hard for us to grasp.
But I think we can admire how profoundly they hold such a responsibility.

What about the billions accrued so quickly in recent years by
our society's unimaginably wealthy? Is it likely they thought of those
monies as important to their actual personal or familial financial
survival? Their fortunes certainly were not of value for regular economic purposes. They were digits held in a bank account, a definition of personal self-worth, control of assets as a source of power or
prestige. This was only exacerbated as most of this money came in
as unearned income — to use the bookkeeping term. Money brought
in money from the multiplier effect of investments and other market

tools, not by the sweat of their brow. The separation from money's value being a combination of the labor and resources it represents was complete. We all witnessed this transformation of money in endless TV advertisements about no longer working for your money but "putting your money to work for you."

Talk about ***moral hazard!*** When money is so divorced from the actual value of labor and resources that it apparently has the capacity to sweat by itself to reproduce itself, our entire social understanding of money has flipped on its head. Money that is only speculative and has no real life or even theoretical economic value is now held in the highest regard. Economic theories no longer apply. Money floats detached from the real work, material goods, and workers of society. And we have fallen through the looking glass.

Derivatives: Where Did All This Loss Come From?

*"I do not think toxic assets is the problem. I mean, you know
we hear this endless chatter about it. You know but the banks
who are in business are lending. But I also remind people that
banks are 25 percent of the system. They're not 100 percent of the
system," explained J.P. Morgan's Chief Executive Officer, Jamie
Dimon, in regards to the overall economic meltdown.*

A J.P. Morgan official says the point of Dimon's comment was that toxic assets are dangerous, but it is the shadow banking system that is the real problem.[19]

Clearly Dimon is right that subprime mortgages were simply the most visible part of the shadow banking industry, the proverbial tip of the iceberg.[20] The term *shadow banking industry* does not really refer to one industry, but to all of thousands of different finance-related institutions which engaged in bank-type activities but were not regulated, not insured, not generally publicly traded. Outside of any government's monetary policy, they existed in the shadows of a global economy which they came to vastly overshadow.

At its height in 2006, $13 trillion worldwide was estimated to be invested in mortgages in the United States.[21] The size of these figures — hundreds of times the cost for the Iraq occupation, for instance — seems staggering. Not until the major meltdown of the subprime lending crisis started or the federal bank bailout were figures in the trillions ever part of the public dialogue. By comparison, the total assets of the entire banking system in the United States in early 2007 was about $10 trillion.[22]

Our regular U.S. banks had had to meet certain levels of transparency for the oversight by the federal government and the Federal Reserve. They had to hold back 17 percent of regular banking transactions. They had to pay into the FDIC and the Federal Reserve to insure that overall there was sufficient money to cover at least our savings and checking accounts. This was to protect us from runs on the banks such as occurred in the 1930s. Our deposits continue to be covered even through this crisis.

The percentages of reserves and insurance payments legally required by all U.S. banks were based on what was supposed to be a transparently assessed value of each banking institution: how much money was in circulation and how much debt. Our pool of financial reserves had not been calculated to include insurance provided by big financial insurers like American International Group (AIG). Regulators decided not to include shadow banking institutions like mortgage companies, nor the even more obscure financial markets created by "new financial instruments" which functioned like private stock markets underground. Nor were regulations applied to the growing number of "off-book" transactions (over-the-counter derivatives – OTCs) by large investment banks.

The total value of the worldwide shadow banking industry was most recently estimated at almost $600 trillion in mid-2008. That dwarfed publicly-traded stocks and bonds which totaled about $62.5 trillion worldwide in fall of 2007 and shrank to about $36.6 trillion a year later![23]

With only a fraction of the banking industry regulated, when the shadow banking house of cards started to fall, the legally required, existing reserves and protections were woefully inadequate to stop the collapse.

While the 1999 repeal of the New Deal-era Glass-Steagall Act (aka Banking Act of 1933), which built a firewall between commercial and investment banks, officially opened the floodgates to speculation, each "new financial" instrument created over the previous decade poked another hole in the regulatory dam. Not because each new financial instrument was really new, but because the officials in charge of interpreting and applying existing regulations failed to apply them.

It did not help that many of the top regulators have been part of the revolving door between Wall Street and government for the last two decades. They believed their own rhetoric about the brilliant whiz kids at investing firms and bank departments with their infallible financial equations and machines. They had told each other over and over again that Greenspan and our financial leaders had solved the cyclical nature of capitalist markets; they mistook bubbles in the market for the promise of endless growth — even though there were plenty of signs and examples from around the world that these assessments were invalid. Nor did the Federal Reserve's regular interventions in the markets adjusting cash flow and interest levels shake some profound belief that Greenspan and so many had built up that the markets were now infallibly correcting themselves.[24]

There were, however, a few people aware of what was happening. The FBI section responsible for tracking fraud in business and banking tried to sound the alarms in 2004.[25] Having been stripped of enforcement officers when their department was raided by the Bush Administration in the wake of 9/11, they still had enough ears to the ground. They were savvy enough to assess what they uncovered in the mortgage industry, specifically in subprime lending, and predict that this far-reaching fraud would dwarf the Savings and Loan scandal when it was finally uncovered. They were calling for more agents and for larger government action, but their call fell on deaf, or perhaps intentionally negligent, ears.

What, in the past, would have been transacted in banks or public exchanges took place in numerous and different shadowy venues for the last decade and half. Various forms of investment — usually from truly huge investors — were used to leverage really big returns where money could be made by essentially betting on investments bought at one price and sold at a higher price. Newer, massive financial institutions had investors so wealthy that they would not need their initial investment anytime soon. Traders could use that additional money to buy longer-term safer investments that would rise in value. This amounted to internationally unregulated betting with large enough sums so that periodic losses could be subsumed by other gains; this seemed safe in a world market that was more often than not still paying out more than it was costing.

Specific examples of these new investment venues included the carry-trade, major investment banks, asset backed commercial paper, auction-rate securities and most of the mortgage companies and hedge funds — some of these segments have completely disappeared since the meltdown. I even tried to follow all of these examples but here is one and its relationship to regulation that could have been applied...

Remember our bucket companies earlier? Folks could invest with higher returns because these bucket companies did not need to pay regular bank deposit insurance nor would they face banking requirements like reserves. Well, one of the "creative" financial tools "developed" in the last 15 years of the last century were auction-rate securities. They became the preferred form of capital for a whole range of institutions because the interest due was lower than regular bank loans. Investors lent money through these securities on a long-term basis, say 30 years, and received interest yields like long term investments except better with no regular bank overhead. The way the auction-rate securities market worked, however, was that once a week they held a small auction — kind of like a stock market — where new potential investors could bid to replace old investors who wanted to get their investment back. The interest rate between auctions was determined by the bid rates of the previous auction. Investors made the typically higher returns from long-term investment rates, but in practice could get out whenever they wanted. If, for some reason, there were not enough new investors to replace old ones, the legal agreement was the interest rate would rise to a much higher penalty rate, say 15 percent. But that never happened so the dodge of normal bank regulation, securitization by reserves and, therefore, bank overhead worked fine.

Until it did not in early 2008. With some $400 billion at its peak, once not enough new investors showed for the first weekly auction, word got out that existing investors could not be certain of getting out whatever week they decided they wanted to. Suddenly, lots of investors showed up at the weekly auction to get out so the weekly auction failed again; penalties mounted and essentially a "run" ensued and the auction-rate securities market vanished — another big domino in the series of shadow banking mechanisms. Of course anti-bucket company regulations existed from 100 years earlier but the big financial players had convinced the regulators not to apply them.[26]

The role of "new" financial instruments

For several years now the names of "new" financial instruments have been making their way into public discourse. Hedge funds, derivatives, credit default swaps — complicated financial tools which are, I suppose, meant to "wow" and perhaps intimidate us a little bit.

Likewise, the complex financial mapping and predicting programs and machines were developed by some brain-children from MIT and similar institutions over the last couple of decades. Faced with incredibly complicated interactions created by a very interactive global economy — complete with floating currencies, massive banks and even more massive individual wealth all seeking to get their money to "work for them." Economists and mathematicians went to work. They created complex computer models, patented the "intellectual" property programmed into their computers and holed up in corners of major financial institutions. The most famous team of wunderkinds were sent to hole up in offices in the top floors of AIG's operations in London, freed from any possible fetters of the U.S. government or its oversight agencies. They served to embody the high tech magic of low risk very high reward investments by the wealthy of the wealthiest. Only, no questions asked, please, about how this was to be accomplished.

Investing in my mother's generation was supposed to be about the investor making calculated risks based on what they felt they could afford to lose versus how much money they hoped to gain. This was a calculated gamble informed by investment brokers based on the track record of a company whose stocks you wanted to buy and guesses about how the stock market was likely to fare in coming months. When you invested in stocks you knew what they were and how much you paid for them. Some people enjoyed the daily adrenaline rush of opening the business pages of some major newspaper and seeing whether their stock was up or down that day or that week. Or you told your stockbroker the kinds of investments you wanted to make for how much risk or gain and let him manage everything with regular reports.

Occasionally you got to gloat about the unusual profit that only you (or your stock broker) managed to pull off.

Then came the magical mathematical formulas which were supposed to be able to predict razor thin possibilities in real-time computer transactions and so greatly lower the risk in investing while being able to capture the kind of large returns only the riskiest ventures were able to capture in the past. Perhaps, the folks who should have been questioning offers from the financial industry that were too good to be true were the wealthiest amongst us — not so much those with few other housing options signing up for subprime mortgage mirages...

There are those who will tell you there is nothing new under the sun, only the same old stuff dressed up in new clothes. From reading through and struggling to understand what all these supposed new financial instruments and off-the-books investment opportunities were, there have been similar ventures before. Most of them had created financial crashes before; attempts had been made and laws were on the books to outlaw or tightly regulate them in the future. These new financial instruments managed in various ways to avoid those regulations being applied to them.

Derivatives

Perhaps the most familiar name of a supposedly new financial instrument is the derivative. Derivatives get their name from being financial arrangements that get their value from some underlying contract. Money, you could say, was originally a "derivative," a receipt of a certain value against gold or silver in a vault.

Any kind of insurance is a bet against the possibility of some bad future; it's an attempt to take precautions now to avoid it or line up the money to fix it. Derivatives started, it seems, as insurance.

Say you are a corn farmer.[27] You have spent a certain amount of money to grow your corn. Rather than worry that the price of corn might drop a lot before you bring the corn to market, you make an agreement with a buyer to pay a certain price for the amount of corn you believe your farm will produce. The buyer will make money on your agreement if the price of corn rises and you only make what was agreed on. But you are guaranteed a certain income even if the price of corn drops at which point the buyer will lose some money. Of course, you need to produce the amount of corn you signed for or you are in trouble.

This contract functions like insurance against future market fluctuations. You might put some of your corn in one contract and another part in another contract based on possible market situations when the time to sell comes. You might let some corn simply sell at the price on the day it is delivered to market. By splitting up your corn in different agreements, you would essentially protect your-self from some risk but also diversify your risk for different possible market outcomes. This could be considered savvy risk management or insurance or gambling. But regardless of purpose, this contract is a derivative, deriving its value from your corn crop.[28]

An investor might buy that contract because they believe the farmer is wrong and the price is going to go up. Or you could buy the contract expecting a loss but allowing you for a time to have a contract with a declared value greater than it will eventually have; you could invest some of that value in the meantime and make some money on it before you are going to have to pay off the loss.

Such contracts, since they depend upon actual execution by both parties according to their terms, are also often insured. That way, if one party defaults, the other party can hope to recoup some of their losses. Such insurance also provides a potential investment opportunity; it can also be bought or sold. It is also called a derivative — deriving its value from the underlying contract, deriving its value from your corn.

Now insurance can be seen as an investment where a third party believes that the principle parties to the contract are going to come through. So you invest, they come through, and you profit by pocketing the fees spent on insurance that was never drawn down.

Each such contract could be insured multiple times, creating multiple paybacks on investment. You could also, however, break the insurance value up and sell it to several parties, passing along the risk. At one point, disbursing a partial risk to so many investors was seen as good; if the insurance was never used, everyone made a little money; if the underlying deal failed, everyone was only out a smaller portion of money supposedly protecting every investor. The other possibility, however, was that if many such deals started to fail, everyone had an investment and the failure could multiply across the whole world market. All these investment agreements are also, of course, all derivatives.

As you may now suspect, the term derivative could be applied to almost any financial instrument. This makes references to derivatives confusing. As a category they also do not distinguish by intent or even your financial relationship to the "financial product."

My farmer in the above example created a contract as a sort of insurance, a hedge, against market changes. But this derivative is clearly anchored in a real commodity; it will be cashed out in the short term. While it may never be recorded by a financial institution, the payout will return to the regular banking industry pretty quickly.

Many such derivatives are mediated by a "clearing house" which provides the legal expertise in making contracts workable and legally sound. Once such a contract flows through one of these service providers or clearing houses (for a fee from both parties, of course), it does end up on someone's books somewhere and appears in an accounting that will be overseen somewhere. And if it ends up in a stock exchange the value could be bought or sold as an investment.

But the types of derivatives out there are numerous and a huge number will never be publicly traded. Even in banks, accounting procedures started listing them as off-the-books and so, unregulated.

Add to this mess that there are millions of these underlying contracts. Even the numerous daily currency exchanges that occur between banks and countries are contracts. A fraction of a cent change in the exchange value between one day's purchase and the next day's sale of a country's currency equals millions per day in "insurance" for the exchange transactions. Such derivative contracts and their insurance can be broken-up into smaller contracts sold at an estimated value or bundled into clumps of investments!

Of course, your head is hurting by now trying to track my descriptions let alone think about how you would know or predict the stability of the value of these contracts over any period of time.

Why do derivatives and the headache I just gave you matter?

Imagine them as the unregulated "insurance" investments, gambling chips valued in the millions that the wealthiest used to bet on vast international financial transactions. The top line in Figure 1.6 shows the exponential increase *in trillions of dollars invested in derivatives* especially between 2002 and 2008. For perspective, two points below in 2008 and 2009 represents the trillions of publicly traded securities, stocks and bonds, the *non-shadow part of the world financial industry*.[29]

One note: Fig 1.6 shows an increase in the value of the shadow banking sector of about 500 trillion dollars worldwide in less than a decade. While I am not an economist, there is no possibility that this represents an increase in real goods and services of 500 trillion dollars worldwide. This value is built on contracts and promissory notes, appraisals and insurance, much like how I described earlier that banks can essentially create money by entering figures in their accounting books. Those trillions may have represented speculation and phantom value built into millions of transactions around the world.

Figure 1.6 Derivative value worldwide vs. publicly traded stocks and bonds[30]

Bad enough that my mother's generation was trying to decide whether to buy oil stock based on somewhat predictable value increases; how do you as an investor today figure out about several dozen different kinds of derivatives? It is one thing to trust your broker when you know what stock they are buying or selling for you. How do you know what is going to happen when they are buying a partial investment, a derivative or a hundred bundled together based on, say, mortgages written by mortgage companies?

Enter the Hedge Fund

Now there have always been traders who were considered brilliant (or some would say lucky). Everyone involved with the stock market watches for indications that the value of a particular company or commodity is going to be impacted. But it is these "brilliant" traders who seemingly know a stock is going to rise when it has been falling (so everyone else is selling it off at a low price they can buy) or who seemingly know it is going to fall when no one else does (so they can sell at a high price while others are still buying) that have traditionally made the significant profits.

With rapid trading in these "complex" new financial instruments often far divorced from the underlying contract, the "brilliant" traders became that select group of wunderkinds I mentioned earlier. Considered the equivalent of geniuses from MIT and other such institutions working with computers programmed with complex mathematical models supposedly able to predict all of this, they became a much rarified crew. The mystique around them grew as they seemed to make money magically multiply.

Over time, investors (individuals and companies) came to trust their brokers at bigger and bigger investment companies more divorced from actual stock and commodity investments, often through intermediary managers of say pension funds or 401(k)s. Finally, big investment transactions became not so much about the track record of the broker as about the prestige of their firms. Unlike my mother's broker, who provided her with the name of actual investments she could even look up on the stock exchange if she wished, more investors, especially the large ones, became parties to hedge funds. The actual investments were not revealed, only the profits under the trusted name of the investment company — Citigroup Hedge Fund, Shearson-Lehman Hedge Fund, etc.

These hedge funds, guided by those whiz kids with their computers (mainly Bloomberg machines) tracking and supposedly guiding these hundreds of derivative deals, started turning over large profits. Investment money came from a few recently enlarged key sources:

- the very wealthy with rapidly increasing wealth not so much through productive investment as through money made from money thanks substantially to significantly lowered tax rates
- larger and larger institutional investors fed by government policies that incentivized investment of retirement funds in the stock market
- funds freed up by the removal of barriers between the huge pools of our deposit money in commercial banks (originally regulated conservatively) and private investment banks that have no such regulations and, in fact, insurance companies, or even mortgage companies as well. A veritable avalanche of investment capital seeking a home…

Hedge funds required significant fees on initial investment. Some put the average investment fee at 5 percent: the percentage fee on earnings at 36 percent.[31] Initially, hedge funds seem to have taken these large initial investments to sell short and buy long; they eventually bought up some otherwise hard to sell investments across the world until the hedge funds cornered certain markets. Thus, when hedge funds ran into trouble and needed to sell assets they either could not sell or sold such a significant percentage of certain types of investment that their selling made prices plummet destroying the underlying investments' value. Either way, the hedge funds could not recoup their losses by selling their basic investments.

So the domino effect, a downward spiral ensued as hedge funds and some of this shadow banking market started to collapse. The tsunami the collapse spawned in the banking shadows swamped the regular visible banking industry across the world.

But I am getting ahead of the story. First we have to visit the most publicly visible part of the shadow banking world, the mortgage companies and their since-ousted bad boys, the subprime mortgages.

Derivatives: Story of a Swaption

Take the Mass Turnpike Authority's situation in 2009. As a quasi-independent agency, they were set up like other quasies to supposedly take them out of the control of elected officials who could use them as graft and political favors for their support-ers — out from being part of a political machine. Unfortunately, this has also mostly meant that quasies have governmental responsibilities and governmental funding but no governmental nor any public oversight!

Now, with no oversight and, apparently as part of the bizarre financial reality distortion field that enthralled top investors everywhere, the MTA in 2001 decided to engage in a huge derivative contract to solve its short-term financial woes. No doubt sold to its board at the time as a prudent fiscal invest-ment, they were as of August 2009 in trouble to the tune of some $300 to $400 million from just one of the debts worth 22 million in 2002. Like the lenders, they are coming to the legisla-tors asking for taxpayer dollars to fix their outrageously risky financial behavior.[32]

Remember this the next time you hear them bellyache about a few toll-takers calling in a sick day. No line worker can turn a few million dollars shortfall into a hundreds of millions dollars deficit in a few years. Of course, there is a popular political spin of demonizing workers, playing into prejudice and just hoping no one turns around and points a finger at the real culprits.

Without knowing all the terms of the contractual agree-ment in this case, a swaption is a "swap" "option," a type of derivative where a new loan is treated *as if* it were a replace-ment — a swap — for an existing one and where there are condi-tions — options — for how the value can be called in.

The Turnpike's swaption, we are told, is too complicated for us to understand; that is patently untrue and undermines our ability to recognize that we can be an informed electorate. In fact, the Turnpike's financial officers, like most such "experts," cannot predict the financial future. The deal was apparently too complex for them to predict and therefore, too complex to have engaged in at all!

Imagine that you wrote a fantasy into a legal contract. Originally, the MTA had signed up for the equivalent of a fixed rate mortgage and signed away the right to refinance it for 10 years. Then interest rates fell *but* they could not benefit from that lowered rate because of their 10 year contract stipulation.

Stuck with their fixed rate mortgage they went looking for some financial institution to join them in a legal game of pretend. What if, they offered, we pretend you refinanced this mortgage at a variable rate to give us lower payments while interest rates are low (if interest rates went up they would pay much more), and you make the payments for the fixed rate mortgage? All as if they had actually been able to sign over the original fixed rate mortgage even though they could not. As part of this agreement they paid $29 million to U.S. Bancorp (USB) to refinance; they agreed that the new lender could call in the loan when they wanted to under certain circumstances (an option).

Like all derivatives this has the scent of a gamble. The MTA was gambling that if interest rates stayed low through the end of the 10 year mortgage, they would save a lot on interest. USB was gambling that interest rates would rise and that they would make more from the MTA than the fixed rate payments they were making on the MTA's original mortgage agreement. There is surely some street lore about the dangers of betting against the bank but then the MTA financial experts probably thought they knew better than street lore.

At the end of the 10 years, the MTA was deeper in debt and unable to refinance at all. The swaption had now grown to a debt of *$300 to $400 million* and USB was talking about calling it in.

While none of the public had a say in the MTA's risky financial choices and the legislature struggled about demanding transparency about this initial stupid contract, we the taxpayers were told that the MTA is too critical to be allowed to fail... (Our schools can fail, our mortgages can fail, but they *have* to spend our tax dollars on keeping the Massachusetts Turnpike Authority afloat).

Signal of the times, Times of signal…

It has been crazy listening to some of what is considered economic policy advice. When Barack Obama was elected, he promised change. One of the noticeable changes in his early speeches from the inauguration forward — for a while anyway — was his forthright statements about the seriousness of the economic situation we face:

> *"That we are in the midst of crisis is now well understood… Our economy is badly weakened, a consequence of greed and irresponsibility on the part of some, but also our collective failure to make hard choices and prepare the nation for a new age. Homes have been lost; jobs shed; businesses shuttered. Our health care is too costly; our schools fail too many; and each day brings further evidence that the ways we use energy strengthen our adversaries and threaten our planet."*
> —*President Barack Obama* from his inauguration speech.[33]

While he was drafting and beginning to lay the conceptual framework in his speeches for a major stimulus push, the economic policy "experts" began to criticize. While some not surprisingly trotted out deficit hawk arguments that had bizarrely been almost silenced while Obama's predecessor dug us into what was the greatest deficit ever, that was not what surprised me.

Has anyone else found it odd that while real people were losing jobs, health coverage, being dumped on the street and unable to locate college loans for their children, that *economists* seem to talk almost exclusively of the need for Obama to change his rhetoric? To them, the problem was not that our economy is in desperate straits and as a country we must come together to recognize and address this problem. No, apparently, the problem was that Obama was not making everyone feel better, giving speeches to calm the nerves of Wall Street, bankers, and investors. That if we could just get over this crisis of confidence, the hard economics of our lives would simply reverse themselves?

I took some solid economics courses in college; I have found myself putting every economic analytical tool I was taught to work in the last several years to try to understand what was happening, especially since everything happening seemed to contradict the official Wall Street and Washington D.C. Beltway insider story. And I found myself almost lost in ironic laughter. Here I am, the trained psychologist, digging deep into my limited knowledge of economics to understand what is going on while trained economists are bizarrely trying to explain everything away as psychological.

A key learning from every economics course must be that our economy is cyclical. The economy goes through growth periods where businesses make more profits, invest more, and hire more workers and the economy expands. And we hit periods where the economic expansion leads to tighter competition and the rising costs of labor and materials — in theory partly because labor and resources get relatively scarcer — and so profits start to decrease, businesses pull back, invest less and then start laying off workers and our economy contracts.

Another thing I learned in a course in third world economics was that not all paths to becoming an industrialized nation were equal. Leaving aside the complexities of colonialism and other systems of control (and many would say exploitation), economically different theories about the swiftest road to becoming a first world economy have held sway at different times. At one point, world powers and economic institutions bought into the idea that it was simply industrialization that brought an economy into the first world. With that as a philosophy, investment dollars were focused on shifting directly from a spread-out farming or hunting based society (without much money or technology) to bringing in and setting up major industrial facilities; they usually opted for production of some fairly significant products such as cars or major appliances. While these products might have a ready market in existing industrialized nations, the countries targeted for this kind of development were hurt economically and did not suddenly enter into the industrialized world.

This, of course, led to a "re-think" on the part of economists. What theoreticians realized was that industrialization which had grown in incremental stages in "first world" countries had brought with it other incremental changes. At its core, simply creating a large product was at best useless to an economy where no one, not even the workers at the industrial plants, could afford the products produced. Flash heavy industrial development failed, because equally critical to our economies is a consumer base that can afford and wants the products of industry. The huge upfront investment in production had overburdened an economy that had none of the associated smaller forms of development; just like a forest consisting only of the largest trees (all the same age) guarantees the forest's eventual demise.

I imagine that these and other lessons played in the back of my head in 1998 when I stood in my office trying to make sense of the larger forces affecting our work as community organizers. All the media reports said we were well out of the recession of the early 1990s. But for the mostly single mothers I worked with, poverty seemed to have stood still — only more intransigent if anything. More searching revealed it was not just my impression that those enjoying major recovery were in the top 40 percent of our economy and those in the bottom 20 percent were being passed by in the "economic recovery."

By the late 1990s, I had many more warning bells playing in my head. Homelessness was seriously on the rise and more and more people were referred to as "rent poor" — that is, paying a lot more than 50 percent of their income for housing expenses. While real wages were not rising, rents surely were. In fact, I remember my deep-seated concern when homeless rates surpassed all previous figures except those leading into the Great Depression.

Moreover, not only were the people I worked with and among doing worse, but according to all official reports, our economy was doing very well. This spin made getting realistic housing, food, welfare, even worker's rights policies heard, let alone taken seriously, almost impossible. Even though most U.S. residents were objectively unable to gain economic ground and many were losing it, policy makers and opinion-makers somehow heard the economic boom language to mean anyone could do better if they just tried harder. With cuts of programs, privatization of government functions and economic choices by government leaders to cut taxes and revenue, it was as if everyone making choices for regular people somehow thought the economy was always going to grow. The government would never need to play a safety net function again. All of these policy choices also meant fewer good paying jobs.

I and others paying attention seemed to recognize that this rising tide was certainly not lifting all boats, even though people continued to use that analogy. So I went looking for answers. It turned out that our economy had taken a right hand turn at some point. The fundamental assumptions we had about economic growth and who benefited how had changed...

Different Economies

Figure 1.7 shows income growth for our whole population divided into fifths from 1947 to 1979 — the lowest fifth of income earners through the highest grew in income about equally.

Figure 1.7   Change in real family income by quintile, top 5% 1947–1979[34]

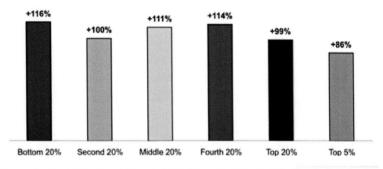

Source: Analysis of U.S. Census Bureau data in Economic Policy Institute, *The State of Working America 1994-95* (M.E. Sharpe: 1994) p. 37.

Figure 1.8 shows the same fifths from 1979 through 2006 when they did not grow together; the more income each fifth started with, the more their income grew and most of our incomes grew very little at all.

Figure 1.8   Change in real family income by quintile, top 5% 1979–2008[35]

Source: U.S. Census Bureau, Historical Income Tables, <u>Table F-3</u> (for income changes) and <u>Table F-1</u> (for income ranges in 2008 dollars).

Lots of explanations exist for why our economy shifted in the mid-seventies — the oil crisis, the fears created by stagflation — which in turn changed how the Federal Reserve interpreted its responsibility to the economy. It no longer concerned itself with job maximization, and therefore changed how the Federal Reserve periodically threw its economic weight around. The minimum wage was allowed to start its decline below the poverty level; the percentage of organized workers dropped off; utility companies were privatized; unilaterally, the federal government decided to detach from the gold standard and float the dollar. The struggle for a guaranteed minimum income failed and even with the supposed War on Poverty, welfare payment levels dropped.

The most salient lesson for me was that over time, we were coming to live in two different economies. One was for the relatively well-off: it got the media attention and their experience of the economy determines whether we were seen as in a period of recession or not. The second is the reality the rest of us live in; over time we were slowly slipping into a worse and worse economy. During each recession, fewer of us were going to climb out. More and more of us were going to be passed by. But the economics that influence the reality of our lives as regular people were going to be harder to understand for those listening to and especially living the official story — that includes most folks high-up in government.

By the late 1990s, the divide between the wealthy and the rest of us surpassed the figures that had led up to the Great Depression. So, finally, did the homeless statistics.

The market started to behave erratically as systems do when they are approaching a potential break-down. So when we were belatedly informed at the turn of 2001/2002 that the economy had entered a recession even before the 9/11 attack, I was not surprised. But while the recession was hard on so many that had never benefited from the last upturn, the bottom did not really fall out and those who had been watching the larger indicators like I had were actually surprised. Why didn't the whole economy crash?

I remembered that part of why the recession of the 1930s was so bad and became a depression was the huge amount of speculation going into it. The huge climb beforehand which had not been based in real value was what made the 1929 crash so deep when the bubble burst. Incredible wealth had been spent not in the creation of more jobs and products of real value; it had been made from money off of money. In a sense, this is gambling on financial ventures: speculation.

With the relatively shallow recession at the beginning of this century, I started looking for where speculative investment must have taken off, masking deeper, more dangerous economic indicators. I was wondering why the recession was described as so mild by economists when there were underlying warning signals like the biggest wealth divide since the Great Depression.

Apparently, the mainstream economists took the short and shallow recession as more proof that our economy, the policies of the Federal Reserve and major financial advisors had reached a new level of brilliance. They could somehow ensure that the world economy no longer need face serious economic cycles. Long-term steady growth could be insured. Greenspan was proven to be the master of the (economic) universe.[36]

Figure 1.9 shows the length of official recessions and you can see the shortness of the recessions in the early 1990s and 2001. The line in the graph shows unemployment increases in the recessions and that since the 1980s recessions, *job losses continued after the official recession ended.* (I deal with that later.)

The fact that the recession in the early 1990s had been saved by what we think of as the internet or dot-com bubble — actually a large stock bubble not real economic value — did not disturb the

Figure 1.9   Historical recessions and timing of job loss and recovery[37]

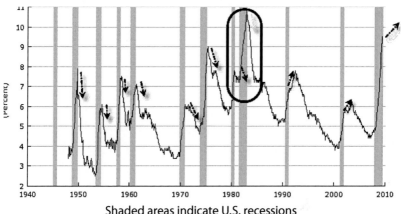

Shaded areas indicate U.S. recessions
2009 research.stlouisfed.org
Source: U.S. Department of Labor: Bureau of Labor Statistics

economists. Even when in 2002 the housing market seemed to take off and cut short another recession, they convinced themselves and each other that housing values could grow forever and it was smooth economic sailing from here on out.

Statistics showed that this time 60 percent of us were still losing economic ground even after the recession supposedly ended. And not the top 10 percent but only the top one percent this time was actually benefitting by the economic upturn. When I saw the sudden uptick in home prices and then found out about subprime mortgages and the unbridled investment money being poured into the housing sector, I felt my gut drop — here was the speculative market, the global venture I suspected had to exist to have temporarily jacked the economy back up before the 2001 recession had even really set in...

What is interesting to me in Figure 1.9 is that major media has not drummed home the shift to "job-loss" economic recoveries. If you notice through the recession in the early 1980s, job recovery started as the official recession ended. Starting in the 1990s, that was no longer true.[38]

The definition of a recession includes a number of economic indicators but somehow by the early 1990s, our jobs and our survival as regular people got dropped from the list of indicators considered important for defining a recession. How come we as regular people stopped counting in the economic equation? Who decided that?

Implications of the Economic Generation Gap

This shift in the economics of income for most of us has created a profound difference in the life experiences of those above and below about 35 years of age; it has created a profound "generation gap."[39] As of fall 2009, a study highlighted the realities that our economics have created in the lives of those 30 to 35 years of age or younger. They include:

- In July 2009, 1.7 million fewer teenagers and young adults were employed than a year earlier, reaching a record 51.4 percent unemployed.
- Since 1999, more of workers aged 35 or younger have lower paying jobs if they have jobs at all.
- 34 percent of workers under 35 live with their parents for financial reasons.
- 31 percent of young workers report being uninsured up from 24 percent 10 years ago, 79 percent of those uninsured report not being able to afford insurance and their employers do not offer it.
- Only 31 percent say they make enough money to cover their bills and put some money aside (22 percent less than in 1999); 24 percent cannot even pay their monthly bills.
- Thirty-seven percent have put off education or professional development because of costs.

Their experience about the accessibility of paid work and certainly the rewards of a hard day's work are profoundly different from those approaching 50 or older.

This challenges a deeply held assumption that our children stand on the shoulders of their parents, especially their parents' sacrifices toward their better future. How many of us carry the stories of how hard our parents worked so that we could stay longer in school so that we could have a better job and make more money? Not all sectors of our society have been able to live this ideal. But it is the profound story of many that their grandparents immigrated to the United States to find a better life, and while like most U.S. immigrants their lives might have been bitter living in crowded unhealthy tenements and working the dirtiest most dangerous jobs, at least their children had access to education and a better life.

But the vast majority of us by 2009 have entered a different life-long reality. For those who fought in World War II and their children there was a reward for their contribution; a huge swath of our society benefited from the G.I. Bill providing education and the means to invest in home ownership. Our economy was set up so that pretty much everyone who worked increased their living standard over their lifetime — as our relatively stable economy expanded and our incomes all grew together. Because of relatively stable employment, education usually meant higher income and access to union jobs or at least job sectors with a high percentage of unions which meant some voice and better income and benefits. This was especially true for the mostly white men who dominated these sectors and could truly say that they did better than their parents. Today, most people still hope for similarly improved lives for their children if they work hard and play by the rules.

Overwhelmingly, the problem is that even for today's sons of these fathers, their work — no matter how traditional and hard — will not reap even the same rewards as their parents. Right now they, and women and people of color, the vast majority of us, will not reap those rewards that especially white men did in the last generation. To change the present economic reality we must return to the government policies, the commitments to broad public improvement and the people's organizations that undergirded in almost invisible ways an economy where we all grew together.

Figure 1.10 Richest 10 percent's share in total U.S. income[40]

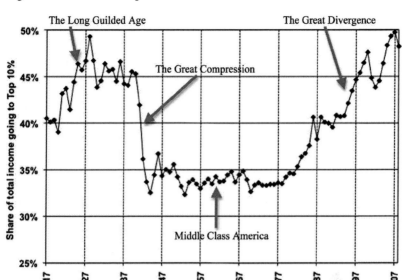

Periods of widely divided incomes (1920–1940 and 1985–present)
and shared prosperity (1940–1985)

Figure 1.10 shows how much of our overall nation's income the top 10 percent received[41] and how that portion has changed over time. As the Great Depression ended and our economy stabilized, their share dropped precipitously, which is called economic compression. The chart makes graphic the period when they had a share closer to the rest of us; from the early 1940s to the early 1980s when there was a growing middle class.

You can see how a reality of shared prosperity built up in those decades. Those who could get work saw a growing economy where their effort contributed and all layers of society benefited. Playing by the rules—the economic and social rules of that time—did, in fact, pay off for the majority. Since then you can see how dramatically the shares in the benefits of our economy have changed. Pay off has come to depend more on what economic position you are in to begin with. A generation gap in life experience and economic expectations has been created. Policy changes underlie those changes in distribution; policies which we need to address to return to shared prosperity...

Part II

Sealing the Holes In the Hull

I n recent years, major areas of economic activity are literally tearing gaping holes in the bottom of our Commonwealth's ship. The foreclosure crisis alone has created gaping financial holes in our state economy — estimates put annual losses to our statewide economy at 29 billion dollars, more than our entire state government budget. Health expenditures represent more than 38 percent of our state budget; they undermine our business economy and our city and town budgets, slice into our take-home pay and were the most common source of bankruptcy before the foreclosure crisis. And, there is no end in sight for steep increases in insurance premiums. Another significant budget expense is our prisons — costing almost 5 percent or 1/20th of our budget.

The crazy thing is that there are policy solutions to all these economic drains that have been proposed. These would not only improve our housing market, our health care, and cut crime, but stop these downward economic forces. They would cost the state government *either nothing or much less* to implement than how much we are presently spending. We cannot save the ship long-term from sinking if we keep taking on water in these areas — and there is no reason not to seal these holes now.

Halting the Foreclosure Crisis and Its Impact

Suppose that the people of our state have lost $58.9 billion in personal wealth between 2008 and the end of 2009?[1] That is more than twice the state's annual budget. Would you think urgent action by our State House was critical especially as our economy bottoms out? The cause is foreclosures on subprime mortgages; the question, how come our elected officials have not yet acted decisively and comprehensively?

One of the concepts I have found the hardest to get across to elected officials is that they need to look at their decisions in terms of the whole economy. They are confronted over and over again with the budget of their own political body. So they forget that their decisions affect the entire economy surrounding that budget. They get conceptually trapped inside the four walls of the State House or city or town hall they work in. This tendency is much greater at the state or local level, where the budgets have to balance unlike the federal budget which is allowed to run deficits.

For that reason, as politicians have gotten more and more scared of talking about taxes, they have focused more and more of their big plans on capital expenditures; for these they are allowed to borrow money through the creation of bonds and let us and our children pay for them later. Operating budgets — which include all regular staffing and program expenditures — bear the almost one-sided brunt of budget cuts, often the day-to-day programs which employ regular people and which we need the most.

As you are probably getting tired of my saying, in a regular economy, consumers provide about 70 percent of our economic activity, business investment 20 percent and government spending about 10 percent.[2, 3] Between the fear of raising taxes and the inside-four-walls mentality, you can see how the government's 10 percent of economic spending in regular times made it relatively easy for elected officials to convince themselves that their choices do not affect the general economy very much.

While that kind of thinking is never helpful, in an economic depression where the other types of spending shrink and shrink quickly, government spending choices are much more critical to our economy. Elected officials have to begin thinking of every dollar they spend as just as impactful on the overall economy as every dollar they raise — or avoid raising.

We do not get mentally trapped inside those four walls and we feel their economic choices all the time. We need to become as vocal about service cuts as about tax increases. We need to become more comfortable thinking about government choices as a whole — it is not like elected officials are somehow magically smarter than us!

We elect officials to help balance our budget, the budget of our state and municipality and our household — not the budget of the government itself in a vacuum. We never have and never will. We must bring that larger picture to our elected officials and *not let them forget it.*

The Subprime Lending Crisis

Because the subprime lending crisis was treated by government officials as a private economic activity, they looked the other way on a huge market sector which was predictably going to undermine our entire economy (the world economy, in fact). Those of us who were watching spoke out and tried to ring the alarm bells.

In reality, as of 2009, economists were just coming to the centrality of this crisis and speaking out on needing to address the banks' "toxic assets" before the economy can turn around. One economist said in summer 2009, since no level of government has really addressed these subprime mortgages which the banks bundled together with other more stable investments, we are no farther along towards righting the fundamentals of our economic crisis than we were in 2007!

On the other hand, pundits are already claiming that this economic downturn is over, that the worst is behind us. Pundits are working to get this period called the Great Recession to avoid that feel-bad "D" word. But the foreclosure crisis along with other new apparently "minor" factors key to economics *such as job losses* make many of us question their assessment. Figure 2.1 is a comparison of much higher percentage of foreclosures predicted in our period and those during the Great Depression:

Figure 2.1   Foreclosure rates for Great Depression and 2008[4]

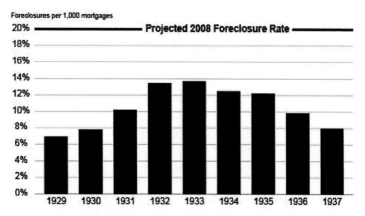

Sources: For foreclosure rates during the Great Depression: "The Federal Response to Home Mortgage Distress: Lessons from the Great Depression" by David Wheelock, *Federal Reserve Bank of St. Louis Working Paper No. 2008-038A*, October 24, 2008. For foreclosure rate in 2008: Center for Responsible Lending <http://www.responsiblelending.org/pdfs/Fclosure-exec-summary-standalone.pdf>.

Too few elected officials are grasping the severity of the foreclosure crisis and seeing it as a government responsibility to act on it. The centrality of the subprime mortgage crisis may be more clear-cut for those of us whose homes are threatened, whose neighborhoods are being emptied and whose jobs and local business's incomes are drying up.

Why are so many of us so over our heads in housing costs?

The groundwork for this crisis was actually laid by a federal policy shift that decided to move the commitment to affordable housing out of government hands and into the private market during the 1980s. While government commitment to affordable housing had lessened over time, the decreases were small and gradual until the early eighties when federal spending plummeted removing $38 billion out of direct housing and subsidy programs. Instead, the federal government shifted to primarily providing mortgage deductions. This took the money out of the parts of the housing market where people who needed it most could draw on it and spend it in our local economies.

Receiving government assistance was made dependent upon ownership of housing, a much more costly housing program not serving
those who need it most.[5]

Figure 2.2   Federal expenditures: home ownership tax loss vs. affordable
               housing programs[6]

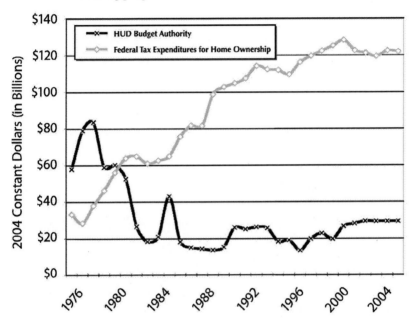

Whenever government leaders make decisions like this, the direct
programs are scaled back and only continue to help the very, very
hardest off amongst us. Many fewer are covered and an artificial
demarcation and threshold are created. Most who need and could
productively use assistance end up facing abrupt cut-offs and large
hurdles to economic advancement as they improve their situation.

This huge shift in the underlying market influence of government
on housing combined with other powerful forces. In the mid-1970s,
income growth which had been benefiting all layers of society split
with the loss in real wages (spending power) of regular people in
comparison with the wealthy — an economic divide that has been
growing ever since. As tax cuts became the cry of the day, local aid
to municipalities began to drop; to make ends meet, cities and towns
became more and more dependent upon the raising of property taxes

which increase rents. With less government spending on housing for renters, there was an opening for more private investors seeing housing as an investment where the priority was to make profits not provide a decent basic human need. Remaining government spending became more indirect — putting money into the pockets of private investors through housing subsidies.

As home ownership continued to slip so that less than 50 percent of people would ever own their own home, more and more people became "housing poor" — more and more of their entire income was going to housing themselves and their families, crossing the line to over 50 percent of their income. The standard guideline in the housing industry remains that at most about 38 percent of your income is supposed to go toward housing, but many, many working class families were spending 60 percent, 70 percent, even 90 percent of their income on a roof over their heads — and taking on more jobs or work hours to try to bridge the gap.

Meanwhile other government policies put in place during the Great Depression of the 1930s were unraveling. One of the great lessons of the Depression was that speculative investment by those with enough money can pull down the economy for all of us. I use "speculative" to mean the attempt to make money without any real value in goods or services to underpin it. The obvious institutions that have huge enough percentages of money in our society to endanger the whole economy if they use them for speculation are banks. Lobbying by the financial industry over the last couple of decades continued to increase, leading to removal or weakening of regulatory policies; many consumer protections went unused through government negligence, if not through intent.

As Vermont Sen. Bernie Sanders said recently: "If an institution is too big to fail, then it is too big to exist." [7]

Under the U.S. Constitution, our federal government is responsible for most bank regulation; since money crosses between state borders, states' ability to regulate is constitutionally quite limited. While deregulation played one critical factor in how the subprime lending scam took off, the real problem was government negligence.

You may recall the Savings and Loan (S & L) scandal of the 1980s: one sector of the banking industry with slightly different oversight used loopholes to invest money without generally recognized safe-guards. They spent enough money so when their risky — sometimes illegal — money-making strategies failed, it sent shock waves through our whole economy. In response, bank regulations were re-drawn. Like today, significant amounts of our tax dollars were paid out to the very investment leaders who had gotten their S & Ls into trouble in the first place!

What has happened in the last decade or two dwarfs all of these examples, however. Those whose overriding focus is making money got creative. A number of financial "products" were created that allowed investors — especially those with huge (and I mean really vast) pools of capital which they would never be able to spend in regular ways — to essentially bet on riskier and riskier prospects in pursuit of larger and larger payoffs. However, because these new ways of making money fell (or more accurately were allowed to fall) outside of existing definitions of banks and regulated financial activities, they avoided the government requirements for checks and balances.

The federal government did not apply existing regulations that came into being for analogous problems earlier. Nor did they create regulations for what became huge sectors of essentially shadow banking industry. Balances that should have occasionally come into play when these shadow activities interacted with existing banking mechanisms failed spectacularly. As Paul Krugman pointed out in his book, *The Return of Depression Economics*,[8] these were by defini-tion banking activities and as such should have been regulated: if it walks like a duck and quacks like a duck, it is obviously a duck. I might add then it should be regulated like a duck.

The most visible of these shadow banking industries were the mortgage companies that grew up doing exactly what banks have always done: write mortgages. Except the mortgage companies did it without the safety valve of regulation. In the years from 2001 and 2006, they went from writing 35 percent of privately originated mortgages while regular banks wrote 65 percent to writing 60 percent of privately originated mortgages with regular banks writing 40 percent of mortgages.[9] In just a few years since then, an entire mortgage industry that minted billions for its investors has disap-peared — leaving huge destruction for most of us in its wake and, at the same time, apparently having served no lasting function in a healthy economy.[10]

If exempting these new mortgage companies from regulations painstakingly created over decades for regular banks unbalanced the playing field, why did no government oversight alarms go off? The very risks of investment and the predatory use of capital impossible with standard bank operating procedures were likely to be fraudulent (for borrowers, investors and our whole economy), why did no alarms go off? One wonders, who was asleep on the job, drunk on making money or was it just wolves in sheep's clothing? It certainly points to why hiring the higher-ups from Wall Street to administer our government financial institutions and fill top economic policy positions is a dangerously incestuous practice.

So how did subprime lending really work?

For most of us whose families ever owned property, we imagine getting a mortgage from a guy in a tweed suit behind a desk at our local bank branch down the street. The bank employees had certain requirements to fulfill and you either fit them (amount of down payment, credit rating, future earning potential, etc.) or you did not. The local bank was not only regulated (one of those millions of government functions our taxes pay for and we are oblivious to) but it also had long-term investments in our same communities where they loaned; they had not only legal but economic reasons to want successful mortgage agreements that would not end in foreclosure. Because of the early 1990 predatory loan scandal (mostly fraudulently exercised against seniors who took out second mortgages and then lost their homes), we had good state-level legal decisions to hold local banks in check as well.

Unfortunately, with mortgage companies almost none of these assumptions were true. While traditional requirements held banks to reasonable lending practices, mortgage companies could loan without those worries. When it walks like a duck and quacks like a duck, human beings are less likely to recognize that it is not a duck. In addition, the less relevant experience a sector of the public has the less likely they are to understand when the duck is not being regulated by the government like other ducks always have been! Borrowers mistakenly assumed that mortgage companies had rules like banks do.

A funny thing happened on the way to mortgage companies lending out all this money. The rating agencies — part of the financial industry that even shadow banks like mortgage companies have to interact with — made a bizarre appraisal: if mortgages were bundled and resold (securitized) in a certain way, then the first 80 percent of the mortgage values (no matter how questionable the actual accounting practices that created them) could be considered AAA (top-safety-rated) investments. With a Triple A rating for the "senior share" of these investments, investment money for subprime mortgages became almost infinitely available. The mortgage companies could lend the assets of others with impunity — *enter **moral hazard** again.*

The federal government took the final step in removing requirement for "skin" in the decision-making of major financial managers in 1999; they repealed the Glass-Steagall Act, ending the legal separation between different kinds of financial institutions. They allowed *private banks,* which make risky investments, to use the capital from *commercial banks* which are supposed to invest very conservatively to protect our checking and savings accounts. In the same period, the executive branch of the federal government had allowed the separation between private and commercial banks to disappear; not applying existing legal protections to various "new" financial instruments which allowed the massive growth of the shadow banking industry. Suddenly, huge reservoirs of our deposits were available to Wall Street. Investors went on the hunt for large new opportunities in what became a competitive scramble to bring in the highest returns; almost no attention was paid to the riskiness or speculative uses to which that huge influx of money might get put... And so we were on our way to rapid pricing spikes based on seemingly bottomless speculative investment.

At the same time, a relatively unusual thing happened: home ownership costs and rental costs — which usually only parallel each other — equalized. Home ownership might be too costly, but so were rents for large segments of society. Mortgage companies — with neither regular banking standards for down payments and conditions nor their commitment to long-term community investments — were perfectly positioned to step in. With much of the return in upfront fees and other closing costs, subprime mortgages became the almost magical cash bull for bloated Wall Street investment firms. Investments of which a very high percentage, the "senior share," were getting AAA ratings from the rating agencies were ideal.

2002: Planets align for home ownership for regular people?

Brokers open up storefronts in up and coming neighborhoods. Heavy advertising on the affordability of mortgages is everywhere. At all levels of our tax-averse government and in the private sector with new credit "instruments," the norm of the day is running regular expenses off of credit. Commercials are rampant promising wealth from purchasing houses with zero down and reselling for profit: house-flipping.

Economists everywhere and especially the government are trying on a new ideological mantra: the possibility of recession-proof economies and ever-increasing housing values. Somehow they are largely ignoring that the only reason that recent recessions have been relatively short and apparently painless is because new speculative economic bubbles have started almost as the last one burst;[11] they are not paying attention to the fact that most of us are not getting to participate in economic recoveries anymore!

Rents have continued to rise especially as investor-owners have passed on ever-increasing property taxes and sewer and water costs as municipalities starved of local aid try to make ends meet. Meanwhile, real wages continue to fall, and so more and more people with apparently decent stable jobs cannot afford their housing costs even if they rent.

Unlike local banks, mortgage companies offer deals with no or almost no money down and with introductory rates comparable to rents. They echo government and public messaging that home ownership is the answer with mortgage tax deductions, promises of building up your credit as you pay your mortgage, and of home ownership building equity. The "American Dream" of home ownership, commercials on television, radio, and the Internet boast "for most people their home is their biggest investment in their life-time representing 68 percent of their life-savings." Financial experts say housing values are going to keep appreciating so why not jump from an unaffordable rent to an unaffordable mortgage? What is there to lose?

Ah, well, everything: your investment monetarily and emotionally, your home and your credit-rating. And in a society where it is hard for people to recognize the larger forces behind the scenes, your sense of self-worth as you get blamed for the situation.

So what happened?

Regular people walked into what looked like the local "branch" of a mortgage company. The staff seemed knowledgeable and well-dressed like local bankers. Unconscious of government regulations that protect them when they walk into a bank, it never occurs to them that mortgage brokers are not licensed, that they have no required education for this job. They do not know that these are not usually employees of the mortgage-company but independent brokers — so neither they nor the mortgage company have longer-term commitments to each other; nor are either the brokers or mortgage companies invested in these neighborhoods long term. Regular people have no way of knowing that longer-term legal responsibility for how these mortgages get written or administered is going to be murky at best. No, for most people, these staff walked like professional bankers, quacked like professional bankers and so they assumed...

Unlike with "prime" mortgages (they used to be referred to as just "mortgages", because only prime mortgages existed), borrowers were not necessarily told about all costs associated with getting their mortgage nor ongoing costs like property taxes, etc. Those who had never owned a home before might not have realized that these additional regular home ownership expenses exist. Unlike with prime mortgages, such expenses were neither regularly escrowed by the lender as part of regular monthly payments nor even mentioned by mortgage brokers.[12]

What makes a loan a "subprime" loan?

By the end of the last century, subprime loan instruments which had been around for several years before the investment floodgates opened had also matured into more complicated instruments— more and more distant cousins from traditional mortgages. If you want to move mortgages quickly and in large volume, key characteristics that became the hallmark of subprime mortgages help.

Lots more potential borrowers exist if you do not require much or any of a down payment; traditional mortgages typically require 20 percent or sometimes 10 percent down. With almost no equity or no equity in the home, the slightest home value fluctuation puts the borrower at risk of having less value in the home than the amount of the mortgage. This is referred to as being "underwater" and makes normal refinancing impossible. Even without loss of home value, refinancing requires additional monies up front for the costs; usually 3 percent of the value of the building (3 points) is needed to refinance. For most subprime mortgages that was already eaten up between initial down payment even with the 100 percent existing mortgage. So unless the borrower has other cash reserves, refinancing may be impossible from the get-go.

Also if you do not require the standard income from a borrower, a much larger pool of potential borrowers exists. Subprime mortgage lenders ignored decades of bank lending experience which shows how much income is needed to afford to pay the mortgage and other regular living expenses.

Not having been in the boardrooms where these decisions were made, who knows what the thinking was. However, these mortgages got written ostensibly using regular debt-to-income standards **but** with a dangerous twist: they had a low introductory rate and only checked the borrower's income against their special lower introductory rate payments. They simply did not bother to check what would happen to the borrowers' monthly financial situation after the lower introductory rates ended two or three years later.

To really move mortgages it helps if these lower introductory rates happen to be close to the already over-inflated monthly rental costs in the area where you are selling these mortgages.

It also turns out that you get more and bigger mortgages sold if you hire unlicensed independent brokers to sell your loans, and you pay them more the larger the mortgage they sell — unlike bankers who are paid a fixed fee for every mortgage deal they close.

In addition, if you do not require any verification of income in the mortgage papers that brokers send up to be approved by the lender, anyone along the food chain has some serious although not legal wiggle room.

How could borrowers take out mortgages with little or no money down, at monthly amounts that are a high percentage of their monthly income? And knowing that there would be a payment increase in two or three years?

Based on lots of anecdotal evidence which is slowly becoming the basis of fraud cases, here is what we understand (only a few of these had to occur in any transaction to set up a borrower): Borrowers thought brokers were licensed employees with legal oversight by the mortgage company that employed them. When brokers insisted that they could afford a certain mortgage, they often felt that it must be their own confusion that they thought they could not. Having provided income documents, they assumed that the brokers had properly and faithfully calculated what they could afford. Perhaps, given that they were signing a loan for 30 or 40 years, they assumed that it was the intent of the lender as well as their intent that the agreement actually last that long.

Borrowers' introductory rates were often the same or less then their monthly rent which was usually already above the 38 percent income guideline used by regular banks. Having managed a rent that was technically more than they could afford, they thought at least an equally unaffordable mortgage payment would build equity over time as they had been told. With subprime mortgage arrangements, building equity was actually quite unlikely.

Brokers were not required to escrow property taxes or water or sewer bills nor even inform borrowers of such regular expenses. Thus borrowers hit not only a bump up in the interest payments after two or three years, but an unexpected large back tax or water/sewer bill!

They were told that payments would increase but just by 2 or 3 percentage points. That does not sound so bad if you are not mathematically savvy or do not understand that they are talking about 2 or 3 percent of the principal of the mortgage, not 2 or 3 percent of what you are paying with your introductory rate. Brokers did not necessarily provide a monthly payment schedule through to the end of the loan as in traditional mortgage documents. At the end of the introductory period, the actual jump in interest was about a third to a half again as much — $1,250 per month going up to say, $1,800 per month. This became known in the industry as payment shock.

Equally common, it has turned out, was a bait and switch: terms at closing turned out to be different from those previously presented or additional mortgage insurance or other costs were added. This is a truth-in-lending violation borrowers could have fought if they had known about it. But for many borrowers, who had already switched their children's schools, made job arrangements and given notice or ended tenancies by the closing date, they were in a very disadvantaged position to then refuse to close their mortgage.

Another endemic occurrence seems to have been that the income shown in closing documents was grossly exaggerated from what borrowers understood they had told their brokers. While a very common, although not universal, characteristic of subprime loans was no proof of income, borrowers report having brought in W-2s and/or income tax forms to their application meetings with brokers. Even when not required to submit such documentation with their application, they assumed that income figures represented at closing on the prepared loan materials were based on the income documents they had presented. With sheaves of papers requiring signature at closing, many borrowers appear not to have carefully read through the income documents or, again, found themselves already committed to the new home even if they noticed inflation in their income figures.

What about having a lawyer present? More often than not, borrowers report having asked their broker and being told that there would already be a lawyer present. It was somehow not explained that the lawyer would be representing the lender, not the borrower.

Finally, a lot of borrowers were concerned about the post-introductory period payments' increase. The mantra repeated in story after story was that the broker told them that after a year or more of good mortgage payments they would have improved credit and be able to refinance out of the loan into a better mortgage.

The problem is that another almost universal characteristic of subprime mortgages were pre-payment penalties — steep ones — extending to the end of the pre-payment period and often beyond. For a household with say only $5,000 to put down at signing, finding an additional $5,000 or $10,000 required a year and a half later put refinancing out of reach.

Just why would the lenders create loans that were predictably unaffordable after the introductory period? Hard to refinance because of the almost 100 percent loan-to-value ratio? And then require a huge pre-payment penalty? Was this not almost guaranteed to trap a huge percentage of borrowers in loans certain to fail?

Justice Ralph Gants of the Massachusetts Supreme Judicial Court when confronted by this combination of loans characteristics said the following: "It is noteworthy that the issuance of such a loan is deemed to be unfair under Chapter 93A even if the lender provides fair and complete disclosure of the terms of the loan and the borrower is fully informed of the risks he faces in accepting the loan. ... The Legislature plainly deemed it predatory and, thus, unfair for a lender to make a high cost home loan, quickly reap the financial rewards from the high points, fees, or interest, and then collect the balance of the debt by foreclosing on the borrower when, as the lender reasonably should have foreseen, he cannot meet the scheduled payments."

"... approval of loans bearing these four characteristics, in the absence of other liquid or easily liquidated assets or special circumstances, was unfair before and it is unfair today, even if we were too blind earlier to recognize its unfairness."[13]

Many borrowers, of course, were also told as new investors in housing that the trick to paying the mortgage was to get renters. No one seems to have pointed out that renting also requires labor and is a legal agreement to provide a service — decent housing — to others. The owner-occupants became not only dependent upon their renter's income and stability but the pretty much predictable foreclosure meant that for every borrower trapped in a dead end deal, there was a renter household unknowingly trapped as well.

A quick clarification: There are those who have claimed that this mess was somehow the fault of the Community Reinvestment Act (CRA). The CRA requires local commercial banks to reinvest a certain percentage of their loans into enterprises in the communities from which they get deposits. As you will notice, these subprime mortgages were not legally allowed to be written by local commercial banks so these mortgages could not legally have been a response to CRA requirements. CRA requirements do not apply to mortgage companies that were legally allowed to write these mortgages.

The Housing Bubble

By the beginning of 2007, estimates had it that the financial industry
was $1.3 trillion into the subprime mortgage market. That was a very
large, unregulated hole that had been created — and it was only part
of the unregulated shadow banking industry that had been operating.[14]
And while rental and home ownership values had been trudging
along almost side by side for years, in 2001, home values just took off.

Figure 2.3   Ratio of home prices to rents 1987–2008[15]

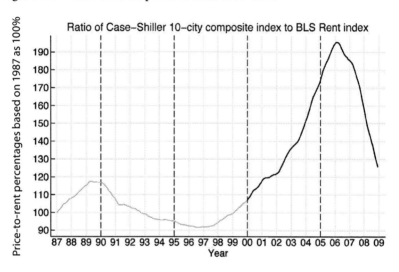

Figure 2.3 shows the ratio of home prices to rental costs. You will
notice for years they stayed around the same level (at 100 percent).
Then, in 2001, home prices did something experts report was unprecedented, housing prices took off leaving rental costs in the dust.[16]

By 2005, Massachusetts housing values doubled! Surely, it was
not the value of living in Massachusetts that had increased so much
since simultaneously our state's population was dropping. It was
not that our aging housing stock had suddenly increased in intrinsic
value — no matter how much we love it.[17] In fact, given the actual
loss in spending power of real wages and no economic reason that
downward trend would end, this skyrocket in housing values made
no economic sense at all.

Not that that stopped the financial whizzes of the world or the voices of economic experts from touting the housing market as a modern economic miracle with nothing but growth in its future?!?!?

The reality was that billions in economic investment pressure had created a demand and the various segments of the housing and financial industry had answered. Since the bubble has burst, stories are oozing out of every corner.

Traditional housing appraisers tell of getting phone calls from brokers and lenders yelling at them for appraised values and being told to go back out and re-appraise higher. If they did not feel it was appropriate to comply, their business as an independent contractor simply dried up.

Hundreds of brokers having accumulated big fee payments upfront packed up and moved away. Some of them have been found guilty in fraud investigations, although at this point thousands will have made millions and may never be prosecuted.

Starting in 2008, some low level bank and lender staff go on record saying that their sections were like little income rewriting assembly lines — day after day going through mortgage applications and writing in increased income figures to make borrowers — otherwise ineligible — loan-worthy for their establishment's purposes.[18]

As the portfolios of Ameriquest, Countrywide, Indy Mac and other major mortgage industry household names appeared to suddenly start collapsing in on themselves, they were bought up, sold or taken over by huge banks (FDIC took over IndyMac). Most of the hedge funds responsible for funneling much of the investment into these doomed mortgages seemed to vanish overnight. A massive amount of bad debt and toxic assets were created by speculative investment and phantom wealth outside of regulated financial markets; these were then transferred with a million problems and contradictions into the regulated banking industry. These mortgage bundles, "securities," ended up on the books of financial institutions that our government does still try to regulate and whose size makes everyone feel threatened.

About a year after those of us on the ground recognized a quickly growing trend of these unusual mortgages hurting our neighbors and neighborhoods — learning that they were subprime mortgages and their structure and far-reaching financing, a story is unfolding in the board room at Merrill Lynch. It is spring of 2007. The story is told, of course, *after the market crashed.*

About that time, Merrill Lynch decided to do one of its routine, periodic internal audits. At their board meeting, the directors were told that they were still early in the audit but that they thought their estimates of the assets they hold had been overestimated by say 4 billion. By the next report, figures showed them overestimated by more like 7 billion. The next report said 11 billion and still count-ing. The ex-board member who told this story, said that the amazing thing was that with these reports — shockingly far off given Merrill Lynch's size and proven track record — even then an alarm did not go off for those in the board room: if they were that far off was this a sign that perhaps the whole Titanic might be going down?[19]

Having been behaving erratically for over a year, the markets finally tanked fall of 2008. We were finally witness to the rating agencies being publicly dressed down by a congressional subcom-mittee for more than a day of public hearings; their contribution to this mess had been hopelessly over-valuing these toxic mortgages to investors. But besides a dressing down, I have heard nothing of charges being leveled at them for their role.

Stories come out now that the federal banking overseers also seemed oddly out of touch with the problems. We all heard ex-Fed-eral Reserve Chairman Alan Greenspan's amazing admission that somehow he "just missed it."[20]

In addition to re-regulation, many of us see a need for a thorough investigation. Charges must especially be leveled at those who headed these, often dissolved, institutions. Accountability must be required for the many in governmental oversight who were amazingly igno-rant or asleep on the job. Re-regulation and passage of other forms of accountability are going to require our voices. Plenty of us saw this coming but not being part of the financial elite in the United States, nor part of the revolving door between Wall Street and the top regulatory or financial officials in our federal government, we were treated as ignorant naysayers.

But this is our time. The time of regular people who knew some-thing was drastically wrong even as those supposedly in the know and in charge were busy drinking the Kool-Aid. Bailout funds are, among other reprehensible uses, being used to the tune of hundreds of millions to fund the next round of the industry lobbyists. We simply cannot allow those who got us into this mess to convince us and our elected representatives that they know how to get us out, nor that we are dependent upon them. We are not and we must insist that we are not.

How big is the crisis and is there an end in sight?

Foreclosure is the process by which someone who defaults on their mortgage loses ownership of their home. It is not, by Massachusetts state law, how you lose your right to occupancy or tenancy. Traditionally, once ownership changes hands new owners can evict occupants if they so desire. But the tenant pays rent and can stay if the new owner is willing. If not, they have the same rights as other tenants to have their day in court and live in a habitable dwelling and not be harassed or pressured while they await their day in court.

But I am getting ahead of the story. To foreclose, a lender has to provide the borrower with notice that they are behind on their payments or have become "delinquent." They have to check that the homeowner is not on active military service. Because of legislation signed into law at the end of 2007, they have to give the borrower 90 days to try to resolve the "delinquency." Once these steps are completed in our state, a lender simply files a petition to foreclose with the court, publishes a notice in the paper and then auctions the home. Often unwilling to accept the amount of outside bids, the lender places their own highest bid at auction and takes the home back into their own portfolio of properties.

While most other states in the country provide a day in court and a chance to address the petition to foreclose before foreclosure, Massachusetts does not yet provide this. This meant many borrowers who might have legitimate legal defenses never got in front of a judge. Those that wanted to had to find a lawyer and initiate a legal process themselves. However, they will get their right to a day in court as the tenant they become by law after foreclosure. Nor does the lender have to provide any bona fide representative or venue to re-negotiate the loan before filing for foreclosure. Stories abound of lost days and weeks attempting to reach someone qualified to negotiate at the lending institutions, whether the borrower, a mortgage counselor or a lawyer, tries. Regardless of the legal authority of who tries to reach a bona fide representative, the vast majority of times the foreclosure will happen before anyone can be spoken to. It breaks your heart. Given some of the legitimate examples of violations of the borrower's rights, it is hard to believe.

The foreclosure process provides different steps by which you can measure and predict how badly the crisis is going to unfold. Initially almost all foreclosures were on subprime loans although as the drop in home values accelerates more and more prime loans become endangered.

Figure 2.4 shows the percentage of new loans in 2001, 2006, and 2008, that were conventional "jumbo" prime, subprime, Alt-A, FHA and VA, and home equity. You can see the percentage of new conventional "prime loans" cut in half at the height of the bubble and the almost tripling of the percentage of new subprime loans by 2006 and then their essential disappearance by 2008.

Figure 2.4   Subprime and Alt-A volume quintupled 2001–2006, fell 2007–2008[21]

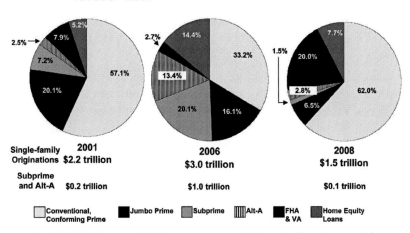

Source: Frank E. Nothaft, Chief Economist, Freddie Mac. Presentation prepared for Milken Institute's Financial Innovations Lab on Housing: Beyond the Crisis, Oct 7, 2008, p. 1 (citing Inside Mortgage Finance, by dollar amount, and updated to include 2008 annual data).

Usually the last step before the foreclosure process starts is falling behind in payments. Figure 2.5 is a snapshot of the extent of delinquencies from 2007 to 2009 in comparison to the number of mortgage rewrites completed under the federal HOPE for Homeowners program and similar programs.

Figure 2.5   Homes-at-risk vs. total lender workouts 2007–2009[22]

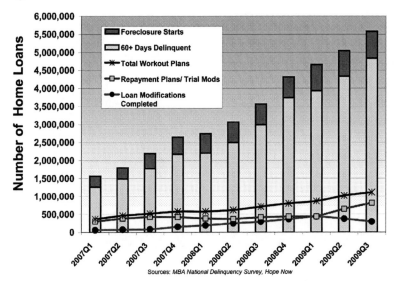

Sources: *MBA National Delinquency Survey, Hope Now*

The first step in the foreclosure process is filing in court of the petition to foreclose. Figure 2.6 gives a sense of the ramp up which is still continuing in petition filings in Massachusetts.

Figure 2.6 represents roughly 16,284 petitions in 2006; 29,607 petitions in 2007; and 21,804 petitions in 2008. By September 2009, 23,931 petitions had been filed representing a 27 percent increase from September 2008.[23] There are apparent slow-downs in these figures but it is not clear these represent an actual change in the overall crisis. Some of the slowdown in rate of petitions getting filed represented the state's imposition of a 90 day "right to cure" in 2008; this significantly elongated the foreclosure process, supposedly to give more time to negotiate refinancing agreements. A study by the Massachusetts Attorney General's office, a great champion in this crisis, Martha Coakley showed that the 90 day period provided had not increased the number of viable work outs. Like all other voluntary programs so far, they have not markedly improved the industry's effective participation in re-writing mortgages.[24]

Figure 2.6   Massachusetts monthly filings of petitions to foreclose
Jan 2006–May 2010[25]

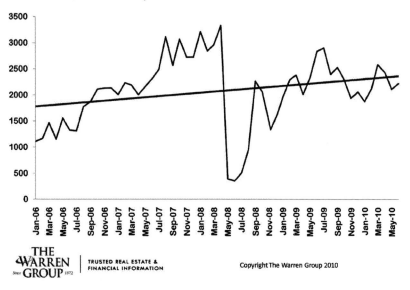

Similarly, rates of petitions and foreclosures may seem to slow because of very short, temporary moratoriums by various lenders as they await the roll-out of different federal initiatives. So far such roll-outs have had little or no effect on the eventuality of foreclosures. As moratoriums so far are all voluntary, foreclosures tend to tick back up after these short moratoriums are lifted by lenders. Finally, the courts responsible for processing foreclosure paperwork in Massachusetts, the Land Court system, are not surprisingly getting more and more backed up — creating a log jam that extended the paper filing process from over six months reported in the second half of 2008 to an average of a year reported in the beginning of 2009.

Or you can track the number of foreclosure auctions and new deed filings, the last step in the foreclosure process. Massachusetts, one of the states relatively hard hit by the subprime crisis and its residents were not as well protected as the majority of states which have judicial foreclosure. There are numerous drawbacks to not having foreclosures reviewed by a judge. In March 2009, a housing court judge confronted by deeds with legal deficiencies ruled that the problems could not be fixed and the foreclosures on the homes represented by these hundreds or thousands of deeds had been illegal;

the rightful owners were still the original owner-occupants who had been evicted! Since mortgages had been bundled and re-sold to different investors, these deeds had been used to foreclose while they had a previous investor's name on them. Because of these continuing deed problems, the rate of the final step in foreclosures in Massachusetts dropped off for a while; this led some to believe that foreclosures had slowed. This is a huge misinterpretation since petitions, the first step, have continued to rise and the foreclosure auctions were only delayed.[26]

Another predictor of the likelihood of the continued foreclosure crisis is the percentages of home owners "underwater" (see Figure 2.7). Regardless of the type of original loan — a prime loan (which usually required as much as 20 percent down payment) or one of these predatory subprime loans — once housing prices start dropping significantly, many borrowers see that initial down payment or investment in equity disappear as the home value drops below the outstanding mortgage debt. At that point, the borrower owes more than the house is worth (or is "underwater") and selling or refinancing can become impossible. Add to that the multiplying impacts of the economic plunge: Actual loss of job hours if not actual unemployment, increasing medical expenses or debt, the need to move to keep a job or the increasing relationship strains likely to increase divorce rates. Being underwater is likely to be the straw that breaks the borrower's financial back.

There are reasons so many of us feel that this crisis cannot be reversed until the balloon in housing values is addressed — and those who created the ramp up and siphoned off all that speculative profit should have to swallow the property value loss. It is instructive to dig deeper into which mortgages are presently underwater. One explanation for this crisis is that predatory lending put people into mortgages they could not afford. It appears more accurate to say that the pressure created by the deluge of capital seeking quick and significant profits led to massive speculation in the housing sector. This artificially ballooned housing values to create huge profits in upfront sales commissions and fees.

Figure 2.7   Snapshot 2009 of underwater mortgages
                  by year purchased/refinanced[27]

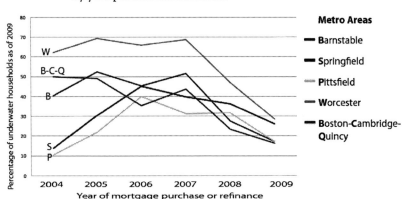

Just look at the unprecedented percentages of mortgages underwater (regardless of type of mortgage) by year in which the housing
was bought. Compare it to the timing of the housing price ramp up
in the price-to-rent ratio chart (Figure 2.3).[28] With the huge property
value loss since the housing bubble burst, it turns out that mortgages, regardless of type, are threatened if they were signed during
the height of the housing prices. Is the primary barrier to putting a
halt to foreclosures this phantom value that is trapping everyone who
bought or refinanced in the midst of the bubble?

We rant against our tax dollars financing the bailout. In addition,
there is the huge burden of speculative housing "value," the bubble
caused by all these questionable subprime mortgage practices. How
about ranting about the huge lenders, their stockholders and wealthy
investors being allowed to shift the entirety of speculative housing
values they benefited from onto regular people who just happened to
buy or refinance their homes at the wrong time?

Isn't it almost over?

The bad news is, no, it is not almost over — contrary to all those
economists who are trying to improve our economy through some
psychological strategy of putting a happy face on the crisis.

Avoiding regulations and requirements is what opened the floodgates and continuing such policy strategy will not magically close
them.

Jamie Dimon, the head of J.P. Morgan stepped in purposefully to rein in the big stock exchange upbeat response when J.P. Morgan's report for the 2009 second quarter looked better than expected: "Prime looks terrible," he told analysts. "And we're sorry, and there's nothing else we can say."

Losses in J.P. Morgan's prime mortgage book could triple in the foreseeable future as the credit mess moves out of subprime and into Alt-A and jumbo loans. "We were wrong, we obviously wish we hadn't done it [investing in Alt-A and other such mortgages]," Dimon told analysts. "We're very early in the loss curve."[29]

Figure 2.8   Distribution of outstanding mortgages by first month of rate reset[30]

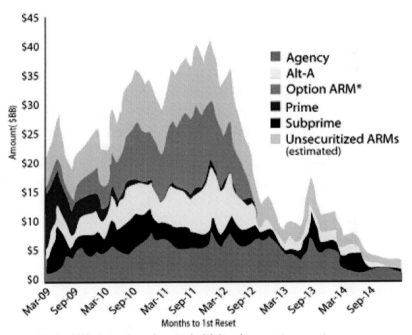

*Option ARMs show estimated recast schedule based on current negam rate;
Source: Credit Suisse (US Mortgage Strategy), LoanPerformance, FH/FN/GN
Distribution of dollar volume of securitized loans outstanding (as of May 2008) by month of first scheduled payment reset.
WWW.AGORAFINANCIAL.COM

This is because "creative" mortgage instruments went beyond subprime mortgages. Of all the bad characteristics of subprime loans, the one that usually precipitated the borrower giving up was around the time of the "payment shock" of the interest payment jump; the buyer lost hope just before the rate jump when they realized they could not afford it, or a bit after when they had tried but were unable to keep pace with the one-third to one-half again higher payments. These significant payment increases are also characteristic of what are referred to as Alt-A and Option Arm mortgages — often requiring interest-only or partial principal deferred payments for five to ten years. The jumps (adjustments) in monthly payments for these loans will present the next round of the predatory mortgage crisis.

Figure 2.8 shows the month when interest rates "reset" by large amounts. Even as the number of now familiar subprime mortgage resets dwindle, the reset dates of other "creative" mortgages multiply; this will sustain the number of borrowers facing payment increases they are unlikely to be able to afford. Credit Suisse recently identified an additional type of reset in this second round.

I am confident both with successes in organizing and real policy change that much of the continuing foreclosure crisis and its damage can be averted. But that is only true if policy action is taken quickly. So far almost none of the "voluntary" mortgage rewrites have addressed the removal of phantom value from the principal. Their just restructuring of existing debt puts the remaining unpaid portions of mortgages based on hugely inflated values into much later balloon payments. Is there some reason, that is obscure to me, that people are suddenly going to have vast sums to pay off these huge balloon payments in 25 or 30 or even 40 years? Or is this simply going to lock people into the equivalent of large rental payments based on inflated phantom values since they are only to lose their home ownership in the long run anyway? Are not such refinancing agreements just postponing the final crash caused by the housing price ramp up from 2002 to 2005 into 2030 to 2040?

Where does the present crisis leave us and what do we do?

"Do not leave!" One Congressional Representative from Ohio, Marcy Kaptur, finally made the public call February 2009 that our national government should have made at the beginning of this crisis.[31]

It is hard to separate the very real and devastating impacts of the emptying of our neighbors out of our neighborhoods from the impacts of the foreclosure. Foreclosure, while it means loss of your mortgage and therefore title to the building, does not end your occupancy nor require forcible vacating of the building. Put the other way, if occupants could stay and lenders had to accept their rent after foreclosure, how devastating would the impact of the loss of the "ownership" alone be on households?

As one of my favorite sister Worcester activists put it: *We have more and more homeless people and more and more people-less homes... that cannot make sense.* The craziest thing is that in over two decades of housing advocacy, I have never heard what I hear from people these days. You knock on their doors and they end up begging you to please make the lenders take their rent or their mortgage payments. Because *they are willing to pay,* but the lenders would rather foreclose and then evict.

In the third quarter of 2007, I pulled together a non-partisan press conference underscoring how devastating the mounting foreclosure crisis was going to be in Worcester, even though we knew Worcester had taken more steps around local home ownership than most communities. One of the key housing advocacy agency heads described the problem: No matter how much had been done in Worcester, this was still going to be much bigger than people realized; it was going to be like a tsunami. And although we were clear about appreciating steps they had already taken, some people in the city administration were upset by the characterization. But the characterization was correct.

In the spring of 2007, when we at the Mass Alliance Against Predatory Lending first filed our three pieces of broad legislation to stave off the worst of the foreclosure crisis, a core Boston activist described it as Katrina without the water. All of this was before we could get practically anyone to listen to us that subprime lending, this predatory lending crisis, was going to be much worse than the one in the early 1990s; it was going to undermine *the whole world economy!*

The impacts are painfully personal — lost homes, lost credit ratings (to get even a rental, certain jobs and forms of insurance), children pulled from schools, made homeless, schools' ability to teach impaired by increasing student turnover. Neighborhood fabric torn. Foreclosed and emptied homes vandalized with gaping holes where not just copper pipes have been taken but the copper wire stripped out of electrical wires torn out through sheetrock. Beautiful old houses crippled or essentially destroyed by burst pipes. The unnoticed ravages of nature leaving growing mushrooms and creeping mold that will make these houses eligible for nothing but demolition. Neighborhood blocks and then streets ruined by abandoned buildings, broken glass, overgrown lawns, ghost towns — a financial and often physical and criminal danger to those who try to remain.

Property values of foreclosed and then forcibly vacated buildings plummet; additionally those surrounding even the first noticeable one in a neighborhood measurably lose value. Local businesses lose customers extending the impact. Finally, municipal governments already stretched to their limit suddenly find themselves burdened with increased inspectional and legal costs chasing elusive property owners — often the foreclosing lenders — who do not keep up their properties or pay their property taxes or water or sewer bills from across the country or halfway around the world. Additional hours must be added for firefighters to shut off unattended water, city workers to board up buildings, police to deal with increased crime. Emptied buildings increase danger of fire, increase danger to the lives of firefighters and huge costs to our municipal governments for each fire.

The statistics bear all of this out too:

- In increasing yearly numbers, foreclosures and the associated evictions multiply the impact on our communities[32, 33, 34]
- Studies released in 2008 show that in Massachusetts, 54 percent of those in foreclosed buildings are former owners, 46 percent former tenants, almost doubling the displacement caused by a foreclosure.[35]
- Homelessness is increasing, even as the Legislature worked its way through a many month process to commit in January 2008 to put the necessary programming and financing in place to end homelessness in our state.

See the chart in Figure 2.9 showing increasing homeless families in our state? The chart only shows the ramp up to 2,600 families in December 2008. From the start of fiscal year 2009 until end of

September, the number of families in Emergency Assistance shelter increased by more than 53 percent. Figures as of September 2009 put the statewide homeless rate at the unprecedented numbers of more than 3,100 families and 3,000 individuals staying each night just in Department of Housing and Community Development-funded shelters.[36] *If the state counted all those doubled up or sleeping in a car, these figures would be higher.*

Figure 2.9   Massachusetts homeless family caseload: fiscal years 2005–2009[37]

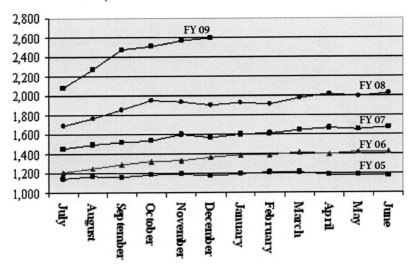

- Crime increases: up 2.3 percent for every additional foreclosure per 100 households.[38]
- Surrounding property values are shown to fall with even just the first foreclosure in a neighborhood.[39]
- The impact on property values increases with each foreclosure and associated vacancy.[40]

The chart in Figure 2.10 shows the dramatic drop in housing values from the peak of the housing bubble to its most recent trough by metro regions in our state. The slight home value rebound is turning out to be as unsustainable as predicted.

Figure 2.10   Massachusetts home prices by region 2006–2010[41]

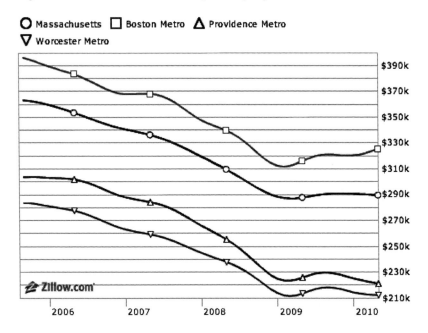

And as the crisis worsens, its reach directly hurts more and more — even without counting the undermining of the whole world economy.

The need for action by our state legislature is most graphically underscored — if the undermining of our financial markets is not proof enough — by the Congressional report released at the beginning of 2008. This report showed that Massachusetts' households would lose $58.9 billion in wealth by the end of 2009 — yes, that figure is for just Massachusetts. It translates into a little more than $1 billion loss to our state economy *every two weeks* of policy inaction.[42]

Legislative inaction

The message from too many state legislators since before the market crashed — when the only apparent problem was the significantly increasing foreclosures — has been "wait for the Feds (the Federal Government) to act." Between a quarter and a half of our legislators have actually supported strong action since 2008. Urgency keeps getting diluted, however, by the endless — and at best useless — debates and supposed federal fixes. These have gotten extensive play in Congress and by both President Bush and President Obama, whether they were approved or not.[43]

National leaders spent months discussing the possibility of creating a program for refinancing; it ended up being totally voluntary for the lenders with limits that made few borrowers eligible. This was partly due to then-candidate Obama's opposition to bankruptcy changes that would allow the courts to force restructuring of mortgages. The final policy then led to refinancing for a tiny percentage of those impacted into loans which often had *higher* monthly payments. Then there was the bank bailout which turned out not to focus on the "toxic" mortgages at all and did not even rein in bonuses, salaries or lobbying expenditures of lenders. Summer of 2009 — thanks to some congressional leadership from Massachusetts representatives — there were some good extensions of tenant law which mostly helped in states with less good tenant laws than Massachusetts has already. Each new federal refinancing program is utilized by fewer people than projected. Once again when borrowers complete the refinance, they did not receive better mortgages in the vast majority of cases.

What the Wall Street bailout and most of these programs do show, is the industry has no overall interest in making mortgages work. That stark reality and the growing number of people sucked into the foreclosure trap have shifted public perception of which party to these subprime deals may have had bad motives.

All the fraud stories and their pervasiveness are beginning to have an impact on the public perception of whose fault the creation of impossible mortgage agreements might be. It is brokers and real estate dealers who are taken away in cuffs.[44] In some banks' departments, workers are exposing wholesale whiting out and rewriting of the income information of potential borrowers so they could get loans approved.[45] Fraud cases in the mortgage lending industry reported to the FBI went from 3,515 cases in 2000 to 25,989 in 2005.

Massachusetts' Banking Division said it filed "377 formal or informal complaints" against mortgage companies including falsifying income of borrowers to qualify them for loans.[46] When Massachusetts finally required that independent mortgage brokers get licensed, it turned out that almost 25 percent (some 1,900) were not even eligible because of questionable criminal records, their own financial

problems or other red-flag issues.⁴⁷ And of course, there are the really
horrifying stories of insider cultures at some huge institutions like
Wells Fargo. Not only were subprime mortgages incentivized over
prime mortgages so that tens of thousands of customers eligible for
prime loans were steered into subprime loans **but** subprime mortgages were referred to as "ghetto" loans and special outreach was
instituted to engage culturally-targeted strategies purposefully to
reach, for instance — their term! — "mud-people."⁴⁸

This then becomes the most visible archetype or lesson *all of us* as
regular people need to learn if we are to get in charge of our destiny.
During the Katrina disaster, it became clear that choices to de-fund
potentially life-saving levees and to ignore research showing the
need for remedial action on canals, etc., was why the flooding was so
extensive and the death toll so high. While people of color were hurt
disproportionately, the long term damage and impact hurt all regular
people. The same will prove true from the targeting of sub-standard
mortgage products from this time period. The potential lesson underscored here is that the breadth and depth of the destructive impact
of these toxic loans on our whole society — just like the levees and
neglect in New Orleans — was too long denied or ignored *because it
was assumed by too many in power to only affect lower-income people
and people of color.* We must learn that warning signals of destructive social impacts demand our attention *regardless* of who seem to
be getting hurt the most first! Or we wait — frozen — until the devastation is already guaranteed to be extensive.

Main Street pushes back

Of course, rather than just wait, people are organizing and pushing
back. Besides strong efforts for legislative change, your neighbors in
many communities across Massachusetts are teaching each other
their rights in this crisis. Trying to make sure the word gets out
that *everyone* in a building becomes a tenant after foreclosure, for
example. In Massachusetts, tenants have rights — rights to pay rent,
rights to a livable home that the lenders/now landlords must provide
and rights to a day in court before eviction after they receive initial
written notice to leave. Where possible local groups like the Bank
Tenants in Boston and some other communities are working hand
in hand with legal service and pro-bono lawyers to push lenders

through public exposure and protest and through legal negotiation to let homeowners refinance closer to the real value of their properties not the speculation-swollen prices of a few years ago. With homeowners and tenants working together they are having numerous successes keeping *homeowners and tenants* in their homes.

Their stories are inspirational and are rebuilding our sense of power when we commit to the well-being of each other.[49] On the other hand, many more must get informed and involved for these strategies to really begin to reach the tens of thousands of households affected across our state. Even with farther reaching successes, policies must be changed to right the very uneven playing field that has been created for both homeowners and tenants.

In 2007, the Legislature did take action which will mostly stave off another round of bad loans for the future — including broker licensing requirements and requiring pre-purchase classes for first time homebuyers. Unfortunately, this crisis is not just going away. While legislation paid for more refinancing counselors, their efforts cannot even keep pace with the crisis nor address the sweeping systemic problems continuing to feed it.

What we need is action at the state level. If the federal government comes in on top of that with additional protections — like forcing mortgage re-writes affordable at present-day values with teeth from new bankruptcy rights — so much the better. Our state, however, can stop the emptying out of buildings by requiring that responsible, paying tenants are allowed to stay. They can bring us in line with the majority of states that require that a judge preside over the foreclosure process and that borrowers get to make their case before they lose their mortgage. We could adopt a mandatory mediation process modeled on the amazingly successful Philadelphia court mediation process and initiate a six month moratorium on foreclosures so all of this can be put in place.

The weirdest aspect of fighting our leaders' inertia and inaction on what is clearly one of, if not the most immediate, cause of a worldwide economic depression: Every proposal that stops the devastation of the foreclosure crisis *will also help the lenders!* After they foreclose and evict, lenders who wrote these mortgages are also losing property value, facing a harder resale as neighborhoods and schools degrade. The house they repossess — their collateral that was supposed to insure all these loans — is degrading faster because of vacancy, weather, vandalism and their own neglect of maintenance. Research seems to show that they are keeping as much as half the properties they own off the market for fear of driving prices down even farther. These houses will degrade even further before resale.

In fact, when the FDIC took over IndyMac's portfolio of properties as part of its dissolution, they did a study showing that the foreclosure route meant they usually only recouped 48 percent of the value of the original mortgage. However, if they refinanced with the original homeowner they saved 70 some percent.[50] So they instituted an across-the-board policy of trying to refinance every homeowner in trouble into a long-term fixed rate affordable mortgage (aimed at payments costing the homeowner 38 percent of their regular income!). Since 2008, Sheila Bair, the head of the FDIC, has been trying to sell Congress on the idea of a federal program requiring lenders to go in this direction instead of knee-jerk foreclosures — still without success even with the proof provided by the FDIC's own program.

Postscript on banks that are too big to fail...

I am sure I am not the only one who had a flashback to Ma Bell and anti-trust laws on the books when "too big to fail" was first repeated. Surely, there must be laws about banks becoming too close to monopolies that would then have to be split up by the federal government and justice department like Ma Bell split into all the little Bells and other phone companies across the country, right? Initially, people told me no, but in fact legal language exists.

The Community Reinvestment Act (CRA) states that no one bank can own more than 10 percent of the deposits (those protected checking and savings accounts the vast majority of us regular folks have) of the residents of the United States.[51] (By the way, unlike banks and other companies, health insurance companies actually *are exempted from anti-trust laws and can consciously and legally manipulate their market and can approach and even become monopolies).*[52]

Prior to the crash, banks had been spending more and more money buying up smaller banks — how often has the name of the institution holding your accounts changed? Then, more frequently buying up each other (their names getting longer like J.P. Morgan

Chase which also purchased Bank One in 2004). Even with the crash and all the supposed bank insolvency, they are still increasingly buying each other up often with our tax money that was supposed to get them lending again.

Meanwhile, smaller banks and the occasional large bank are folding at an unprecedented rate. In October 2009, the FDIC reported 106 banks had failed. In June, the agency reported that 416 banks were at risk of failure — the highest level in 15 years. While a significant and increasing number, it does not rival the number of bank closings during the Savings and Loan crisis which peaked at 534 closures in 1989.[53] Another dynamic is in play this time. It is small banks that are failing because the really big banks are getting bailed out. The really big banks are using much of that bail-out to take over lots of smaller banks. I do not have figures on takeovers but I wonder whether, without our tax money-based blood transfusions to the biggest banks, more banks of all sizes would be failing. These national bailouts are not only against our expressed wishes but are now taking away our local banks which support our local economies. Yet another example of tilting the playing field away from our local economies and concentrating more wealth higher up.

All this merging meant that by the time our national elected leaders were having public meltdowns about some of these financial institutions being so large that we could not afford to let them fail, those biggest name banks had in fact become so large that *they are illegal*. Bank of America and Wells Fargo, to name two, hold over 10 percent of our bank deposits.[54]

So why not just dismantle these institutions? The FDIC, which insures our checking and savings accounts at these institutions, has not raised concerns about its own ability to guide any dissolutions necessary and still protect our insured deposits. These mega-banks clearly have not only enough market share to endanger the market and potentially manipulate the financial markets, but also seem to have the financial resources, mostly our financial resources, to manipulate our federal leaders. National leaders said there was no way to split them up.

Turns out splitting up the banks is exactly what was done during the Great Depression.[55] The formula still applies and it is relatively simple: just reinstate the Glass-Steagall Act. Regulators would take each institution and re-separate the traditional investment bank activities from the traditional commercial bank activities — putting the riskier investments (like those mystery mortgage bundles that include subprime mortgages) into the portfolio of investment banks as they have traditionally been and put the large investors, the large and small stockholders in charge and allow them to sink or swim on their own. They would take the more conservative investments and allow those to continue from the financial base of traditional savings and checking accounts in commercial banks. This has been the successful model since the Great Depression until recently and these institutions would again be on a stable and predictable footing.

Finally, as of fall 2009, such legislation has been filed at the federal level. Will it have legs to swim in the deluge of financial institution-funded lobbyists and elected leaders beholden to these interests? Especially while the financial advisors and economists from the Wall Street revolving door are filling the airwaves? Maybe. Because even some of these players like Greenspan are having moments of truth themselves. And folks like Representative Ron Paul, R-Texas, and many in Congress are waking up to the real economic and popular demands for legislating the transparency of the epitome of the bankers' backroom, the boardrooms of the Federal Reserve System.

Federal Reserve window

Most of the huge loss was started in the shadow banking industry — both unregulated and "invisible" to the publicly traded financial markets and most of the world. That huge and now contracting economic sector had contributed nothing to financial "pools" that make up the various Central Banks like the Federal Reserve across the world. These are the banking industry's "insurance" pools, supposed to be available to lend out when a "run" on a bank is imminent. The Taj Mahal of cards began to fold, taking the air out of the huge international speculative boom. When its huge tsunami bore down on the regular banking industry and regular people, it was far beyond the "reserves" of the Central Banks to impact.

The most recent solution of the Federal Reserve was to open the Federal Reserve banking window to huge segments of the financial industry not normally allowed to borrow reserves they never contributed to nor were regulated to protect. Since the Federal Reserve's

lending is a primary part of the creation of "money" through debt
that banks do almost all of, one could argue that the Federal Reserve
is "printing" literally trillions of new dollars. The Federal Reserve is
responsible for most of the $23 trillion in loan and loan guarantees
out to the financial sector as of fall 2009.[56]

As of fall 2009, the Federal Reserve was lending at .02 percent
interest. The U.S. Government treasury bonds were at 3.5 percent.[57]
All these new and old Federal Reserve borrowers, can (and have,
in fact), borrow money and lend it back to the U.S. government by
buying Treasury bonds and make 3.3 percent on each dollar. These
trillions of "new" dollars provide an almost endless blank check for
U.S. government spending and other financial companies — including
a few not even based in the U.S. But this "minting" requires no actual
production of goods or services to give this money real value in our
economy, nor does it even have to play a role in the financial markets
of "earning money on money." It does not require transparency to our
Congress, let alone Congressional action in the creation of money as
required by our Constitution. Our elected representatives have no
meaningful say in the creation of all of this debt although the Federal
Reserve is legally guaranteeing its value on the back of taxpayers.

This is production of money with absolutely no economic basis
and no one has any skin in the deal as far as I can tell. This is the ulti-
mate in speculative value explosion and quintessential **moral hazard!**
Literally, the Federal Reserve has the proverbial money printing
machine in its basement and it is printing all the time.

*Is an unregulated, unsupervised Federal Reserve trying to create
enough monetary value to bail out the shadow banking industry?* And
since this money had no real value, is this not essentially a huge currency devaluation?[58] What happens when so many U.S. dollars based
in no value at all are created?

Halting the Health Care
Crisis and Its Impact

S urrounded by many of the world's greatest teaching hospitals
and an extensive health care system, we have one of highest costs
for health care as a state in the most costly health care country in the
world. Our state, with a creative agreement with the federal government, has made a commitment to try to get everyone health coverage in a way guaranteed to break the bank; it already cost us $13.112
billion of the 2008 state budget of $34.213 billion which equals 38
and 1/3 percent of the budget and rising.[59] And yet, like the rest of
the U.S., our health care outcomes fall at the bottom of developed
countries — worse than some of the poorest countries in the world.

In a classic inability to see beyond business as usual and see
beyond the four-walls of their government building, our state government's leaders have ignored the health care impacts on the budgets of
municipalities, residents, and businesses. No one can afford the spiraling costs of health care — not just our state government's budget.
Health care costs dampen the ability of municipalities, businesses
and individuals to participate economically — at a time when we need
it most.

Funnily (or sadly) one version of the answer lies not far from Massachusetts. In fact, close enough that there are publicly organized
trips to take advantage of some of the great benefits of the Canadian
health care system. Because they serve everyone, even Americans
can cross the border and benefit from Canada's much cheaper pharmaceutical prices and certain medical care:[60] Bulk purchasing drugs,
coordination of care and creation of the largest risk pool possible
minimizes costs and uses medical resources as efficiently as possible.

Recently, with hard work from a number of players, Massachusetts has taken some steps towards the efficiencies of a government
sponsored single system of care (referred to as "single-payer" which is
mostly *not socialized medicine* although some pundits keep trying to
confuse us).

Already on the Massachusetts books is a law that provides for the state government to bulk buy all of its drugs. We are not the size of Canada and we would only be buying for state programs. Still, lots of pharmaceutical companies would find themselves having to sell to that big a pool of buyers allowing us to push down the cost of our drug expenditures. Because of lack of coordination and lack of taking the long view, no administration yet has managed this. Not even the Patrick administration has implemented this cost-saving measure, even though our present governor campaigned on bulk-purchasing drugs and it is already authorized by the legislature. Some of us have done the research; we know which internal State government systems are saving the most money while providing the necessary services. In 2007, depending on whether our savings would have matched Virginia's 17 percent savings or the 31 percent of the Minnesota multi-state savings pool, Massachusetts could have saved $200 million to $250 million in its state budget.[61] We hope we can get the present administration to move on these savings soon given the fiscal crisis.

In addition, a couple of parallel efforts bore fruit during the legislative session that ended in 2008. We got passage of a uniform overhead billing requirement. Overhead is consistently estimated at some 30 percent of health care expenditures. Uniform billing removes a significant percentage of wasteful bureaucracy. It means one set of forms formatted the same for every health care transaction. Presently, every health insurance company has its own forms, definitions and procedures, as well as a number of complex plans. This extra paperwork complicates the lives of every patient and health care provider. To some extent, it affects insurance companies too, since the number of administrative staff necessary to fill out paperwork — but not provide additional care — is astronomical. One might imagine streamlining this system might be tough given the many variations of billing forms in existence. However, there is one billing system that pretty much every provider knows and is familiar with: the Medicare system. While insurance companies do not like it, fast-tracking the implementation of uniform billing would be a gift to all of us, another no-brainer in this plummeting economy. Implementation is stalled a year and a half after the bill's passage at the end of 2009.

Even if you just switched these administrative billing jobs over to
health care provision instead of administration they would generate
more economic activity. Paper-pushing is just not very economically productive while jobs that increase the health of our workforce,
decrease the collateral costs of illness, increase preventative care and
long term health have an economic multiplier effect. A recent study
commissioned by National Nurses Organizing Committee/Cali-
fornia Nurses Association looked at the expanded amount of direct
care needed were we to actually provide, nationally, a single-payer
version of genuinely universal coverage; it would create 2.6 million
new jobs nationally infusing $317 billion in new business and public
revenues.[62] Why shouldn't Massachusetts access our percentage of
these benefits?

What about the rest of a single-payer system? It would require one
comprehensive standard of care; this would move us away from the
health disparities almost guaranteed in our present separate systems
which we know from history are never equal. **One system means all
doctors are available to any patient.**

What about our present spiraling costs for businesses which
try to provide care? Or workers whose percentage cost of employer
provided care is also more and more unaffordable? What about those
whose medical insurance does not cover care sufficiently? What
if you lose your coverage when you lose your job? Especially, in an
economy that is nose-diving...

And what does it say when likely illegal trips to purchase drugs
out of country are still publicized and organized? What does this say
about overriding need and public acceptance?

Going without care

*"Of all the forms of inequality, injustice in health care is the
most shocking and inhumane."*
— *Martin Luther King Jr. in a speech to the Medical
Committee for Human Rights, March 25, 1966*

The impact of lack of health coverage is both traumatic and much
more far-reaching than many realize in our very stratified society.
Many of us who have health care insurance would be shocked to

know what is not covered; until we have a major illness or something catastrophic happens we may falsely believe we are covered.

I have been personally and deeply affected by stories and, worse, personal encounters with the life-costs of lack of (or inadequate) health care coverage. I remember working with a young woman whose single father had molested her repeatedly, so she ran away from the home with nowhere to go. Still claimed as his dependent even though she was 18, getting state-sponsored MassHealth was not straightforward. Homeless and on the street, she tried to ignore that she was pregnant. Although she did eventually go to the hospital for free care, she had almost no prenatal care and ended up unexpectedly giving birth in the middle of the night in the elevator in her father's apartment building. One of her newborn twins died before she could ever tell anyone that she needed an ambulance.

Or I think of one of my friends — counted in the statistics documenting the "success" of Massachusetts' miracle plan, known as Chapter 58 — whose health is slowly deteriorating; his condition has become life threatening and likely to get worse. He has been a very effective advocate on issues in the past and works on and off as his disabilities allow him. He has some mental health difficulties and serious diabetes — both conditions that he has managed for years through diet, exercise, and careful drug regimens. But our supposedly successful plan pushed him from "free care" through various federal options and finally onto MassHealth. Getting people off of free care and onto MassHealth is touted as a success. However, with his very limited income and numerous medications and medical paraphernalia required for his diabetes, he cannot afford numerous new monthly co-pays along with food and rent. Unfortunately for him, the revolving door of having to adjust to alternative drugs for his mental illness has compromised his methodical control of his psychiatric condition. Different plans denied him access to his time-tested medications for his illness. At present, he can only afford either his diabetes medications or his mental health medications. This, of course, threatens his control of his diabetes both financially and in terms of his capacity for self-care.

As an advocate, he has tried to negotiate, cajole, beg and even threaten (based on his knowledge of his legal rights) his way through the various medical institutions he is required to deal with, and with almost no success. I worry that I will hear that he has lost his battle and is in a hospital, dying.

Stories many find unbelievable in a civilized, "first world" country abound about serious but treatable conditions increasingly leading to death.[63] In early 2009, as many states faced severe shortfalls in Medicaid funding, 19 reported having cut back on fundamental care.[64] Such cuts along with more and more of those on unemployment losing their medical coverage and finding COBRA — where one can pay the full premiums of their prior employer covered insurance — unaffordable, stories become common of diagnosed but untreated cancer, heart attacks, diagnoses too late to save lives, increasing meningitis and more.

Figure 2.11   Un- and underinsured: risk of forgoing care and medical debt[65]

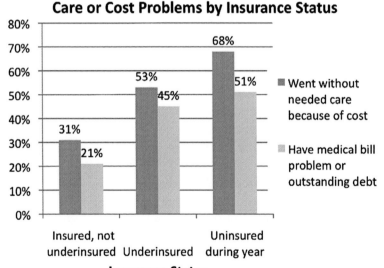

Notes: "Underinsured" means insured all year but experiencing:
a) medical expenses equaling 10 percent or more of income
b) medical expenses equaling 5 percent or more of income if low income (<200 percent of poverty), or
c) deductibles equaling 5 percent or more of income.
Data: 2007 Commonwealth Fund Biennial Health Insurance Survey.

The problem here is that whatever successes programs such as Massachusetts' present health care arrangement can claim in their first few years (and there have been similar attempts made in various states over the years) they always depend on special underwriting with federal dollars and none of them address the fundamental problem of cost control. Thus as private health insurance costs continue to rise at rates well beyond regular inflation, these plans that extend coverage to those previously uninsured become an increasing burden on their state budget. And sectors without government subsidy, such as employer and employee funded plans break the bank on our businesses, local governments and residents across the state.

The answer is often to then cut back on coverage or increase costs to those paying for these plans. Both of these actually create a negative feedback loop where people get less care, later in the progression of illness, and lose money to fund those things that keep us healthier such as nutritious food, less stressful lifestyles, even paying for healthy places to live.

The obvious reason that government-funded health care is cheaper is because it removes redundancy, complexity, and the waste of money on administration, advertising and the costly parts of competition created by numerous private insurers. I do not need to see another billboard advertising which hospital has the latest heart machine. Part of why state-funded health care is also cheaper is that it creates seamless, consistent, high quality and convenient care.

Imagine health care

Close your eyes for a moment ... breathe easily and relax. Feel the bottoms of your feet on the floor and your back straight and tall. Let out a slow breath and imagine this...

Imagine going about your daily life. Then imagine that you are feeling sick, trying to decide whether to go home and rest. You reach into your pocket and feel your medical card, which all Massachusetts residents have. A nurse practitioner you like works at the nearby hospital who you could call for advice on what you might have. Not only do you know her, she will also have access at her fingertips to information on the latest flu and viruses going around. The conditions of all patients treated in your area are entered anonymously into a network that provides an up-to-date overview of the concentrations of diagnoses every day. Or, you think to yourself, you could just drop in on the clinic on your way to pick up your child from daycare.

Because all medical institutions and practitioners are part of one system, you can call your nurse practitioner or go to any clinic you want for free — no extensive papers to fill out, no issues about who is in network, no massive administrative hurdles or numerous different forms for different health care plans for your medical center to fill out.

Because early treatment is more effective and more accurate with early diagnosis, everyone is encouraged to seek immediate care. The economic emphasis is on the improvement of early diagnostic tools not incredibly expensive heroic measures and fancy equipment for end-stage interventions. You live a generally healthier life with state economic incentives towards public health, eradication of diseases and education about healthier lifestyles.

Likewise as you consider whether just to get advice from a practitioner you know personally over the phone or drop into a convenient clinic, you are mulling to yourself that you doubt you caught this at work, since people rarely ever show up sick at work anymore. Since you are less frequently sick yourself — even with higher allergen rates due to increases in global warming — you also still have paid sick days available in the morning if it makes more sense to stay home.

Many major public costs have decreased significantly. Social costs created by untreated addictions that lead to crime, domestic violence, inability to be employed, homelessness and imprisonment, which plagued the U.S., are driven way down. This was predictable given the experiences of nations across the globe that have universal care provided through single payer systems. They provide what is called "treatment on demand" — that is, addicts can access immediate treatment even if they surface only briefly to a desire to get clean. In Massachusetts, in 2009, the wait for a treatment bed is usually many weeks by which time active addicts have likely lost the lonely struggle to stay clean enough to remember why they wanted treatment to begin with.

The public costs of partial, emergency treatments will also be mitigated. In 2009, the worst stories are of people who come in for emergencies and are expelled from hospitals before treatment is completed because of lack of health coverage. Stories such as the mother of someone I met in Worcester who was escorted from a hospital and ended up on the streets and then at a homeless shelter with bone sores and no medications. She eventually lost a leg.

Or the less obvious but now documented increases in those who have medical procedures and are released from hospitals before they can recuperate properly without continuous care and supervision. They must then return to hospitals for lengthier more expensive follow-up care! This is such a recognized problem that as of 2009 some medical plans are actually trying to penalize patients for return visits!

For me, the most dramatic and clear cut example of how government-sponsored single-payer care saves on long-term social and health costs is the story of Canada's implementation of single-payer coverage. I know it has become commonplace in U.S. political discourse to talk down Canada's health care system. But it is used by hundreds of U.S. citizens who cannot find affordable care here. That raises the question: How much of this criticism is funded through channels by the U.S. private insurance industry whose existence is threatened by the success of single-payer coverage across the world?

Canada's transition story

It is often said that the greatest determinant of future health is your health at birth; that healthiness is profoundly affected by the amount of prenatal care a mother receives before giving birth. The impact of Canada's transition to single-payer care is as important in its impact on pre-natal care as in any other aspect.

Canada did not transition in one step as a whole country to a single-payer system but actually transitioned province by province — which is why we know that single-payer can be effectively enacted at the state level in the United States.

As is true in the U.S., women, especially single mothers, are one of the populations most likely to be low-income, most likely to have jobs without employer-sponsored health coverage. They are likely to have been battered or have been through other trauma. As such, they are least likely to be able to afford and therefore, access prenatal care. More than one out of five children are born into Massachusetts families below the federally defined poverty level with serious implications for longer-term health and social productivity. The federal poverty line is inaccurately defined as too low by all other standards.

So the percentage of infants who did not receive good, prenatal care is probably much greater than we think.

With access to the new single-payer system, Canada found that pregnant women quickly and consistently availed themselves of that good free care; the health of their infants improved measurably. In the years immediately following the province-by-province transition to single-payer care, neonatal care costs also dropped markedly in a similar time-delayed rolling pattern province after province. This improvement alone increases the long-term health of the Canadian people as a whole.

Chapter 58: the story of the Massachusetts Miracle Plan

I am often haunted by that definition of insanity as doing the same thing but expecting a different result.

Political leaders confronted by increasing rates of uninsured and demands for action started the process of negotiating for changes in health care delivery in Massachusetts. After over a decade there was growing grassroots organizing in support of single-payer (government-funded care more like Medicare). In 2001, a campaign was initiated for a statewide ballot question that would require employers to provide decent health insurance or pay a significant amount of money into a government fund to cover those not presently insured (referred to as the Play or Pay initiative). Reports showing how much our tax dollars were paying for state insurance — MassHealth — to cover workers in major businesses like Walmart fueled the flames. We suspect the growing support for a government-sponsored program — which would provide universal coverage for less — really scared the private insurance and drug company friends of some of our elected leaders.

Thus, a round table process was created, bringing together the now typical major industry and political players. While they immediately excluded single-payer activists, they did include some community voices considered safely in the Play or Pay camp. While this insured strong community voices, it took systemic problems that have been feeding huge health care cost increases firmly out of the conversation; voices were excluded who might suggest that private industry not feed at the trough of profits as more people lost all access to health care.

After much fanfare and complicated negotiations, Chapter 58 of The Acts of 2006 of the Massachusetts General Court was written — primarily behind closed doors. The more than 100 pages of complicated health care reform legislation were submitted to legislators the night before the vote. Those touting the proposal included industry, key Play or Pay advocates and political leaders from the right like then-Governor Mitt Romney, a Republican, as well as strong Democrats like the late Senator Edward Kennedy. It was touted as a new miracle, the Massachusetts Health Plan, catapulting Massachusetts leaders once again onto the national stage as forefront policy leaders and touting a new "solution" to the health care "crisis."

Like the 1988 Dukakis-era initiative to cover all children in Massachusetts and a number of other "solutions", plans for public coverage expansion in the last 20 years (Minnesota, Tennessee, Vermont, Washington, Maine and Oregon), the Massachusetts Health Plan was to expand government coverage to all the presently uninsured in our state. Like the similar "miracles never before attempted" ours would predictably succeed in decreasing the number of uninsured for a few years and then fail because it was too expensive.

Figure 2.12   Percentage of uninsured in Tennessee 1987–2005[66]

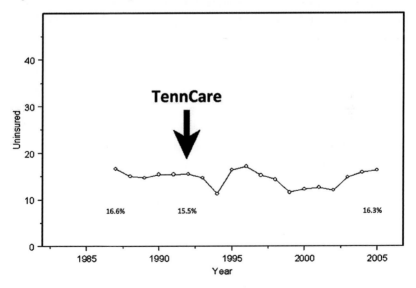

As an example of how these "miracle" plans tend to impact rates of the uninsured, in Figure 2.12 we see the effects of one of the larger attempts known as TennCare out of Tennessee; you can see it did bring down uninsured rates for a few years until it became unafford-able because it had not addressed spiraling costs.

A relatively unusual piece of Chapter 58 was a mandate for those not insured but also ineligible for government health coverage. These individuals would have to purchase health insurance at their own expense or be fined through the state's income tax system. A unique addition was a large new bureaucracy to solicit and oversee the private health plans offered and sort the uninsured into free, sliding scale, or completely self-funded plans; this adds an additional layer of administrative costs of 4 or 5 percent to our state health expenditures.[67]

The plan has led to higher percentages of insured state residents; it now covers 67 to 80 percent of those uninsured when the law was first passed. It has been heavily subsidized by federal dollars (beyond normal Medicaid funding). It also defunded most free care as part of a spending shift to make the plan more affordable to the state. This caused many who were receiving care to receive no or inadequate care since they cannot afford the new additional fees or co-pays and deductibles on their extremely limited incomes. The primary safety net hospitals also saw their free care revenues cut back severely, although the number of free care patients they are seeing has only decreased by a third statewide. Chapter 58, the Massachusetts Health plan, included a payment formula that also skewed payments away from safety net hospitals and has created a two-tier hospital system where doctors at the state's largest hospitals may receive on average from 15 percent to 60 percent more per procedure (up to 300 percent reimbursement) than doctors in the rest of the state's hospitals.[68]

The Massachusetts Health Plan has also cost more than projected, costing $1.1 billion in fiscal year 2008 and $1.3 billion in fiscal year 2009. And it is costing more every year. Individual mandated plans — even with attempts at stiff negotiation by the new government administrative layer, called the Connector — have been much more expensive than projected. They have had to jettison commitments to comprehensive and quality standards to even get the more "affordable" plans they have to offer those mandated to purchase coverage; these often include high deductibles and co-pays that make use of such care likely to be prohibitive. They are regressive: for instance the same plan for a 54-year-old may cost twice as much as for a 35-year-old.[69] Such high costs made the goals of the plan for savings from preventative and early intervention evaporate. When you add the large numbers of those newly unemployed, many of whom have lost coverage, the picture gets dicier.

Much of the Massachusetts "Miracle" Health Plan depended on special dispensation for an unusually high federal contribution without factoring in the exacerbating cost of continued health insurance increases for everyone including 100 percent government-subsidized coverage. Drains on the public coffers seem prohibitive for the federal government to replicate it. All this was true before the economic plummet.

The fundamental failure here is not the attempt at universal coverage but the denial of the interrelatedness of cost and coverage. We have to remember that the most common cause of individual bankruptcy before the sub-prime lending crisis was unexpected and runaway medical expenses. As I said in my 2006 run for governor, as someone who has often not had health care coverage, *no one wants to go without coverage.* As a state our commitment to necessary care regardless of insurance mitigates the anxiety of lack of health coverage. It is still like walking around with a ticking time bomb: you never know when it might explode. The low-level fear that uninsured carry around — especially those with children — takes its own toll.

Contrary to public messaging, most people are not avoiding the reality of possibly needing care nor ignoring potential catastrophic costs; health insurance simply costs more than they can afford. Like most things, if people feel they can get something they need for what they can afford to pay, people are willing to pay for health coverage.

Making care costly

In our culture we tend to make policy decisions, well, any decisions, toward the average, mean or norm of a group — like *the normal life expectancy after a second heart attack is...* or *the average savings from cutting such a tax program is...* There is, however, often as much to learn from asking about the extremes and finding out why they are different. Average life expectancy after the second heart attack is not nearly as useful as knowing the average for the age group to which you belong. It is even better if they tell you that if you can change your cholesterol by changing your diet that you are likely to live as long as anyone who has not had a heart attack at all! Many of us wish that when they propose a tax cut that economists would share more real information. Will the vast majority of us save a little in comparison to the top 20 percent who get most of the savings? Will we get a little money and then suffer most of the service cuts?! In trying to understand increasing health care costs, research on specific examples can also prove helpful.

Special points to Atul Gawande, a surgeon, who decided to research McAllen, Texas — the community that has the dubious distinction of having the highest per-person health care costs in the country, second only to Miami, Florida, which has much higher costs of living in general.[70] In 2006, Medicare, which is a good barometer of all health care spending, spent $15,000 per enrollee in McAllen, almost twice the national average, while the town's per capita income was only $12,000. On top of high poverty, it has a 60 percent higher incidence of heavy drinking than the national average.

Poverty and alcohol, however, do not explain McAllen's high health costs. El Paso county, about 800 miles away, has the same demographics (size, public-health statistics, percentage English-speakers, undocumented immigrants and unemployment) **but** Medicare spent $7,504 per enrollee there in 2006: half of the expenditure in McAllen. Health conditions were the same, so that did not explain cost differences. McAllen had state-of-the-art hospitals but so did El Paso and the same number of doctors per population.

Was the increase in costs because of better health outcomes? Apparently Medicare ranks hospitals on 25 measures of care. On all but two, McAllen's five hospitals performed worse on average than El Paso's.

Gawande dug deeper for answers. It was not malpractice because Texas has some of the toughest legal limits on malpractice awards.[71] Gawande had an experienced economist look at statistics based on Medicare's payment data and searched two private industry data sources. It turned out McAllen got more of pretty much every kind of billable care — more tests, more hospital treatment, more surgery, more home care than El Paso and nationwide.[72] The statistics from

2005 to 2006 show staggeringly higher figures, including two to three times as many pacemakers and five times as many home nurse visits.[73]

Contrary to that oft repeated phrase that "you get what you pay for" that is not true in medical spending. It may be the exact opposite.

Two Dartmouth economists found that the more money Medicare spent per person in a state, the lower that state's ranking quality of care on average. In contrast to McAllen, the Mayo Clinic in Rochester, Minnesota, has fantastic medical facilities and quality but is in the bottom 15 percent in Medicare spending, more than $8,000 less in per-patient spending than McAllen.[74] In another 2003 Dartmouth study, researcher Dr. Elliott Fisher found not only much more medical "care" given in higher-spending regions with equal or less good outcomes, *they received less low-cost preventative services, like vaccines, primary care physicians or quick access to emergency rooms and doctor visits.*[75]

But the key question is why? Why in some areas is more measurable medical "care," in terms of quantity and cost, given than in other parts of the country — especially with no measurable difference in outcomes, except perhaps worse outcomes?

Gawande kept digging but when he brought his data to the top hospital administrators in McAllen, they had no idea care was more expensive in McAllen, let alone knew why. Nor did doctors he spoke with although they were the ones doing the procedures and ordering tests.

Dr. Brenda Sirovich, an assistant professor of medicine at Dartmouth Medical School, surveyed some 800 doctors broken into groups by high-cost, low-cost and in-between-cost cities. For totally standardized cases and protocols, the doctors' answers for course of treatment were the same. However, for the many more cases that were not clear cut, some doctors ran the maximum number of tests and procedures, some the minimum. It depended upon where they practiced. In case after case, outcomes were not necessarily improved by more medical activities. But in the most expensive cities, doctors made the most expensive choices.[76]

So if McAllen doctors and hospital administrators were unaware that they were charging more than the national norm and that they were following the most expensive courses of treatment, what was creating this phenomenon? Context really can be everything.

Gawande compared the culture surrounding care in McAllen to the Mayo Clinic and places like Grand Junction, Colorado; they have achieved some of Medicare's highest scores for quality of care while charging Medicare in the lower percentages.[77]

Woody Powell, a sociologist at Stanford University, identified an effect he called the anchor-tenant theory of economic development.[78] Stated simply, if the biggest fish in an economic arena functions, for instance, more cooperatively, then so will the smaller economic fish. If they function more cut-throat so then will the smaller economic fish. In McAllen, where fee-for-service predominated and doctors came to see themselves playing more of an entrepreneurial than a medical role — purchasing their own clinics, increasing their billing through purchasing their own testing machines to use in-house, for instance — the norm of care came to emphasize maximizing what is billable.

The Mayo Clinic consciously built its organization around the tenet that "the needs of the patient come first," not the convenience or income of the doctors or anyone else in the food chain. The first thing Mayo Clinic leadership recognized was the need to get rid of any financial barriers to care. It pooled all the revenue doctors and the hospital system received, and put everyone on salary so patient care was not influenced by what increased the doctor's income. Doctors, nurses and even janitors met almost weekly to figure out how to improve care and service. When the Mayo Clinic opened campuses in other states, its process and payment arrangements made hiring staff and getting properly established take longer — at least a decade. But they found that "when doctors put their heads together in a room, when they share expertise, you get more thinking and less testing."[79]

Medical leaders in Grand Junction, Colorado achieved comparable results for their community, even though in Grand Junction doctors still receive piecework fees from insurers unlike Mayo Clinic doctors. Years ago, however, these doctors created a system where they all got paid the same fees regardless of the pay schedule of the insurers — Medicare, Medicaid or private — to avoid competition over type of patient. The main health plan in town, an HMO, got the doctors to agree to meet regularly on small peer-review committees to go over patient cases together and address "poor prevention practices, unnecessary back operations and unusual hospital complication rates." Problems went down and quality went up as it did in 2004 when they created a community-wide electronic-record system. The health costs per patient remain one of the lowest in the United States as have the costs in other localities that adopted these approaches.[80] These are what Fisher of Dartmouth (mentioned above) calls "accountable-care organizations."

While organizations with these underlying values repeatedly provide the win-win model in the U.S., Gawande ultimately argues that this success is not a function of how we pay for health care. Economists, he says, have pointed out that as a society we generally pay doctors for quantity not quality and they sometimes point out that we pay them as individuals not as members of a team. He makes the analogy that if you build a house by paying electricians, plumbers and carpenters each separately, you will likely get more outlets, faucets and cabinets "at three times the cost" however no one would be surprised if it fell apart a year later because no one was coordinating the effort.

Gawande rightfully argues that simply putting individuals in a position to decide what to pay for themselves will not work; we have neither the expertise nor the leverage when we need an operation to negotiate with each surgeon, nurse or anesthesiologist in the hospital room.

What is clear, however, is that uncoordinated service, piecemeal payment systems driven by profits by multiple insurance players create an "anchor-tenant" in most of our health care system. That anchor-tenant is increasingly one for-profit insurance provider per region (although different regions are dominated by different such providers out of a handful or more throughout the U.S.). What Gawande has described as the highest quality care, lowest cost systems inside the U.S. are actually locally organized single-payer systems: care is paid for at the same rate, information is cooperatively shared, and they coordinate care especially to address system-wide problems or deficiencies and identify creative improvements. These are the strengths of the best non-profit systems. By Gawande's own detailed exploration, he has argued for a specific, decisive role of an anchor-tenant, a dominant health care force driven by goals of care not profit. This is the opposite of our health care systems nationwide that are dominated by institutions driven by profit first, then care.

Can international comparisons teach us anything?

Although I know we Americans do not like comparisons to other countries — I suppose like younger siblings still out to prove ourselves — it does not mean there are not things to learn from other countries.

Most U.S. health care reforms continue to focus primarily on trying to extend medical coverage to everyone. But that goal has been shown again and again not to be sustainable without addressing the other key problem with our health care system — costs. As our economy contracts, the high cost of health coverage for all of us — individuals, government and businesses — is undermining any chance for meaningful recovery.

In 2010 costs of private insurance are projected to rise at least 9 percent and 10.5 percent for businesses.[81, 82] Those projections represent unaffordable costs, especially at this time. Small businesses providing health care plans for their workers nationally have dropped from 68 percent in 2000 to 62 percent.[83] Massachusetts employers have so far slightly increased coverage because of our "miracle" — while it lasts. But employees accessing those plans have dropped by 7 percent[84] and the percentage paid by employees for individual coverage went from an average of 18 percent to 25 percent. That does not take into account increased co-pays and out-of-pocket expenses. Those costs are increasingly unaffordable to people who are employed just as they are for those in the Massachusetts subsidized plans.[85] Figure 2.13 shows the percentages of people who needed care but ran into cost problems both for the uninsured and underinsured. But it also shows the increase in numbers reporting a cost barrier since 2002 even with the Massachusetts health care reform in the last three years.

Figure 2.13   Underinsurance has increased under Massachusetts Reform[86]

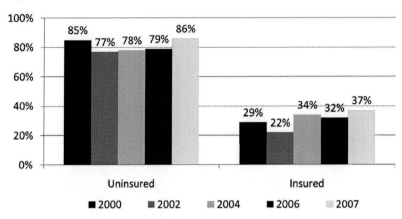

Massachusetts Division of Health Care Finance and Policy, "Health Care in Massachusetts: Key Indicators," November 2008: p. 33.

For businesses' health plans designed to meet the state's legal mandate, few employees are finding them affordable enough to buy into, given the cost of employee shares, co-pays and out-of-pocket expenses. Nationally, with no employee required contribution, employees opt for coverage 89 percent of the time. If employees have to pay 37 percent or more, the percentage of employees opting in drops to 68 percent. Trends towards increasing the employee share of health coverage will clearly undermine any chance of nearly universal coverage and any of its potential health or economic benefits.[87]

How do our high health care costs compare with the rest of the developed world?

They compare badly; we pay roughly twice as much as the next most expensive country, Canada — both per capita at $6,697 compared to Canada, the second highest in per capita costs, at $3,326 in 2007, and as a percentage of our Gross Domestic Product at 16 percent instead of 9.8 percent for Canada.[88] Figure 2.14 compares health care expenditures per person in industrialized nations and breaks out those expenditures by sector of spending.

Figure 2.14   Health care expenditure per person by funding source 2004[89]

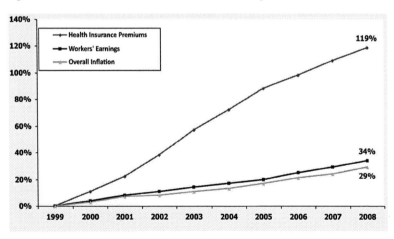

- Private Spending
- Out-of-Pocket Spending
- Public Spending

THE COMMONWEALTH FUND

	United States	Canada	France	Netherlands	Germany [a]	Australia [a b]	United Kingdom	OECD Median	Japan [a]	New Zealand
Private	$2,572	$483	$444	$806	$342	$354		$148	$28	$113
Out-of-Pocket	$803	$472	$239	$238	$313	$582	$370	$396	$389	$359
Public	$2727	$2,210	$2,475	$1,894	$2,350	$1,940	$2,176	$1,917	$1,832	$1,611

[a] 2003
[b] 2002 (Out-of-Pocket)

Source: The Commonwealth Fund, calculated from OECD Health Data 2006.

If we look over time at increases in health care costs, it has not always been this way. The recent period of health care costs outstripping inflation started in 1980.[90] Figure 2.15 shows the average per year increase in health care costs in the United States compared to

Figure 2.15   Insurance costs vs. workers' earnings vs. inflation 1999–2008[91]

- Health Insurance Premiums
- Workers' Earnings
- Overall Inflation

119%

34%

29%

Kaiser/HRET Survey of Employer-Sponsored Health Benefits, 2000-2008. Bureau of Labor Statistics, Consumer Price Index
Adjusted for differences in cost of living

both inflation and overall wage increases. Compare these increases: From 2002 to 2009, as U.S. residents, the average premiums we paid to large U.S. health insurance companies: up 87 percent. The profits of the top 10 insurance companies: up 428 percent.[92]

Figure 2.16 National health spending per person (U.S. 2000–P.P.P)[93]

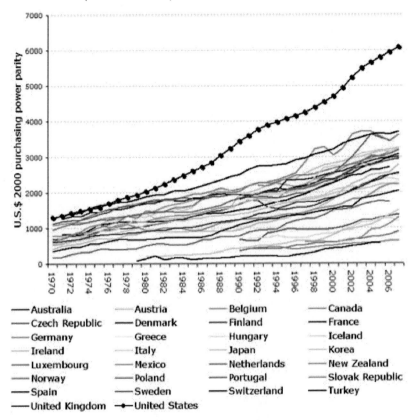

While the costs are rising, I think we assume as regular people on the ground that this is inevitable. We simply are going to have to find money we do not have to pay these increases or live the scary life of having no insurance. While our leaders discuss subsidies, stopping actual cost increases seems to be considered impossible.

For better or worse, comparison of the costs other countries are paying **and** the inevitability of insurance cost increases show that we are unique as a country in facing such high costs (see Figure 2.16).

That certainly implies something can be done. When surveyed, most Americans agree about what can be done: we must shift over to some version of the various types of single-payer systems out there. We are told that we will give up a lot if we make this switch.

Health care experiences of people in other countries.

We are continually told the United States is a leader in health care — with our amazing machines, huge pharmaceutical companies and in Massachusetts, huge teaching hospitals. Studies show, however, that *we are unique in that we pay more per capita for fewer hospital beds, fewer ICU beds, for shorter ICU stays, and for fewer practicing physicians per capita.*[94]

Unfortunately, it turns out the ways we "lead" in health care outcomes are not so rosy. If we are willing to put down our assumptions for a moment, here are the facts according to the World Health Organization[95] (WHO has to produce studies that are pretty much irrefutable by power elites across the world, so they are about as careful as you can get).

The United States ranks:

- 31st in life expectancy (tied with Kuwait and Chile).
- 37th in infant mortality (a U.S. child under 5 is 2.5 times more likely to die than in Singapore or Sweden — a statistic deeply connected to access to good prenatal care).
- 34th in maternal mortality (a U.S. mother is 11 times more likely to die in childbirth than a mother in Ireland).

These statistics get even more frightening when you look at subpopulations in the U.S. that have worse health outcomes even when you correct for amount of insurance coverage, access to care and educational attainment. For one frightening statistical example, an African-American in New Orleans has a shorter life expectancy than the average person in Vietnam or Honduras.[96]

Is this all because of lack of real health care coverage?

Certainly our burgeoning numbers of uninsured suffer major health problems because not having coverage often leads to coming too late for care. In Massachusetts you have a legal right to care but late care means more expensive, more extreme, and much worse health outcomes. At the end of 2009, we are near 50 million uninsured nationally with a predicted uptick of 1.1 million for each percentage point increase in unemployment. Projections approach 20,000 deaths per year directly traceable to lack of insurance.[97]

Just as bad for health outcomes, however, are those who are officially underinsured; they knowingly have barriers to care; they add another estimated 40 million or so to our total of insufficiently insured.[98] In addition, we have high turn down rates when people who believe they are fully insured file for significant services; there is between 15 percent and 50 percent chance of having your policy dropped nationally.[99] Seven out of 10 people file for bankruptcy because of medical bills.[100] Chances are that those who find themselves actually underinsured when the rubber hits the road is much higher than estimated.

But it is not just explainable by lack of insurance or insufficient insurance. A more comprehensive measure from a recent study by the Commonwealth Fund (health insurance company financed) show that of the 19 advanced countries included, we in the U.S. have by far the most preventable deaths. The study looked at serious illnesses with known courses of successful treatment. It found our system fell shorter on life-saving outcomes than the other 18 countries. If our system attained outcomes comparable to any of the top three study's countries, *100,000 fewer Americans would die each year.*[101]

Real financial access to care matters in whether people try to get timely care: About 37 percent of us report not seeking care for financial reasons. See Figure 2.11 which shows both the diminished use of care and the significant increase in medical debt for those under- and un-insured.

While, yes, the people of every country seem to fall into the human condition of complaining about their health care system, only in the U.S. do 34 percent want the whole system scrapped — twice the percentage in any other country.[102] While the media is filled with pundits talking about longer waits for care in other countries, actual studies show that we are only on the faster end when it comes to seeing specialists. With the exception of the oft-touted examples of Canada and England, 16 other systems get appointments for your primary care doctor faster than in the U.S. if you have one.[103] These appointments can be *mostly scheduled the same day*. Emergency care access is also, on average, better in *all* other industrialized nations.[104]

While we may think we are paying more because we support a more productive pharmaceutical industry, for instance, that turns out not to be true either. European pharmaceutical companies are ahead of us in creating productive new medicines.[105]

We do, however, pay more out of pocket and more for administrative overhead (about 30 percent of our medical dollars). It also turns out that much of our supposedly "frivolous" over-spending complained about by economists in recent years — including the stereotype of people in trouble for spending too much of their home equity — was increased medical expenses. Figure 2.17 shows that if you hold constant the medical expenses we have had to pay, we would have saved measurably more money.

Figure 2.17   U.S. personal savings rate with and without medical expenses[106]

In the midst of all this stark reality, we are told we must await a uniquely American solution. And anything that could even smack of government intervention gets splattered with accusations of "socialism." The purpose of that label is to conjure long lines, with centrally controlled health disbursement, government-employed doctors with worse education assigned to patients without a say, in a system under-resourced and inefficiently run; the death panel image is just being thrown in as icing on the cake.

A uniquely American solution

Let's take a breath. Pure socialized medicine is the system in only some countries, with the British system being the most well-known in the U.S. Socialized medicine does mean that the doctors and hospitals are directly employed and run by the government. Single-payer systems simply mean systems that are paid through one financial mechanism — usually the government. Even if you use the comparison chart (Figure 2.14) a few pages back, you can see there are few absolutely pure single-payer systems and actually a very small subset of those could be properly described as socialist with directly employing government doctors, for instance. In those countries with socialized systems, doctors generally report very high satisfaction. Medical school costs are also much lower. Almost all of the work performed by doctors is actually patient care (unlike in the U.S., where frequently doctors must get permission from private insurance companies to treat at all). In all other industrialized countries, treatment is overwhelmingly directed by the patient and the doctor.

Here comes the real unraveling of the images of less desirable systems that were recently splashed across the media. We do have uniquely American examples of single-payer systems in the country — a more pure example before some changes in recent years. And we have an example of a socialist system already in the United States.

Before discussing this issue, I need to first ask for your forgiveness. One segment of the U.S. does have longer life expectancy than the average of other industrialized nations even with the highest rates of sickness, fewer financial resources on average and the full spectrum of race and ethnicity: Americans over the age of 65.[107] Evidently once we enter Medicare, the only single-payer system in the United States, we all uniformly increase our life expectancy, regardless of our medical history, poverty level and disparities of past health issues.

We enter a different world where almost all doctors are in the system (close to universal choice). Financial incentives shift to prevention and early intervention (since this system has to pay for our increased medical expenses if care is delayed or inadequate). And there is universal coverage. In addition, most medical decisions return to the doctor-patient dyad with insurance staff and adjusters removed from the health care equation. This is the world of Medicare.

In recent years, the breakup of Medicare into different pieces and more direct use of private insurance systems have increased the overall costs of Medicare and out-of-pocket expenses for participants. But Medicare patients still have greater access to care than those with private insurance. In a Commonwealth Fund study released in May 2009:

- Only 10 percent of Medicare recipients report problems with physicians accepting their insurance compared to 17 percent of people with employer coverage.[108]
- Sixty-one percent of those on Medicare reported *"excellent or very good quality of care"* in the past year compared to less than half of those with private insurance.[109]
- Only 15 percent reported problems with cost or being hounded to pay bills compared to 26 percent on employer plans in the same study.[110]

In contradiction to our images of single-payer plans:

- 70 percent of patients in traditional Medicare say they *"always"* get access to needed care, including specialists and tests, compared to 63 percent in Medicare-managed plans and only 51 percent of those with private insurance.[111]

Of course, one other system in the U.S. has even better health outcomes, especially those they have targeted for quality control. That is the Veterans Health Administration (VHA), part of the Department of Veteran Affairs (VA). This research was reported in August of 2009.[112] The study compared hundreds of patients from across 12 areas of the VHA system with a hundred randomly identified, comparable aged patients.

- The VHA scored 16 percentage points higher than the providers for the random sample — 67 percent to 51 percent — for overall quality of care
- For chronic disease care, the VHA finished 13 percentage points higher: 72 percent vs. 59 percent
- For preventive care, the VHA finished 20 points higher: 64 percent vs. 44 percent
- The comparison the VHA did not win was for acute care

- The VHA held the strongest advantage in processes targeted by VHA performance measurement, where the VHA finished 23 percentage points above: 66 percent vs. 43 percent
- In areas where the VHA has not instituted performance measurement, it scored weakly: just 0 to 10 percentage points better.

The irony, given the present health care debate, is that the Veterans Health Administration, which is required to care for many of those with the greatest health challenges and has many of the best outcomes is the *only* health care system in the U.S. which fits the definition of socialist. It directly hires its doctors; patients can get care at any facility near where they are from any doctor available that they choose; all care is covered; and the cost for care is some of the lowest in the U.S. even though the care needed may be some of the most extensive.

With a state level version of single-payer health care, national health expenditures like Medicare and Veterans Health Administration would ideally become revenue streams to the state. Otherwise all medical services would become available to seniors and veterans — wherever they live and with complete choice of any health care provider and the state would provide wrap-around services. At present, while VHA hospitals are specially prepared to address veterans' particular health needs the most effectively, the reality is these services continue to get cut back even when needed more and more with more returning veterans. Gaps in needed care with services often long distances away from where veterans live, are generally covered by and paid for by our state. A single-payer system would mean both much more comprehensive services and care for our veterans and significant savings for our state budget in this area as well as the numerous savings identified above.

A Real
System of Corrections

It is not overlooked in the eyes of the rest of the world that we have the highest incarceration rates worldwide. The human costs are not to be underestimated. What is rarely, however, addressed is the outrageous, and by any standard ineffective and unnecessary costs of such high rates of imprisonment. The situation is only getting worse. Without changes, the costs of prisons are likely to increasingly tax our over-stretched government and social resources. Massachusetts has one in 24 people under correctional supervision (probation, parole, prison or jail), putting us in the one-fifth of states with the highest percentages of residents under supervision.[113]

Already, our Commonwealth paid $1.25 billion in 2008 for corrections — at 4.6 percent or almost 1/20th of our entire state operating budget. In addition, the building of new prisons, especially maximum security is very expensive. Our incarceration rates have increased from 1982 to 2007 by 420 percent and parole and probation rates by 485 percent.[114]

Even worse, national studies show that increased incarceration rates do not mean less crime. There are actually diminishing returns as more and more are incarcerated for less and less serious crimes. The Limited Importance of Prison Expansion study of 2006 showed that, *"after exceeding a threshold in the range of 325 to 430 inmates per 100,000 residents, incarceration fails to reduce crime — and may even increase it."* We surpassed those rates in the early 1990s. Increased incarceration, on the other hand, does mean spiraling costs to the state and so to us, the taxpayers.[115]

Crime

We all understand the anger and outrage when our safety and sense of rights have been violated — especially, when the chance of direct restitution seems small and the absolute assurance that victimization will not happen again is lacking. The next best option would seem to be the deterrent created by the certainty of punishment.

In the face of increasing crime and, I suspect, the breakdown in community which seems to increase the randomness of victimization, we saw for a couple of decades an increasing call for punishment of criminal behavior. Somehow, if we could identify the "bad" strangers amongst us who might be considering criminal behavior, and we could either convince them that they will be punished or lock them up and throw away the key, then we could feel safe again.

Some basic principles are required to accomplish this — like the idea that the punishment must predictably fit the crime (deterrent value). So stealing should incur a particular punishment but murder should incur a proportionally greater punishment; the first incidence of molestation one punishment, the second instance of rape, a much greater one.

No matter how these punishments were calibrated and no matter how certain, the great majority of those punished would, of course, have committed lesser crimes and so face lesser punishments than life in prison or death (no throwing away the key). No matter how punishment-oriented our system has become, therefore, some 97 percent of those incarcerated do eventually return to our communities.[116] Lesser crimes are punished mostly by our larger and expanded community corrections system, especially probation.

Figure 2.18 shows not only the over one hundred percent increase in overall correctional population by 2008 but breaks it out by type of supervision.

Figure 2.18   Total correctional population (Massachusetts)[117]

		Probation	Parole	Prison	Jail	Total
Population	**State**	175,419	3,209	11,300	13,394	206,241
	Federal	214	1,012	1,693		
	Combined	179,854		26,387		
Share of Adults		1 in 28		1 in 190		1 in 24
National Rank		3		47		5

A successful system, by any definition, would decrease crime over time and, so, would require that our criminal system at least decrease criminal behavior — be an actual system of *corrections* or more accurately *rehabilitation*. We cannot have a system that both punishes proportionally and "throws away the key" on everyone who gets caught stepping across the legal line.

While penalties were stiffened to try to clearly delineate consequences believed to strengthen deterrent, the financial costs of our system have skyrocketed while doing less to decrease crime. This assessment comes from across the political spectrum by those who have studied our correctional system's actual functioning.

A visit to our present system of imprisonment

The minimum length of prison terms is generally agreed to have increased. There is no dispute that the number and severity of security designations have increased. With the incarcerated population increasing, maximum and super-max cells have multiplied and minimum security and re-entry programs have decreased significantly.

One might reasonably ask, has the increased severity of incarceration been a greater deterrent to recidivism? The simple answer is "no"; it appears that it contributes to increased recidivism! In the last couple of decades, the severity of crimes committed has not changed measurably at all. Criminal behavior has been impacted more by improvements in the economy and police strategies like community policing.[118]

At the same time, costs for our criminal system have grown significantly; as of 2009, Massachusetts ranks at the top in the country with per inmate prison costs of $130.16 per day.[119] And even though there is a very broad consensus that this increasing in security levels is actually failing to decrease crime, reversing the trend has been difficult. There has been almost no success in getting the word out to the public that policy moves towards "throwing away the key" are actually increasing both costs to the taxpayer *and crime*.

The annual incarceration costs for a minimum security imprisonment per inmate per year is $41,392 for Massachusetts; medium security annually — $45,117; maximum annually $54,240.[120] And yet, we have moved more prisoners to higher security facilities and constructed more prisons of higher security classification.[121]

Why are we caught in a spiral of increasing costs and crime?

Central to this trend is the impact of more and more prisoners with less and less constructive activities to engage in; as of June 2009, our prisons were at 142 percent of capacity.[122] Add to this, less access to appropriate medical care and to possible diversion to other more targeted facilities and programs, and you have a recipe for real trouble — that is, increasing violence inside our prisons from all possible parties. Lack of medical care increases bad psychological conditions for those suffering, for those exposed to the suffering of others and for guards who may or may not be able to sort out the reality of illnesses nor have the interpersonal skills to handle such complex human dynamics. We know they have less time per inmate and that increasing physically unpredictable, and possibly threatening, situations has led to significantly higher absentee and measurable injury rates. This is bad for the workers and bad for our budget, paying for more guards needing to take medical leaves and for replacement workers. Increased violence is bad for inmates.

The Point Classification trap

Without evidence to sort out the relative impacts of the different factors, increased dangerous behavior serves as a real basis for inmates to accrue increased points in the point system that defines at what level of security a prisoner is held. There have been attempts to adjust the point system but for whatever reason — from being overwhelmed and on edge or an attempt to increase control through punishment — adjustments have not led to prisoners receiving fewer points. Increasing point assignments are moving prisoners into higher and higher security classifications even though the initial crimes that have placed people in prison have not increased.

Increased point classifications have led to the need for higher security cells and facilities. These also have the consequence of denying inmates access to rehabilitative programs during the term of their sentence and to paroling or other "step-down" programs toward the end of their sentence. The Hampden County Massachusetts system has been an exception in recent years. They are keeping comprehensive statistics that show that their increased use of parole instead of imprisonment has helped reduce recidivism rates.[123]

Increasing points also tends to get relatively minor crime inmates moved into facilities with higher crime offenders—leading to inculcation of more dangerous behaviors, connections, and different life expectations. "Step-down" programs, which used to be common to help increase life skills and work and educational options toward the end of prison terms, have almost disappeared. Inmates have fewer, if any, opportunities to begin a more personally and socially positive reintegration process before they leave prison; pre-release activities in the past included even specialized job placements, on-grounds halfway houses, etc.[124]

It is not only the internal dynamics of the point system that decreased the use and existence of rehabilitation and step-down programming. An odd side-effect of the increase in minimum sentencing guidelines was a decrease in the preparedness of inmates to reenter society. Prison system legislation recommends that prisoners first become eligible for most rehabilitative and/or work-related pre-release or step-down programs at the two-thirds point in a sentence, and that has to be after you have served the "minimum" sentence for your crime. But with mandatory and increased minimum sentences, judges much more often sentence the minimum mandatory amount of incarceration. Prisoners have more and more often been eligible for release the day after the minimum sentence runs out. No rehab, no step-down. With the punishing attitude of a more intimidated and less rooted public and therefore elected officials, the decreasing use of rehabilitation programs led to their faster defunding and shuttering as other prison costs continued to rise.

In addition, while some may be less interested in the human costs on inmates of the loss of these programs, the impact is that the majority of inmates move from prison facilities abruptly to being out on our streets with no incremental adjustments. A much higher majority of those abruptly discharged come directly from months of isolation or isolation-type confinement. With little or no financial resources, someone whose hour-to-hour activities have been determined by an absolute authority possibly for years and who may have had little human interaction day to day, is suddenly expected to function productively in numerous social interactions. They need to function from internal motivation and internal discipline often with few or possibly no more additional social and work skills than they had when they entered prison. A study by the National Research Council reported probability of arrest is twice as high in the first month after release as in the 15th month (based on 240,000 offenders released in 13 states).[125]

How have our prisons gotten so overcrowded?

Some overcrowding has been caused by budget cuts, where we have increasing numbers of open judgeships usually created through attrition: a judge ages and retires and is never replaced. Some governors have seemingly preferred not to replace judges so that they do not have to worry about an appointment making some ruling that creates political scandal coming back on them. With the economic downturn, our judicial system has seen significant cuts like so many other governmental systems. All of this has greatly increased the backlog of criminal cases.

Second, bail and bond costs pre-trial have skyrocketed because of fear of those already booked either committing another crime before their trial or seeming like a flight risk given increasing instability of employment and long-term residencies. Few can afford many of these fees for what in earlier times would have been much lower amounts. Many more people are actually incarcerated pre-trial, and given the backlog on cases, many stay in prison for months awaiting a trial date; many are held up to two years before trial. Many more who are found guilty are sentenced to time already served for minor offenses. The dangerous flip side of this is that many who are found not guilty are actually serving the same sentence as if they had been found guilty. The communities hardest hit by crime, therefore, are often losing family and productive workers who simply sit in our prisons costing millions of government dollars without even having been convicted.

In 2006, it was estimated some 8,000 people were being held awaiting trial at any one time, overpopulating our prisons. If three-fourths of those prisoners were released with supervision, it would cost one-seventh the cost of imprisonment. At the time, the annual cost per inmate in our county facilities was $35,000 annually. With increases since then, this means a savings of considerably more than

$210 million in direct prison costs without measuring the other posi-
tive impacts of decreasing the prison population numbers.[126]

Third, because of easy access to guns on our streets, the severity
of incidents is greatly increased. For instance, what in a country with
fewer guns might have been a fistfight or a knifing, in the United
States tends to escalate to gun fights and serious injury or death. This
contributes to the high rates of youth violence and death. I am tired
and heart weary of marches and vigils in many of the cities in our
state, grieving the loss of young lives; too often these deaths come as
they are trying to avoid getting dragged into street violence or have
turned their lives around and are trying to get out of gangs. This is
too high a price for a society to pay. The cost in lives lost and impris-
oned and tax dollars is just incomprehensible to me.

We also get overcrowding because of the increased recidivism
rates of those released in the untenable ways described earlier. We
get increases because of significant probation or parole violations
that some jurisdictions are successfully addressing without increased
incarceration.

Life for the 97 percent who are released

Three-quarters of returning prisoners have had histories of substance
abuse; two-thirds do not have a high school diploma. Half of returning prisoners earned less than $600 per month at the time of their
incarceration.[127] These were hardly well-employed people with easy
pre-incarceration employment records to fall back on.

Confronted with the much higher hurdle of lack of preparation
for re-entry into regular society, those leaving prison have faced
another, perhaps greater, incentive to recidivate (commit more
crimes and return to prison). Having supposedly served their debt to
society, returning, often low-skilled, offenders face more-narrowed
job and housing options.

The Criminal Offender Record Information System (CORI) was
created to catalogue every interaction with the police that might be
of a criminal nature. It lists any arrest, any court appearance in a
criminal proceeding whether it led to a guilty verdict or not. Clearly
for the legal purposes of assessing potential criminal behavior this
information could be useful. And for a long time, it was only available to police and court personnel.

Since actual convictions are a matter of public record, in the past those with a legitimate need could travel down to their local courthouse for public documents if people did not move so much. Years ago, employers started asking about arrests although they actually only had a right to know about any convictions.

Enter the modern era with both increased concerns about pedophiles and sex offenders and mobile and vast populations. If you were hiring a teacher or overnight nurses on a children's ward, someone who might have just moved to the area or not had references, checking for potential sex predators with vulnerable populations was urgent. So a process was developed where state criminal history boards would require an application of an organization and if they met certain conditions and made a successful argument for the right, they could receive the CORIs of potential employees.

At the time, I worked for an organization that ran a boarding house for mostly single women, some of whom had a child. We took to calling applicants' parole officers — if they had a record — to make sure it did not include any charge of sexual molestation to make sure children in a house with shared bathrooms, for instance, would be reasonably safe. As far as we knew, that worked until we got told by a parole officer that they were not allowed to divulge the actual nature of someone's criminal history! We had to apply to the Criminal History Board system to check the nature of criminal offenses. We also had to go in and argue for the justification of our application at a hearing to get approval. In more recent years, however, the acceptable reasons for getting CORI access and the number of authorized organizations skyrocketed to over 10,000 in the state.[128]

Criminal history record problems

It is clear when you get a CORI report on a potential employee or tenant why these reports were never meant for untrained, non-police reviewers. While we claim to believe in innocent until proven guilty, it is hard to ignore a series of arrests on someone's record even if none of them even went to court. Worse than that, there was no training requirement for reading the reports we were approved to receive. Was the average person receiving a report likely to understand what "continued without a finding" really meant? Or a "case dismissed with prejudice" — which means that the case cannot be brought again as opposed to the implication that the case was dismissed with some doubt as to the defendant's actual status. Some see our courts as too lenient and so ascribe guilt where none was found. Or they worry about a conviction of shoplifting 20 years ago; never mind that you were a teenager then and the job you seek is for landscaping. Then there are even issues of how decipherable the CORI reports are. And how prone to errors they are when common names are added to the mix (they used names not social security numbers as identifiers).

Convictions are what should matter in a democratic system (suspicion is just too easy to foment). For hiring or renting purposes, even convictions should only matter if they are relevant to the position and recent enough to have any relevant bearing. Massachusetts Department of Corrections data show that recidivism rates for those formerly incarcerated are high in the two years after release, drop in the third year, and approach zero risk by the fifth year. By the seventh year after the release if they have not re-offended there is less than one percent chance of them ever breaking the law again.[129] Since offenses from years more than seven years previous cannot predict future criminal behavior, how can it make sense for those outside law enforcement to even see them? Unfortunately, no matter how obvious these failings, CORIs have become too commonplace in recent years; they also turn out to be too easy to obtain for a fee from unscrupulous or unauthorized, and often inaccurate, sources.

In the last few years, even if those at my non-profit knew how to read CORIs and to exclude irrelevant convictions, we found ourselves being required as a subcontractor to sign legal documents that required that we abuse the CORI system. In one case we could hire "no one with a CORI." That meant if someone had ever gotten a record filed in the CORI system, we were supposed to refuse to hire them. For instance, if they had ever wrongfully been arrested (we all know about the higher likelihood of being arrested, for instance, as a person of color simply for being in a traditionally white setting at the wrong time) or had a bench warrant issued for not showing up for a hearing on a parking ticket, we could not hire them! And this was a contract for government money and they were insisting that we violate potential hiree's rights or we had to lie on our contractual agreement or void our contract!

Needless to say, the vast over-expansion of the use and often abuse of the CORI system has put not only ex-offenders but anyone ever picked up at a terrible disadvantage. It is certainly not true that all positions are CORIed. The more professional and privileged the positions, the more independent and self-managed, the less likely that CORIs are required. This disadvantages the very entry-level positions most likely for ex-offenders to apply for — the entry-level positions more likely to be filled by women, people of color, those with less formal education or economic advantages. Fifty-six percent of employers in 1996 used initial applications to screen for ex-offenders; by 2004, 80 percent did.[130] Similarly, the housing most likely to require a CORI check for renters is subsidized! All of this adds to a multiplication of barriers for those trying the hardest to find new avenues of survival besides whatever pursuits may have gotten them in trouble no matter how long ago.

All of these factors make successful transition to a constructive life in our society that much more unlikely, they increase recidivism and lose more human potential to our society and costing our state budget more revenue!

The 87% under Correctional Supervision not behind bars

Massachusetts, with only 13 percent of its correctional population behind bars, has actually bucked the national trend of increasingly incarcerating those who are sentenced through our courts.[131] This is particularly important since our prisons are the most expensive per inmate **and** we have such a high percentage of our population under some sort of supervision. We spend a much higher percentage of our correctional dollars on our prison inmates than probation and parole (for each prison dollar we spend 4 cents on community supervision);[132] this puts us well outside the national average and that may not be helping us accurately address criminal behavior nor lower our overall costs.

Our lower percentage behind bars, as opposed to in the community, does not mean we have not increased the numbers we have behind bars; we have — like the rest of the country — just not as fast. But since increasing incarceration does not correlate with less crime, this still needs attention.

A closer look at the deterrent value of punishment and imprisonment reveals important facts. Deterrent value is based on three characteristics — swiftness, certainty and proportionality.

Length of time for trial in prison because of fewer judges and an increase in pre-trial detention has ruined the relationship between swiftness/proportionality and punishment in our state. In many cases today, the certainty of punishment has essentially shifted to being based on getting arrested and bail bond decisions. While as the public we fear that people awaiting trial might recommit, the legal purpose of bail and bond decisions are about the likelihood of flight, that is, whether the defendant is likely to show up for trial: they are, therefore, more a measure of how stable someone's life circumstances are. If you are accused of rape but have a visible and steady, well-paying job, children and own your home you are less likely to be held than if you are accused of theft but are alone, homeless and without a job. There has been a huge increase in the numbers held over for trial. There is a comparable increase in those held for so long they get sentenced to time-served if found guilty. They will have served the same sentence if they are found not guilty in that belated trial. Therefore, if you are being held so long for trial for a relatively minor crime, you are serving the time whether you end up being found guilty or not — completely destroying the deterrent value of proportional punishment by imprisonment for minor offenses. What matters is if you get arrested in the first place.

The lengthening of minimum sentences even if we imposed them in a swifter procedure also appears to lose their value beyond a certain point. Without even considering the loss of step-down and re-integration programs specific to the Massachusetts system, increasing minimum sentencing does not necessarily address other aspects of criminal behavior. Some criminal activity like drug dealing is so driven by demand — where the street dealers at the bottom of the food chain are easily replaced when they are arrested — that the length of sentencing does little to decrease criminal activity. Much of the most common criminal behavior also tends to be the purview of the young so lengthening sentencing until prisoners are old has little deterrent value. Thirdly, since it is the swiftness of imposition that matters most, the first few months of quickly imposed sentences matters more than the last few.[133]

In studying behavior change around criminality, an interesting reality has come to light. It appears that carrots are usually more effective than sticks — rewards are working better than punishment[134] — not only for criminals but for the community supervision agencies as well.[135] In policy shifts reflective of a deeper focus on effective crime deterrence from Kansas to Hawaii, the following outcomes are proving effective:[136]

- Initial more detailed risk assessments have helped probation and parole agencies put more of their resources on the individuals that need it the most; this assumes they are given enough resources to begin with.
- Increasing swiftness and more response to initial probation and parole violations. With better initial targeting of attention, supervisors are finding out about violations more promptly. With a range of possible sanctions and use of alternatives to incarceration such as ankle bracelets they are able to halt a downward slide with finer tuned sanctions than the sledge-hammer of incarceration after the delay of a new judicial review. Some locales are moving more probation and parole officers into higher crime areas for more hands-on presence.
- Better assessments of effectiveness — often through increasing use of team coordination of all of those interacting with criminals out in the community. These assessments pull practitioners out of traditional ruts and shift attention to what actually works and to fine-tuning that. Acknowledging differences among criminals and their behaviors is increasing better outcomes.
- Finally, establishing a system of rewards instead of only punishments; these include appropriate shortening of parole or probation for good behavior, increased access to training and other programming and even passing back to the agencies themselves some of the financial savings of decreased use of incarceration for their charges. These all have improved outcomes.

New York State proves another outcome is possible

Massachusetts managed not to grow its prison population as quickly as the national trends and kept more of those convicted in community supervision systems. New York State's new strategies meant an actual *decrease in incarceration* and *a much greater decrease in the overall incidence of violent crime than the declining national average.* New York State led in both least prison use **and greatest decrease in crime** in the last 10 years, according to recent statistics as seen in Figure 2.19.

Figure 2.19   New York cuts crime and incarceration 1997–2007 [137]

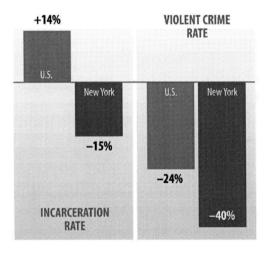

SOURCE: The Bureau of Justice Statistics "Prisons at Yearend" series and the Federal Bureau of Investigation Uniform Crime Reports.

In reports I first saw in 2006, New York had embarked on a different strategy for addressing criminal punishment. Rather than focusing on harsh punishment and disposition of major offenders, they decided to focus on small offenders to interrupt the escalation to bigger criminal offenses. The goal was to keep small crime and first-time offenders out of jail as much as possible. They did assessments diverting pretty offenders to drug and alcohol treatment if needed, mental health treatment if needed, and community probation options. The courts focused on diversion options in sentencing and the state put its money behind it. While it required a shift in focus and funding, the intensive focus on those traditionally of least interest to the legal system worked: recidivism plummeted, bringing down both crime rates and prison population numbers. Addressing sometimes underlying causes of criminal behavior, like addiction — statistically much more prevalent in prison populations — early in a potentially criminal life had a significant and measurable impact.

Prison as punishment

As many have pointed out, the punishment of going to jail is supposed to be exactly that — the loss of freedom, removal from the opportunity of the minute-to-minute choices, human connections, even seeing the full arc of the sky that those not incarcerated enjoy. So sentences provide a certainty of a minimum number of years of incarceration, possibly followed by a defined period of heightened supervision and still limited freedom circumscribed by parole.

The sentence is not supposed to include heightened likelihood of death from wildly inadequate medical services, unsupervised involuntary withdrawal from dangerous narcotics, nor often inadequately attended isolation for potential suicide watches...

I was at a legislative hearing May 2007 where a report on prison conditions was presented; the hearing had been prompted by a significant uptick in prison suicides in Massachusetts.[138] This inspection was performed by national experts in the field. No matter how disturbing those of us listening found some of the graphic details, the presenters remained surprisingly matter-of-fact. The report was not good and their assessment was our system needed urgent, significant reform. I was most struck by the answer to a question asked by one of the legislative committee chairs at the time.

We had been regaled with stories of the treatment of those on suicide watch who were often stripped naked, then re-clothed in a hospital gown, and put in an isolation cell inside a medical ward which was transparent. Oddly, these transparent cells were not positioned so that they could be viewed from the staffed supervision station. This was the worst of all worlds: Leaving someone in serious emotional distress, completely isolated, totally exposed and yet not actually supervised to ensure the prisoner's safety. In their interviews, they found most prisoners in serious emotional trouble dreaded being identified as potentially suicidal. Because of the suicide watch cells and procedures they did their best not to inform anyone of the emotional danger they were in!

After these graphic descriptions of medical facilities in prisons — lack of sufficient medical personnel and then almost no

training of prison guards, the chief presenter of this investigative
study was asked, *"But in terms of those overall prisons and prison
conditions, how would you described them?"* The investigator, in his
three-piece suit after his very matter-of-fact presentation, stalled
searching for words and finally said, *"Well, sir, I can only say {pause}
gothic."*

Images of medieval prisons of stone, dark, dank cells with rusty
bars, malnourished prisoners, and involuntary outcries echoing
periodically through the corridors flashed through my mind. Nudged
about his choice of words, the investigator was not persuaded to
move off of that description.

Under these conditions, then, the worst stories that get told of our
prisons are not surprising.

I remember stopping a prison guard on the street at one point
during a public outreach activity during my 2006 gubernatorial campaign. This guard recognized me whether by sight or at the mention
of my name, I am not sure. She started to walk away saying that she
suspected there was little point in our talking since we were unlikely
to see eye-to-eye on anything. I asked her why and she told me what
her job was. I had replied that from what I knew about our prisons,
her job was probably very difficult.

Surprised, and yet clearly feeling somewhat understood, this
entire story tumbled out of her. She said she had originally become
a prison guard expecting her job to be about keeping order among
criminals. Instead she said she felt more like an involuntary witness
to the sick and mentally ill. She said it felt more and more like all she
was dealing with were addicts detoxing without any assistance — the
sounds and smells, the human anguish and to her, evidently dangerous involuntary processes of cold turkey withdrawal were deeply
disturbing. She got very upset just talking to me. While a clearly controlled person, she became halting in her attempt to describe what
it was like — clearly traumatic to her as an untrained and essentially
helpless witness; she now hated her job.

My reaction to her story — including a churning stomach — comes
back to me as I write. None of this is surprising: 75 percent of the
prison population have histories of substance abuse;[139] 22 percent
have open mental health cases, but up to 65 percent of female
inmates do (since this only measures open cases, it is a significantly

underestimated indicator); 47 percent did not have a high school diploma, 14 percent had not graduated 8th grade.[140] In addition, we have treated addictions as crimes and incarcerated more and more people for victimless crimes often connected to drug possession. Part of the impetus for the passage of the recent very partial decriminalization of marijuana bill in our state was that such victimless incarceration led to prison overcrowding and pushing of violent criminals back to the streets.

This guard's story was particularly unsurprising because of the increase in the holding of those arrested because of increasingly unaffordable bail and bond costs. Those being held are not usually screened medically at all; even at initial incarceration, medical paperwork can take a few days before inmates are eligible to be screened and they only receive medical care in clear-cut extreme cases. In addition, those awaiting hearings are not usually held in prisons with the fuller range of services but in local temporary holding facilities. Not surprisingly, active addicts generally start withdrawal in a matter of hours not days. Unsupervised or unassisted detox is not only scary and painful, it can have serious life-long and even life-threatening medical consequences.

Other countries which have government-sponsored universal health care (single-payer health care) incorporate provision of treatment of all addictions as part of any person's health care. This creates "treatment-on-demand." An addict who surfaces even briefly between being high and active drug use can seek and immediately receive treatment. Not only does this greatly reduce ongoing health impacts and thus costs of addiction, it decreases crime directly connected to the acquisition of drugs *and* decreases collateral criminal activities *and* significantly decreases prison populations. In Massachusetts, even if you are eligible for drug treatment through insurance or can afford to pay for it, the wait can easily be six weeks or more for actual treatment. By then most addicts have not surprisingly given up trying and gone back to active drug use.

In 2007, experts in the addiction treatment field estimated that while Massachusetts had 400 treatment beds, it needed 700 to cut waiting times enough to make treatment accessible. Each 100 beds serve about 5,000; with requirements for reimbursement for patients with private insurance, upfront costs to the state would be significantly less. The prison savings of an effective diversion program for addicts is significant.[141]

Lack of proper medical care in our prisons led to other stories almost unbelievable in a 21st-century nation: Inmates with dental problems unable to get seen for days, stretching into weeks in incredible pain, involuntarily moaning and having teeth literally split down to their roots and getting dangerously infected before getting any kind of care; prisoners with psychiatric needs not being seen; or more invisible illnesses such as what turned out to be cancer going without treatment because guards interpreted requests for medical attention as "bellyaching" or simply "attention-seeking" behavior or acting out.

Prison guards are generally acknowledged not to be trained to discern what real illness-related behavior is and what is not. Instead, "cost-saving" measures have meant less and less available medical care in prisons and, many would argue, the quality of care available has been dropping. Medical services have been outsourced to larger and larger, recently even national for-profit chains with terrible outcome ratings by arms-length reviewing organizations.

While questions of human rights can and have been and must be raised about these issues, there are additional financial costs. One of the reasons that universal health care saves money as well as improving lives is that it necessarily affords continuity of care. That is, if you have health care always available, people seek health assistance early in a possible illness. Illnesses are even picked up in regular screening or annual exams. Without a single system of care, continuity of care can still result in monetary savings as well as improved health and life-expectancy outcomes.

I was reminded of this after the passage of Chapter 58, the Massachusetts Health Care Reform law passed in 2006 towards the end of the Romney administration. Having created a commitment to provide MassHealth to those leaving our prisons if they could not afford to buy their own presently mandatory health coverage, the state medical system is today inheriting the "pre-existing medical conditions" created by our sometimes dangerously inadequate prison medical practices.

The most heart-rending story of this type was of a woman who had been incarcerated while pregnant. She had also left behind children at home. She managed to give birth to a healthy child in prison who was immediately whisked away from her but was sent to live with the other children. In the next couple of years, while serving out her term, she began to experience pain in her breasts beyond what she had experienced normally during her monthly cycle. She requested a medical examination. She was told it was in her head. But the periodic pains continued, so she requested to be seen again, and at more frequent intervals. For whatever reason, she was repeatedly denied. When she finally finished what was supposed to be the term of her punishment, she was released. Reunited with her family including the young child that had never known her and now having access to our state's Medicaid system, MassHealth, she went to get a regular check-up. She was immediately diagnosed with breast cancer, and not early-stage cancer any more either. After very invasive (and expensive) treatment that the state paid for because of lack of earlier state spending, she died in several months.

Part III

Into
Deeper Water
For Safety

I
t may feel counter-intuitive, especially for land creatures. But as the waves get bigger and controlling the ship gets harder, sailing as far away from land as possible — steering away from those reefs and rocks near the shore — offers the greatest chance of survival. As our government resources shrink, cutting anything not absolutely necessary seems logical. The problem is that our government does not exist in a vacuum. It is the health of our whole economy that matters and turning it around is what will turn our state budget around.

Shrinking the government has become an accepted mantra in recent years for helping our economy. But many cuts actually undermine our economy by hurting the economic lives of those of us who spend the most reliably and the most locally. This, in turn, hurts the revenue base of government itself. Other cuts increase government expenditures because they delay and exacerbate addressing underlying problems that are cheaper to prevent earlier on. Some cuts hurt our state because they increase economically destructive cycles. We have to learn to assess policies for their real impact on the whole economy — counting everyone. So, no matter how much extra fuel we must spend to get the ship into deeper waters, we need to judiciously prioritize spending that actually takes us to greater economic safety — not just follow our unexamined, often false, concept of what increases safety.

Housing the Homeless First and Prevention

Homeless shelters can be pretty oppressive places; family shelters with families squeezed into a single room can be untenable arrangements. Children screaming, running around; anger and frustration abound. Not surprisingly, many such shelters become heavily regulated, unyielding places, as those in charge frequently face nearly impossible stress. Add to all that periodic untenable cutbacks or unattainable expectations for residents as the state fluctuates under very high shelter costs and some forces seek punishment as a way to force families to stop being homeless....

Conditions for single adult shelters, just regular everyday existence in them, make family shelters look like a cakewalk. Assigned usually a cot in a huge open space, moment-to-moment existence includes an edginess of holding onto your few belongings, uncertain who might have wandering fingers. How exactly do you sleep soundly and make sure nothing is ever stolen? The number of hours per night when things are genuinely quiet are few and most shelters have very early hours by which you must be out, having showered, gotten food and repacked all your stuff to be back out to probably wander the streets all day. The negative health impacts of lack of sleep are well documented, especially for chronic lack of sleep.

On top of this, many adult shelters are "wet" shelters, meaning they do not bar people who might be inebriated or high. For the shelter system itself that makes sense since they have a limited number of facilities and some of the beds in an area must be for those who are also not clean or sober. Otherwise, those who are drunk or high are likely to get an overnight in jail — socially more expensive and not necessarily at all appropriate. The police are also generally trying to focus on bigger fish.

This is my description of staying in an adult shelter from the perspective of someone who is not at all on edge mentally, not prone to insomnia, and who hopefully has a reasonably non-obsessive relationship to their belongings. What if you are a more marginalized person already? Losing your home and probably most of your belongings is traumatic enough. Often such happenings are triggered by other trauma. No *how-to-survive-life-on-the-streets* guide magically falls into your hands should you suddenly find yourself with nowhere to stay.

For those who are lucky, homelessness only lasts for a few months and is weathered in admittedly difficult circumstances on someone's couch. For those who actually end up on the street and in shelters, hopefully that condition only lasts for several weeks. When it lasts longer, the chronic pressures can make even the sanest person go a little crazy.

Why do I describe this? Because in recent years there has been a breakthrough that for many seems counter-intuitive. The concept is called Housing First.

For longer than I can remember, the conventional wisdom or assumption about housing long-term homeless folks has been a slow step-by-step phasing into shelter, then a dry shelter or a therapist, then a program plan with counseling and building up an income and then, if you get that far, a place of your own.

For many, however, normalizing their lives by having their own space with a roof over their head is actually the first step. This has been shown to be the foundation in fact, for normalizing the other areas of their lives. Given the insane-making reality of adult wet shelters, you can imagine how impossible that situation can be for anyone who has a fragile hold on reality for lots of reasons. For many of the long term homeless, staying in their own space or territory on the street becomes preferable to being sardined with strangers in an enclosed space where it may easily be noisier, brighter and less easy to control others' access to your stuff and your space. So the next best thing to your own space on the street turns out to be your own space inside. That stabilization then apparently opens the door to being able to heal mental and addictive problems which often need to be healed for anyone to stay in any such housing situation. Housing First does not replace the need for services concurrent with housing; it only means that housing cannot wait for other services to be completed first; it must be part of the first step itself.

Some say this is the difference between seeing housing as a privilege humans gain if they prove their capacity to meet certain societal expectations and seeing housing as a basic human need that makes other human dignity possible. For some of us, it is less of a theoretical argument and more of a practical reality. Housing First shows us that meeting the human need for our own space is a piece of dignity humans apparently need fundamentally to function in society.

It turns out that Housing First is also cheaper

Studies show what I suppose many of us might have suspected if we had bothered to think about it. You can try to cut people out from using public services like homeless shelters, food stamps, etc., but then their interactions with our social systems simply get postponed until they are in much greater trouble.

A small percentage of homeless people, the most chronically homeless, use many more social resources than most homeless people — 10 percent of homeless people consume more than half of homeless resources.[1] The chronically homeless only access services in crisis so when they do it is the police and emergency personnel and emergency rooms. In their incredibly fragmented lives, reaching such crises turns out to happen more frequently than we think.

A study in Boston showed that 119 chronically homeless people had 18,384 emergency room visits and 871 medical hospitalizations during the five-year period from 1999 to 2003, costing on average about $28,436 annually compared to $6,056 for a comparable group who obtained housing. While housing someone with chronic problems may seem unlikely to last, the initial Massachusetts Housing First programs that provide housing with appropriate voluntary services has an 84 percent success rate![2] For these Massachusetts efforts, estimated annual costs per participant before housing for Medicaid, shelter and incarceration was $33,108 and after housing, these costs dropped to $8,691 and Housing First itself cost $15,468. While those not able to take advantage of such programs remain a concern and danger to themselves and a strain on emergency resources, the savings in human and economic terms of Housing First programs speak for themselves.

It seems a human truism that prevention is always cheaper than early intervention which is always cheaper than trying to repair what is already broken. Although fixing is still better than end-stage heroic measures.

Addressing family homelessness

While homelessness figures especially for families have been growing during the last few years and have taken off with the foreclosure crisis, some folks in New York City and city government had a brilliant idea. For years, researchers have been studying the causes of homelessness in an attempt to understand what causes it beyond anecdotal stories. They have been honing in more and more. NYC decided to take the data and create a comprehensive program to move backwards up the likely chain of events and decrease homelessness before it occurs. Figure 3.1 shows New York's profound decline in homelessness since implementation of their new program.

Figure 3.1   NYC Homeless Outreach Population Estimate (HOPE) 2005–2009[3]

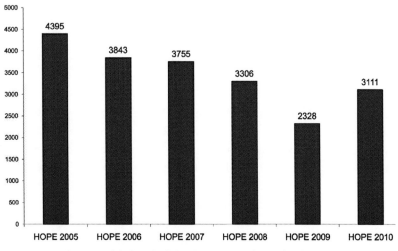

Courtesy of the New York City Department of Homeless Services

While Housing First has become a successful model for returning most of the chronically homeless to housing, in 2003 New York's focus went towards keeping people, especially families, from becoming homeless in the first place and to keep them from returning to shelter once they had left (a significant number of those in shelter were returning households). Some components of New York City's Homebase's strategy are familiar to many who have advocated policies like housing mediation; Massachusetts has a very successful model in the jurisdictions of the state where Housing Court exists and Massachusetts' own flexible short-term assistance program, Rental Assistance for Families in Transition. However, Homebase went smarter.

New York ended up getting back into the people business because of the impact on communities and drain on city resources of homelessness. Some grassroots advocates had an idea that if you could get resources to people before they lost their home, you could significantly decrease the number of people who lost, in these cases, their rental. That brought down the negative and serious impacts on children through homelessness and loss of the community fabric — jobs, schools, religious institutions, and community activities — that family life is an intimate part of. Built out of this preventative consciousness, Homebase's initiative reminds me of old-style government; government, using its greater reach and ability to coordinate resources, used to see itself as in the business of outreach and connection with its people. This is the opposite of recent decades of "outsourcing" most often to non-profits which then end up functioning as small silos without the resources or the reach of the government programs they were contracted to replace.

Many policy people these days complain about the negative impact of "silos," programs and/or policies that function separately from each other even though in the real world their functions overlap. I remember, long before one-stop shopping policy language was being developed, arguing for instance, that agencies — not just community organizations — needed to do something as simple as give people food stamp information when they went to a food pantry. In recent years, the concept of one-stop shopping for services has been talked about and implemented to a limited extent. However, Homebase designers recognized not only that anyone at risk of homelessness needed the full range of options to increase their basic income but also that they make different contacts for different kinds of help.

This was the more important piece of their work: brainstorming and researching the many access points where a family or household approaching homelessness might receive assistance before it was too late. In a complex life in a complex society, who might have an inkling that a household was in trouble and could maybe link that household up with New York's initiative? Thus, by identifying all entry points and teaching intake/receptionist people in each organization key identifiers of risk of homelessness, they could compile lists of households at risk *before these people became homeless.*

Obtaining this critical contact information meant organizing agencies to share information with the city's departments *and each other.* These interactions became the basis of team meetings; they combined information on help seekers and also built a better overall picture of who needed help and how to get it to them. As their understanding grew, they created public/private initiatives to issue stopgap or bridging resources that could get households over the crises that might otherwise have rendered them homeless.

Homebase put money into experienced community outreach workers on the street who went through the neighborhoods with the highest numbers of households typically becoming homeless. They met with churches, small pantries and other very local helping groups that people with housing troubles might contact. They even went "door-to-door" through local businesses and drop-in spots to identify the informal networks. Recently, they created a general public outreach and poster campaign for the holiday season and times of the year when people might get into financial trouble and lose their housing.

Homebase has been an affordable and highly successful deterrent to homelessness. It has provided $9.6 million in flexible, short-term financial assistance to families at risk of homelessness. Out of the 15,300 households who have received housing mediation, financial counseling and employment training, nine out of 10 were still in their homes at least a year later. At an average annual cost of $3,000 per household, Homebase cost one twelfth of what sheltering a family costs per year — comparable to the Massachusetts costs of $36,000.[4] It has modeled the role of government as not only committed to the well-being of its people but the most effective use of the people's resources they are responsible for.

For years, Massachusetts advocates have pointed out that it is cheaper to provide housing subsidies than pay for shelter. In 2009, the average family with a Massachusetts Rental Voucher Program voucher cost the state $539 per month for the state to supplement their income to stay in their own home; besides the stress and damage of homelessness to families and their children, a shelter costs about $3,000 per month. The average stay in family shelter was six months and the state had over 3,000 families in shelter and motels. While I suspect housing subsidies have been politically challenging because so many Massachusetts residents struggle with our own high housing costs, it makes fiscal and long term social sense to increase vouchers and end shelter costs.[5] Homebase is, of course, a step ahead, using these kinds of expenditures to avoid homelessness before there are shelter costs to have to reduce.

With homelessness skyrocketing in Massachusetts, a key contributor to the increasing numbers facing the destructive experience of homelessness is the foreclosure crisis. For the state's 2008 commitment to ending homelessness to be meaningful or even economically feasible, the huge flow of people being evicted from their homes because of foreclosure has to be stemmed. Any move towards a Homebase-style cost savings approach to *avoiding homelessness in the first place* just makes fiscal sense. Combining this approach of educating front-line workers about risk indicators for homelessness (including foreclosures and post-foreclosure evictions) with the fuller range of helping services would be the key to ending the present escalation in our state's ratio of homelessness; it would end this drain on our social fabric and our governmental resources.

Community First

We have all heard horror stories of nursing homes — people essentially warehoused until the end of life. The reality is that this is only the worst end of the spectrum. There are numerous care facilities and senior communities that create their own internal and active communities. Some of these cost a great deal more but not all of them.

We may have personal fears ourselves of growing old or becoming disabled; without other options, we could be thrust into a nursing home that is directly contrary to our individual life-fulfilling needs. We may have been party to or witnessed the angst of a family or individual friend about when and where and how to leave an older or disabled family member in a nursing home. Either way, we know how scary and devastating the decrease in connection and loss of regular daily living can be.

Nowadays, while statistically measured as increased worker productivity, those of us who are paid for our work are working longer hours for the same or less money. So are our neighbors. Fewer families can afford for one parent to stay home and welfare programs were changed to prohibit such families from having a parent stay home. All of this means there are fewer regular interactions among neighbors. Some of us rarely see our children nor have time for friends outside of work hours.

In addition, the long term trend is that most of us have lost financial ground slowly. We live in more cramped housing, without storage, a den, or extra bedroom, to take in a physically needy relative.

This is why our dependence upon nursing homes has increased; people have less free time and fewer financial, community and other resources. Changes in our economic lives have meant that our elders and disabled friends and family have needed more often to be cared for outside our homes.

Nursing homes have become commonly used for two types of situations: the long term disabled and aged, but also as aftercare for operations and other hospital stays before someone returns to the community. Roughly 120,000 people in Massachusetts are admitted to nursing homes each year and 100,000 of these are MassHealth members leaving hospitals.[6]

A number of disabled people and seniors, recognizing the sometimes very poor quality of care and certainly loss of life choices in a nursing home, started organizing. They fought for the right, if they were capable with potentially available support services, to continue to live in or be cared for in their own homes. They fought to get public and health care policy changed. They sued. Eventually, the courts agreed that it was a violation of their right to a reasonable human life to force them into a nursing home when community services would allow them to continue a normal life living in their own homes.

Then, something interesting came to light which we can advocate for on both the grounds of our own shared humanity and because of the economics — for Massachusetts, it goes like this...

Some of you may remember my wonderful 2006 lieutenant governor running mate, Martina Robinson, who taught us all so much during the campaign. One of the many insights I learned from her as a significantly physically disabled person (which surprised and stuck with me) was that even with all her disabilities, if she were sent to a nursing home, her annual care would cost more than when she lived in her own home; even with unusually severe disabilities if she drew down every available community support service, the state saved money. In addition, she lived a full life and even offered her commitment to a better society for all in service through our government.

Very few people living in the community instead of a nursing home would ever draw down that wide a range of support services. On average, six people can receive home care for the cost of one person in a nursing home. For those who require more specialized care, three people can receive services to the cost of each person in a nursing home. In fact, the average nursing home cost, as of 2008, is almost $58,000 per year. Regular home care is a little more than $9,000 and enhanced care approaches $16,000 per year.[7]

The savings seems clear — both in human and economic costs. Think of the extra effort community programs and volunteers put in to try to create cross-generational programs to reconnect children with seniors, or simply volunteer to increase the quality of life for those in nursing homes.

The state budget savings may be less clearcut because the federal government pays half the bill for nursing homes. Still, it is hard to believe that senior and disability groups have to lobby their legislators to make policy choices that are *cheaper* to the state as well as better for their own constituents and our communities. Recent budget "cuts" in 2008 set programs back to 1996 levels — losing the average savings of $335 million annually![8] Only by some bizarre inverse dictionary definition can these "cuts" be considered monetary savings. And that is without figuring in the significant human costs.

The final kicker here is this: Remember those court cases I mentioned that disabled and seniors had won that determined they had a right to the greatest quality of life that could be provided by the least restrictive living arrangement? There was a significant financial settlement. And there were of course also national policy initiatives. So guess what? Not only are these services cheaper to provide but there are also federal and settlement funds available to come into the state to undertake the shift in provision of care and pay for some of these services.

A healthy forest is characterized by not just a diversity of species but also by trees of different ages providing longevity and also an integrated variation of contributions by different-aged trees. So too, our human communities are healthier when all different ages and abilities — including those who do not have to be absent for work responsibilities — are there to naturally pay attention to each other....

Fork-ready Stimulus

Suppose I told you the Massachusetts state government could spend $5 million additional dollars to provide 150 plus jobs directly which would bring into the state economy $340 million in stimulus dollars which in turn would generate $600-plus million in economic activity. Oh, and would bring the state $7 million to $10 million in revenue. That is $2 to $5 million more than the initial outlay. You would think it would be a no-brainer, right? And those are conservative estimates.[9]

I like to use the example of food stamps when I talk about government spending because whether a Republican or Democratic presidential administration, the statistics on success are always the same: for each food stamp spent about $1.80 in economic activity is generated.[10] It guarantees our farmers an income and is our best program for combating hunger and malnutrition which were still rising even before this economic downturn.

There are numerous studies of other programs such as welfare and other forms of unemployment insurance that show the relatively swift uptick and bigger bang-for-the-buck in economic activity from stimulus spending at the bottom of the economic ladder. Those programs, however, have never managed multi-partisan political support like food stamps even though statistics show they stimulate the economy.

Food stamps are, by definition, stimulus. They are spending for a basic human need by those who survive below a livable income and so must spend quickly every form of revenue they can bring in just to try to get by. The monthly allotment of food stamps, even with the recent increase some of us fought so hard to get, remains insufficient to cover a month's worth of food and so food stamps are close to being guaranteed to be spent. Even with food stamps, these households remain under-resourced to cover basic expenses and so are also pretty much guaranteed to spend any cash freed up from food costs.

Food stamps are completely funded by the federal government. They draw down tax money we have already paid as workers and consumers. It costs the state budget nothing; the feds even provide advertising grants to let the public know about food stamps if the state draws them down. What the state must provide are food stamp workers to intake and administer food stamps.

By spring of 2009, food stamp demand was way up in Massachusetts with food stamp workers facing double the case loads of years earlier and still growing! This is not surprising with the most recent Massachusetts figures showing 13 percent of our children — 182,000 children — live in poverty, up 4,000 children between 2007 and 2008. Advocates have used the image of the 138 mile Massachusetts Turnpike with these children lining the length of it; there would be one child roughly every four feet![11] Surveys show that 8.3 percent of our households face food insecurity; 3.8 percent have actually gone without food; both figures are up from the previous measurement period.[12] Even without specific post-market crash figures for Massachusetts, one can expect that the sharp national increases in hunger are mirrored in Massachusetts. With major impacts from even short-term hunger on educational attainment and longer-term more serious health impacts, now is also the most critical time for us and our state to act on behalf of our neighbors and our future.[13]

I remember years ago being angered when our state changed the food stamp system. In an emergency, a person had been able to walk in and get a small allotment immediately if you qualified. Given the incredible stigma attached to seeking any kind of assistance in this country, I knew folks who mostly waited until they had used up every can of food in their cabinet before they went for help. Then they changed the law so now *emergency food stamps* means you get them in *seven to ten days* usually *after* the last food ran out.

Although it is against even the ten-day law, emergency food stamp applications by early 2009 were taking a month to fill simply because of an extensive backlog of applications. With job losses in our state in the tens of thousands each month, this will only get worse!

What a loss. While our farmers are in trouble, our cities and towns denied local aid could really use local stimulus investment and that is **exactly** what food stamps are. It would be more effective and reliable than our already vastly over-burdened food pantry system; in Worcester County in 2008, our regional food bank provided food to 17 percent more people compared to a year earlier, approximately 12,000 more people.[14] Food stamp dollars are an influx of income from outside our state, not a drain on limited state government dollars. I remember when food pantries were really for emergencies. They have become the refuge for the everyday emergencies created by chronic household budget deficits. However, only about a quarter of households experiencing hunger use our food pantry and meal programs, which makes getting all our hungry families on food stamps only more urgent.[15]

Food stamps are also a greater investment in human capital, a long-term investment in quality of life and a healthy workforce. Just as good prenatal care is the best long-term predictor of lifetime health, childhood malnutrition is the best (or should I say worst) predictor of long-term ill health. Even when hunger does not do long-term physical damage, we are all familiar with the studies showing the barriers to learning caused by hunger. And what about the psychological and social impacts on our young who see markets full of food and yet learn that they are not worthy of a decent, regular diet — do we really think this goes unnoticed?

So yes, if the state government puts in $5 million, it can hire 150 to 160 intake workers, who can process the large and growing backlog of food stamp applications. If only half of those applications are approved (a quite conservative figure that does not include a likely continued growth of demand), $340 million of food stamps will enter and be spent in our state. That will generate $600 million in economic activity, mostly at local stores and with some careful targeting, benefiting local farmers, and, yes, generate $7 million to $10 million dollars in state revenue.[16] The financial impact is created in one year. And that is not counting all the other savings from better health, greater school performance, and fewer absences from work for parents in these households.

So long as the economy is bad, the stimulus impact of this small investment of state money remains each year. If hunger continues to grow as this economic downturn continues, then the stimulus impact of the state expenditure actually continues to grow! Our local economics will benefit first as will our municipal government budgets. It is called a positively reinforcing system.

This section detailed four programs: Housing First, New York's Homebase initiative, Community First, and food stamps. They all save a significant amount of government money or, in the case of food stamps, actually generate significant economic activity and therefore state income. There are, of course, other specific program examples like these. I share examples, however, because if we ever needed to fine-tune our thinking about government spending, now is the time. Given our economic times and the habits of our state leaders, the initial increased state funding required for these programs contradicts the simple cuts they are used to—even though simply slashing jobs and services is often just worsening our overall economy. We have to turn away from the familiar shoreline and put out a little fuel to get to clearer safer waters.

Part IV

Ensuring A Deep-Sea Worthy Vessel

With the realities of the great economic Depression having receded into indistinct images and distant stories, the need for governments capable of weathering a massive storm out in the safer waters of the deep sea was easily forgotten. Almost all of our political and economic leaders had convinced themselves that our economic climate had become fundamentally more benign. They pointed to their own successes as proof even as their own economic "solutions" fed the size of the waves and strength of the winds. Those of us unschooled in formal economic meteorology pointed to danger signs of our lives already becoming topsy turvy.

Instead our political and economic leaders have argued to and actually dismantled much of government preparedness claiming all we needed was a swift racing boat. I am all for government being efficient. But government's role is akin to insurance in an economic downturn unlike private companies. It needs to step in and turn our ship around while businesses are contracting and withdrawing along with the overall economy. Government needs to have resources stockpiled and reliable sources of fuel to weather every type of storm. It needs the perspectives, insights and efforts of all people—from the engine room to the crow's nests high on the masts. It is responsible for all its passengers not just the ones with money to pay what businesses want to charge. Also, the government is responsible for the preparedness of all its future passengers and workers.

A government by and for the people needs reliable revenue, a voice for its workers and successful education for all. Decades of efforts to dismantle the deep-sea worthiness of our ship have left us poorly prepared — economically and ideologically.

Taxes, Taxes, Taxes

"Taxes are the price we pay for a civilized society"
— Oliver Wendell Holmes, Republican,
Supreme Court Justice from 1902–1932.

I always wonder why U.S. citizens resent taxes so but I think it has to do with two things: First, the lack of transparency about where our taxes go; and second, even if we find out we have no say about how our tax dollars are spent — violating that so fundamental American concept of "no taxation without representation."

Polls that ask generally get the same answer: U.S. residents do not mind paying taxes as long as they are not squandered. How can any of us not feel like they are being squandered today?

Never having been big on government spending myself, I have always been concerned not with big or small government but effective government (President Barack Obama said this but based on his choices I wonder if he means something different from what I do). Ironically, the greatest expansion of government spending in my lifetime to-date had been by President George W. Bush, a supposed Republican conservative who could claim he cut taxes only because he deferred payment onto future generations. The politicians' complaint against regular folks spending beyond their means is ironic when our federal government continues to draw down wild amounts of credit only possible because of the government's special "good faith and credit" standing. The U.S. federal government can truly extort credit from the rest of the world for being "too big to fail."

I end up reflecting on the railing against our local government the way any of us drivers do when there are huge potholes in the road — and our plans to sue the government if we get a flat tire or hurt an axle if we hit a really bad one. This is mild compared to complaints from friends who have traveled abroad — especially in developing nations — about how whole segments of roads have washed out or have had all the paving worn away. Or friends who return from overseas with stomach parasites — angry about bad water they must have drunk somewhere and angry at themselves for not having remembered to always use iodine tablets to purify water before they drank it.

I remember trying to explain to co-workers that most state and federal tax money spent in our country is never talked about in budget debates; it is spent on a million unspoken protections. It is not that earthquakes leave massive debris and huge death and injury tolls in other countries because the earth quakes worse elsewhere in the world; it is that we have government-enforced building codes that ensure construction standards that withstand more shaking.

As this book went to press, we had the disturbing earthquakes in Haiti and Chile; our prayers are with the people of both countries. The loss of life and devastation unfortunately underscores the importance of larger governments with the greater everyday protections that richer countries can and do afford — like stricter building codes. Haiti, the poorest country in the Americas, had an estimated 230,000 deaths with a 7.0 magnitude earthquake; Chile, the richest country in South America, had about 500 deaths with an 8.8 magnitude earthquake.

A friend and I had once tried to enumerate how many interactions with tax-funded protections the average U.S. resident has in the first 15 minutes in the morning: fire retardant requirements protect us from our mattress, our blankets and pillows; we do not worry about parasites in the water or dangerous chemicals in our tooth paste when we brush our teeth; we do not worry about turning on a light or plugging in a hair dryer — because of both building codes and electrical product standards; we do not worry about e-coli in the milk in our coffee or overly health-endangering pesticides on those coffee beans. The list got too big and complicated for us to complete.

On top of these protections, we are used to citizen advocacy groups tracking and fighting for improvements in such government standards all the time. We may be absolutely furious when unacceptable lead levels are found in the paint on toys made in China. We are not at all surprised that someone in our country discovered this and mounted an effort which forced it to change.

In short, much of taxes we pay go to basic living standards, which we just assume should be part of Oliver Wendell Holmes' "civilized society." We generally only become aware of them when the government fails: such as, in an e-coli break out, the reappearance of meningitis which had almost been eradicated in the United States, or during a government-driven product recall.

The real question is not big or small government but how effective and transparent it is, who is paying for it and what is the balance in who is benefiting from it. In short, are we getting represented in what we are paying for?

Five pots of money plus one to pay for it

Suppose you were left to decide about raising funds to sustain our state services. Suppose I gave you five pots from which to raise the funds.

The first two pots of the five I gave you were pretty small to begin with. Both have been steadily decreasing since 1980 and we expect them to plummet in the next few years at least. Pot number three used to be decent sized and pretty predictable. But even pot number three has decreased consistently since 2001. That decrease will accelerate in the next few years. Pot number four has a significant amount of money; for decades it grew and until eight years ago was growing at significant rate — but then it too flattened out; in this downturn it appears to be decreasing but it is much bigger than it was 20 or 30 years ago. Finally, pot number five has burst its seams and had to be re-potted a number of times in the last 30 years. The largest percentage of its contents has tripled over the last 15 years alone and while the contents have shrunk in the last six months, it remains overflowing at levels well beyond where it was 10 years ago.

It seems prudent that — if you wish to protect a reasonably healthy budget with the most crucial of services — pots one and two are not going to provide any meaningful revenue these days and are hardly worth considering in the near future. Pot number three, while it could provide some resources, is not going to provide

a decent foundation for future funding any time soon. Pot number
four at least has built up a significant basis even though it is losing
some ground in recent years. Clearly, however, the most logical place
to seek a longer term base for funding is pot number five — assuming that those who contribute to all the pots value a vital state and a
vibrant economy.

Increasingly over the years, the norm of thinking for policymakers (not all of them, thank goodness, but the majority!) has been that
we need to incentivize preferred spending options for those with the
most wealth and power and make punitive the less desirable spending options for low-income and working-class folks — with grada-
tions for those in between. In short, the more financially well off you
are, the more public policy money was added to increase the size of
the carrot it offered; the less well-off you are, the more public policy
money was withdrawn to increase the size of the stick it threatened
you with.

Somewhere in here, the considerations of the value of our communities, our relationships and even the value of a decent future as
motivation for people's choices in our society, were lost. Policymakers
were so convinced of the centrality of the "me" concept as motiva-
tor, that they have hastened our loss of mutual bonds and protection
by never speaking about those bonds or, more importantly, to their
value.

The five pots I have described to you are the pots created when
economists divide our state's residents into five groups based on
income. Economists call them "quintiles." The first two quintiles,
pots one and two, as I described them, represent the bottom 20
percent, and 20 percent to 40 percent of income receivers. The third
pot is the middle 40 to 60 percent of income receivers. The fourth pot
is 60 to 80 percent of income receivers and the last pot represents the
top 80 to 100 percent of income receivers. Pot five therefore includes
the very top income receivers whose incomes have skyrocketed in
more recent years while the vast majority of the rest of us have lost
purchasing power.

Figure 4.1 shows the stagnation of income of the "bottom" 90
percent of workers as well as the take-off in income of wealthier individuals since 1979. If you separate out the bottom 90 percent, most of
us have actually lost ground during the last 10 years.

Figure 4.1   Growth in annual earnings by wage group, 1979–2007[1]

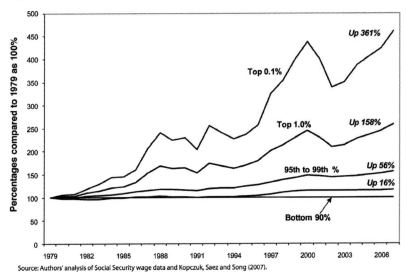

Source: Authors' analysis of Social Security wage data and Kopczuk, Saez and Song (2007).

The reason I opened this section simply describing the relative money available in each segment is that if policymakers were blind to social assumptions and simply wanted to balance our budget so that we created the most effective government and economy for all, the tax choices would be clear.

Our economy fails when we do not have a strong consumer base and the stronger the consumer base, the hotter our economy; so making sure as much as possible that *everyone has enough income* is the best for our whole society — including for those who glean the most profits from a strong economy. Policies that prioritize income beyond what individuals and households can and will regularly spend have diminished returns for all of us. Similarly, a reliable and effective government which can ensure that people live the healthiest and most productive lives best serves our whole society.

Pot Number Six: Corporate Taxes

Of course, depending on how you slice the pie, there is another, at least one other, significant pot of money out there: corporate taxes. I know in our society that we tend to be sloppy in our language not making a distinction between "businesses" and "corporations." But in tax policy, the distinction is important. We have learned to our dismay that banks, which have been much regulated, and lenders, which include the up-until-now unregulated mortgage companies, are also not interchangeable terms.

Small businesses in our society are mostly taxed as an additional tax schedule in the owners' personal taxes. Large businesses that are incorporated submit their own tax forms and have their own tax policies that affect them separately. When policy makers talk about business tax policy, they are generally talking about policy for corporations which are big enough and separately taxed. They are not talking about your local shop owner. So when they talk about special corporate tax breaks, those are incentives that pass by local business owners; the ones most of us are likely to know and have our local economy and job creation depend upon.

As we end this century's first decade, how are taxes distributed in our state? Do those taxes do their best to ensure the greatest economic activity? Do they provide a consistent and predictable base for making the best policy choices by our government? And how does our failing economy contribute, change or detract from present tax policy choices?

State Tax choices

It turns out that state taxes, over time, have depended more and more on individuals rather than corporations. And among individuals, state taxes have depended more and more on low-income, working class and middle class taxpayers — the bottom three quintiles or the less-than-60-percent income receivers. And which pots have been losing money in the majority of the last decade? And which were smaller to begin with? These same three pots.

Let's step away from the unquestioned assumptions of who is supposed to do the right thing because of incentives and who is supposed to do the right thing because of the threat of punishment. Unclouded by assumptions, the shift in tax base is simply ineffective, short-sighted policy which will only become more ineffective and worse for both our state economy and our state's ability to provide services.

If we step away from the ideological gun perhaps we can make sense of what we need to do for tax policy that will help pull us out of this hole rather than mire us farther into it.

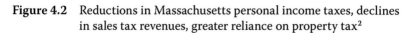

Figure 4.2   Reductions in Massachusetts personal income taxes, declines in sales tax revenues, greater reliance on property tax[2]

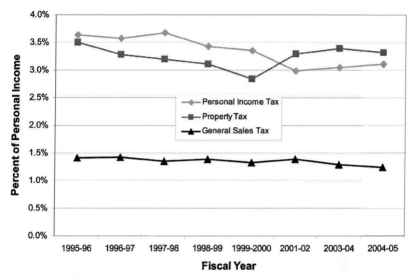

Note: "Personal Income" includes capital gains.
Sources: U.S. Census Bureau, *Governments Division*;   Bureau of Economic Analysis, *Regional Economic Information System*,   March 2008; Mass. Dept. of Revenue. Census data are not available for fiscal years 2000-01 and 2002-03.

For many years, individual taxes at the state level consisted primarily of income and secondarily sales taxes. More recently, as the state's financial commitment to our cities and towns dropped, property taxes — which are levied at the municipal (city and town) level — have come to rival individual and household income tax burdens (see Figure 4.2).[3] It is important to understand that property taxes are **not** just felt by homeowners. Property taxes are one of the taxes generally passed directly onto renters and so are renters' taxes as well. This tax is partially responsible for Massachusetts' high rental housing costs.

Also, as the government has shied more and more from the big bad word "tax," they have turned more and more to hidden taxation. The state has vastly increased fees and huge dependence on borrowing through use of bonds. Dependence on bonds, for instance, still shows up as an increase in the regular debt payments as part of annual government operating budgets. However, bonds mostly pass the financial burden onto future budgets and taxation and probably future generations.

So what kind of taxes tax which of our pots? They do not fall at all evenly it turns out; "a flat tax" is not at all flat because types of spending are wildly different for different quintiles. Thus, the types of taxes that a politician supports say a great deal about who they think should be paying for our governments' services. If we are all in this together, surely it makes sense for everyone to pay in some sense, right? And at present in our worsening economy, some of us would argue that those who have benefited by far the most from state policies, should perhaps be required to pay the most — although in this crisis it would be good if those who make up the biggest pots even paid as much as the rest of us!

Figure 4.3   Distribution of personal income dedicated to state and local taxes in Massachusetts, 2006[4]

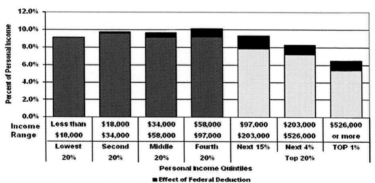

If you think about it the higher percentages in taxes paid by regular folks in Figure 4.3 is not surprising. Including federal tax deductions just exaggerates the differences.

Take sales taxes, for instance. Our state does not put sales taxes on most services that higher income people buy, like accounting help or legal advice. Lower income and working class people spend pretty much every cent they bring in on taxable goods (store-bought food being the one non-taxed type of regular expenditure they make). So those of us in the first two pots/quintiles are paying out the most per dollar in sales taxes — many times more than those at the top (see Figure 4.4).

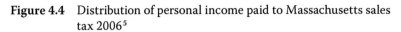

Figure 4.4　Distribution of personal income paid to Massachusetts sales tax 2006[5]

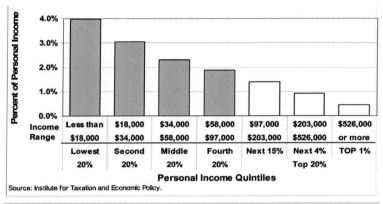

Everyone pays property taxes; tenants pay it because it gets passed on in their rent. Those wealthy enough to own investment properties pay those taxes by increasing the rental payments they charge and taking them as a business cost, not paying those taxes as part of their personal income. The problem is that the percentage of the household budget that goes towards housing costs is high for moderate and lower income people while for the very wealthy it drops *significantly* in comparison to their overall income (see Figure 4.5). This means property taxes not only impact those with the least more, it is really property taxes of the top 20 percent that drop off measurably.

Massachusetts has a flat income tax (constitutionally restricted) unlike our federal taxes which are graduated (traditionally the more you make, the more you pay per dollar over a certain amount). Given the above situation with sales and property taxes, Figure 4.6 shows how state income taxes are the only major tax that really impact those in the growing pot number 5, the top quintile of income receivers.

Figure 4.5   Distribution of personal income paid to Massachusetts property taxes 2006[6]

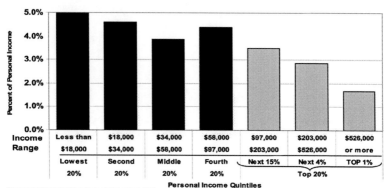

Source: Institute for Taxation and Economic Policy.

MASSACHUSETTS
BUDGET AND POLICY CENTER   February 2008

Taxes that are higher for those who bring in less money are called regressive; those that are higher the more income you receive are referred to as progressive.

Figure 4.6   Distribution of personal income paid to Massachusetts income tax 2006[7]

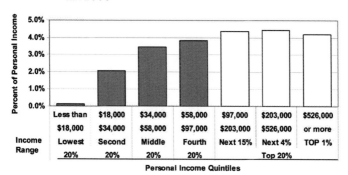

Source: Institute for Taxation and Economic Policy.

MASSACHUSETTS
BUDGET AND POLICY CENTER   February 2008

As the great Republican Oliver Wendell Holmes said, *"Taxes are the price you pay for living in a civilized society."* No conservative who is truly by definition a conservative — who wish to conserve resources and the longevity of our communities — opposes taxes. Like the rest of us, they oppose frivolous taxation. The real debate should be about what is frivolous not about whether we should be committed to having a civilized society.

So what, you might ask, about other taxes? Well most fees, again because we generally only charge them on government services that are used by regular people, tend to be regressive. Taxes that can only be charged at the municipal level because they tend to be essentially fees, sales taxes or property taxes are usually, although not always, regressive.

And sin taxes? I am always stopped in my tracks by this question because our society has moved to a definition of sin that, I think, would have our Judeo-Christian fore-fathers and -mothers gyrating in their graves. Surely, all the most basic lists of sins would place greed above the over-indulgences of tobacco or liquor. And while we tax gambling when it is state run, we do not tax gambling when it is done on the international markets and pulls down the entire world's economy!

I think one could make a moral argument for sin taxes if the sins were more inclusive and taxed people regardless of venue, but they do not. The problem with sin taxes in our very stratified society may be that what is sauce for the goose is not at always sauce for the gander. The terminology presently used only identifies "sin taxes" as those that are the escapes of regular people with a comparatively limited choice of such "sins." The term, and so the taxes, do not equally target the wider range of huge "sins" available on the world's stage. If we want to argue that logically all over the counter items should be taxed even if these taxes are usually regressive, at least that argument is consistent — in arguing it is because some of these items represent "sinful" behavior, I think we have wandered off the cliff of moral reasoning.

Legally, the state budget must balance annually unlike the federal budget. All major revenue sources are falling at this point, and if we tax those whose economic activity we need to increase the most — that of regular consumers — then we are only digging a deeper economic hole! Realistically and effectively, to supply the most basic needs for all at this economic juncture, we must figure out how to shift the tax burden back to the pots that are full and still filling.

Corporate Tax shifts, past and proposed

Why do the people of Massachusetts feel like we are paying more and more, and getting less and less, from our government? Because we are! We are paying more because we are making up the share that used to be paid by corporations. Regular folks have been paying more and more of the share that wealthy households used to pay.

Corporate taxes in our state provided about 16 percent of state revenues in 1968. By 2006, they were providing less than 4 percent. Individual, household and small business taxation had to fill this revenue gap. In 1968, corporate excise taxes amounted to $7.43 per $1,000 of personal income. In 2002, corporate excise taxes amounted to $2.36 per $1,000 of personal income. This is a drop of more than two-thirds.[8]

In concrete terms, this has increased dramatically tax burdens paid mostly by residents. In 1968, the state's take from sales taxes and corporate income taxes were nearly equal; correcting for inflation, sales tax provided $760 million and corporate income tax $815 million. Personal income tax provided $1.6 billion roughly twice sales or corporate income taxes. By 2004, sales taxes were providing six times as much revenue as the corporate income taxes and personal income taxes were providing 13 times as much! If corporate taxes had remained a constant share of personal income between 1982 and 2002, the state would have brought in an additional $1.1 billion in the year of 2003 alone.[9]

After years of advocacy in 2008 the state legislature instituted a version of combined reporting: certain corporations could no longer use complex book-keeping shell games to avoid Massachusetts tax levying. They could no longer set up "holding" corporations in tax-free states and shift their profits onto those books to avoid Massachusetts taxes nor engage similar strategies. This slightly increased the corporate share of the state revenues although much of the gain was offset by a bizarre legislative decision to drop the corporate tax rate as a whole in the same legislative session.

Why if corporations have been increasingly employing what Governor Deval Patrick described as unfair techniques for years, would our legislature then turn around and reward all corporations with a tax break? Even as our economy was beginning its downward slide? In Patrick's first proposed budget in 2007, he had continued former

Governor Mitt Romney's call for combined reporting to close this tax loophole. At his first budget conference after election, Patrick said he knew from his own experience that corporations will take advantage of such loopholes if they exist; he was referring to his own role in getting Texaco's profits off the federal tax rolls when he was their corporate counsel; he got their federal tax payments basically down to zero dollars.

Elected leaders consistently argue that we need to provide tax breaks to get corporations to create jobs in our state or express fear that we will lose them. Numerous studies show that corporations do not make location choices based on relative tax levies by states. For instance, a 1996 study by then assistant vice president and economist for the Federal Reserve Bank of Boston, Robert Tannenwald, compared 22 states' corporate tax burdens and found no measurable impact on the location of new investments.[10] Other negative impacts of tipping the playing field to benefit large corporations, which do not create as many new jobs per dollar as small businesses, are discussed in the final section of this book.

Not only have Massachusetts corporate tax revenues suffered from increasingly creative bookkeeping techniques in recent years, our state government also made numerous choices to shift the tax burden onto people and away from certain corporate sectors in steps that were supposed to save jobs. With lots of reassurance by industry leaders but no actual regulatory requirements, the Massachusetts legislature opted to cut corporate taxes in eight separate acts between 1991 and 2001 for defense contractors, manufacturers, mutual fund companies, banks, and insurance companies for purposes of "keeping jobs" from leaving our state.[11] Contrary to promises, jobs in these industries have streamed out of our state and tax revenues as well; in fiscal year 2004, these exemptions cost the state an estimated $382 million in revenue.[12]

Clearly, we cannot afford further erosion of the percentage contribution of corporations in our state by allowing the 2008 corporate tax rate roll-back to be implemented. We have to close industry specific loopholes and tax breaks such as implementing the telecom tax. We need to institute other protections on corporate bookkeeping techniques that allow some corporations to avoid tax burdens that more responsible corporations contribute to our state.

Inevitably, there will be those who say this is a bad time to focus on corporate taxes with corporate profits down in many sectors. There are three problems with this argument.

First, the Massachusetts Budget and Policy Center highlights an important 2001 study by the Nobel Laureates for economics, Joseph Stiglitz and Peter Orszag of the Brookings Institution. The study found that during recessions targeted tax increases especially on the affluent are less damaging to the economy than either direct spending cuts or cuts in transfer payments to low-income individuals.[13]

Second, too many of those voicing these concerns have also historically been part of seeking corporate tax breaks or fighting closing loopholes when the economy was doing well — implying that *corporations should never be expected to contribute* a reasonable portion of state revenues where they do business.

Most importantly, however, as we know corporations make site location and investment decisions based on quality of life factors such as an educated workforce, infrastructure and the cost of living in a region, surely it does not make sense for them not to contribute to the societal upkeep of such quality of life. It is akin to undermining their corporation's own future productivity.

Are there tax solutions in this crisis?

We can balance our state and municipal budgets without exacerbating our regional economic downturn and move towards longer-term re-balancing the health of our economy. Instead of isolated government budget balancing and short-term strategies, we need to stop silo-thinking — in this case imagining that government budgets function separately from the economies in which they exist; we need to stop allowing candidates and elected officials to abdicate responsibility for the overall economy.

In addition, corporate cultures that have moved to shorter and shorter-term thinking have also influenced our policymakers. We have both an economy and an environment which require of us long-term thinking and an interdependent perspective on the impact of our choices.

When large corporations drain profits out of our local economies without contributing even reasonable taxes or the wealthiest amongst us multiply their control of more and more income *and assets* while paying back much less than the rest of us, economic failure is guaranteed for all of us — corporations and wealthy as well.

To rebuild the spending capacity of those who spend, we need to avoid tax increases that continue the shift on to pots one through three, working and middle class people. Especially that means, in terms of tax sources, we must avoid standard sales and property tax increases. For taxes that fall more evenly on all segments of society, we need offsets that do not add to recent decades' tax increases on working and middle class segments.

What could tax that fifth and perhaps fourth pot while not increasing taxes on everyone else? What tax revenue increases are not drawing on the most quickly diminishing sources? In terms of existing revenue sources we have to look to taxes like income taxes with offsets to protect regular people and much smaller revenue sources that do not tend to tax everyone else much at all like dividend taxes, capital gains, etc.

Figure 4.7   Combined federal and Massachusetts dividend tax rates, 1992–2007[14]

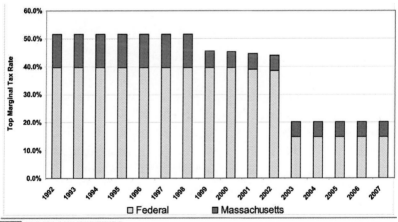

An example of one possible area of state taxation is dividends. Figure 4.7 shows the cut in dividend taxation in 1999 and 2003 and the loss of income from them.

And which pot benefited from this significant tax cut? See Figure 4.8. In fact, this tax cut benefited really only one pot (you guessed it, pot number five); in fact it benefited the part of the pot that has burst its seams and led to that pot having to be repotted. Some tax sources clearly exist where money can still be raised for our state budget without drawing on the pots that cannot yield much; such taxation will help re-balance our state revenue sources. It will help shift the tax reality undergirding the sense of regular people — who have continued paying our taxes and yet our services have been cut — that others are no longer paying their share.

Figure 4.8   Dividend rate cut beneficiaries[15]

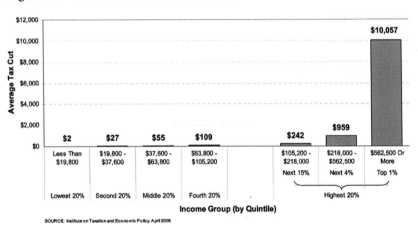

Income taxes cannot be graduated in Massachusetts and certainly increasing taxes on those of us experiencing job and income cutbacks will not help. But other means of increasing income taxes and offsetting them with deductions or even tax credits can at least protect if not free up some money for increased consumer spending.

There is no money is only true for some of us

"There is no money" has become the too oft-repeated refrain from government voices these days. Because there is supposedly "no money," they are playing slice and dice with our state budget and — for many of us — our futures and our livelihoods.

Simply repeating something often enough does not make it true. Our previous president played that one out about as far as it will go.

Massachusetts has been the third richest state in the country for a while. While everyone has lost a lot with all the air going out of the speculative bubble, small segments of our state population have primarily benefited from the huge economic gains in recent years. Those people include some whose gambling in the world economy got us here. Most of them still have enormous wealth.

Here is a sample snapshot, from spring 2009, of how the state might raise $2.5 billion in tax revenue in ways that will continue to bring in revenue and that are most likely to not exacerbate our economic situation; in the long run, these types of tax changes may move us back toward a sustainable economy, partly because they do not increase taxes on regular people, but they do bring in revenue to start paying for the jobs and services we have a right to expect our taxes to leverage for us all.[16]

1. Freeze the corporate tax rate reduction. This lowering of the corporate tax rate was in 2008 when we finally got the legislature to close two of the largest corporate tax loopholes that existed in Massachusetts. That is, say $100 million in revenue.

2. Close the telecom loophole. This is an outdated law on the books that exempts telephone companies from paying property tax on their poles and equipment from when the telephone was a public utility. That is $77 million in revenue.

3. Rescind the tax cut on dividends and interest (this was a tax cut passed in 1998 that reduced the tax rate from 12 percent to 5.3 percent). Estimated at $534 million in 2008.

4. Even without a progressive income tax, our flat income tax is the most progressive large revenue source in the state. It is not as progressive as a graduated tax but it is still progressive, unlike sales, gas, etc., which are all regressive. The state can generate an additional $1.2 billion if the income tax rate were at 5.95 percent.

5. To protect, if nothing else, the spending power of those already hard hit by this economy, we should offset the income tax increase with an extension beyond seniors of the property/rental tax circuit-breaker. We should increase its cap to protect many of those who have been in recession since 2001. We give up $150 million in revenue.

6. Close the sales tax loophole created by Internet shopping that should be charged sales tax. State action to close this loophole

can increase revenues $35 million. Federal action closing this loophole increases state revenue another estimated $500 million!

7. Close several industry specific corporate tax breaks originally created with the explicit purpose of keeping jobs in our state. Remember what was referred to as the Raytheon tax break? Or the Fidelity tax breaks? I do not have the specific revenue increase from this but we are in the vicinity of $2.4 billion. They simply have to be willing to raise revenue from where it still exists.

Where's the money that used to feed a healthy economy?

While most people are shocked when they actually see the vast income divides across our society at this point (compare minimum wage to "retention bonuses" at AIG), these are miniscule compared to the exponential wealth divide. Figure 4.9 shows that the *top one percent has almost half the wealth in our country.* The bottom 80% of us have *only 7 percent of the wealth.*

Figure 4.9   Where the money went[17]

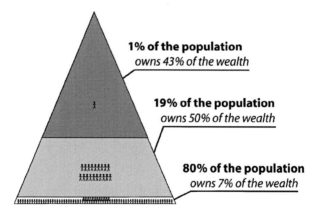

1% of the population
owns 43% of the wealth

19% of the population
owns 50% of the wealth

80% of the population
owns 7% of the wealth

A tiny, truly small wealth tax of one half of 1/100 of a percent would bring in millions. This could be offset with a property/rent tax circuit breaker to exempt those whose primary asset is their home and where tax would represent a significant percentage of their limited income.

Paying your share

Inevitably someone out there is going to scream that these policies amount to soaking the rich. Given that it is only the top quintile as a group that has continued to benefit from government policies during the last nine years, it is the rest of us that the government has been soaking for a while. Even more exaggerated has been the top 100th of one percent of income receivers who had pretty much tripled their income in the 15 years before this economic downturn — clearly government policies abetted that almost incomprehensible accumulation of wealth.[18]

This is true even in Massachusetts, just looking at state tax policy alone: According to the Institute on Taxation and Economic Policy, the top one percent of taxpayers in Massachusetts received half of the savings from the total cut in state taxes between 1989 and 2002. *The top 20 percent received almost all of the aggregate tax cut.*[19]

One might argue then that turnabout is fair play. A chunk of the wealth at the top has in fact fizzled since it was never real wealth; it was speculative value won at the roulette table of global financial investments and never actually more than a mirage. But a deeper reality exists here.

In fighting for more equal fiscal policies, we are in fact fighting for the economic future of the wealthiest as well as the rest of us. Those of us who struggle to conceive of our society as one interconnected system were right: those with wealth cannot endlessly accumulate from the rest of us because even market economies slow down and then collapse when money is increasingly unevenly distributed and the consumer base dries up!

For those who have a hope and vision of the future no matter their economic status, we were right. A deeper human truth that we are all in this together has come home to roost!

Tax brackets and highest income receivers

I made a reference that although we have been told that taxing the very rich a lot is bad for the economy, in the 1950s under Republican President Dwight Eisenhower the tax rate on the top national tax bracket was at 91 percent.[20]

I entered my adulthood under President Ronald Reagan and have been told more times than I could measure how taxing those with the most disposable income hurts business investment and how that hurts the economy and ultimately jobs. Yet I know from stories and history (see Figure 4.10) that in the 1950s and 1960s the U.S. economy just hummed along — profit margins were small but reasonably good because of the high productivity of the U.S. economy.

Figure 4.10   After-tax corporate profits as share of national income [21]

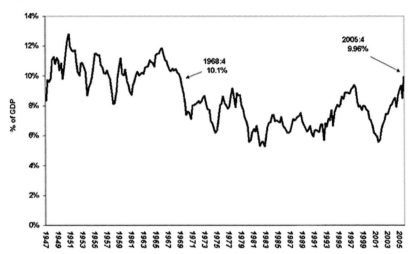

I hate to let the facts get in the way of a good story, but what if it turns out that when the top income-getters pay a very high tax that this not only equalizes things but it actually is part of a stable, healthy economy by several major measures?

Nationally, we have what is called a graduated income tax. There are a series of thresholds and when your income crosses one, each dollar you make over that threshold has a higher tax taken out of it. As of 2008, for a single person the tax brackets come out as:

- 10 percent on income between $0 and $8,025
- 15 percent on the income between $8,025 and $32,550
- 25 percent on the income between $32,550 and $78,850
- 28 percent on the income between $78,850 and $164,550
- 33 percent on the income between $164,550 and $357,700
- 35 percent on the income over $357,700

Most of us make $40,000 or less, so if they raise the top percentage on monies made over the first $357,700, that will not impact our tax rate. In fact, you could raise the top two tax bracket rates and only impact 1.9 percent of U.S. households — the 0.7 percent of U.S. population paying the top tax bracket and the 1.2 percent that tops out in the second highest bracket.[22] While outside of our present experience, a tax of 70 percent to more than 90 percent was normal for decades and the very wealthy paid. When policy makers ended that practice, the tax burden shifted primarily onto middle and working class folks.[23]

In direct contradiction to what we have been told, statistics prove that tax increases have a different impact on working people than on those at the very top. Theoretically, if your income is $75,000 annually, your after-tax income is $60,000; your boss knows it. This is the money you and your boss expect you to be willing to do your job for. If, however, your income taxes go up so your take-home drops to say $55,000, both you and your boss know this amounts to a cut in your take home pay; in just a couple of years, history shows that your salary will usually go up enough so you are once again taking home $60,000 — even though the tax rate went up.[24]

This is a well-known affect: wage inflation. Apparently former Fed Chairman Alan Greenspan ranted about it and the Wall Street Journal and other papers have written about it. Historically, if your income taxes go down, your take-home out of that $75,000 rises; in a few years, your wages and those of the people around you would drop returning your take-home to that same $60,000.[25] This is because, for most people, their take-home pay is what they live on and spend.

What happens for those at the top, who have more annual income than they can actually spend? They apparently pay their taxes out of what is called discretionary or disposable income — the part they usually put in savings somewhere. Therefore, if they used to save $4 million when their top tax rate was low, but that tax rate jumps significantly, they *simply save less.*

A loss in savings does not push wages up over time. It does not decrease wealthy people's spending on everyday expenses. It has no measurable negative impact on our struggling economy. If workers lose spending power that hurts our economy directly. In addition, our wages will end up increasing back to where our take-home pay remains the same, thereby impacting our employer's bottom line.

This is the opposite of what we have been told: If the taxes of those of us who mostly live on our after-tax income go up, our wages will generally rise in the next couple of years to cover that loss in take-home pay; if our taxes go down, so generally will our income, again taking us back to the same take-home pay. On the other hand, once the income tax is mostly being paid out of disposable income — money a high income-getter does not normally use to live on — the wage inflation effect goes away: they bring home less when their taxes go up and more when their taxes go down. Tax increases on those who pay them out of their regular spending money hurts the engine of our economy and may push up inflation, not tax increases on the wealthy.

The economy and the impact of taxes simply are not the same for regular people as on the very wealthy. Apparently, political commentator Thom Hartmann who wrote about this got quite the ribbing in Europe that we as Americans do not know this about income taxes while it is quite common knowledge in Europe.[26]

Top tax brackets

Although my Reagan and post-Reagan sense of reality did not prepare me for this information, the top tax bracket (affecting only the most wealthy) was at 73 percent before the "roaring" 1920s and between 70 percent to a little over 90 percent from the 1930s through 1980. For those 50 years, our economy grew steadily. We had no economic crashes and no significant bank failures or financial industry fluctuations. Working people's wages and other programs grew steadily, building the strongest middle class in American history.[27]

But what happened when the Republicans dropped the top tax bracket from 73 percent during the 1920s down to 25 percent? We had the roaring '20s stock market bubble, temporary boom, then crash, rampant foreclosures, bank closures and the Great Depression starting in 1929.

What happened after 1980 when Reagan cut the top tax bracket from 74 percent to 38 percent? There was a huge surge in the market, a housing bubble, the worst crash at that time since the Great Depression, and the Savings and Loan debacle.[28]

Since Reagan, the changes in the top tax bracket were smaller for a while; the economy did not get back to the underlying stability and growth like before nor surge and crash. Then President George H. W. Bush cut taxes — mostly benefiting the top, debt soared and wages for regular people fell. President Bill Clinton slightly raised the top bracket on the very rich but President George W. Bush slashed taxes on unearned income (that is income made from assets and investments not from wages and salaries) down to a top rate of 15 percent. *The wealthy now pay, in total, less taxes per dollar than what anyone making a middle class income is paying per dollar of their earned income.*[29]

Figure 4.11 Top US Marginal Income Tax rates, 1920–2009[30]

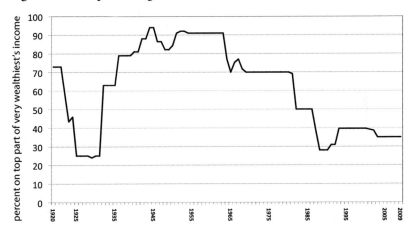

Figure 4.11 shows the tax rate percentage for the incomes that reach into the top bracket. You can see the huge cut in percentage of tax on the wealthiest in the 1920s. Then, coming out of the crash, the climb back up as the federal government tried to stabilize the economy. You can see the almost 50 years of relative stability and the huge cut in the 1980s. Between the predictable surges from the new "found" discretionary wealth created by top tax bracket rate reductions, the deregulation of the financial markets, we got a series of increasing bubbles, and then the foreclosures, the bank failures and today's second economic Depression.

Figure 4.12 shows the market fluctuations fed in part by top tax bracket rate changes.

Figure 4.12   The Stock Bubble: price surge not based in increased value[31]

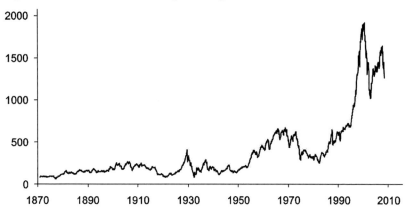

It is painfully clear. While there are a number of forces at work here, when the very wealthy are taxed a high percent, our economy does well; money is plowed back in through our government and wages for working people rise. When taxes on the top are slashed, loose money goes searching for risk to mint money off of money and we end up with economic Russian roulette.

The underlying reality is that while the very rich complain when taxes go up and they lose some of their discretionary income, if our taxes go up our wages will follow. The economic realities are not the same and we have been told that our economic future is tied to lower taxes for the wealthy so they can invest, when in fact *the opposite is true.*

We have also been told that when regular people's wages go up so do prices. Turns out there is no evidence for that either.[32] The evidence seems to prove the opposite: when prices rise it may force employers to pay more so our take-home stays the same, or we are likely to quit... But that is another story...

What is the impact on government revenue of such lower tax rates for the top bracket? Nationally, as an example, according to the Institute on Taxation and Economic Policy, *if the top tax bracket rate on Americans whose yearly income exceeds $10 million were raised to 70 percent, and the rate for those who earn between $5 million and $10 million a year were raised to 50 percent, federal revenues in 2008 would have increased by $105 billion.*[33]

The shift to huge CEO salaries

In trying to highlight the often huge and growing profits of companies in a struggle with their union members, union leaders have increasingly focused on the incomes of the top corporate officers, the CEOs. While it is often easier for people to focus on the concrete example of one person, the policy logic of focusing on CEO salaries seemed odd to me at first; that logic has clarified as the divide between pay packages of CEOs and their top corporate staff and those of regular workers has grown significantly.

We used this comparison again in looking at the relative amounts people pay in Massachusetts with a flat rate for income tax versus if we could institute a graduated income tax (which requires a complicated process to amend our state constitution). Looking at high salaries of corporate CEOs and their workers (see Figure 4.13), it is easier to see the contrast in their economic and tax situation.

Figure 4.13   Ratio of CEO to average worker pay, 1965–2005[34]

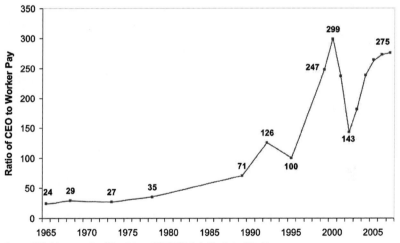

Source: Mishel, Lawrence, Jared Bernstein, and Heidi Shierholz. The State of Working America, 2008/2009. An Economic Policy Institute Book. Ithaca, N.Y.: Cornell University

As pointed out earlier, in my mother's day the highest incomes were those of investors but as our economic policies and economy has changed since the 1970s, the corporate leaders themselves not only made more of the profits of large companies but were often paid in their own corporate stocks — blurring the lines between CEOs, their board members and the rest of their investors. Numerous policy choices have affected both the type of economic activity inside the U.S. (such as NAFTA and other trade agreements) and the loosening and ignoring of regulations on money making money from money. The greatest "performing" sector throughout this period has become the financial sector itself by a significant margin.[35] Along with that, among the highest income-receivers have become the top CEOs and financial brokers in the financial industry itself.

Figure 4.14   Hedge and private equity fund managers[36]

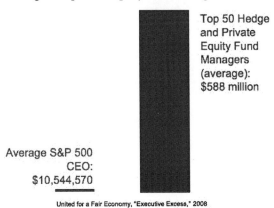

Top 50 Hedge and Private Equity Fund Managers (average): $588 million

Average S&P 500 CEO: $10,544,570

United for a Fair Economy, "Executive Excess," 2008

While these corporate higher-ups have come to receive some of the highest remuneration in the world, with the highest per capita incomes globally, they have gotten these incomes through fees for handling the incredibly risky gambles of the largest investment blocks in the world *with no real skin of their own in the deal.* By the end of 2009, top financial organizations rebuilt their financial strength through tax-payer money, loans from the Federal Reserve, successful lobbying expenditures and the continuing acquisition of other financial institutions. They rewarded themselves and their top echelons with higher bonuses than at the height of the bubble in 2007: *$149 billion in 2009 holiday bonuses* in the top six U.S. financial institutions.[37] Between the use of Troubled Asset Relief Program (TARP) moneys to pay out "retention bonuses" in 2008 and the December 2009 set of bonuses, they made themselves immune from not only prosecution but from any financial punishment for their role in pulling down the world economy.

The idea that these salaries are necessary to fill these corporate positions with the most qualified is debunked by the realities across the world. In 2008, three of the five banks with the greatest assets were in China, paying CEO compensation in the $200,000 to $250,000 range. Whereas, the largest British bank paid $2.8 million and the largest American bank, J.P. Morgan Chase, compensated its CEO, Jamie Dimon, nearly $19.7 million; see Figure 4.15.[38] The European Union's government, for instance, is not sitting still, it is going after the bonuses and salaries (and breaking up the big banks).[39]

Figure 4.15   Bank CEO compensation by bank size and continent 2008[40]

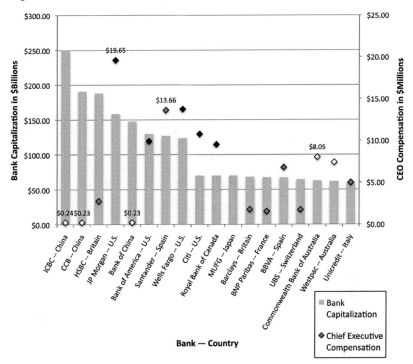

And that tax cut of the unearned income rate to 15 percent by President Bush instead of another decrease in the top income tax bracket as you might have expected? The top CEOs and other top financial executives today generally get paid in stock and other "unearned" income so this was to cover them. Cutting the top income tax bracket again would not have benefitted such a targeted group. With most of their income "unearned" they pay at the same tax rate on those "salaries" as those who make anything over about $8,500 in our society and pay only in the lowest federal tax brackets of 15 percent. Almost all of us are paying more per dollar of earned income than they are!

Social stratification nationwide

I remember when I first discovered the American Profile Poster (excerpt in Figure 4.16). Stephen J. Rose compiles this wonderful break-out of the financial status of the U.S. population every 10 years or so.[41] Color coded with pictures representing census data by household, it breaks all of us into 1,000 representative households — laid out by income level. So you can look at the overall spread and where most of us are concentrated by income. Or you can zero in on the household picture closest to your own and get a graphic sense of where you fit in the whole (you can see example households on the left of Figure 4.16).

This clear exposition is a special gift in a society that is so stratified. We get a glimpse of the lifestyles of the rich and famous on TV and a bizarre Hollywood version of mostly professional and stable working class homes. But for so many years, I could never get most of the people I talked to to even recognize that significant numbers of people *go hungry* and children actually *die of malnutrition* right here in the U.S., in Massachusetts, within a few miles of where any of us live. The American Profile Poster begins to help us form a more realistic overview of the spread of our society.

Let's look at Figure 4.16.[42] Note that the bulge (where most of us fall in the U.S. distribution of income) in this excerpt of the 2005 version has slipped lower on the income ladder since I first saw this in the 1980s. Rose says this points to the almost disappearance of a real middle class.

Most remarkably, when I first purchased the two and ½ foot poster, when you got to the top of the curve they told you that the household graph would have to continue up *17 more stories* of a building to include the household graphic representing the income of top income families in the United States!

Figure 4.16 American Profile Poster excerpt[43]

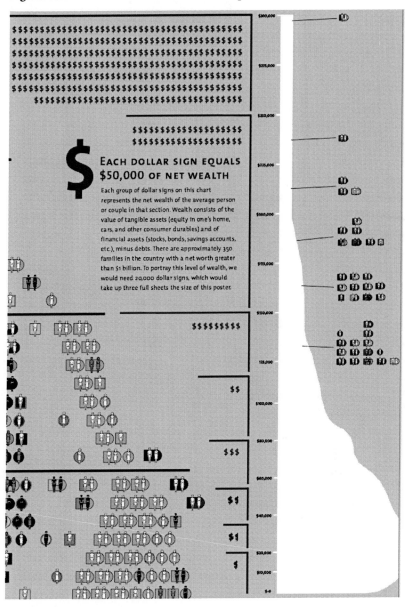

Imagine the 2005 graph presented here blown up 32 inches. But for this 2005-corrected profile, the top 1/1000 of U.S. households, the poster only needs an added 8 feet. Why? Not because the

192 Main St. $marts

very wealthiest are not as far away from the rest of us. Remember how much of the "income" of highest income receivers has shifted to unearned sources? To include the top 20,000 more people who declared more than 10 million in annual income on their tax returns the poster would have to *reach to the 20th floor* (the poster is based on government surveys which do not include unearned income like capital gains)![44]

Once you have caught your breath, there is an even deeper reality in the profile. See the '$' signs on the left side of the line opposite the income levels? *That is the wealth* held by the average household in each tier as you move up the graph: $50,000 in wealth per dollar sign. Through the first eighteen thousands of income, the biggest point in the bulge, there is essentially no wealth — that means no assets: not a car of any significant value, not a home, not even a stable savings account. Compare this with the wealth of the top 350 families included in that graphic on the 20th story of our imaginary building; it would take 20,000 $ signs to represent the $1 billion in wealth, filling three 21" x 30" posters.[45]

Most of us can look at the figures for income shown in the diagrams included in the last section and be disgusted or jealous trying to wrap our imagination around what having that size income could really mean. But the difference between our incomes and theirs is like drops of water in a lake compared to the differences in wealth. They are staggering.

The economic bottom-out slashed the number of billionaires in the world by 30 percent. Their average net worth dropped by 23 percent and their collective net worth dropped from $4.4 trillion to $2.4 trillion.[46] For many more of us, this economy is threatening not only our income, it literally multiplied the number of homeless and hungry. The downturn will undermine the basic building blocks of our communities like schools, health and housing to an extent we could not have conceived even a few years ago. When one looks not just at the incomes but the wealth of those in the higher echelons of our society and our state, there can be no moral argument for why they cannot be expected to contribute in at least the same percentages as the rest of us — especially given the wealth shift upwards to their benefit in recent years.

Still, the profile makes graphic that the greatest divisions amongst us are not even income but wealth. With that amount of wealth, even the smallest percent returned to the well-being of the *Common Wealth* could make more of a difference than we think; as shown in the last section it would essentially make no difference to the status or purchasing power of the wealthy. However, a relatively tiny contribution of wealth from the wealthy would go a long way towards the good of the whole including beginning to reverse the fundamentals of our economy.

> *Ex-Treasury Secretary Robert Reich looking at IRS data estimated that "a tiny [national] annual wealth tax of one-tenth of one percent on all net worth exceeding $5 million — a tax that would affect only 50,000 households, or fewer than one-tenth of one percent of the nation's taxpayers — would yield an additional $100 billion."*[47]

A similar, miniature state wealth tax would be legal by our state constitution. While I have been unable to ascertain exact figures, Massachusetts is the third highest income state with the fourth fastest growing wealth divide.[48] Our overall state budget was at $27.046 billion at last reckoning October 2009 (although dropping fast); a few billion in new income would save our cities and towns, our schools and a chunk of our public health.[49] By Reich's proposal, if a similar tax were imposed at the state level, we might raise 2 billion or more.

At some point economic sense must win out even if common decency — let alone morality and justice — cannot.

Jobs, Jobs, Jobs

Walking around my home city of Worcester, it is clear that our buildings are disintegrating—especially when emptied and left vacant by foreclosure. We have too many children per classroom because there are not enough teachers. We have people unhealthy because they can not access health care; lead paint still needs to be removed from our buildings, and lead from our soil. Children need daycare and after school activities. Our seniors and disabled could use care and transportation to live in their own homes and still be active in our communities. We need frequent, reliable and comprehensive public transportation. We need to clean up our streets and beautify our neighborhoods. Our present trees need inoculating and we need to plant many more. Manufacture trolleys, windmills, and energy-saving appliances. Weatherize every building, move to clean energy production, clean up our environment and old toxic sites… The list seems endless—we ***do not lack for work or workers,*** we ***lack for pay!***

I found it annoying long before I ever ran for office when campaigning politicians would promise to create jobs. Jobs always seemed the hardest to predict. I think when people listen to a politician promising "jobs," they do not think that you might create a few jobs. The promise is really that there would be more jobs not fewer when you were done! Short of actually putting money in the government's budget to hire particular positions, this always seemed like a very popular but highly unrealistic promise. How do policy changes make private businesses hire or not hire? How can you prove that it was your policies that created jobs?

Having been on the receiving end of too many broken promises from politicians, I have never been big on promises. I really believe actions speak louder than words. But as I have found out over time, just as policy choices underlie many trends in our society, the same is true of job creation or loss.

The easy way out for politicians who promise jobs would be to raise taxes and expand government to hire people. These days most elected officials are so afraid to raise taxes that they would avoid this option. When they even appear to provide job opportunities some may go to friends and it creates quite the scandal.

The only other way, it seems to me, to easily claim job creation is for an elected official to provide government incentives to large enough businesses so they move to the area and hire people. The politician can cut a ribbon and claim to have directly brought those jobs to their district. The problem here is that we have to ask if such government spending creates *a net gain of jobs* or is this simply a privatized version of raising taxes and hiring people?

The second perception problem about job creation highlights our particularly disturbing social amnesia. Although our birth as a nation was stained for its first century by our acceptance of the inhumane practice of slavery, we seem surprisingly adept at forgetting that **not** every job is a good job. Slavery is a job. Indentured servitude is a "paying" job. Yet these are morally, socially and constitutionally unacceptable. Why do we have a minimum wage if reasonable pay for reasonable work was insured by market forces? Why did people have to organize to end child labor? Why did tens of thousands fight not only for a minimum wage, a 40 hour work week, over time pay and, just as importantly, right-to-know laws for use of dangerous materials, disability protections and social security? Today, we remain horrified when victims surface of sex slave trafficking, domestics denied basic human rights and the general human slave trade. Sometimes it surfaces in even our most seemingly stable and homey suburban communities or in the homes of our public leaders!

I remember years ago when welfare was restructured and eligibility seriously curtailed. The literal slogan of the Massachusetts public welfare program was *"any job is a good job"* even though, as I said, our history teaches the opposite. The impacts of those welfare policies reached beyond just those directly affected: 65 percent of single mothers on welfare had been victims of domestic violence but 87 percent of the families who went through shelter had been battered; the Department of Transitional Assistance (DTA) public messaging shamed them for being on welfare.[50] We feared the messages and polices would scare many into staying in dangerous personal relationships or even bad jobs.

As the Coordinator of a community organization at the time, I remember picking up my office phone one day to the voice of a woman clearly scared and speaking quietly. She explained she had no income **but** proudly assured me that she had a *new job* lined up and would start in six weeks; she just needed to know how to get food stamps to feed her children in the interim. I started talking her through how to get food stamps although I sensed there was something disturbing about her situation. Food stamps are critical for food but if she had children, how were they to cover life necessities besides food? Heat, electricity, for instance? Rent?

As I walked her through the food stamp process I told her she would need proof of income; did she have her last four weeks of pay stubs and, maybe, a letter letting her go from her last job? "No, no," she got very insistent; she had none of that. And there was no way she could go back to her previous boss to get those. In as matter of fact a manner as I could muster, I pointed out some such documentation would be necessary. She got very agitated on the phone. So I could not stop myself from asking, how did she expect to get through the next six weeks with no money for utilities, rent or transportation? Why not just apply for welfare? "No, no, no!" She said she was not going on welfare. She had worked and she had work lined up. And besides, she said, hadn't they cut all of welfare anyway?

I told her making sure her kids survived had to come first, that they not lose their home. And why could she not get evidence of her previous income? And **then** the story came tumbling out.

She had been hired through a hiring agency as an administrative assistant more than six months earlier. The office was in one of those new office buildings that cater to very small businesses; they provide a number of very small offices with access to shared large meeting space and copiers, so each business does not have to be able to afford its own. She and her boss were the only ones in the business's office space. Isolated with her boss, he had shortly become verbally abusive. Apparently, he was yelling and screaming at her but was inaudible to others in the building since no one ever asked or checked on her. Then, he had begun to slap or hit her if she made mistakes, sometimes chasing her into a corner in the office. She told me she realized that she needed to leave but with welfare "unavailable," she also knew her kids depended upon her for survival and she could not leave until she found another job. It took several weeks — meanwhile the physical abuse escalated — but two days earlier she had received written confirmation of a new job and had just walked out!

I wish this were the only story.

It is worth remembering that people have organized and literally died rather than face certain treatment as workers. Slaves revolted, were beaten to death, tracked down, shot and killed, publicly lynched to keep them in their place; still thousands risked and succeeded in escaping. Towards the end of legalized slavery in the U.S., slave revolts, the Underground Railroad and other anti-slavery organizing were threatening the institution's continued existence. The history of union organizing too has its share of bloodied and killed advocates. Many have given much to organize for and to institutionalize protections of a decent job.

In this recent economic debacle, central to the stall-out of our economy is loss of the spending power of the majority of everyday U.S. residents! Compare this to the 1950s economy that was on the upswing and in which the benefits of economic growth was shared across the population. A critical component of both the present failure and the previous success was the distribution of decent paying jobs and the corollary spending capacity of most consumers.

I am also struck by the numerous studies, one after another that show worker productivity increases at work places when policies are instituted that directly assist workers or provide them with more choice. Little things like the color that the walls of a workplace are painted. Big things like having input into how an assembly line functions. Business school experts have shown how the informed input of line workers can improve procedures and overall efficiency. "Pro-worker" policies such as paid family leave — often vigorously opposed by employer associations — actually decrease absenteeism and improve productivity.[51]

The proposed paid sick day legislation in the Massachusetts legislature in 2009/2010 is a perfect example. The benefits are clear for workers and the public immediately. Those most likely not to have paid sick days include many of those paid the least, a huge percentage of which serve the public. Almost 80 percent of wait staff and childcare workers cannot earn paid sick days.[52] For those of us who frequent restaurants, it would be comforting to know that those serving are likely to go home when sick and not continue to serve us. For the over 40 percent of Massachusetts workers without paid sick days, such legislation immediately conjures the possibility of taking time to heal when we are sick, of ensuring very sick children are not at home alone; we could stop ignoring basic personal care like medical check-ups or time to protect ourselves from a batterer. Seventy-five percent of the poorest families lack any regular paid sick leave.[53]

But the real challenge is for business owners. Large corporations may be less likely to see the benefits, but small businesses are generally more dependent on their workers and the impact of high turn-over and retraining is real. While employers are estimated to have to put out about $1.49 more per worker per week when this legislation passes, with savings especially from lower turnover costs, they will save $2.38 per week with a net savings of $0.89 per week. The net gain for all Massachusetts employers is $130 million annually, with $218 million in additional costs delivering a savings of $348 million.[54] Will our indigenous business leaders start to reach for best practices that make them more money even if it requires them spending a little more on their workers? Can they embrace spending to save and really putting their money into their greatest asset, their workers?

As well, women legislators have taken the lead trying to get the state itself as an employer to reclassify jobs to reflect pay equity for women. Such policies are often opposed because of fears of increased costs or by some men for fear of somehow coming up short. Even if the evidence shows we are not hurt and possibly helped by a change, many of us have been scared of the removal of a social stratification we previously unfairly benefited from.

In this case the Massachusetts bill has a carefully structured phase-in based on what worked in Minnesota. In Minnesota, after the complicated reclassification was phased-in, employee retention increased and wages evened out; not only has the wage gap in Minnesota government lessened significantly but it has spilled over into private industry policies that improved employee retention there too.[55] In Minnesota, these changes not only increased retention, it meant savings balanced out the cost of bringing up the pay for all jobs in each classification; no group of workers faced a pay cut to accomplish this!

The reality is that we need to institute policies that will rebuild our economy such as increasing economic activity in our local economies and through small, locally-owned businesses to create jobs. If we want to ensure the biggest policy impact, we need decent pay with the best safety codes and an insured baseline of benefits. This will ensure the most productive workforce and the best consumer spending base.

Since evidence shows that good baselines for workers are good for business's bottom line and yet corporate and business trade associations tend to oppose such governmental policies, there has to be a countervailing force for government to pass such policies.

Unemployment Skyrockets

With increased unemployment come increases in violence, perhaps best measured by increases in incidents of domestic violence. Boston City Councilor Chuck Turner, a former counselor of male perpetrators of domestic violence made this observation: Men are raised to measure their worth by the property they own; losing financial access to other forms of property, they are left focused on the successful ownership and control of their girlfriends and partners.

Unemployment is demoralizing in a society that so very much defines us by our work (the most common question after "what's your name?" is surely "what do you do?"). Unemployment also creates a core negative economic pressure on our economy. When people can make money and provide for basic necessities, the government is not called on to step in. More importantly, for those without significant savings, every additional unemployed person generally means a cut back on local spending, over time including less spending in the housing market and greater use of health resources.

Since the spending of regular people is 70 percent of the engine of our economy, increasing unemployment or cuts in hours, wages or benefits means an increasing drag on our overall economy. These days we are all at least a little on edge about possibly losing a job.

The uptick to over 10 percent official unemployment in the end of 2009 is not even half the picture.[56] You might reasonably assume, for instance that official unemployment statistics actually measure how many people are unemployed or not able to get enough work hours.

They do not and when you research it, even the government departments responsible for statistics admit it.

Official unemployment rates

I was amazed during the first few years I started working as a community organizer mostly with single mothers. The public welfare program in Massachusetts, the Department of Transitional Assistance (DTA) by law, was supposed to track two figures for welfare: the payment standard and the standard of need. When I first started in 1985 these two standards reported different figures; the standard of need was markedly greater. In other words, the payments were falling far short of the reported economic need for survival. In addition, the federal poverty standard was quite a bit lower than the actual costs to live in Massachusetts. The federal poverty figure is even more irrationally (under) estimated. The federal government takes the regular budget for food for each family size and assumes that is a third of our living costs! Who can afford to spend a third of their budget on food? Not in my adult life span!

Anyway, some state government whiz figured out that if they wanted to stop being criticized for not providing enough public assistance for families to live on, they should just change the mathematical definition! The real impacts of homelessness, hunger, social and economic tolls notwithstanding, the state government simply started reporting that the *standard of payment was the standard of need!*

Some years later the official state figures for homelessness stopped trying to account for families doubling up with friends, people sleeping on someone else's couch, nor those camped out in their car, or where available, out in the woods! The official homelessness figures were redefined as how ever many families were in shelters or state-funded hotels. (You get the idea — cut the money for shelters and that can lower the official homeless rate!)

Not all those immersed in these fields have just let the dumbing down of government reporting go by. There have been periodic lawsuits, occasional improvements and there is the very important homeless census that advocates in Massachusetts try to do yearly. For transparency in government if nothing else, this kind of misreporting renders impossible real public engagement with policy or even an accurate reflection of what we experience going on around us.

Why digress about government reporting?

Unemployment statistics have been misleading and apocryphal for a long time. For some segments of our society, where unemployment has been ravaging communities for many years, even the official statistics have been devastating. Yet the real picture has consistently been under-reported. This is why media's periodic comparisons to other countries' unemployment rates is pretty useless; other countries use unemployment measures that more accurately measure how many people do not have the work and hours they want and need.

For years, the best way to get an accurate handle on real unemployment has only been through infrequent economic studies by private economists. Rather than relying on government program usage and surveys, they essentially take adult population figures and subtract from them the number of full time jobs and full time job equivalents. Allowing for those over or under work age, disabled, parents who stay home and do the unpaid labor of raising children, etc., such studies are much more accurate. I have not seen one in years. They yield higher figures than even a more careful and transparent calculation based on the official figures.

Without that level of careful accuracy, guess what? Even simple translation of various federal labor department categories yielded *an unemployment rate of about 20 percent before the worsening downturn late in 2008!*[57]

At that point the official U.S. figure for unemployment was 8.1 percent and rising. Yet from the U.S. Department of Labor's own unemployment chart the figure was 16 percent; why were almost half of these workers not added to the "official" rate?[58]

In their own words, to fit the narrow federal definition of "officially" unemployed you have to be "looking for work." But almost half of these unofficially unemployed workers are: *"Marginally attached workers... persons who currently are neither working nor looking for work but indicate that they want and are available for a job and have looked for work sometime in the recent past. Discouraged workers, a subset of the marginally attached, have given a job-market related reason for not looking currently for a job. Persons employed part-time for economic reasons are those who want and are available for full-time work but have had to settle for a part-time schedule."*[54] Apparently, half of the unemployed want paid work and *"have looked for work in the recent past"* but are not considered "looking for work."

In addition, the following categories of workers are excluded by the Department of Labor even though *they are presently looking for work:*

- Students seeking work are never counted as unemployed. So even someone taking college classes at night and seeking a full-time day job is not counted as unemployed.
- Pensioners seeking work are never counted as unemployed. This includes those who receive a minimal monthly pension because they retired early, often forcibly. Soldiers in the U.S. military can retire with a small pension as young as age 37, yet they must find work to support their family. However, they are classified as retired and not counted as unemployed.
- Anyone seeking a full-time job who works a few unpaid hours a week at a family farm or small business is not counted as unemployed.
- People seeking their first job, such as recent high school and college graduates, and housewives are excluded. The logic is that since they were never employed, they are not unemployed.

In Figure 4.17 the bottom line is "official" unemployment, the one announced in the media all the time. The middle one includes the official underemployed (and unemployed). But the top line includes all the categories I just listed that I think most of us would agree are jobless against their own best wishes.

When you add these all together, you get more than 20 percent unemployed when the market crashed. This percentage is based on the numbers on the Department of Labor's own less rigorous measures. *That is more than double the official figures before the continued rise in unemployment.* If you dare to look at official figures among, say, African American men, who are officially up at 42 percent and have been for a while in various parts of Massachusetts, you would then realize those are likely to be less than half of a real estimate...[60]

Figure 4.17   Unemployment rates: official, enhanced official and all reported categories[61]

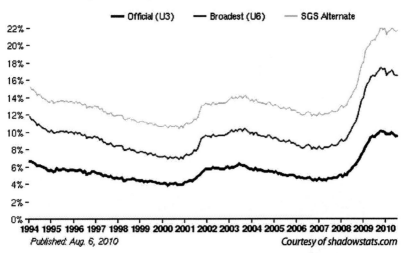

Published: Aug. 6, 2010   Courtesy of shadowstats.com

At some point in the 1990s as homeless rates continued to rise and we seemed perched on the point of getting used to dangerous levels of chronic homelessness, some of us got together to see if there was any ready-made solution. We took just the city of Cambridge because we had statistics on the number of housing units standing empty; looking at statistics for the number of area homeless, it became clear that there were enough empty units to house them even assuming the government's under-reporting statistics. The huge drain of temporarily housing the homeless in hotels (which is incredibly expensive) and in-state shelters was in fact a creation of rental prices and property-owners' choices — not a real housing shortage.

Today, when our entire economy, not just the state or the country but the world, needs the engine of regular U.S. residents working and purchasing, the rising unemployment rate simply cannot be an afterthought. We do not lack work that needs doing as a society, nor workers — it's that those with the finances are not willing to pay workers to do the needed work.

A comparison of job loss by recession makes graphic (so to speak) the undeniable seriousness of the situation.

Figure 4.18 Job losses in recessions as share of employment[62]

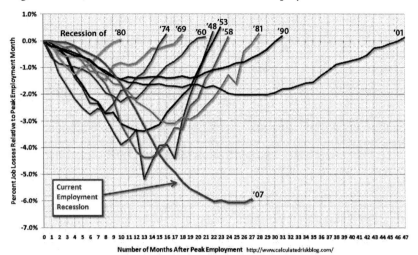

Figure 4.18 shows job losses for each recession since 1970. Regardless of the official unemployment before the beginning of each recession, it shows how much worse the job situation became once each recession started. This time job losses have been spectacular. Even with the slight cushion of the first stimulus package, there is no end in sight.

Government policies and spending priorities that continue to put our resources into the "credit crisis", and into only large corporations for supposed job-creation and retention is destroying us — not just workers and large segments of our communities, not just the economy but even those whose incomes place them at the top. If the economic foundation is crumbling, no amount of temporary scaffolding will hold the structure up.

Inflation is not gone … they just re-did the math!

How often do we go to the market and think: *"How'd that get so expensive?"* I know for years it has felt like the money seems to go less far. On the other hand, nothing in the papers said inflation is a major problem. The Federal Reserve and financial pundits were telling each other that low inflation was because they had tamed market cycles — before their rude awakening when the market crashed in fall 2008.

But we, the regular people, have been living this rude existence: it is why we felt something was deeply wrong long before they did. But it is confusing when our experience is so out of sync with everything we hear in government statistics and on the airwaves.

Here is the reality of inflation — the official story is the bottom line, and the "reality" of *our lives,* without the legislated redefinition of inflation since 1980, is the top line (Figure 4.19):

Figure 4.19   Annual consumer inflation: official (rev) vs. original formula[63]

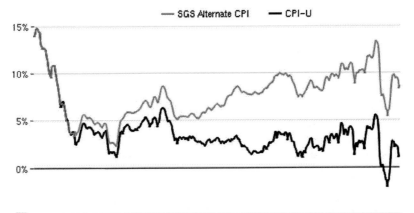

We have been paying more and getting less! *By just before the crash, inflation was over some 12 percent.*

What happened is they did not like headlines about inflation. Beginning in the 1980s and accelerating under President Bill Clinton, changes were made to how the Consumer Price Index (CPI) was calculated. Since World War II, the CPI was based on a standard set, a "basket," of goods considered regular household purchases. Periodically, the government would go out and price those same goods; change in the price of those goods defined the inflation rate.

In the 1980s, however, Alan Greenspan and others suggested, for instance, that when steak gets too expensive, consumers will switch to hamburger so as products get more expensive, they should substitute a comparable but cheaper product. They constantly assumed we were all having less income so they could *lower the value* of what they were using to measure inflation and pretend they were measuring the same consumer goods; this incorporated into their definition an ongoing degradation of the value of the products in our lives. On the other hand, they claimed that if we buy improved products, like safer cars, then that increased value can be subtracted from the increased cost — so not all the increased cost of cars we all buy is included in government's inflation estimate because safety standards have increased. But of course, we have no choice and there is less real money in our pockets.

Then they also literally changed the mathematical equation, so real increases in the costs of the new *devalued* "baskets" *are not even reflected!*

The CPI is considered key for business planning and *our incomes* as regular people have often been tied to it. The CPI is the baseline for Social Security payments, many union contracts and public funding for certain programs. Not angry yet? For seniors reading this: *Social Security payments would be almost 50 percent more than they are today* if they had not messed with the math![64]

Minimum wage as stimulus

Like other influxes of money to those who live closer to the edge, minimum wage increases serve as a local stimulus. Such changes cost our diminishing state budget nothing and in fact, bring a small influx of income tax and then sales taxes from increased purchases. While all business trade associations line up against minimum wage increases, not all businesses are equally affected by them. *Many businesses benefit from increases in the minimum wage.*

The concept that our minimum wage should guarantee a full-time income sufficient to lift a family above the poverty level seems almost definitional and certainly just. Yet the minimum wage has failed to keep pace with even official cost of living increases.

The last time the minimum wage paid enough to be above the federal poverty level at full-time work was in the early 1970s. Remember, the poverty level is pegged to an absurd formula that assumes you can take a family's food budget and multiply it by three to get a reasonable measure of a minimum living standard. In addition, the poverty level was supposed to measure the minimum you could live on *temporarily* for a few months; such a limited amount of time meant that longer term minimum living necessities like clothing did not need to be included. Federal poverty for a family of four is defined at about $20,000 annually as of 2008. Reality and studies based on it, in recent years has shown that minimum living standard in Massachusetts, an expensive state, is more than $54,600 per year.[65]

All of this means that increasing the minimum wage in Massachusetts will, like food stamps, put money in the pocket of those who need to spend any such increase quickly on life necessities and most probably locally. Like food stamps, this money represents an influx to our local businesses and economy—a powerful economic stimulus.

Funnily, many of the *local business owners* who have been encouraged over the years to speak out again minimum wage increases are not hurt by them but *are in fact helped*. The employers who pay strictly the minimum are generally the larger, chain businesses. Local business owners traditionally pay a little more than minimum wage and so increasing the minimum wage actually contributes to leveling the playing field with their larger chain competitors. Longer term studies show that the higher the minimum wage in the state, the better small businesses thrive. The lower the initial income of those who receive the increase, the more locally they tend to spend their money. Combined with consumer education—that our taxes subsidize the Walmarts in our communities, and that spending in locally-owned businesses improves our local economy for all of us—a minimum wage increase would be a greater win for our local businesses.

The state minimum wage increase to $8.25 was estimated by the New England Policy Center of the Federal Reserve to mean a $255 million increase for low wage workers and our local economies—a significant stimulus for our state economy we should look at again.[66]

We seem to just work harder and have less to show for it

Every year or so, there is some headline about how proud we should be as workers because we have increased productivity. Technically this is a measure of how much we produce in the same given number of hours of labor. But for years, my friends and I have joked sardonically that this is a measure of us all working harder while we make the same money.

The reality for U.S. workers used to be that producing more products per hour meant more money for our workplace and we shared in those profits until the 1970s. My friends' joke, however, has become the reality in recent years; the more productive we have become, the less and less that translated into increases in our income and living standard. That productivity has simply increased the profits of business owners. From 1980 to 2008, United States worker productivity grew by 75 percent; our inflation-adjusted average wages increased only 22.6 percent; workers were paid for only 30.2 percent of the increased productivity their work created.[67]

Figure 4.20   Typical workers' compensation lags productivity growth[68]

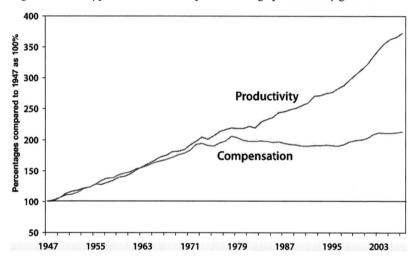

The shocking reality today is that productivity in fact spiked in the second quarter of 2009. That productivity increase is being used against us as workers in 2009: as long as productivity increased, businesses still cut jobs and as of the beginning of 2010, did not re-hire. U.S. Department of Labor reported that productivity rose at an annual rate of 6.4 per cent in the April-June quarter of 2009, while unit labor costs dropped 5.8 per cent.[69] So companies reported better than expected quarterly earnings even while sales fell and we worked harder while falling farther behind!

More jobs, better paying jobs, more productive jobs come from the best worker policies, from shifting funding to real local businesses that create jobs, stay in communities and *have an investment in their workers and communities.* Government policies that cut line jobs but save administrative jobs at the top just add to the problems. Government pay scales at the top that try to mirror huge and destructive income differentials in large corporations only compound the problems. In contrast, government policies to improve working conditions — that come into being often in the face of opposition from corporate trade organizations — benefit us as workers, our whole economy and even most of these companies themselves. Quality of life improvements such as good public education, healthy neighborhoods and recreation, are not only what improve our lives but actually are the basis of big companies remaining and relocating to an area.

The force that provides the most reliable improvements not only in the wages and benefits of workers but the creation and retentions of all of these types of policies? Healthy and thriving worker organizations, also known as unions. (Remember that I asked for that agreement to put aside ideological assumptions and to listen through the facts?)

Worker organization

It seems like in this society, you were either raised to respect unions or to blame them. That divide in respect seems to have only gotten worse as prices have risen and government budgets tightened in recent years. As most of us lost ground financially, this seems more true even though our political leaders would not talk about it. As the economy bottomed out, I heard the situation blamed on unions in especially two venues: in statements by many — especially local — government leaders and during the potential bailout of the three major car manufacturers. You will hear all the time the comparison of what some group of relatively highly paid workers are getting as wages or benefits compared to the bad or failing incomes of most of the rest of regular folks.

It feels like for decades that I have heard people complain when the baseball players went out on strike and how ridiculous it was when they make an unbelievable amount of money. I always wondered why folks never thought about how much more money the team owners make if their players were making such huge salaries.

But for some reason, even in the bank bailout with CEO salaries and bonuses part of the conversation, it was not until the big three automakers' CEOs went to beg for a bailout in Washington on their private jets that their perks seemed to become the focus of public conversation. *Lots* of people were furious at *AIG retention bonuses* but few questioned the *underlying* **outrageous** *salaries* paid to those who buried the world economy. Nor did complaints focus on investors, the speculative gamblers at the very highest income levels in our society who literally tripled their incomes and socked away most of that money. Savings they are still sitting on — starving our economies of the needed flow of cash to function let alone turn around.[70]

So what is the reality with unions, anyway?

They say that history is written by the winners. I think at this point it is clear that the present winners have been the leaders of major corporations and the very wealthiest amongst us. If we put aside the arguments they make and those of much of the so-called major media they own, what can we learn from a more even-handed tale about unions? After the demonization of unions in the McCarthy years when unions were still on the rise, *the public rhetoric did not become increasingly negative until union membership dropped off.*

But as the economic situation of the majority of us has worsened more and more obviously in recent years, that may all be changing. While corporate bad-mouthing has moved more and more over to government leaders, regular people are increasingly convinced they need help to hold their ground on wages and benefits.

At their simplest, unions are democratically-run membership organizations for workers to come together and struggle around workplace issues. Of course, "democratically-run" can mean a range of things in reality.

> *Remember Churchill's famous pronouncement: "Democracy is the worst form of government, except for all those other forms that have been tried from time to time." (House of Commons speech Nov. 11, 1947).*

Like the government in this country, union democracy and leadership was pretty much reserved for white men. Like government, there are plenty of examples of corruption. I suppose like our government, union democracy's strides towards real inclusion and more democratic function has been as much about internal struggles and outside organizing for inclusion — especially for workers of color and women. I have known plenty of people with real personal stories

of exclusion or discrimination by unions or of union ineffective-
ness. I would separate these from the more rhetorical complaints in
political maneuvering around issues (which may have more political
motivations).

While there are plenty with stories of union corruption—and I
have some doozies of my own—I think it is hard to argue there are
not many more examples of corporate corruption and greed these
days. We have yet as a society to oppose the existence of corporations
because of their miserable track record recently, the same balanced
acceptance of their existence must surely apply to the more democratic institutions, unions.

There is almost no major institution in our society that has not
excluded or discriminated against those with less social privilege.
Look at how long it took for men of color, women, even people
without property to fight and get the right to vote. Only in 2008
did female membership in the Massachusetts legislature surpass
25 percent.[71] Hardly a sterling example of inclusion and equal access
to participation—and this is our central democratic institution! But
we do not give up, because while we have our work cut out for us to
approach our goal, real democracy matters; we cannot give up on it.

As with all human institutions, transparency and vigilance are
our best safeguards against the worst human excesses; democracy
and full participation are our greatest tools for the positive role of
institutions. Making sure all workers in a workplace can participate
fully in their unions will improve unions the most.

There are plenty of studies in recent years showing the success of
companies with unions when compared with non-unionized companies in the same market. For example AT&T, always a major market
shareholder, has been unionized for decades. They merged in recent
years with Cingular which had also been unionized and had a standing neutrality agreement with their union—both sides agree to not
interfere with workers' right to decide if they want a union. AT&T
has had a labor/management alliance since 1986 and Cingular's
union had a voice in the merger negotiation and process. AT&T and
the Communication Workers of America have a history of working
together and recently brought outsourced jobs back in-house![72]

Accepting failings that a number of unions have struggled (like other democratic institutions) with real full suffrage and with corruption, what have they accomplished that has been important?

Unions remain the primary voice for overall policies that ensure decent pay and working conditions and benefits. Without the voice of unions, these economic pillars for both business productivity and the overall strong functioning of our economy erode.

Sometimes our only societal memories of life without unions in the United States exist in some shadowy memories or tales of early industrialization and the waves of immigrants from the 1800s and early 1900s. Rickety tenements in filthy streets, with families doubled and tripled up, working long hours in pollution-driven factories. Accidents were all too common with workers losing arms or worse. There were dangerous health conditions with typhoid, scarlet fever and other contagious diseases periodically blowing through neighborhoods leaving death in their wake. And of course, tales in books or even movies of the child laborer, aged by an early life of hard labor.

While working conditions can be quite bad, there has been an overall transformation in the U.S. The source? Unions. While unions in America have been mostly based workplace by workplace (unique among countries where most union protections are actually written into the government laws), they have struggled against bad working conditions and for larger social protections all along.

There are in the history of our own state of Massachusetts miraculous stories that contradict the images of unions being uniformly run by big white men. My imagination of life pre-unions certainly fits the city of Lawrence at the turn of the 20th century. In 1912, overwhelmingly women garment workers, who purportedly spoke 38 different languages found the common purpose of needing safer and more reasonable work lives, came together, formed a union, struck and won! Known as the Bread and Roses strike, with 20,000 in the streets they stopped a wage cut, won overtime pay and stopped retribution against workers for their strike activities.[73]

Early strikes and organizing led to the end of childhood labor, cut sometimes 80 hour work weeks eventually down to forty while creating the requirement for double pay for overtime (a necessary economic incentive to stop employers from ignoring the forty hour work week as all of us who work professional, non-unionized jobs know happens all the time). They stopped the ability of corporate owners to lock workers into factors during work hours, deny bathroom or food breaks, or insist that workers stand for 14 hours days.[74]

During the Depression, it was joint action by unions and other people in the street that demanded cradle to grave minimum income and basic health benefits.[75] Without these actions, we would not have Social Security, Medicare, Medicaid, unemployment benefits, welfare benefits, the creation of a minimum wage and other minimum economic baselines from New Deal legislation. These have been eroded since the early 1970s (when union density noticeably started to lose ground).[76] These programs have saved countless lives and undergirded the survival of hundreds of thousands of families when their bread winner(s) were unable to find or hold onto paid work.

In more recent decades, union organizing in response to chemical and health hazards has exposed the impacts of asbestos and other toxic chemicals. Those activities led to the outlaw of these products not only in manufacturing and workplaces where people were injured or killed by them but in our communities and homes as well. Right-to-know laws about what chemicals are present in workplaces and even household products came from these union battles.

Numerous studies show that if you correct for other major factors and you compare within comparable jobs and workplaces, it is union-ization that explains most of the difference between wages and bene-fits within a job sector:[77] Between 2004 and 2007, unionized workers' wages were on average 11.3 percent higher than non-union workers with similar characteristics.[78] See Figures 4.21, 4.22, and 4.23.

Figure 4.21   Unions and health insurance[79]

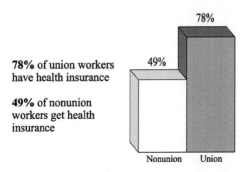

78% of union workers have health insurance

49% of nonunion workers get health insurance

Source: BLS Employee Benefits in Private Industry: 2007

Figure 4.22   Unions and pensions[80]

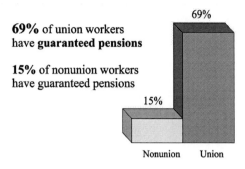

69% of union workers
have **guaranteed pensions**

15% of nonunion workers
have guaranteed pensions

Source: BLS Employee Benefits in Private Industry: 2007

Figure 4.23   Union and wages[81]

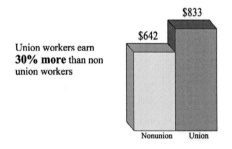

Union workers earn
30% more than non
union workers

Source: BLS USDL 07-0113

Over time there is a clear parallel between wages, health benefits, and other basic worker protections on the job. Level of unionization can be shown two ways: by looking at the overall numbers of unionized workers or by what is referred to as "union density," that is the percentage of unionized workers in the overall labor force.

While union membership in sheer numbers continued to rise thru 1980 (see Figure 4.24), the impact of unions beyond their specific workplace depends on density — the percentage of workers unionized overall. In Figure 2.25 we see that density of union membership started to fall as even more non-unionized workers were entering the workforce. It was not until absolute numbers of unio members started to fall that union leaders awoke to the already lessening impact of the voices of us as workers in the overall economy.

Figure 4.24   Union membership, 1945–2008[82]

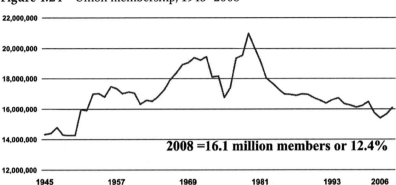

2008 = 16.1 million members or 12.4%

Union presence matters in the overall quality of our lives as regular people. Not only does their density impact wages and benefits in unionized workplaces and employment sectors with higher concentration of unionized workers (sector density). Also, having organized voices for the issues and perspective of most of us who work for a living impacts whether public policy prioritizes our needs. The examples of such policy priorities are all around us.

Figure 4.25   U.S. union density 1945–2008 (12.4% in 2008)[83]

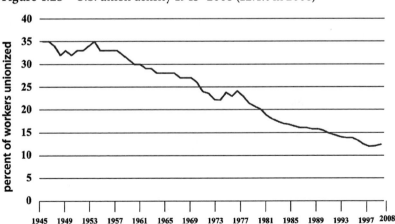

I have mentioned how I have heard municipal leaders in public settings blame their economic challenges on unions. Possibly the highest cost faced by our cities and towns these days is health coverage for their workers; since most of top government leaders are not willing to address the real sources of waste in our health care provision, cutting workers who need that health coverage seems like the answer on the surface. The problem is that our local governments are central to the quality of life in our communities. Municipal workers are central to local services; they also know health care coverage is undermining municipal budgets. This also means, not surprisingly, that municipal workers are also worried about spiraling health care costs and concomitant job cuts.

In Massachusetts, there is a law known as Section 19 which municipalities can adopt so that they bargain on health care costs with all their unions and their retirees together, "collective bargaining." This takes health insurance out of the separate bargaining with different municipal unions for wages, working conditions and other benefits. It turns out that the few municipalities that instituted Section 19 have found working "collectively" with all their municipal unions *has kept health costs growing at a much slower rate* than those municipalities that did not.[84] Municipal workers were able to identify savings, move more quickly to new plans and accept coverage cutbacks that they helped to craft as least damaging to their members.

Three more policy priorities for regular people are education spending (a direct predictor of public educational attainment), unemployment insurance and workers' compensation.[85] Figure 4.26 shows the relationship between a state's union density and these wide economic priorities.

Figure 4.26   Unions and public policy[86]

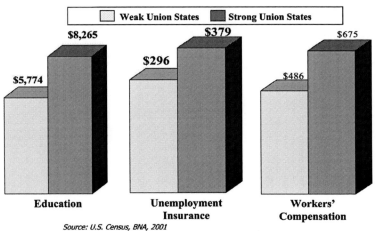

| Weak Union States | Strong Union States |

$8,265

$379

$675

$296

$5,774

$486

Education

Unemployment Insurance

Workers' Compensation

Source: U.S. Census, BNA, 2001

In fact, key supports for working people in general have trends that parallel union activity. For instance, while unionized workplaces generally pay above the minimum wage, unions have still been the primary organized voice for minimum wage increases to directly benefit primarily non-unionized workers. Line up Figure 4.27 on the rise and fall of the minimum wages with Figures 4.24 and 4.25 on union membership and density.

Figure 4.27 The value of the minimum wage, 1939–2006[87]

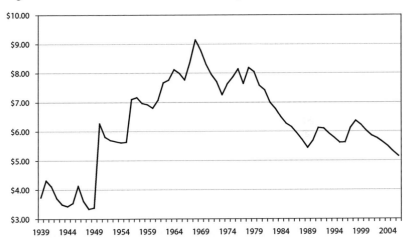

NOTE: Adjusted for in!ation using CPI-U. Real values for 2006 are based on averaging the price index from January through August of this year.
SOURCE: Author's calculations based on data from the U.S. Department of Labor.

We cannot reverse this economic depression until regular people start having the income necessary to provide fuel (the consumers' 70 percent) for our economic engine. Since historically as working people, as regular people, our income is always small compared to those at the top of our society, an organized voice matters. Just as an organized voice for those who are small business or small property owners is important since they are now dwarfed economically by huge corporations and large slum landlords. In terms of economic measures of which I have only highlighted representative examples, organizations explicitly for workers provide us a democratic vehicle to ensure not only our survival but our thriving which in turn feeds the economic life of our overall society.

Luckily, many more of us have realized this. As people have realized their economic needs are less well met even when working full-time, they have also realized they may be better off organized to negotiate for their rights.

Figure 4.28   Strong support for unionization[88]

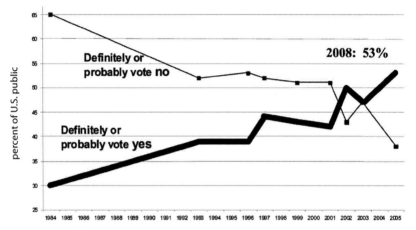

Poll results from when people were asked "if an election were held tomorrow to decide whether your workplace would have a union…"

Earlier, I mentioned that the Federal Reserve was tasked with three focuses in making financial interventions: one was to increase employment. Yet, when the inflation leading into the economic challenges of the 1970s was blamed on too much emphasis on monetary adjustments to create jobs, this key focus was dropped going forward. Creation of jobs critical — to our livelihood as regular people — was no longer a priority for the Federal Reserve although it remains legally part of the mandate for its existence.

In discussing Figure 1.9, I pointed out that through the end of the recession in the early 1980s, there was no such thing as a jobless recovery. But once again something changed; the rebound in jobs, our jobs, disappeared from the economists' definition of economic recovery. Since then, unemployment and inflation have become statistics to manipulate for political messaging. If you look at job loss in the present downturn, which I still believe will be seen as a depression in the future, you know jobs cannot be ignored. There will be no real recovery without us, without jobs. For us, neither employment nor inflation are theories to be played with for political spin.

We need to act and rebalance the playing field so we can get back in the game.

Education:
Whose Silver Bullet?

Education and education reform have always gotten so much attention from others that I have tended to observe and not comment. I know plenty of good advocates. After all, it is considered by so many to be "the silver bullet," it did not seem to need my advocacy. Silver bullet for …? Well, almost every social wrong it seems if you listen to the public dialogue.

Public education did not just appear; it was the result of a very large movement on the ground over decades. Although Boston Latin School was founded in 1635, the movement for common schools started in the early 1800s. The "common school" movement's first statewide success was in Massachusetts in 1837,[89] then Connecticut. Eventually, by the 1900s, grassroots activists around the country won when local schools were paid for by tax dollars. Shortly after, mandatory attendance was passed into law, over time that came to include attendance at public or — originally parochial — private schools up until a certain age. Before schools were mandated, education was guaranteed only for the wealthy through tutors and then, in piecemeal, scattershot form, for others usually through local denomination-led schools.

One recurring purpose of schooling has been moral uplift. At various points seen as a vision of a unitary standard in a very diverse nation, schools were to be answerable to non-denominational local and statewide standards. Early on, just after its signing, a number of the architects of the Constitution called for schools as a necessary building block for a democracy. The people of a democracy must be educated so they can participate meaningfully in our form of government, one uniquely dependent upon their informed participation. As industrialization progressed and apprentices as the basis of work skill transfers became less common, schools were seen as more important for basic literacy for all workers.

Funnily, the different purposes of education continue to weave through debates about public education; they echo the same tensions between local versus state control, and input of parents. More importantly, early tensions over the social benefit versus the social burden of schools persist, as does the more outright privileged argument over why those with enough money to pay for private schooling should care about and therefore help subsidize the schooling of all children. Although then as now, the lack of meaningful access to education seems a factor in the increase of criminal behavior.

While Massachusetts was the first to outlaw legal segregation in schools, it was not until 1855 when the state Supreme Court reversed an earlier 1845 ruling.[90] Yet, today public schools in our state's major cities rival the level of segregation that drove the need for legal action in Brown v. Board of Education of Topeka (1954) in the Jim Crow South of the United States only a little over 50 years ago. Education is a constitutional right in our state. Whatever the many uses of having an educated people, it is supposed to be an equal right for all.

Fast forward to the 1990s: A series of cases in different states across the country challenge unequal funding formulas since funding has remained primarily district-based since public schools began. This local-based formula, of course, has lead to significant differences in funding since race and class segregation between school districts is still common. In pursuit of fairer educational opportunity, some folks finally sued. The result from the Massachusetts case was a requirement for education reform through shifted financing, at the state as well as local level.

At the same time, concerns about the uniform value of a high school diploma were increasing. For decades, students had been held back when not doing well enough but it later came to light that repeating grades was directly increasing dropout rates. In response, holding students back decreased while concerns about the value of a diploma increased.

These forces and no doubt other less visible ones led to education reform in Massachusetts in the 1990s. Many believe this was really the first major change in public schools since the original legislation founding public schools in the state. The Massachusetts Education Reform Act (MERA) included key components: significant funding increases primarily for low-spending districts; a review of what proficiency meant—to be measured by a spectrum of measures from traditional pencil and paper tests to measures of other aptitudes including the creation of a portfolio for each student to showcase their area of greatest educational attainment.

Even after decades of struggles to mitigate race and cultural biases in our nationalized standardized tests succeeded, all paper and pencil tests still test a limited range of aptitudes. Non-standardized testing also might be harder to evaluate and more expensive. However, it is worth capturing and accurately reflecting other aptitudes which can provide avenues to success. Testing was to be not only a per student measure for advancement but also a measure for the performance of specific schools and their teachers. The impacts on advancement and penalizing for students, schools and teachers were to be phased in over time.

Before MERA even reached full implementation, however, its relatively lofty goal of a more robust and inclusive testing format was inadequately funded. The only piece of testing for students, teachers and schools, became the now infamous Massachusetts Comprehensive Assessment System (MCAS) test, based on standardized pencil and paper models. Because Massachusetts did not use only nationally vetted tests but developed its own test, it has required revisions to correct for renewed cultural and race biases. But more importantly it became the only measuring stick for pass or fail. The MCAS measures math and English proficiency primarily. If all else fails, those two courses alone become the litmus test for students, schools and teachers.

A visible battle has raged over the MCAS: who benefits, who gets penalized and how ultimately its results will be used. The more significant change accomplished under MERA, however, may be in the funding for low-spending schools. There has been a lot more research since the legal suits in different states required financing reform: some trying to measure the impact of funding; some assessing other education reform changes.

MassInc's recent comprehensive study *Incomplete Grade* concludes with an incomplete grade on the MERA, 15 years after passage.[91] It represents a comprehensive look at the funding changes and impacts on not only overall educational changes or between the quartiles (splitting schools in four tiers) of school performance. It also takes a deeper look at the relative impact on what was initially the lowest-spending quarter of schools — presumably the schools most central to the court's demand for evening out school funding in the name of justice.

MassInc's study, *Incomplete Grade,* demonstrates some startling and not very comforting results. They believe based on their results that it has been the change in funding levels that has been responsible for what changes have occurred not the heightened accountability (the various sticks and carrots of the MCAS). The monetary influx directly impacted students through improvements like teaching and physical resources. This impact was even greater where it was supplemented with combining school districts and a commitment to decreasing administrative overhead — although combining actual schools wiped out any benefit. While the funding impacts were significant — bringing the bottom quartile comparable to the middle two quartiles in spending levels — the budget cuts of the early years of this century decreased some of those gains. The funding changes, unfortunately, never helped the bottom three-fourths of schools close the gap on the top quarter of schools.

More disappointingly, MassInc's research does not show testing gains simply by correcting for standard socio-economic factors (that is standard measures used by statisticians to correct for the very impactful factors of money, social status, etc.). By such measures, MERA has produced no measurable results. They posit, perhaps correctly, that this is due to the lowest-spending districts facing significant increases in the percentage of lower income students and students with very little English in the last 15 years. MERA's most important gift is that these districts did not lose even further ground as those changes would predictably have pushed test scores even lower. They do point out that while education reform monies increased some as those population increases added strain on these school districts, those funding increases probably did not keep pace and actually cover those increasing costs.

If you look at existing trends when MERA was implemented and account for school-specific baseline characteristics, then MERA funding increases had a significant improvement on schools. At the time of education reform, there was a wide divide between the top quarter highest-spending schools in the state and those in the lower quarters. The lowest-spending schools in the state already had a measurably widening gap in achievement in math and English. Likewise, they argue, school-specific baselines could be caused by problems in school cultures or other long lasting features that simply increasing money cannot really change. Once you add in these factors, there is a noticeable improvement, a statistically significant improvement but the importance and implications of these factors are unclear.

Exploring the relative success of the initially lowest-spending schools in comparison to each other is more interesting. While the percentage of lower income students and low-English proficiency students increased across Massachusetts,[92] they were highly concentrated in districts that had already struggled with low funding. These lowest spending schools had an average of 40 percent lower income and low-English proficiency students in 1992, and up to three-quarters in some districts in 2006. Even among those initially lowest-spending schools, the bottom fourth, there were some districts where those percentages did not increase, in fact even fell. These smaller percentage of schools in particular were where most of the MERA improvements can be seen. Specifically the challenges facing non-native English speaking students have been least addressed by MERA and so they have tended to drop out in higher numbers.[93]

MassInc points to other more in-depth studies that seem to show what underlies the improvement for the historically lowest-spending schools: an increase in teaching hours — both as part of the regular school day and in outside hours, and a change in overall school culture toward a "disciplined can-do attitude." An attitude I too remember from the best teachers I ever had. They were usually disciplinarians, yes, but for them part of that was the higher expectations they lovingly but firmly held us to.

MassInc's solid piece underscores lessons we might pretty much expect. Additional funding that goes right to the teaching of children is what makes the difference. Good teachers who continue to improve really make the difference. Of course, increasing class sizes does not help. Additionally, more students from backgrounds with other economic stresses and less educational attainment by parents are a great challenge for schools. Coming fast on the heels of an end to bilingual education in the state, I cannot say I am surprised that MERA seems not to properly address the needs of non-native English speakers.

On the other hand, MassInc also falls into some typical, familiar assumptions of our time. In trying to figure out how to improve education with less funding, they do not address more progressive funding sources for the state. They suggest cutting health care benefits — not only from present teachers but from retirees, a fair number of whom retired well before recent increases in teacher salaries. Their pensions reflect much lower pay levels and are hardly in a position to face double or triple health cost outlays. Both of these reflect the widespread recognition that spirally health costs are hurting government budgets along with the rest of us but they do not entertain real cost-saving universal coverage such as single-payer care. With the recognition of the value of smaller, more student-focused teaching situations, they go for the obvious desire to put more money toward charter schools but only performing ones.

Clearly, charter schools are seen, by some, as the real silver bullet, the way out for students in struggling public school districts whose parents do not have money for standard "private" schools. On the other hand, only the most rabid charter school advocates do not recognize that publicly funded charter schools have allocated more money per student and grab a higher percentage of local public school budgets per child. Thus, they strip comparable resources from the student in traditional public schools. Given court cases saying that it is unjust to underfund the lowest-spending schools, it seems clear that applies whether it is by an unjust funding formula between districts with less money on their own or policy that actually siphons money away from them for a small minority of students in those same communities served by charter schools. I can hear already the cry, *"But what about my child?"* from a parent who is willing to fight to get their child into a better school but does not have money to pay for it by themselves.

What if the charter school is not making the difference?

I have always agreed with those who understood that an educated electorate is fundamental to a functioning democracy. As Jonathan Kozol, long-time educator and researcher says, for civic engagement the three 'R's' — reading, writing and 'rithemtic — are necessary but it is the fourth, critical reflection that is most basic. He brought down the house at Worcester's 2009 Martin Luther King, Jr. celebration.[94]

I cannot help but think of my friends and colleagues who are single mothers...all the single mothers we worked with and advocated with. I knew their desperation then, trapped in poverty and desperately trying to access a better future for their children. Such a desire can only be so much more vivid for many parents these days — with long-term and increasing unemployment rates for young men and women, especially of color. That is the desperate hope: that a good education or access to specific skills from sports to carpentry might spell a ticket out of poverty for their kids. We are told education can make the difference in that...

An important study, "School Sector and Academic Achievement," by Lubienski and Lubienski compared different types of educational institutions and their impact on educational success for students.[95] They compared not only regular public schools with "private schools" as a whole but broke out their analysis to compare the national test scores of regular public vs. charter vs. Lutheran, Catholic, conservative Christian evangelical and "other" private schools. They carefully analyzed the raw data from not just the tests but the household characteristics of students and demographic data to create an incredibly robust study. If you are shocked by their results take comfort in the fact that they were also sufficiently surprised to try reassessing some of their interpretation of raw data; the results held.

What led Lubienski and Lubienski to their study were initial results by other education researchers based on 2003 national test scores. These studies showed if you took into account some of the characteristic differences in school population for public versus private schools, *private school students tested equally or worse on average than public school students.* While the national test scores of private schools always come out better in general than public schools, this research showed that it was not the *school* that was making the difference. The difference in test scores might have more to do with the populations that attend different kind of schools! There are many studies out there showing these types of results but the Lubienskis' is particularly comprehensive and my education researchers say it may be telling a more carefully derived story...

What the researchers did is this: The National Assesment of Educational Progress (NAEP) test records more than just scores; it records demographics and some detailed background questions on each student. It has results from all types of schools (although Lubienski and Lubienski are cautious about their results for conservative Christian schools and "other private" schools because the samples, though consistent with their other results, were very small). They looked at math scores because such skills are usually more dependent on school teaching (compared to reading, for instance) and on home environment conditions that are unlikely to be influenced by the school — like the presence of regular newspapers, access to computers, and the number of books.

When they checked for the impact of type of schools on test scores corrected by home environment, demographics and school location (rural versus urban and U.S. region) this is what they found:

Fourth grade national test results

- Without correcting for any other factors, charter school students perform worse on math than regular public schools and public school students scored generally lower on average then private school students (Catholic, Lutheran and other private schools showed significantly better scores).

- When you add in the impact of student demographics (such as race, economic status, language proficiency), all of the private school advantage disappears and conservative Christian schools perform noticeably worse. Charter school scores, while still below average public school scores, become even worse.

- Once you add the impact of overall demographics of the student body on the mean (average) scores of schools, all charter and private schools perform on average measurably worse than public schools. Conservative Christian school scores plummet. The impact of those who make up the student body is significant and public schools fair much better.

- With all of these characteristics (variables) accounted for, African American students on average have significantly lower scores than white classmates, and Latino students followed by Native American students also had a significantly lower mean (average).

Eighth grade national test results

- Again raw scores showed even larger differences in averages between public and other types of private schools. Charter school scores were about equivalent to regular public schools.

- Once you add the impact of student demographics even these larger benefits for most private schools disappeared although Catholic and Lutheran schools retained a statistical advantage.

- Once you add the impact of overall school demographic composition, public schools perform significantly better than Catholic and conservative schools and the same as other schools.

- The lingering affect of student race continued in the eighth grade sample as well.[96]

While the researchers, as researchers are wont to do, are cautious about the meaning of their results, the implications are that moving to private schools can hurt (including charter schools, although their eighth-grade sample was too small to be conclusive) and that given demographics, the most significant educational advantages are actually provided by regular public schools. Since charter schools and school voucher programs assume it is the *school type* that improves scores, we have heard all sorts of explanations for why private schools must be better — including explanations that it's public control of curriculum or some negative impact of unions that is making the difference. These results could be seen to put that argument on its head since in fact public schools are performing better; public control and unionization are — if anything — helping!

The other implication is that most of the difference in scores is explained by school composition and even more student-level demographic differences. Race, gender, etc., matter more as do the number of educational opportunities in the home. The magazines, newspapers, computers, atlases, encyclopedia and just plain books make the difference. While this is not different from findings in the health field of the impact of "lifestyle" characteristics on overall health, it has important implications for what we must address for the better education of our children ... **and** we need to look at what public schools are doing *right!*

I know I can get pegged as conservative when I posit things like this but I simply cannot see the logic of spending more money for programs that do not perform. Even if we have all sorts of ideological arguments for why certain types of schools should perform better, anecdotal stories about their significance or their mystique has somehow captured our hearts and hopes. When you combine the Lubienski results with the Massachusetts focused study, *Incom-*

plete Grade, whose authors worried about decreasing financial resources for our schools, the argument for charter schools is clearly ungrounded. There is no legitimate policy argument for the drain of resources from our regular public, "district" school students for higher cost-per-student charter schools which appear to perform significantly less well than our "district" schools.

While there is evidence that smaller classrooms especially in younger grades make a difference in educational attainment, ensuring smaller classes for more of our public school students can only be facilitated by concentrating all our public resources where they are more effective: our regular district schools. We must oppose policy that allows the resources to be siphoned off by good intentions. Policies that keep the best teachers in place and allow them to flourish are important. It is arguable that the high turnover of teachers in charter schools may be part of what hurts their educational success.

Both studies underscore the significance of the achievement *gap*. Turning our attention to the measurable impact of home resources on learning seems clear. Considering what exacerbates the relatively harder road for students of color and especially non-native English speakers is clearly underlined. *Incomplete Grade* especially highlighted recent work that points to the emergence of the potential predictive power of what is already happening for children by the time they reach third-grade; by then early predictors seem meaningful for predicting later dropout rates. This is the educational point, as researchers say, when students move from learning-to-read to reading-to-learn.

The Massachusetts Comprehensive Assessment System test

Like charter schools, testing can be a hot button topic. There is no question testing is necessary. When we take in-class tests, we know how important they are: from everything from the impact of deadlines on all of us to the potential as a future teaching tool — so we know what we have understood and what we still need to understand. A good teacher can also learn what concepts they got across and for what kinds of students, and which ones they did not.

When MERA was under consideration, it was not only the fulfilling of a court mandate. There was a larger felt need to provide real measuring sticks and some sense that, for instance, a high school diploma or movement to the next grade signified certain educational attainment. Is this what the scaled back Massachusetts Comprehensive Assessment System (MCAS) tests — without its more in-depth and comprehensive multiple measuring tools — got us?

As pointed out earlier, the paper and pencil MCAS test is a scaled back version of the larger recognized truly comprehensive test. We got MCAS because of scaled back funding. Unlike national tests, it is given every year.

Looking at different school environments based on school population, the results of using MCAS seem to vary by quartile of schools. For high-performing schools the impact on teaching where the test content is already mostly covered and students tend to already perform well on paper and pencil tests has been minimal. For middle-performing schools, where test preparation can have a significant impact and content can be covered sufficiently, teaching seems to have shifted over to a focus on the test.

For the least well-performing schools, the scramble is on. To some extent in these schools, it has all become about the test. Many of them must bring up the scores of some of those on the edge of failing or they are likely to get in trouble with too low a score as a whole for the school. In these schools, the best performing students may lose the attention of teachers focused on the students right on the edge of passing. However, the real danger is to the kids who are deemed to require too much time to be helped to pass and may simply be written off. Such a dynamic only gets exacerbated by the state cuts to extra tutoring and after-school and summer school programs to help students who do not pass the MCAS.

The term teaching-to-the-test has become well known; responses to its use among teachers I found instructive. In talking with teachers in what is clearly *not* a random sampling, I am always surprised at the range of response. Many of the teachers who have been around longer do not bridle at the phrase; some are angry overall at expectations that they feel are almost irrelevant in classrooms and disciplinary requirements that they find overly challenging. Some really resent a test they can see cutting into their valuable time to teach lessons more relevant to the lives and challenges of the children in their classes, hamstringing time they used to use for more in-depth learning and critical thinking skills that they value more highly.

Interestingly to me, resentment of the test seems least among newer teachers for whom it has always been part of their expectations; some even feel that it guided their early study plan development and focused their early teaching struggles. And some of them *really bridle* at the use of the term teaching-to-the-test; they felt their work demeaned by it.

With Ed Reform in place in Massachusetts for some 16 years, like other state reforms in response to legal rulings to improve equity, we actually have some of the most comprehensive studies of high stakes testing.[97] *High stakes testing did not correlate with student achievement, nor did it narrow the achievement gap.* But denying diplomas in Massachusetts in 2007 did disproportionately impact students with disabilities: 2,000 did not graduate on time. Holding children back because of their scores does increase drop-out rates just as repeating grades historically has: 29 percent of those who do not pass drop out compared to 2 percent of those who do pass the MCAS.

MCAS tests are not cheap. They are not helping our schools prioritize all our children nor helping our failing schools get the resources they need. They are costing our state 36.5 million without counting any extra support program costs.[98] They cost our municipalities by diverting resources from teaching hours, materials, substitute teachers' wages and other items in the schools that need those resources the most to really help our children learn.

Given that Massachusetts has one of the widest achievement gaps in the U.S., is it more important that we design policy on our assumptions and wished-for outcomes or on the facts? MCAS are expensive and they are not meeting what are reasonable goals — that diplomas measure achievement in some sense and that all our kids have an equal right to achieve. Nor will sending our children to Charter Schools which powerful evidence shows provide less add-on educational value than our regular district schools and cost more per child. In addition, anything that makes the retention of teachers harder especially in our toughest schools will undermine efforts to close our achievement gap.

We need to change the cultures in our schools to expect solid but diverse achievements for all our students. In order to get there, we have to stop spending money on what does not work — no matter what our personal feelings are — and put that money into what does work.

When Groups Get Scapegoated

It always amazes me when groups get scapegoated for a problem — especially one that they clearly were not influential enough to cause.

It is not that I am naive about the power of assumptions or prejudice. Trust me that as a woman and a lesbian, I understand just how pervasive prejudice can be. Never a day goes by that I am not reminded in any number of little ways and often a few big ways that I am treated by society as less than others in certain aspects.

Nor am I less cognizant as a white person who grew up with some class privilege that there are an equal number of ways in which I am party to race or class dynamics even though I was raised to be less aware of them. I know whether it is being comfortable in a health food market — which one of my dearest health-conscious Black friends hates to frequent without a white friend because of how white such venues still are and how she gets looked at when she shops there. Or whether it is a particular Brazilian friend of mine who often asks me to make cold calls for her to stores or bureaucrats because she knows how much more easily the call will go without her accent in the mix. Or it is the more structural but more punitive reality that friends of color face when applying for jobs or driving through white, well-to-do neighborhoods at night. They are more likely to have their criminal history record checked and have it get a door shut in their face or get them scrutinized by the police.

What seriously surprises me is this: given we all know we were raised exposed to prejudice, why can we not step back and agree to try to look at the facts? Why not do our best to listen to each other and make choices based on those facts? Instead we seem to get tangled up in feeling like we have to justify, not listen.

Take our electoral system. We know that we have poor voter turnout. We can have 25 percent of the electorate show up in most elections compared to sometimes even struggling democracies which will have 75 percent, 80 percent, or even 90 percent turnout. When you look at the number of U.S. folks eligible to vote who never register, it is really chilling.[99]

With less visible sectors of society, the rest of us do not necessarily know what is going on. For example, I remember sitting with teenagers from South High in Worcester several years ago. Stories from the lack of textbooks, paper and pens to study; days spent trying to pay attention in their winter coats because of faulty heat or classrooms like sieves in the depth of freezing winter temperatures. Or stories from home lives with cracks in walls or not enough to eat.

We may not hear these stories but clearly they underlie the problems in our hardest hit schools – designated underperforming. Add to these details serious cuts in the numbers of teachers and increasing class sizes. In these conditions, the logical solutions clearly do not start with laws that target and remove the legal rights of not only teachers but custodial, cafeteria, and clerical staff. Yet removal of the legal standing of these groups as workers was a central component of the 2010 education reform legislation in Massachusetts. It also included additional changes to public education that run counter to all the studies on what is effective for our children and closing the achievement gap. We need to be careful when scape-goating starts replacing actual solutions to real problems. We cannot become about fighting each other on the deck of our ship of state thereby ignoring taking the steps to stop it from sinking.

But we, as a society, do not give up on the basic concept of democracy. We know we have to keep improving our system. Some of us expend significant energy in that direction. We must think real education reform (based on the facts) at the service of every one of our children. We know an educated electorate is foundational to truly functional democracy. From Colonial times, we knew that deep democracy, *all inclusive participation and control of the purse-strings,* is fundamental to a just society. Real democracy in unions is also fundamental to their being healthy enough to play their role in keeping our economy balanced and functional.

Part V

Rebuilding a Better Ship After Storm Damage

There is already significant storm damage to the people, businesses and government of our state. If we are going to lose the mast off the ship, if we are going to have to jury-rig to survive this crisis, why not take advantage of the opportunities this provides to rebuild the way we want? Healthier, saner, more stable lives and communities; a strong democracy with more representation for all of us, and input on use of our tax dollars in our economy and environment; the institution of new policies that support rebuilding communities, local control, direct economic benefits to all our people and a sustainable future.

Storm damage may have to be fixed when it happens — no waiting for the ship's captain's order to put out the fire in the boiler room. Nor is the ship's captain best prepared to identify the breech in the hull far from where he is stationed. If we see it, we use our smarts together to fix it, saving ourselves and each other. Line staff frequently spot potential problems first, and have the specific skills to address them. And if our warnings have gone unheeded we cannot afford to wait now. Where we can, we will have to work from the bottom up to solve our problems together.

Greater Opportunity

I often refer to the Chinese sign for crisis, which they say is a combination of the signs for danger and opportunity. What I had not realized until this crisis is that the greater the danger a moment brings, the greater the opportunity.

One of the misconceptions that the powers-that-be continue to put out is that this is just a short-term dip in the road. It is in fact a far-reaching crisis in the world economy. Trends that have been exacerbating for decades are bringing our economy to its knees. Many of the avoided or voided regulations at the national level will have to be reinstated, some fundamental human rights will have to become guaranteed such as the right to a single, universal, affordable standard of health care. We will have to revamp education so that it can actually meet our state guarantee to public education for all.

But along with these regulations and restructurings to undo increasing harm (to segments of society, yes, but just as importantly to the overall functioning of our economy), come opportunities to re-envision the world we want to live in and address real changes in our world situation.

There is no politician anywhere along the political spectrum that I can think of who has not at some point harkened back with approval to the time when as children we were watched over not just by our own parents but by whole neighborhoods — like that African proverb that it takes a village to raise a child. Our villages may have been a set of blocks in a city, a cul-de-sac in a town or adjoining properties in the countryside, but such references always seem to elicit knowing nods at least from those over a certain age.

The first stimulus bill by the Obama Administration is unlikely to be the last, given the likely length of this economic depression and no matter what "hopeful" spin many of the more quoted economists are trying to put on this. Estimates pointed out that the pace at which our economy is worsening would make the impact of the initial stimulus package barely enough to fill the widening hole. While it seems to have slowed the downward slide, predictions that it won't reverse the economy look accurate, unfortunately.

It behooves us then to think well and strategically about how to spend this money and to use it to tailor longer-term answers to longer-term problems — everything from rebuilding those communities where children were treated as a shared responsibility to economic and environmental models based on sustainability.

Whether you want to have arguments about what percentage of global warming is due to human activity, at this point scientists of all stripes are no longer arguing about whether there is global warming, only about what portion is human contribution. We know we are using up natural resources faster than they replenish and polluting at rates that threaten our health, and faster than our environment can clear naturally by itself.

It is not only that we are somewhere around having used up the majority of easy to reach petroleum reserves (peak oil), but may also be approaching that for the most useable coal. And river specialists at the state say we are in fact using more fresh water in Massachusetts than nature can replenish; we may have peaked there as well.

In the face of so many problems reaching critical points at the same time it is easy to despair. It is easy to feel like we have to just focus on one problem at a time so we can fix it. But if instead we think of this as a systemic crisis of which all of these are expressions, then we know to turn our attention to solutions that in fact will put us on a new road — a road to many kinds of recovery at once. Trying to somehow solve each problem separately in isolation simply will not work because none of these crises are disconnected from each other. *I stand by my belief that you cannot fix a problem until you can name it and this is an interconnected problem.*

Imagine, instead, that this is an opportunity to guide all these many shifts together towards a different scenario — closer to what in our best selves we would want? Imagine for a moment experiencing the shifts and unpredictably not as a sign that what we care about is going to end? Imagine such shifts are challenges for us to reach beyond what we have been told we should want and expect and *reach for what we really want...*

For instance, if being dependent on petroleum is no longer realistic, how can we create better versions of the old trolley systems? Live our daily lives with our homes closer to our work and our children closer to us wherever we are moment to moment? We may have to rebuild communities where we know each other again!

Or if incredibly long work hours for a few of us — that deny us daily time with our children, friends and neighbors — have to be cut so there can be jobs for everyone — that would be a welcome change! We need to address how incomes can be sustainable for everyone and the benefits and stresses of working more evenly shared. We might come to have time once again to know not only our own children but to become stewards for all the children in our neighborhoods.

If we cannot keep using and disposing of material possessions without hopelessly polluting and using up natural resources, maybe we can really learn to reuse and recycle and change over our industries to do that. We can replenish our soil with compost and come to grow food locally and live more on local foods.

What else do you imagine? And how might we manage an economic shift during an economic downturn?

Shifting from coal and petroleum to other oils

Given that there are numerous reasons to cut back on our use of petroleum and burning coal and mining uranium, what does that point to as new formulations for how we live day to day? Natural gas is a byproduct of petroleum production and less polluting. It is currently more plentiful in these early 2000s and does not cost as much. Transferring dependency onto this likewise limited resource however will not help us in the long run. Similarly the environmental impact of methane in the atmosphere is even worse than carbon dioxide. The cleanest burning, least polluting type of coal — bituminous — is what we may have mined the most of and be closest to hitting its peak. That is also the kind of coal we make steel out of, which lasts longer to serve our needs than burning through such a critical resource.

Simple substitution of one source of oil for another can be equally fraught with danger. For a long time, our federal government has subsidized corn to provide ethanol as a corn derivative to supplement or replace petroleum. Unfortunately, the way we grow corn is petroleum intensive and transforming corn into ethanol remains energy intensive even after decades of research. While not yet economically viable as fuel, corn is fundamental to the world food supply. The role of corn in our world food supply is being endangered by using corn to produce ethanol as ethanol becomes more profitable as an extender for our gasoline.

Another, more promising, substitution in terms of the energy intensiveness of production and potential competition with our food supply appears at first glance to be palm oil. And many have seized on this as a likely answer.

I remember with almost mystical wonder descriptions of the rainforests and the literal layers of ecological worlds created by giant trees that dwarf much of our forests. Even visiting and being awed and engulfed by the size of redwood trees apparently cannot prepare one for the overarching size and worlds of ecological complexity of the rainforests. Seriously, if you have never considered what rainforests are like, treat yourself to an online search of pictures of humans up against the base of some of the huge trees that anchor the rainforest or one of the discovery or travel channel shows.

The carbon draw down in the regular breathing of one of these giant trees alone each day is staggering. Indonesia, Brazil and the Amazon, and the Congo Basin contain the vast majority of the rainforests, which function like the lungs of the planet, breathing in carbon from the air. Figures from 2003 show two billion tons of CO_2 enters the air from rain forest destruction. The remaining standing forest was calculated to contain 1,000 billion tons of carbon, double what was calculated to be in the air worldwide in 2007.[1]

Why you might ask have I digressed into the rainforest? Because the great palm oil producers, the giant corporations that have grown up in some parts of the world as palm oil has become more used in preprocessed foods, have happily stepped up to make greater profits producing oil to run engines. Palm oil tree varieties vary greatly in how much oil they produce and vary significantly as well based on the fertility of soil they are planted in. Guess where the highest oil-producing palm trees produce the most oil the fastest? When planted in recently cleared rain forest soil — at least for the first few years...

We may be used to worrying about oil (or should I say petroleum) companies. There are incredibly destructive oil spills like the Exxon Valdez oil spill in 1989, and wars we know are fought over access to ever more scarce oil reserves (no matter what the latest spin on why we are sending our sons and daughters to face and wreak danger and death). When gas prices were gouging us the most and turning our economic lives almost upside down, these were the quarters when oil companies made the most profits! Besides being on the receiving side of constant federal subsidies, they had no conscience about telling us how they were just increasing prices because supplies were down. In fact, they were at best using the opportunity to increase their profits.

The problem is that in this part of the world we have not been paying any attention to the growth of other kinds of oil companies and their impact politically, socially or even environmentally. We cannot simply trade a new source of oil for our engines for the world-wide environmental impact of clearing rainforest for its production. Palm oil is trading one destructive oil production for another.

Switching from petroleum but contributing to deforestation–especially of the rain forest – demands attention. *"In the next 24 hours, deforestation will release as much CO_2 into the atmosphere as 8 million people flying from London to New York."* That is a quote from 2007, and the *rate of deforestation has accelerated since then.*[2]

According to the Stern Report, deforestation amounted to 25 percent of global greenhouse gases; transportation and industry each accounted for 14 percent; and aviation only 3 percent. So this is critical. In 2007, Indonesia and Brazil were third and fourth as greenhouse gas emitters *even though they have little heavy industry* compared to the European Union, India or Russia. The only two countries that contribute more to greenhouse effects are the U.S. and China.[3] It may make sense to do the math on how much rainforest we have destroyed and continue to destroy daily. We need to consider that our carbon contribution may be as much about the amount of the earth's regular air recycling process we have destroyed as how much pollution we have put into it.

You might ask why I am spending so much time on fuel sources from other parts of the world when this book is focused on state and local solutions. We are the economic driver behind fuel transition choices — we and the rest of the U.S. and the developed world. Our policymakers in Massachusetts have tried to get out in front of the global environmental crisis so we are trying to lead; we better be leading in the right direction. Municipal and state legislation has been passed emphasizing biodiesel as an alternative to petroleum. This creates a big market and economic pressure to shift to vegetable based fuels. We need to not create economic pressures more destruction of our environmental and economic futures than petroleum.

There is one source of plant oil that could be produced according to early research without having such dire collateral impacts on our environment. It could safely serve as a transitional option or provide for whatever applications we end up still needing oil for even after other forms of ingenuity have been mostly exhausted. That is switch-grass — a weed that has been seen as the enemy of agriculture in the bread basket states. There is industry to harvest it already, so maybe if we are more intentional about growing it, we could avoid other pitfalls. Switchgrass grows happily in environments like the foothills of the Rockies, where regular farming does not thrive because of the soil and unevenness and rockiness of the land. It also grows in the plains where we need to make sure it is not *displacing necessary food production.* Its growth could be nurtured (even if it may require more human labor — not a bad thing in a down economy with huge unem-ployment rates) in areas not used for human food production nor dis-placing a critical world environmental habitat as palm oil production does today. In that scenario, research shows that significant growths of switchgrass in its own indigenous environment would be enough to replace all other ethanol and vegetable oil production for engines in use today. It could go far beyond that replacing much higher per-centages of petroleum production.[4]

Imagine: no new drilling in Antarctica. No new oil rigs off shore threatening our oceans, our coral reefs or our fisheries which we need to preserve and be able to harvest sustainably for a long time to come. No "drill baby, drill."

[As this book goes to press, we are witnessing the British Petro-leum oil breach in the floor of the Gulf of Mexico — which a simple automatic shut-off valve, as required of oil platforms in Brazil and Norway, could have stopped.[5] This will be the worst, widest impact spill in history by the time it is done. This not only underscores how critical alternatives are but may also make the public believe that new drilling will be discouraged. Unfortunately, new deep water drilling permits are still being expedited under the Obama administration[6] because of the same forces that got U.S. rigs exempted from the shut-off valves — large oil lobbyists with massive amounts of funding. Change comes when we as regular people are vocal and organized and insistent — not because business as usual has been exposed as widely destructive.]

So we have to change our state policies internally to protect our trees but even more importantly, we cannot just blindly transfer our dependence to any petroleum substitute; we must define acceptable sources and prohibit palm oil. In general, if we are serious about our environmental future, we have to evaluate existing and new policy choices that can contribute to the clearing of critical rain forest.

What if we were left in charge?

It turns out we have some important anecdotal evidence to answer that question.

When I ran for governor in 2006, the hottest example of alternative energy development was the first white windmill in the community of Hull, along the Massachusetts shore line.[7]

Hull, one of the smallest communities in Massachusetts, is essentially a series of islands connected into a peninsula with a history of fishing and especially shipwreck salvage and life saving. Yet, it built its first electricity-producing windmill—the iconic white wind turbines—before any other community on the east coast of the United States. Hull is touted for its residents' inclusive process and a conscious poster child for wind energy, having won numerous awards. We have to ask, why did Hull get there first and why have imitators apparently been so scarce?

The central focus during energy and environmental proposals touted by the various 2006 gubernatorial candidates, Hull in 2009 has two windmills providing more than a tenth of the community's energy, with four larger off-shore windmills in the works. Together they will provide essentially 100 percent of the community's electrical needs. They have even sold some energy credits. In mid-2009, Hull remains nationally unique in this successful transition to 100 percent renewable energy production to be accomplished in the next few years.

The answer to Hull's unique success rests primarily with the often referenced but to my knowledge essentially unexplored implications of the inclusion of the residents in the decision-making, the regular people, the people like us. Treated as a quaint and admirable step, most recounting of Hull's story misses that resident inclusion was not quaint or so much admirable as required.

Hull is one of 40 communities in Massachusetts that has its own municipal utility.[8] Decades ago when electric utilities were public, some communities or small blocks of communities had their own separately run public utilities. When statewide energy production became privatized, these utility companies remained owned by their municipalities. The consumers were the residents of the community — much more directly benefiting or losing based on the utility's choices; and the utility's profits or losses were directly passed on to the residents; the basis of their decisions were more transparent and locally accountable.

Renewable energy has significantly different economic dynamics. The upfront costs of building any electricity generation plant are significant. With traditional electricity generation the ongoing costs of fuel are significant and dependent upon production. For renewable energy sources, the costs of ongoing generation is much less — essentially the cost of maintenance.

When a private company complains about upfront renewable energy costs and seeks government assistance, it knows that once initial costs are provided for, all savings from then on turn into windfall profits with "fuel" drawn from our free public natural resources. This incredibly inexpensive electricity generation will be one of a number of energy sources they control; it will flow into their production stream and, given its small percentage of electricity across the entire market, not measurably decrease the price for electricity. Instead of the savings lowering electricity prices for a long time to come, producers will simply price their overall electricity at the same going rate as other producers and reap the profits of their production from our free resources.

In Hull, through public meetings, concerns by residents were directly solicited and answered before bids for a windmill were even solicited. Since the residents have a municipal utility, those huge production savings are theirs directly. There was, not surprisingly, widespread support.

While our present governor and then-Speaker of the House Sal DiMasi got into a bit of a spitting contest about who would provide a viable green energy plan for the state first, they both overlooked the quintessentially New England process that had fired Hull's success. The source of the success is the same town meeting democracy that when threatened, led to the initial non-violent ouster of the English King's forces prior to the famous bloody phase of our Revolution. The State House did pass a green energy plan *but with both corporate incentives and policy pressure on municipalities for the siting of alternative energy production by for-profit companies.* Renewable energy projects by major for-profit companies from mountaintops in the Berkshires to offshore have hit significant local resistance. This is not surprising since local democratic control was not only not included in the legislation, there were pressures to override it. Meanwhile, Hull's initiatives continue to expand and move forward.

As the economic downturn hurts especially our local communities and municipal governments, local control of clean energy generation could make such production more likely to succeed. Cheaper energy will create communities that are economic havens from the seemingly endlessly increasing costs of energy; with significant savings for our increasingly defunded municipal governments as well as enticements for local business expansion. Not to mention it will keep more money in the economically critical pockets of regular residents instead of big private — out of state — utility companies.

The cost for power from municipal utilities today represents a significant savings for customers from for-profit utility bills: for the first half of 2009, National Grid, NStar and Unitil charged 25 percent, 51 percent and 53 percent more than our state's municipal utilities.[6] We do not have good enabling legislation for communities to transition to municipal utilities in Massachusetts laws as of 2009 even if residents want to. This is, however, exactly the kind of revenue neutral legislation a strapped state government can give to its financially ailing municipalities and the people and local businesses which are the engine to its future long-term recovery.

In the meantime, electrical production can be broken into three stages which could be paid for differently. Presently, whether we pay private utility companies or have our own municipal utility, these are bundled together. They are the electricity source production, the transmission of that electricity and the local poles and wires and maintenance. Presently a municipal government can take over the last two and bulk-buy its electricity from whatever production sources it wishes. Apparently such bulk buying saves the residents and local businesses of municipalities that bulk buy together roughly 10 to 12 percent off their electricity bills.

As we use up petroleum, who chooses the uses of the remainder?

I remember what I think was a commercial when I was much younger. In a daily glass of orange juice, if you looked at what you were actually paying for, it was 80 percent the cost of the gasoline to transport it — and they showed a glass of 80 percent gasoline and 20 percent orange juice!

What else is petroleum an ingredient in? We know we use it for heating and gasoline but here is just a suggestive list:[10]

- Clothing products from polyester to purses and sneakers;
- Office supplies from pens and printer cartridges to telephones;
- Numerous types of sporting goods from fishing poles and footballs to cameras and skis to sleeping bags and insulated boots;
- Baby/children's goods from toys and baby bottles to pacifiers and baby lotion;
- Furnishings from shades and rugs to wallpapers and patio furniture;
- Kitchen goods from refrigerator shelves and cake decorations to trash bags and teflon coated pans to utensils and microwave dishes;
- Health and beauty products from perfume and hair products to vitamins and sunscreen;
- Building materials from caulking materials and glue to floor wax and solvents;
- Miscellaneous goods from fertilizer, food preservatives and flutes to lighter fluid, pillows, flags and dyes;
- Automotive supplies like coolant and fan belts to car seats and sport car bodies; and
- Medical supplies from allergy medication, aspirin and anesthetics to latex gloves, heart valve replacements, artificial limbs, and hearing aids.

Petroleum functions as an ingredient, a component cost, in almost everything we buy that was transported over a significant distance.

Some of these have non-petroleum-based alternatives. But if we are reaching peak oil, would it not be critical to stop running through these hundreds of different products we dispose of every day without thought? And also prioritize heart valve replacements or necessary medical uses? Should plastic and petroleum producers simply be trying to expand their present markets and supplying the most expensive uses? And should we really be eating, inhaling and slathering on our bodies and our children's bodies significant amounts of petroleum?

Instead of being shielded from the uses and using up of petroleum as a natural resource — belonging to all people as part of the common — we should know what is happening. Through our government by and for the people, should we not have some say before we suddenly hit shortages that no amount of existing subsidies for the petroleum industry are going to fix? Do not alternatives make sense for possible health impacts as well? Not only as we burn petroleum into the air we breathe but soak it into our pores as skin cream when alternatives exist?

Petroleum is an ingredient in an almost inconceivable range of products. But if you think of petroleum as if it were a limited amount of water to get across a desert, you would want to use it only for what we needed the most!

As various natural resources fundamental to our life styles and society move towards the unfamiliar reality of being used up, do not we the people need to be informed? Policies already influence how these resources get used and used up. When will we demand more of a say in revamping policies that will change so much that we have taken for granted?

Why Not Rebuild
What We Want?

Imagine getting up in the morning, after getting the older children ready and off to school, you grab the hand of your littlest one and walk a few blocks through the neighborhood. You greet your neighbors similarly getting their days started. You share stories of the weekend's community activities, worship services and check in on the health of a neighbor's ailing parent. Joined by another parent also walking their preschool-age child to one of the neighborhood home day cares, you drop off your children together, and chat on the walk back home.

You grab your work materials and coat to travel the few minutes to your job — either grabbing the local bus, joining one of the local carpools to work, or to cover a few errands to your local clothing place on lunch — you climb into your pre-arranged use of a car that is part of your local shared auto service. You have planned your day on Tuesdays to work the early shift. That way you will be able to grab the early bus home, walk to pick up your youngest from daycare, stop by the local grocer and bake shop on your joint walk home and still get back in time to oversee the local neighborhood children (including your own older ones) who are scheduled to play at your house or at least outside within sight of your windows.

Can you imagine having a life with time to work full-time and still have time for walking twice a day? Seeing your youngest child off to daycare and picking up groceries in a matter of minutes from your home? Not needing to pay to maintain your own car and yet having affordable and regular transportation options available? And having time for regular community activities that allow you to know those around you easily and coordinate regular schedules that allow your children to play safely with supervision while you go about the rest of your daily activities?

This is the vision of a philosophy called "Smart Growth" which could improve our environment and our economy while returning real quality to our lives…

Smart growth studies looked at a number of factors from quality of life to our environmental footprint. What they found, not surprisingly, is that if instead of commuting long distances to work and shopping malls, if instead of living in separated off single plot suburban homes, we live nearer to where we work and shop, nearer to our children's playmates and in more walkable mixed-use residential and small business communities, we would address many of our present day problems.

Over the last number of years, even as gas prices rose, the average commute for the vast majority of us who drive a car to work continued to lengthen. Studies show that much of this increase is not by choice. The distance from affordable housing and livable communities to available employment simply grew for most workers. In Figure 5.1 you can see in the last section that the growth was significant — up 20 percent from 1990 to 2005.[11] On average, commuters lose between 42 and 51 hours per year to sitting in traffic.[12] When you multiply our growth in vehicle miles by the hundreds of thousands who commute in Massachusetts alone, the impact in terms of time lost, wear and tear on roads and vehicles and pollution is staggering.

Figure 5.1   Average commute distance and duration by mode[13]

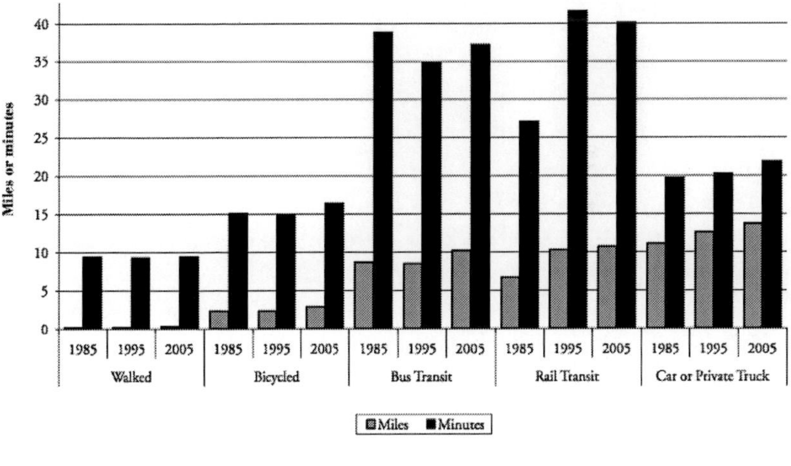

Anecdotally, people were not happy about it either. Commutes have continued to grow to the point where many people leave before

7 a.m. to arrive at work for a 9 a.m. start.[14] We can afford neither the pollution, nor the gas, nor the time away from our home lives.

We are less and less likely to be able to work near where we live so many of us need to have a car to get to paid work. While the average cost to maintain a car is an ever more unaffordable $8,000 per year, the longer distances required by our commutes have made public transportation a much more difficult (sometimes impossible) solution.[15]

We have also been losing more and more of our natural open space. Clearly this is not good for our wildlife and ecosystems, but similarly it is bad for humans. People rest and recreate in natural open space and benefit from the trees sharing our air and generating our oxygen. Such spaces moderate sweltering summer heat and chilly winter cold.

Building out into what was natural open space has a disproportionately negative impact on the environment as well. Clearing for lawns and the still common practice of heavy fertilizer and pesticide use are damaging the smaller waterways that feed our bigger waterways, closer and closer to their source. The earlier that damage, where chemicals are a higher percentage of the nascent water flow, the less likely that fresh water life will be able to withstand the overwhelming onslaught of contamination.

When human building encroaches on more and more habitat, we also tend to lose important flood land and wetland that serve as nature's hedge against flash floods and rivers overflowing their banks. The natural back-up of high water levels into such areas is an integral part of the health of such habitats. Simultaneously, these act like sponges in heavy rains quickly absorbing excess water and then slowly draining that water back into streams and rivers, decreasing the height and rapidity of peak river levels.

In the spring of 2006 and then again in 2010, because of slightly higher temperatures in the atmosphere, Massachusetts experienced major rain instead of our more common March snows. Areas hardest hit by rain did not have the normal slow melt of snow, and the loss of wetlands meant fast and destructive rises in river levels — seriously hurting some people's homes and businesses. Such events can put increases in property insurance for effected areas out of reach in the future, making these home-owners and business-owners dependent upon Massachusetts' back-up public insurance plan; this essentially shifts the insurance burden onto tax-payer backed systems. The widespread flooding in 2010 was described by some as a unique "hundred year" rain event but these types of rainy periods are likely to become more common. A direct contributor to the flooding has been the loss of wetlands as a buffer; many of these wetlands actually still exist but have been cut off from their rivers and streams by manmade road beds, rail beds and other structures which we can rebuild with culverts and other means to reattach them. And we all have an economic incentive to insist our government step in and make those changes happen.

Meanwhile, the stock of vacant housing in established communities has been significant and in some large cities growing, even as housing costs and homeless rates have continued to rise. Smart growth advocates recommended in-fill building, where empty lots are built up before sprawl is allowed to continue. All of these housing options existed before the predatory loans of the subprime lending industry imploded, the tidal wave of foreclosures started to hit, and the lending industry decided to empty areas of our communities in a wholesale way.

We cannot afford to lose all of this usable housing. Our neighborhoods cannot suffer the degradation of housing stock or the undermining of community and local businesses that provide most of our job growth. On the other hand, loss of natural open space is endangering more fragile ecosystems, minimizing any sizable wild space and undermining natural systems that protect us as well — such as wetlands, flood plains and even the trees that naturally clean our air.

It takes a village to raise a child. It also takes a village to reclaim our family-time and neighbors, to re-establish our economy and reverse our negative impact on the environment.

Fundamental shift in our "development" strategies

Smart growth studies surmised correctly that what is environmentally healthier and better for our quality of life requires a fundamental shift in our "development" strategies. When you add the lessons from this economic crash, it just becomes clearer.

Unfortunately, we have inherited numerous zoning assumptions that turned out to have very adverse consequences. They have us building farther apart, eating up remaining natural open space, locating businesses farther from our homes making effective public transportation harder, and prioritizing large, distantly owned companies.

Zoning laws throughout the Northeast were fed by the idea of avoiding density and protecting nature by forcing distance between buildings and not letting noisy dirty industry too close to our homes. The image of the New England town led to building limits on multiunit housing. In the long run such zoning laws have led to sprawl. Urban areas have continued a relatively flat expansion outward and more sparsely populated areas required large plots to build new homes. These policies have led a seemingly endless spread into more and more remote areas, eating up remaining wild space. While industrial areas were once loud and dirty, much of our business is not industrial anymore. Much of industry's toxicity is better addressed and waiting legislation, once passed, can address it even better.

All of these zoning requirements combined with other forces to exacerbate these identified clearly destructive trends.

Local control and pad ready development

When I ran for governor of Massachusetts in 2006, I was surprised by the huge emphasis put by other candidates on the creation of "pad-ready" development and their emphasis on other state programs to override local ordinances in order to attract huge, outside development and streamlining of business regulations — again, primarily for large businesses.

I doubt anyone questions that complicated and obscure regulations are a problem for many parties dealing with the government, whether businesses or individuals. But what concerned me most about the other candidates was not their desire to make the process for business permits clearer and more user friendly, but the emphasis on the government subsidizing especially large companies.

Small businesses create most new jobs and feed our local economies. Numerous studies show that corporations make siting deals mostly based on factors besides tax incentives. As gubernatorial candidates, we got asked specifically about the state developing a significant area in Fall River to make a large pad-ready parcel including building a special expensive off-ramp from the Interstate.[16] Why commit to such a large investment with no promise of return? Why continue the very type of economic development that Smart Growth proponents such as Governor Patrick claimed to be, must know was antithetical to that mission?

As a state, we are in trouble with the amount of toxic sites we need to address and redevelop. Brownfields reuse is the redevelopment of contaminated properties into revitalized productive uses. The Massachusetts Brownfields Act of 1998 established the Brownfields Redevelopment Fund (BRF), which provides loans for site assessment and cleanup to both public-and private-sector parties. Brownfields funding and projects put consciously to that end make sense. Since state government chose not to recoup money from the companies that created these environmental messes to clean them up at the time, these sites have become a public liability. But such cleanup should primarily be for the public benefit. As well, any business benefit should surely not be skewed to only large, often out-of-state corporations.

Why not pass prospective laws that would stop the use of toxics in present day industry so we do not continue to create a future public burden — especially given the large number of toxins for which non-toxic alternatives exist? Otherwise, we doom ourselves — the public — to paying endlessly for the Superfund (the Massachusetts Department of Enviromental Protection's program to clean up abandoned, accidentally spilled, or illegally dumped hazardous waste) and Big Dig disasters of the future with no corporate accountability in sight. It is cheaper and healthier to remove toxics from our residential and business life than to avoid mixing business and residential development for fear of toxins.

With much fanfare Governor Patrick, the self-identified Smart Growth proponent, announced closing the deal with Bristol-Myers Squibb on development at the former Devens Air Force Base. The logic? Bristol-Myers Squibb committed to build a facility that would employ 350 people (earlier estimates seem to have been 500) at an average annual salary of $60,000.[17] At the earlier estimate that would have been a payout of $30 million in salaries, once built, per year. How much did the state invest in building a plant that was far from people's homes, would require significant commutes, not provide local business growth nor keep the profits in our state?

The state package that was supposedly fundamental to bringing Bristol-Myers Squibb here? A $34 million state subsidy to build out infrastructure around the plant, plus another $30 million in state investment tax credit. Bristol-Myers Squibb also lined up a break in local taxes, plus a discount on the 80-plus acre site from the state development agency that controlled the Devens site.

The overall package was more than twice the entire salaries that Bristol-Myers Squibb would pay in its first three or four years of operations. I am not enough of an economist to estimate what the company would pay in corporate taxes or what its employees would likely produce in pay-roll taxes toward our state coffers; still clearly just the state subsidies alone will take more than 10 years to recoup.

The magnitude of those tax giveaways is underscored as our legislature stresses out over trying to pass any taxes that look to either completely close corporate loopholes or touch the incomes of the wealthiest amongst us. Our elected leaders seem to find it hard to stand up for any taxes. They even struggled over a sales tax increase which let them avoid facing wealthy interests. It continues to shift destructively the tax burden onto working class and middle-income residents, and would raise annually half of what the state gave away to Bristol-Myers Squibb in one year.

A $58 million state investment in one of our state-based green companies, Evergreen Solar, meant a one-year infrastructure investment for a company that has now announced moving its manufacturing to China.[18] Why do we keep making huge tax-deals with corporations with the hope they will stay committed to our state instead of requiring a contract to stay? As a growing industry critical to our green economy, that infrastructure money could have been used to both economically persuade Evergreen Solar to stay and benefit our residents and the future of all of us.

State monies could have been invested to prime the local market for a period of time for solar energy products like theirs; for instance, a state fund to decrease the cost to our residents of purchasing residential or small business scale renewable energy units. Such funding in Germany has decreased the cost of solar panels, making them affordable to many more residents, and making Germany the leader in residential solar panels. Imagine an initial $54 million subsidy such as a revolving loan fund for the technological early risk takers.

Such a strategic choice could have fueled the early stages needed to ignite the public's imagination while significantly increasing the domestic solar panel market. Evergreen Solar would have had a significant, and potentially long-term, local market. Hardly something to move away your manufacturing from and then have to pay expensive shipping to sell back to. We have a pronounced environmental and economic need for these types of creative win-win initiatives.

On the heels of this failed multimillion dollar, taxpayer-funded infrastructure development, in August 2009 our governor advocated using stimulus funds for a $9 million dollar footbridge to nowhere at Gillette Stadium, which in 2002, replaced Foxboro Stadium. Patrick said he needed to incentivize keeping another huge investment group in Massachusetts.[19] This is yet another deal with no contractual commitments from a private investor when all studies have shown that *this kind of investment is not what guides capital investment.*

I remember talking about where to put our development dollars during my 2006 gubernatorial campaign. I was always surprised with this huge corporate investment focus when the evidence is that small businesses create more new jobs, recycle the most consumer dollars in our communities, not to mention donate more dollars on average to their local communities. Local businesses are rooted in their local communities. For them, it is not some calculated strategy. They are genuinely home-grown and small enough to have a local presence and personality. If a large company can site anywhere and we try to use tax incentive and pre-development and infrastructure development dollars to bring it here, it still retains the reality that it could have been sited somewhere else.

This local business reality is understood by most of the people with whom I have ever talked in our state (except some fairly high-up in a major company) and it resonates with them. I had the most remarkable experience walking through a festival in the northern Pioneer Valley, and talking about this very issue with randomly selected people. I spoke with one couple about an alternative to this large-corporation focused strategy, and they said, *"You do not need to tell us, when Gillette moved into Devens, we got hired. Pretty good paying jobs, too."* I was about to apologize if I had offended them, when they continued, *"Of course, that lasted for five years until they moved on again..."* They could not have agreed with me more...

Smart Growth, smart investment

The logic and necessity of Smart Growth is only enhanced by the incredibly destructive impacts of the economic bottom-out.

When we look back to what really re-footed our economy after the Great Depression, one of the major economic investments — ever — of our federal government was the G.I. Bill. I am told this is the only time that our government used a significant amount of taxpayer funds to invest directly in asset development for regular people. A big chunk of the G.I. Bill gave money to families to own their own home — the largest asset that most regular people ever own. The G.I. Bill made real what the subprime mortgages promised but ultimately further undermined. True, having learned the moral lessons of the civil rights and women's movement we are aware of the unjust impact on those primarily excluded from the G.I. Bill. Yet this example demostrates the huge positive social impact when government funds directly help regular people create economic investment and long-term financial stability.

Not all neighborhoods are equally vulnerable

In the early 1980s, the core of Roxbury was already filled with emptied and disintegrating buildings. Community people were fighting to save their neighborhoods. Thanks to a particular coming together of events, a neighborhood organization, the Dudley Street Neighborhood Initiative (DSNI) found itself empowered by a mayoral run by Melvin King. The near success of King's campaign was leveraged into a unique housing arrangement — as a community non-profit, DSNI captured eminent domain powers usually reserved for governments.[20]

DSNI had a different vision: regular people should own their neighborhoods. Generally this area of Boston was home to housing owned by absentee landlords who tend to see housing as an investment to make money not as a service to be provided properly for a fee to tenants. We know from experience even without the numerous studies — that when people have control over their own housing, they can stay long enough to invest emotionally and financially in their homes.

DSNI wanted to be able to force market purchases of abandoned land and buildings and rebuild in a way that the people of the area would always be able to afford to own their house. DSNI has spent over 20 years slowly and deliberately acquiring land, rebuilding and selling individual houses built on land now owned in common through land trusting. While some observers have complained this is a different standard of ownership — not somehow considered as "complete" — DSNI's approach made the housing itself much more affordable because buyers do not have to be able to afford the cost of Boston-priced land. They instead sign a contract that they cannot resell the houses for a huge financial gain. DSNI has built and created home-ownership for literally hundreds of people.

Today, look at a map of the impact of speculative home values and spreading foreclosures in Boston. An amazing island of safety, of unaffected homes emerges. That island is the huge effective vision of the Dudley Street Neighborhood Initiative made real over all these years: an effective bulwark against predatory investment in residential property. This provides a concrete yet visionary model for rebuilding our foreclosed, ravaged neighborhoods that could include mixed-use, smart-growth neighborhoods.

Government possesses the legal if not always the financial tools to help us rebuild our neighborhoods. They range from eminent domain rights to neighborhood stabilization funds. Will the economic downturn get us to force our elected leaders to shift over to using such tools for the benefit of the majority of the people of this state?

Local Shopkeeper

Almost all of us have good memories of living in a neighborhood or even a small town with a friendly grocer we knew by name or a hair stylist or barber shop where community people might gather and swap stories. Or even a candy store where the clerk knew what we liked or a restaurant where our favorite meal was always on tap. How else would "Cheers" have been such a huge success on television?

I have heard envious descriptions of life in France. Friends describe how the local family they stayed with would decide in the afternoon what was wanted for dinner. On the way home from work, one parent might stop by the local baker for a fresh baguette; another stop at the local cheese or wine shop. And arriving home with the freshest of food — specific to the desires of the day — they would enjoy a wonderful meal together.

Whole "quaint" towns or waterfronts have been rebuilt to re-create this world with unique shops. They are an attempt to make each walk an adventure with specialties and quirky individualities of stores a centerpiece for tourists, creating an ambiance of slower, more restful lives. Of course, we also spend money in such places but with a greater fullness of sensory experience and fun.

In the craziness of our busy lives these days, few of us can or do take the time for such an existence. Instead we have created a culture or fallen victim to marketing that tells us in advance what our options are and entice us into chain stores. Moving frequently and commuting over longer distances, our lives have become elongated. Rather than build a relationship with a unique shopkeeper in a unique business, we develop relationships with a brand name or a chain store: a predictable relationship of trust that we can fulfill our needs whenever we find a free moment to pop in and purchase a uniformly-produced branded product quickly so we can hop back into our car or onto the bus and get back to our overly busy lives.

Most of us know, I think, that when we spend at chain and franchise stores, the money mostly goes into coffers far from where we live or work. I was struck especially, though, by the following description by some friends.

The Philippines remains a fairly rural struggling economy with city centers, now common in developing countries, where those seeking work or a "better life" than the countryside too often end up in desperate living circumstances on the edge in squatter-like communities. The main metropolis of Manila, the capital city, is like this. Apparently, when word went out that Walmart was going to build its first store—a super Walmart—people were excited by the usual fanfare of increased economic opportunity and jobs. However, when the store finally opened, something much more graphic happened than what we usually experience with Walmart stores. Each day at the end of business, the cash receipts were literally placed in a crate, driven to the airport, lifted on to a plane and flown off the island, out of the country and across the ocean. I have this image of upturned faces of those who had hoped for an economic influx, starkly disappointed as the plane flies off into the horizon. This situation created a graphic sense of how money flows out of—not into—our communities.

While some chains can provide cheaper prices because of the economic savings that bulk production and purchasing brings, much of the "savings" is reflective of lower wages and, sometimes, the loss of quality of the goods themselves.

What if we turn our attention from the preferred community-building and local character building to a more pragmatic focus: our spending power as consumers? If we can help rebuild the spending power of regular people, our neighbors going about their properly resourced lives will reverse our overall economy's direction. Increased income to the wealthy that goes to tax-shelters and continued accumulation of wealth simply will not flood our markets with spending the way we will.

It turns out that spending at local, independent businesses begets more spending locally which in turn begets even more local spending. There are actually studies that show this—I am not making it up! It makes intuitive sense. Unlike our image of the plane with Walmart's cash-takings flying off into the wild blue yonder at the end of each business day, local business owners naturally take their profits and in the normal course of their local lives are going to spend more of it locally. They are also statistically more likely to have relationships with other local business people and to purchase their own goods and services locally. They give more money and in-kind contributions to local community efforts because they are personally more likely to know about and be invested in them.[21]

Local businesses are more likely to hire locally. They tend to pay somewhat more and to be more flexible employers than chains and franchises because they function more interdependently with their workforce who are also their family, friends, and neighbors.

Spending locally

The practical economic impact of increased spending at local independent businesses is reported repeatedly in anecdotes by those local business owners. Some local advocates have put their mind and energy towards first paying attention to local spending and then working together to create such a shift in consumer spending behavior. There is a growing movement across the country to get local residents to consider buying first from local businesses. Begun in the early 2000s, the Local First movement is seeing success.

Here is what studies show us: The multiplier effect of spending money at local independent businesses can result in as much as three times as much money staying in our local economies, dramatically increasing the quality of our neighborhoods and lives. As of 2009, the most recent study was of the Grand Rapids' area of Western Michigan. Civic Economics reviewed business ledger sheets in four segments of the Kent County economy: pharmacies, grocery stores, restaurants and banks.[22] The study found that:

Spending at local pharmacies generated

- 77 percent more local economic activity
- 330 percent greater local benefit per square foot of store space

Grocery store spending created

- 17 percent greater local impact
- 60 percent advantage in productivity per square foot of store space

Local restaurant spending brought

- 52.4 percent more local economic advantage
- 9 percent more productive use of space

Given the lessened transparency of banking transactions, exact figures for this sector were not possible to extrapolate. Local banks, however, have to invest locally because of the federal Community Reinvestment Act (CRA). Their economic future is tied to their local economy while chain banks, on the other hand, consistently move investments to the highest yield markets in the country — essentially draining money away from many local communities — or when investments almost everywhere seem to provide less return, they can (and these days do) sit on their assets. Local institutions tend to keep lending in order to stay in business. Given the huge assets of national chain banks, the multiplier effect of even small economic benefits from shifting to local banking seems clear.

Putting these specific market segment figures together with other similar studies, the results of the Grand Rapids study are marked. Looking at a simple shift of 10 percent of the $8.4 billion in retail spending to local businesses by the 600,000 residents in the area in 2007, this is what that $840 million shift would produce:[23]

- 1,600 more local jobs increasing employment by 0.5 percent for the county
- $53 million more in local wages
- $137 million more in economic activity as well — benefiting the entire local economy

These results mirror other studies in Chicago, San Francisco, Phoenix and Austin which sometimes fleshed out other segments of the market and yet yielded similar results.[24]

Clearly, this is an area where local resident action can make a difference in our local communities in a matter of months. We can focus on individual spending — our own and our neighbors. We can support initiatives for our local independent businesses to get together and form a Local First initiative. An initial project of a Local First organization is usually a creation of a local shopping guide which lets us as consumers know which businesses are in fact local and independent. Thus, those Local First campaigns create a tool to support local shopping exploration as if we were adventurous tourists in our own communities, rediscovering our own local gems. Get to know that genuinely local pharmacist before all our local drug stores go out of business! Or make a friend of your local general store manager again. Or reach for a little more adventurous courage in your travels, explore a local restaurant instead of a chain. In doing so make your small contribution to the local economy.

As our cities and towns struggle to balance their own budgets, our own spending behavior can offset some of the losses from reduced state local aid. As housing values continue to plummet and erode the local property-tax base, and until we make distant lenders stop emptying and destroying our neighborhoods, local spending may be a key tool we have to make a significant difference.

Consider as well the economics of small businesses in the context of our economic mess. Local businesses, depending on whose study you believe, provide between 60 to 80 percent of new jobs. While the impact of a relatively big retailer moving in may seem impressive, it is nowhere near as reliable as growth provided by local businesses. Many of the big retailer's "new" jobs may simply be picking up workers displaced from local independent competitors. This is the proven economic impact of new casinos — often providing no net increase in jobs after initial construction but undermining the local economy and tax base.[25]

We all know the anecdotal stories of local business owners putting what profits they have made back into the business to help it grow. This is even truer in bad economic times — and there are studies as well as stories that document this: small business owners will invest significantly more money to keep their business afloat. They will increase their hours, solicit the assistance of family members, and cut their own and their own family's wages before risking losing the business.[23] A recent study showed that many small business owners will go without any income from their business for months as the downturn hurts their businesses. With the increased financial commitment of their own income and savings and the hidden economic resources of their own and their family's labor, local independent businesses are actually better suited to survive and provide the first real new jobs if and when the economy improves.

Can you imagine our big banks' CEOs giving up their salaries, plowing back in those stock deals, giving up their own Cadillac health packages and then getting their senior staff, board members and more importantly, major shareholders to do the same? The laugh you are holding back tells you exactly why we should be more committed to our own local independent businesses who will re-invest in our own local economy at levels that some of the wealthiest will not even consider.

What does this mean for state and municipal policy? How often have we heard — over and over — that we cannot tax big businesses and must instead provide all sorts of economic incentives to get them to stay or site in our communities? Where do most of tax incentive packages go? And when people, including those I ran against for governor in 2006, refer to "pad-ready" building sites, made "pad-ready" through the investment of tax dollars — they were not referring to those kind of investments in our local independent businesses, let me assure you.

Siting Incentives

The reality of tax incentives, tax increment financing (TIFs) and industry specific tax loopholes is that they are not a deciding factor in the location of large businesses, nor the keeping of jobs or tax revenues. They are, however, benefiting large corporate entities not the small businesses that we and our economy need the most. As such, they cost not only taxpayer money but are likely undermining economic opportunities for our local independent businesses.

I was struck by this when I went to the State House for the hearing on closing the telecom loophole in our state tax system — that is, making phone service providers pay taxes on their property and assets, as other companies do instead of benefiting from a tax loophole that was created when phone service was still a public utility. As always, if I have time, I like to go hear testimony before I testify; it gives me a sense of the flow of the presentations, what has already been said (so I do not repeat it) and what have been the salient arguments by the other side. It also gives me a chance to gauge the reaction by the legislative committee members and which arguments are reaching them that I most need to either reinforce or expose.

The Verizon executive who introduced herself as being in charge of operations in Massachusetts and Rhode Island spoke at length. She presented figures showing how much the increased tax burden would impact Verizon's budget, their profits, and what percentage it would be of their investments. She spoke of Verizon's financial projections, the future of investments they were contemplating — some for which legislators had fought as upgrades for their own communities. She implied that these might all be endangered by closing the telecomm tax loophole.

Finally, legislators were given an opportunity to ask their own questions. After a few of them had made their inquiries, one of them asked what turned out to be the most revealing question. Since this Verizon executive ran operations in two states, he asked her to compare the relative impacts of the different tax liabilities imposed by the two states and how that impacted comparatively their business choices in both states.

She replied immediately that one simply could not compare them at all — that the business environments were completely different; that what affected Verizon's decisions was the overall quality-of-life issues in the two states, not tax packages. For instance, she said, Massachusetts is one of the most expensive states in the country to live in, given the cost of housing and transportation; Verizon looked at the quality of schools and other opportunities. The two states were simply too different to compare those kind of decision-making factors, she noted. And then she returned to her discussion of Verizon's opposition to increased taxes.

Of course, all the studies underscore that large corporations do not in fact make location decisions based on tax costs but on other larger economic and quality of life factors.[27] As someone once pointed out, we would hope that taxes which represent a tiny percentage of large corporate budgets would certainly *not* be that decisive a factor; if they were that would be a sign of true fiscal incompetence. Still, I had not expected such a crystal clear and forthright response from a top executive at a legislative hearing. I underscored her statement in my own testimony hoping to emphasize its compelling implications.

In 2008, our legislature finally took some action on the bait-and-switch bookkeeping procedures that Walmart and other large corporations have used in recent years to vastly undercut the amount of taxes they have to pay.[28] Court rulings in recent suits had pointed out that a corporation making a division on paper into different entities to avoid paying taxes is not legal. Most commonly this is done to transfer ownership of assets or even income from a locale where they are taxed to one where they are not. The answer used increasingly by states has been imposition of combined reporting; that requires a company to combine all its and its subsidiaries' financial transactions and then allocate the percentage that they transact overall in a particular state and pay taxes on that percentage. Apparently the version our legislature passed was not as strong or clear-cut as it could be but made significant progress in closing the loophole.

Then, the legislature turned around and lowered the overall corporate tax rate! It is mind-boggling to me, and, I imagine, to others, that having forcibly removed the hand from the cookie jar they then took the cookies themselves and divided most of them among all the corporations. You would think the legislative goal was to bring the language of the law in line with its intent that large corporations doing business in our state pay their portion of state taxes. You would also think our elected leaders would not somehow turn around and pay large corporations off for having finally had to do what they should have been doing all along! That lowering of the corporate tax rate was not a temporary measure. In 2009, and for years to come, these large corporations will pay less unless our legislators wake up and require that they pay closer to a reasonable share of our state's tax burden. After all, if they do care about quality of life issues in Massachusetts, and if they are going to do business here, they should have to pay a reasonable share of the costs.

Surely, as we become more informed participants in our society and government, especially as we untangle our economic reality and become greater players in it, we need to latch onto these widely proven facts. Even though these facts contradict so much that we have been and will be told by many of those who have led us into this economic mess. Our elected officials have also had this misinformation drummed into their heads. We need to lead them with a new drumbeat.

Every day tax subsidized prices: Walmart

It seems to be particularly easy to focus on Walmart. They have notorious labor practices. During 2009 they were touted as leading up a new mechanism of determining their workers' hours. Instead of providing normal work hours and a reliable (if low) wage for their workers, Walmart moved to a complicated formula to cut labor costs. They crafted a computer program so everyone would work split, and often incredibly disparate, hours so that during high-volume relatively short periods of the day and week workers would be scheduled in larger numbers — whenever during the week or weekend or night these hours might fall. This "economic efficiency" breakthrough, of course, wreaked havoc not only with the attempts of workers and their families to lead a semblance of normal lives, but also meant workers' pay became dangerously unpredictable. Even before this policy, unions had worked to unionize Walmart store-by-store and had begun to make some inroads. Hopefully, such a work scenario does not represent our job-life of the future!

We are not surprised that Walmart pays poor wages, or about the sweatshop conditions in the countries where products sold at Walmart are made. However, there is a further reality we uncovered a few years ago: Walmart is subsidized by tax payer dollars. Through today's economic lens, we would call the multiple, often hidden forms of corporate subsidy a bail-out with our tax dollars.

As part of a larger coalition that was looking at welfare, low-wage and union worker policies at the state level in the late 1990s, we had begun to dig up how workers received health coverage at their jobs (if they did). A startling study came out showing that many of the largest employers in our state were not only not providing any health insurance to their workers but that they were getting away with it because they were feeding at the public trough![29] Some of our bigger employers traditionally provide health coverage to their employees partly because their more organized and often higher-paid workers had continued to expect it, and if necessary, fight for it. An uneven playing field was created by some large employers such as Walmart who do not offer health coverage. Because the chain was neither paying decent wages nor providing medical coverage, they had positioned most of their workforce to be eligible for and to get medical care through accessing state-funded health care such as MassHealth (Medicaid)! It was not simply that Walmart was paying poor wages in order to charge lower prices and still make significant profits; the corporation had policies to leverage your and my tax dollars to subsidize their low prices!

This health care subsidy became even more infuriating when it came to light that we, the taxpayers, were essentially paying taxes for them as they exercised complicated bookkeeping practices to write-off all those big, fancy stores located in our state. How did they do it?

Essentially Walmart broke itself on paper into separate legal entities. The mother company transferred the title of its properties to a shell holding company which had no employees but held title to the properties. When Walmart filled out its tax forms for business transactions in our state, it deducted the rent from all its stores in Massachusetts using tax loopholes to claim that it was paying rent to a "separate" company that owned the land. This holding company claimed Delaware as its home — a tax-free zone much like the Cayman Islands — and then paid back the Massachusetts rent as corporate dividends to Walmart stores in our state, making it untaxed income for the store owners.

Take an example in 2006. In Massachusetts, Walmart said it paid nearly $19 million in state and local taxes that year. Assuming roughly $11 million of that was state income tax, the retailer also avoided $5.4 million by deducting rent it paid to its Delaware-based real-estate holding company as a business expense, lowering its taxable income in Massachusetts. The company also cost taxpayers $7.2 million in health care costs for 6,000 Massachusetts Walmart workers and dependents on Medicaid. The net result is that Massachusetts taxpayers actually lost money on the 45 Walmart stores located here.[30]

How often do we hear that borrowers should have been worried about subprime mortgages that were too good to be true? Yet we have clearly been given corporate pitches that were too good to be true for a long time — and they are counting on our not smartening up! Walmart's "low, every day prices" are just one more example of hidden taxpayer subsidies where we are literally paying the biggest players to make money off of us!

Rain, Pollution, and Climate

Over a month of rain and more to come. In June and July 2009 as I sat through another evening downpour, my Facebook site and personal emails from friends were chock-a-block full with postings about the rain in the Northeast. Finally, I started posting in response that this is global warming coming back at us. Someone took the plunge and asked directly how this could be global warming, all this unseasonable rain?!

I am reminded always of people's responses to my example from the 2006 gubernatorial debate in which I pointed out that if global warming went ahead unabated we in Massachusetts might not have our traditional fall foliage. I remember the shock and dismay, sometimes fear and in some cases annoyance and denial that I triggered. As a city dweller myself, I know how hard it can be to sense global warming locally; I brought it home by pointing out that fall foliage as we know it may be gone in 20 years if we do not act. While to some this felt alarmist, for many this was the first example they could put their hands around. The climate debate had felt vague and scientific; the only regular people deeply concerned about it seemed to be environmentalists or polar-bear lovers.

Oddly, the next day a report came out of the Union of Concerned Scientists whose worst case scenario underscored exactly the same thing. When the newspapers called the next day, I could point them to that report — our hardwoods, Massachusetts hardwoods, as we know them, could be essentially gone. Of course, then I had to explain to one reporter what a hardwood is and have her look up the common Massachusetts varieties.

The Union of Concerned Scientists created the map in Figure 5.2 in 2006 based on now somewhat out of date global warming data. It shows two possible future scenarios for our state's weather: one, where we expedite changes needed to lower our carbon emissions quickly; one where we do not.

Figure 5.2   UCS Massachusetts climate scenarios[31]

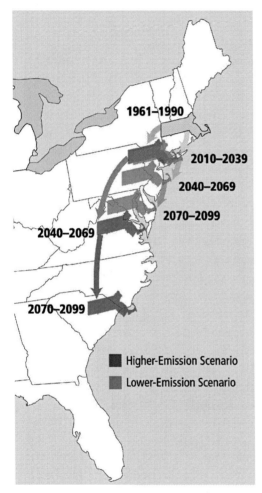

Changes in average summer heat index—a measure of how hot it actually feels, given temperature and humidity—could strongly affect quality of life in the future for residents of the Northeast. Red arrows track what summers could feel like in Massachusetts over the course of the century under the higher-emissions scenario. Yellow arrows track what summers in Massachusetts could feel like under the lower-emissions scenario. The higher-emissions scenario assumes continued heavy reliance on fossil fuels, causing heat-trapping emissions to rise rapidly through this century. The lower emissions scenario assumes a shift away from fossil fuels in favor of clean energy technologies, causing emissions to decline by mid-century.

I had used the fall foliage example because polar bears are far away and so are melting glaciers, although anyone who has even seen footage of glaciers "calving" and falling off into the ocean has to be impressed.

How is global warming predicted to look in Massachusetts?

Ten years ago, early on before an international consensus of scientists was building (U.S. scientists lag way behind), National Public

Radio was interviewing a climate scientist about global warming. The interviewer asked, at the end, what many of us think when we first hear the term: Did this mean that every year it was going to get ever so slightly warmer? The scientist had replied: Well, in New England, no, the climate models predicted it would get more temperate. A temperate climate has more moderate temperatures and much more rain — more like the west coast climate.

Scientists, in predicting what Massachusetts will face, point to increasing sea levels; it is in part why private home insurers moved out of the Cape Cod market in recent years — leaving people dependent on the state-provided insurance (another shift of the for-profit market out of the less profitable parts of their field and abandoning need which our taxpayer dollars are often forced to pick up!). An additional effect of global warming will be wetter wet spells and drier dry spells. Also, it turns out, higher concentrations of carbon in the air are best tolerated by ragweed, poison ivy, and many other plants that humans have allergies to; not to mention increased wetness exacerbates molds and mildew problems.

The impacts of global warming are becoming more marked; the really bad news is that every benchmark that scientists identify in their climate models are coming faster and in larger scale than scientists predict — from ice melt to loss of coral reefs.

The most dramatic measures seem far away and our tendency to assume that change is linear confuses us. The capacity of human beings to ignore or in more extreme cases deny change that is either very small, very slow or very far away is well documented.

In fact, the more the system of our planet's climate as a whole becomes stressed, the more that predictable or "regular" weather patterns will break down. The "regular" climate of regions will shift fast enough to be easily perceptible by us in our regular lives. Then we will experience more unusual even outlandish weather incidents. Nothing in a complexly interactive and interdependent system occurs in some linear, step-by-step fashion.

On the other hand, understanding that change is not linear and that most systems in our life are too complicated for linear ways of measuring to work does not require advanced degrees. Our formal education may tell history as if it were a linear progression of distinct events but our experience of the larger forces of nature tell us this is not an accurate portrayal of even human history.

Cycles of change

You can ask a small child who grew up by the ocean if the breaking of a wave and the rolling of it up the beach means the tide is coming in; they will know to tell you that it does not. If they have not been watching the beach for a while, they may go look for the reasonably recent mark in the sand that is the farthest inland mark of the edge of a wave. They will tell you to sit down with them and wait and watch. I knew from my childhood that waves came in cycles, starting smaller and then growing and then getting smaller again — regardless of the overall size of waves on a particular day. The child will sit with you through a cycle or two of waves; they will point to the earlier highest up mark. If the edge of the most recent large waves surpassed it, they will tell you the tide is coming in; if the waves did not reach it, they will tell you the tide is going out.

So too, over the decades, you can watch a beach and tell if the beach is building up. Neither a regular incremental removal of a few grains of sand by each wave nor the devastation created after a hurricane determines the beach's future. Neither incremental predictable forces nor single incidents tell us the overall pattern of change. Even when we argue over global warming, we, all of us, have experience that tells us that not one hot summer, one extra cold winter nor one unusual storm is an accurate predictor of larger systemic change.

Larger measures tell us that unprecedented ice melt is occurring at the poles of the earth much faster than climate change models predicted. Remember our child on the beach? These are like world-scale high water marks. Like the marks on the beach, they cannot be easily tracked to tell the tide by those of us swimming among the breakers. However, weather balloons spread across the earth together show overall increases in temperature. We know pollution — especially carbon in our air — is increasing and trapping heat. Water levels are rising and the cycles of water that heat and cool oceans across our world are shifting. This has far-reaching effects in weather as the oceans' temperatures' warming and cooling impacts temperatures and the life cycles of many thousands of species.

Instead of arguing over how much of global warming is created by human impacts, suppose only part of this effect is because of human pollution? Given the potential gravity of sea level rising two meters or temperature rises wiping out Massachusetts' indigenous hard woods, would it not make sense to stop contributing whatever we can to this incredibly destabilizing and destructive change? Especially when increasing carbon in our air is contributing to serious increases in asthma, especially in children? Increasing pollen and mold levels in our air and living quarters? And hurting our health in other ways?

As well, by lowering our carbon footprint, we lower our dependence on foreign oil and liquid natural gas, decrease our military interventions, protect our shorelines and arctic wildlife, stop the damage created by coal and uranium mining, and lower our energy costs. If we bring our regular lives — working, shopping, childcare facilities — back into our neighborhoods, we increase our time for ourselves and each other and help recreate vital local economies. If we shift energy sources today, we should be able to remove our dependence on limited and diminishing global resources like oil and coal before their scarcity causes higher prices, more human conflict and dangerous senses of scarcity.

Rather than argue over the size of the human contribution to global warming, this can be our moment to shift many imbalances in our lives back toward healthier and more sustainable ones.

Urgency and the possibility of change

After years of supporting those most impacted by social issues to work for change, I understand a sense of urgency. I have worked on issues where my coworkers were directly impacted by our successes or failures, or even delays in the coming of those changes. Some of them died ... and I helped the families bury them...

The vastness of system impacts and changes to our planet's ecosystem and the sweeping life-threatening impacts of our economic meltdown can overwhelm us. The sense of destruction and urgency for action can be immobilizing when we stretch our necks back as we try to look up high enough to see the top of the tsunami — or should I say tsunamis — that are bearing down on us.

I can only offer a few insights that may or may not be of use. First, humans (together) got us into this mess and so we, of course, have the capacity (together) to get out of it.

Second, the depth of human capacity cannot be measured by our regular daily lives. Our true capacity is only measured in periods of extreme challenge. In times like these, if we harness the best in ourselves, our capacity may prove almost limitless.

I think back to the story of World War II. The United States was asked to fight a war across a vast ocean; it was a war we were going to have to fight. We were a young industrialized nation with almost no planes. And yet, our president knew we were going to need to get across an ocean. So he called on us, as a people, to build 50,000 planes in four years: a task that seemed impossible at the time. The government, in fact, changed time to do it, instituting year-round daylight savings time. With the dedication of pretty much every aspect of our economy, you know what we did? We built 100,000 planes. As that wonderful children's book, *The Phantom Tollbooth*, says: *Impossible only means it hasn't been done* yet.[32]

Finally, I remember the words of that song that says, *"We are in danger, we must work slowly."* In haste not only may we reinforce our past mistakes but change only moves as quickly as we work to make it move. It cannot go any faster. As I have said to many who toil diligently for a better world, no matter how many responsibilities you pile on your back, you can still only do as much as one person can; there is no point to piling on more.

Our faith in each other and in the greater good will have to carry us through the coming times. For surely, there will be times when our sense of hope will fail us, but we can still succeed if we persevere.

Where is Massachusetts' energy use and pollution?

Massachusetts gets its electricity from the electric grid and is mostly generated within New England. We have no real coal nor petroleum sources, nor uranium for local power generation. Today's transportation fuel and heating fuel are mostly from other parts of the world.

We think of energy production and transportation as the major contributors to global warming. But we have underestimated the contribution of other factors: insufficient energy conservation and weatherization, insufficient recycling, loss of trees and green space, continuing sprawl development, and toxic use and pollution that effects the usability of what we have left; the ongoing impact of these last two will have more dramatic effects as we near the limits of our natural resources like peak water or loss of enough open space for ecosystems to self-perpetuate.

In Massachusetts, our energy is generated from the following fuel sources:

Figure 5.3 Fuel sources for Massachusetts electric power generation 2005 (trillion Btu) [33]

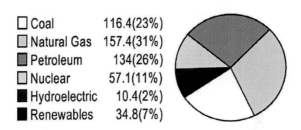

☐ Coal	116.4	(23%)
☐ Natural Gas	157.4	(31%)
◼ Petroleum	134	(26%)
☐ Nuclear	57.1	(11%)
◼ Hydroelectric	10.4	(2%)
◼ Renewables	34.8	(7%)

There has been some renewable increase since 1990, but most of our renewable energy still comes from hydro-power. Figure 5.4 shows how our different social uses of fossil fuels contribute to the carbon we release into the air.

Figure 5.4 New England carbon dioxide emissions by sector, 2004[34]

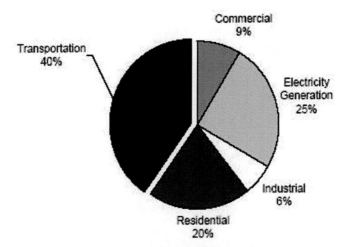

Source: Environment Massachusetts Research & Policy Center and Clean Water Fund

When we talk about the need to transition from fossil fuels and strive for a zero carbon contribution (footprint), the feasibility and transition costs of renewable energy are always raised. In the face of existing energy industry opposition, cap and trade and other formulas and regulations have been proposed.

What if renewable energy could already provide for us?

From childhood, I was intrigued by renewable energy. Maybe it was the pollution of New York City, my home; maybe it was my mother who was more environmentally aware than many of us brought up in cities. Maybe it was about the dangers of nuclear fusion power while I was too young to be jaded. In more recent years, as larger segments of our society started seriously looking at a significant transition to renewable energy, I became particularly interested.

Hydro-Power

The largest source of renewable energy production in Massachusetts is hydropower, water-propelled turbines that generate electricity. No surprise, since our history whispers around us in community after community of a time when these thousands of mill buildings were the center of our state's economy; each was fueled by a river and its water driven turbines.

There is an impetus in our state to save our rivers where their fisheries and natural life can still be saved; the procedure is to remove dams and free up the living length of rivers and streams for fish to swim. On the other hand, a study by our national civil engineers showed that some 100 to 300 dams had additional potential to provide hydro-energy in Massachusetts.[35] A number of these will be found to conflict with the Massachusetts Riverways Program salvaging priorities.[36] Many other existing dams will be usable and are locally owned by neighborhoods or even municipalities. These create local opportunities for development of renewable energy where long term savings can accrue to local residents.

In addition, water turbine technology is also improving. Without changing the flow and drop of our rivers, low-flow hydro-power opportunities exist. Partial dams with proper protection for fisheries may allow for additional hydro-generation. Micro-turbines are also available, the possible uses of which are only beginning to be explored. Even without conflicting with uses for our waterways, a great deal more hydro-production is available.

Wind Power

Although I have not seen it, friends who have visited Scandinavia say that windmills are a frequent part of the shore line landscape. The beautiful, white, and amazingly quiet turbines provide a noticeable percentage of those countries' energy as of 2009. Those countries are the primary location of present day production of such turbines. They are graceful and are not so much a distraction from the seashore's beauty as a seemingly integral part of it.

Denmark is probably farthest along and so far is only providing slightly less than 10 percent of its energy needs from wind.[37] But like our most successful wind energy-based community in the United States, the town of Hull, Denmark has built so much energy production from wind quickly because it incentivized wind-power through neighborhood and municipal ownership. Although total public ownership has dropped a little recently, 75 percent of Denmark's wind energy is publicly owned and savings therefore benefit the public as opposed to private investors.[38]

Like Denmark of centuries past, New England was famous for its windmills from over a century ago: the town wind-powered mill was where all households took their flour to be ground. No one would have considered complaining that these mills somehow disrupted and ruined the picturesque nature of their community. In fact, like lighthouses, for decades they have been a tourist draw, taking us back to another time.

Those who have studied our winds in New England and mapped their velocities believe *we could today provide for all our electricity* by simply harnessing existing wind energy.[39] This is looking at wind production from the relatively large white windmills that Hull and some other communities have erected in heavy wind areas. A next generation of windmills is also under construction. These windmills are even larger and are placed offshore at some distance but could provide even larger amounts of energy without needing so many windmills.

It is equally possible, however, to go smaller and have business- or residential-size turbines; these are not terribly expensive and provide a fairly predictable and not insignificant amount of savings at the household level. Unfortunately, many Massachusetts communities have not addressed the zoning changes to allow for such installations. These small turbines have significant advantages. They do not require high wind speeds to function at peak capacity. They bring savings directly to the households that install them.

They also address another problem: long distance electricity transport dissipates power. In heavy concentration, it changes magnetic fields significantly with impacts of which we only have initial investigations of. Should we not move toward greater neighborhood and household control of our energy with all its benefits?

Companies diversify their activities for good survival purposes; similarly, if households weatherize and utilize other energy saving measures combined with wind or solar generation, we can move many of us toward a significantly shrunken carbon footprint.

A whole field of architects and builders has developed incorporating numerous passive solar and energy saving designs. If you are building from scratch or doing an entire overhaul of an existing home, the opportunities to change your energy consumption will boggle your mind if you explore them. Some are more expensive but many are design shifts that do not cost a cent more!

Geothermal Energy

Existing geothermal energy production is mostly being pioneered in the U.S. West, where geological conditions are most favorable; there the deep underground flows with tremendous heat, while far underground (thousands of feet), are not so far as to be prohibitive.[40] While there have been recent technological advances in drilling techniques to make future geothermal energy more financially feasible, such geothermal energy production is unlikely to ever be appropriate for our geological part of the country.

However, geothermal energy as a more passive energy source is already being tapped in Massachusetts. The overhaul of the 1826 Whitin Mill in Northbridge as a community complex will have as its energy centerpiece a modern water-driven generator — not far from the old water turbine that drove the mill itself almost two centuries ago. In addition, they are drilling down several hundred feet to underground water that stays a constant 55 degrees as an ancillary source of energy. It can provide a regular 55 degree water source: the basis for all air conditioning in the summer and with only a relatively small increase in temperature, the basis for heating in the winter.[41]

This kind of geothermal water source has potential in large areas of the state; it provides significant savings, even including initial drilling and equipment costs. There is no real danger of geological disruption from this use. For larger developments where subterranean water is reasonably accessible it can provide an excellent renewable, locally owned resource.

Heat Island effect

I remember as a child driving back from Long Island to New York City in the heat of summer. No matter how incredibly hot it got on the end of Long Island, I always felt I was able to breathe, move around and there was hope of relief from the heat — especially at night. But in "the city" it would be blistering and on the drive back I knew with some dread what we were headed for.

As we got closer, first you would see what appeared like an arc in the sky enclosing what seemed like a greyer atmosphere. At some point it would feel like you had hit an invisible wall, a thick curtain through which you could physically feel your passage. The air smelled different, bad. The density of the air seemed to weigh down your breathing and condense on your skin. I had no problem understanding what was meant by the term "heat inversion." It felt like the universe itself was reflecting the heat back down to you in the city, the air trapped so that even at night there was often no real escape. One of my most dreaded memories of the worst of the hot days in New York City was when it would rain even in the afternoon.

Rather than providing relief, you could hear the water sizzle as it hit the pavement and immediately turn into steam. The rain would stop and there would be no darkening of the cement because it was dry already. But you were not. You were coated in endless sweat from the more than 90 percent humidity *without* rain.

New York City, of course, is huge and the "heat island" effect was obvious even to a child. All that wall to wall dark asphalt and cement, mostly straggly trees trying to make a life out of squared holes of the cement and, no doubt, black tarred roof tops. All of these surfaces served to absorb as much heat as possible during the day, only to release some of it during the night; this reversed any possibility of expected cooling and, of course, pollution as well trapped the heat and reflected it back.

What was more striking to me, because it was more subtle, was living as an adult in Massachusetts. In Cambridge first and then in Somerville, the number of oppressively hot days followed by oppressively hot nights were very few every summer. But when I could, I planned to spend nights that promised to not cool down at the houses of board members of my non-profit out in Metrowest.

It was not until I met my then-girlfriend who lived just outside of Route 128 that I realized a marked, if subtle, phenomenon. The weather when I crossed over Route 128 was often noticeably different. It was most obvious with snow: I would find that while it had been snowing at home, it was sticking and accumulating outside Route 128. Or rain would start after crossing over the highway. Cloud accumulations would often change. At first, I seriously thought it was my imagination or a fluke of timing. But it happened frequently enough that I started to notice that weather forecasters often gave reports demarcated by Route 128 or I-495.

It was not simply shorthand on the part of the weather reporters, nor my personal insanity. Boston, too, has a heat island effect — far more subtle than New York. In fact, studies show that not just mountain ridges can change cloud formations and tip a downpour but that Route 128 and I-495 create curtains of heat rising up from the ground that alter weather behavior, trapping heat or tipping downpours. If black asphalt roadways with associated heavy automobile traffic at rush hours and industry can noticeably alter weather patterns, the potential weather impacts of our daily collective unconscious behaviors is a little frightening.

To lift our human footprint and significantly decrease our impact on weather patterns, a simple opportunity is to change colors: it only requires a little public education. Black asphalt absorbs significantly more heat on our roads than more cement based formulas. More significantly, black asphalt roofing materials make the top floors of our buildings like ovens in the summer. They unnecessarily contribute to our heat island. In cities, they represent more square footage than our streets. Imagine an aesthetic movement for white and light gray tile roofs.

The green roofs movement had even more dramatic results. While some cities in Europe have moved over to grass and garden planting on roofs with dramatic decreases in heating and cooling costs, my favorite example comes from the Midwest.

In Chicago, the story goes that City Hall fills half of a huge building. Like many buildings in our cities, the roof was sealed with a coating of black tar. Needless to say, at the height of summer those roofs really heat up, absorbing the sun's rays. This roof gets as hot as 170 degrees. Standard air-conditioning set up in large buildings is the opposite of ecological or economic sense. Air is drawn in from outside through vents and is then cooled to supply the air conditioning system. This air is drawn from — you guessed it — the vents on these sizzling tar roofs.

The Chicago city government prioritized not only a green roof to be built for the top of City Hall but they tested the green roof's temperature against the still black-tar roof on the other half of the building. When temperatures were taken on the hottest days, the temperature differential was 50 degrees. Not only did City Hall avoid that heat bearing down through its roof, but the air it drew in for its air-conditioning system was that much cooler.[42] The cumulative impact on the heat island of numerous green roofs in a city like Chicago would be significant. The savings in air conditioning for City Hall already are.

Solar Power and the size of the problem

I remember when considering the large amounts of energy production needed for conversion to 100 percent renewable energy, people started bandying around options for sufficient magnitude. Of course, one problem with large-scale renewable energy production like solar energy has been the square-footage needed to output significant wattage with existing technology. People started focusing on large open spaces. One idea that I know has caught the fancy of some big investors has been the "unproductive" land occupied by desert. The image fills one's head of miles of otherwise pure white sand covered with end to end photovoltaic panels wired together. As this image unfolded in my mind's eye, like a slow roving camera, over meter after meter of black glass slabs stretching as far as the eye could see in every direction, my stomach curled in on itself. I thought not of energy production but heat islands and huge weather impacts and dangerous heat increases in already arid deserts.

On the other hand, my childhood reminded me that we already have large black covered spaces — they are roofs and they are in great abundance in our cities. While you can build a garden on the flat roof of an office building, many of our pitched roofs will not sustain a garden. But local roofs with small solar units or household size windmills do not require huge rebuilding projects. They will not require huge utilities being willing to change their investments or us continuing to assign our energy future or environmental impacts to their desires for profit margins.

If we can get past wanting to have someone else in charge of producing our energy and our belief that their expertise is necessary to accomplish energy production, our own alternative energy production makes more sense. It fits better with regaining our democratic control over our future. Since technologies in these areas have become quite stable and straightforward, why should we as people not benefit from the long-term savings instead of big corporations?

Solar panels properly installed on roofs or even in gardens — that are angled to get the most advantageous angle of the sun for our part of the planet — are more affordable. New technology makes them relatively maintenance free. A reasonable estimate is a third of your annual energy use can come from a solar installation.[43] It is estimated that savings from regular energy conservations measures can save from 30 to 50 percent of your energy bill.[44] So depending on how much savings you get from conservation measures in your home, some households can easily provide more than half their energy needs from a solar installation. There are also good "passive" solar installations (capturing direct heat from the sun) that can provide for most water heating.

One recent study looked at renewable energy generation options for Massachusetts. It estimates that we could get 21 percent of our needed energy from that solar energy alone.[45] Even the study's authors pointed out that this is the most decentralized solution — granting the most control to regular people. While costly for individuals to install, the cost becomes substantially affordable if subsidized by tax dollars that could be saved from electricity costs taxpayers presently subsidize. For instance, we all currently pay for electricity transmission and Congress is considering increasing significantly our contribution as taxpayers. This subsidy is *only* beneficial to the huge energy operations to continue our apparently unnecessary dependence on long distance production.

While using small, personally-owned or neighbor-owned energy opportunities, residents can still use electricity from our national energy grid. Laws exist in our state to provide for two-way electric meters so that when your home solar panel or windmill is providing more energy than you need at the time, you do not need elaborate batteries to save the additional energy. That energy can feed into the grid and then be used to lower your payments when your household needs to draw energy off of the electric grid.

One note on this as we transition to these locally owned, roof-mounted solar panels and windmills: remember that the trees that overhang our roofs and grow up near our homes also provide significant cooling in the summer (cutting air conditioning costs 13 to 15 percent) and heating in the winter (saving 30 percent of heating costs).[46] Psychologically, local trees in developed areas also help us as human beings feel better; they actually improve school performance, especially of girls, and decrease crime!

> *As one solar installation company owner said, "Just remember, I want you to buy our product. But do not take down a tree to do it — you will get more reliable energy savings from having that tree shade your roof!"*

Tree Loss: Worcester's example

Worcester and our trees are a perfect example.

Urban trees are invaluable—they do everything from help clear pollution from our air to help warm and cool the houses they grow near. They actually help students do better in school. While talking about trees could get you accused of being a fuzzy-headed tree-hugger, Worcester found itself in 2009 right in the path of the Asian Longhorned Beetle infestation. Reaching up from New York City, it has apparently been in the Worcester area for a decade. Not only are large swaths and a high percentage of susceptible trees infested, but there is a question of how to save those that are not infested but could be. While our local government was getting briefed and trees were being marked for infestation, in some areas the federal government started essentially clear-cutting.

At this point, the psychological, the community and the emotional impact of clear-cutting our urban trees has been marked and impossible to ignore. Besides the complex containment measures that have to go along with cutting, it turns out that even though we are the second largest city in New England, the federal planners decided we were (our trees, that is) not "worthy" of the inoculation option. The clear-cutting that we thought was a mistake was not a mistake in their eyes. In New York City, they were doing the more costly innoculation of trees but they said they could not afford to do it in Worcester (do not get me started but this is the federal government that can afford to give trillions to Wall Street to bail them out...).

Part of Worcester's problem is that our most prevalent trees are maples (unhealthily lacking biodiversity because of overdependence on one species). The ancient maples that arch beautifully over our streets and houses are signature for their fall colors and profoundly interwoven with our sense of place. However, if the infestation of our trees creates a bridge north, it threatens the economic base of significant parts of Vermont and Massachusetts near the border. The federal government's critical focus was to protect those huge stands of maple trees—sugar producers and their tourist base.

Of course, we have seen infestations and tree diseases brought in or spread from farther away before and without a built up immunity, those have had severe impacts as well.

But something is also different here. Do we think of the impacts of global warming as gradual changes, not, for instance, that one day the predicted hardwood trees will simply fall down and die? Likewise, increasing sea levels will not mean that one wave will simply arrive one day bringing a meter or two of standing water with it and it will never leave.

No, the problem is that as the climate changes, historically, gradual changes will become more rapid. Our maple trees are stressed by weather that is not what they are used to (just as we stressed by not getting to see the sun as much as we are used to or how walking around with nagging allergies wears us down). This stressing and weakening over time of their regular health and defenses means that things like the onslaught of a new disease or infestation is likely to overpower many more of our trees and kill them. In the past they might have been able to build up a resistance as a species. This weakness made it appear, for instance, that our ice storm in the fall of 2008 was able to just tear apart an enormous numbers of trees. In fact, the damage was more extensive because more trees were already weaker.

Trees, especially the huge ones, also naturally absorb and store huge carbon concentrations, known as sequestration capacity.[47] I was shocked when I started seeing the tonnage they process and the clean air they release.

- One large sugar maple can remove the airborne lead emitted by cars burning 1000 gallons of gasoline.
- One tree can absorb 50 pounds of particulates per year.
- One tree can absorb 26 pounds of carbon dioxide per year or 2/5 tons per acre, and replace it with oxygen.

A key component of a natural carbon reduction plan would be to emphasize the saving of our largest trees and the growing of new ones.

So we stand at one of a million choice points. Our federal government is racing to cheaply contain the Asian beetle in Worcester; before local action they clear cut many of our largest indigenous trees — to save money from inoculating. During the same period, our federal government was putting out special stimulus grants for research into artificial means of sequestering carbon — a technology not expected to be sorted out for more than a dozen years! We have natural sequestration in Worcester that they slashed (literally). One acre of forest absorbs 2/5 tons of carbon dioxide and gives off 4,280 pounds of oxygen per year.

On the other hand, to re-forest our city a wonderful project has been put in place to plant trees. These are not the little ones that you can often get on Arbor Day which are frequently and too offhandedly not planted or tended properly. These trees are already partially grown; those who receive them also participate in training in how to plant and tend them. Such projects are precious and need their own tending to be sure to succeed and grow. Boston has had such a program for a number of years, and I have suggested Worcester might want to replicate it. Both, I believe, were started before the magnitude of this infestation was known. We must create such programs across the municipalities of our state for their numerous benefits.

Oddly, the Worcester program had not, as of the date of this writing, committed itself to looking at the overall ecological goal of rebuilding our indigenous ecosystem. Instead, it has chosen hardy local species as one set to plant but also "non-invasive" non-indigenous species. While we are going to potentially have wiped out the local hardwood species most prevalent in our city, we may be planting new trees, mostly non-indigenous ones, that will not rejuvenate our present ecosystem.

There is painful irony here. In our lack of attention to the holistic implications of trying to contain the Long Horn beetle **and** of re-populating our city with non-indigenous trees, as human beings we may actually hasten my heartbreaking image of the loss of our fall foliage.

Conservation

Just as trees and conserving green space prevent environmental degradation, conservation in its various forms protects our environment, our health and our economic strength. There are various estimates, but the Massachusetts Climate Action Network says relatively simple home conservation measures can save 30 to 50 percent of household expenditures. That is money we could be more usefully spending locally on our daily lives and fueling our economy.

Conservation includes weatherization, the huge energy savings of replacing appliances, and choices about water use and creation of solid waste — that is, *trash*. We are all familiar with the reduce, re-use, recycle graphic. Clearly we can make more choices to fix rather than throw away things in our lives. We can re-use or pass stuff along to someone else who wants it. Bad economic times tend to foster swaps; by 2007 local clubs and websites existed devoted to finding new homes for what you no longer want — check them out!

Elsewhere I have discussed at length the win-win-win of weatherization and energy conservation through moving to much more efficient appliances. I now want to focus on the longer term movement to increase recycling.

Recycling

Recycling plays a number of roles in improving our environment and our economy. The obvious role is that it lowers the amount of waste we dispose of saving landfill or incineration and the money for that disposal. Additionally, though, some recycled materials such as paper are both heavily in demand and *are purchased by recycling companies.* Equally important is the savings of reproducing products out of recycled waste rather than the more costly production from virgin materials. For communities that make people purchase expensive trash bags, recycling can put more money in the hands of those of us whose spending is needed to turn our economy around.

Through the 1990s, Massachusetts communities were on a constant and significant increase in recycling. However, this has disappointingly leveled off. In a number of communities, rates are dropping. The state average is at 47 percent but some communities like Nantucket, Foxborough, and Needham are at more than 90 percent recycling and reuse.[48]

In 2009, Massachusetts generated more than 12 million tons of solid waste. About half is recovered through recycling, composting and reuse. However, more than half of our potential recyclables still end up in the trash. Two-thirds of potential compostable food and yard waste do too. Particularly important for their environmental impact are aluminum, plastics, glass and paper which when recycled and used for production compared to virgin materials save 95 percent, 70 percent, 40 percent and 30 percent of environmental impact respectively![49] Our solid waste also includes paper products which not only costs $110 million per year to bury or burn but represents about $75 million in lost revenue.[50]

Paper recycling is a perfect example of a win-win-win but I know I did not realize the economics of it until researching it for this project. Demand for recycled paper — which as of 2008 can include even envelopes with cellophane windows, paper with staples and paper clips, cereal and other dry food boxes — makes this a potential cash cow. In 2009 the city of Newton, for example, saved more than $130 per ton in trash disposal costs and gets paid $40 per ton of recycled paper — that is a total of $170 per ton![51] Imagine those savings accruing to your city or town or even a more targeted school funding campaign to save needed services.

Our state Bottle Bill, which requires beverage containers to have a deposit and producers to recycle returned containers, did not cover all beverage containers although it covered the majority at the time it was passed in 1982. Only 35 percent of non-deposit containers have typically been recycled compared to 75 percent of deposit containers. However, the original law does not cover water, juice, tea, and other non-carbonated drink containers which have grown by 2009 to about 30 percent of the market! Updating the bill will save our struggling municipalities from $4.3 million to $7 million per year and generate about $20 million in new state revenue.[52]

All of this connects to larger recycling goals because initially Bottle Bill revenues went directly to statewide education and support activities to increase recycling. In 2002, the state invested $15 million toward recycling outreach and support to communities to purchase bins and provide residents with information. By 2009, only $2.1 million was proposed but only $1.6 million passed as part of the state budget. This is one of those clear examples of needing to spend a little but *save much more.* This short-sighted cut also means lost jobs. Passage of a revised Bottle Bill that covers all the present drink containers would mean not only the significant revenue increase of $20 million per year but that at least $5 million would be earmarked for state recycling activities. Major drink manufacturers will squawk but the focus here remains our future economy, health and local jobs.[53]

Transportation

While much focus has been on alternatively fueled cars, transportation technology is not as far along as alternative electricity production and heat.

Clearly, technology already exists to vastly increase the mileage standard for cars; there are alternative fuels already for diesel vehicles. These higher Corporate Average Fuel Economy (CAFE) standards should already be required. Many options to put economic pressure as well as political pressure on the automotive industry already exist. If the EPA continues to have power to address carbon released into the air, and CAFE standards are allowed to be raised, states are poised to move several state markets out of the reach of vehicles with CAFE standards that are too low; this will quickly shift the economic pressures on all automakers. State governments can use their economic power to purchase entire fleets of vehicles at the highest standards available and negotiate for reduced bulk rate costs. If such requirements are also added to vender contracts for outsourced state government work, then shifting the pollution impact of fleets of vehicles beyond the government's own is also possible.[54]

Private vehicles are the hardest to impact, given that most cars are on the road for about 15 years (even if they change hands several times).[55] As part of moving to Smart Growth where we live nearer to work, shopping, and each other, we can help cut down on the use of private petroleum-dependent cars. While it is well documented that the federal government has long subsidized the private vehicle industry, we as individuals still pay on average $8,000 per year to maintain a private car.[56]

By comparison, forces in our state tried to convince us that saving an average of $3,000 per year was worth the destruction of government services as we have known them when they proposed ending the state income tax in 2008.[57] They did not mention that the $3,000 average was incredibly skewed by the much bigger savings that would go to the inconceivably wealthy minority in our state. Regular people would each have actually only received a few hundred dollars of tax rebate.

But $8,000 dollars in saving is a far more significant amount. Like many things, it is the savings created by pooling resources that makes public transportation several magnitudes cheaper. Zipcars, a car-sharing service, for example, have flourished. Even with additional for-profit cost margins, Zip-car users still experience savings and convenience.

Weaving together existing transportation alternatives

Barcelona, Spain, maintains a fleet of some 6,000 bicycles with 400 parking stations throughout the city; by the end of their second year, they were providing 35,000 rides daily with 186,000 subscribers, about 9 percent of the city's population.[58] Established as a share arrangement, those who become members of the service can pick up a bicycle at a nearby parking station and ride and leave it at the parking station nearest their destination.

Such a system could be combined with an extensive public transportation system. In a number of significant metropolises, well designed subway or tram systems have become the overwhelming and preferred method of travel, including for commuters. With thoughtful planning and a committed vision, these municipalities have instituted bus lanes that give the time advantage to those commuting by bus while individual car drivers face longer traffic delays.

In Massachusetts there are numerous routes where regular travel or heavy commutes would make institution of regular bus service an obvious first step towards a functional public alternative. For instance, Route 44 is a 38-mile stretch of road through Southeastern Massachusetts which runs from Providence, Rhode Island to Plymouth, Massachusetts. The rush hour traffic on this artery can triple the normal travel. However, parking areas at each exit could be used for commuters to board buses. On-demand computer design programs became available shortly after 2000 to input each rider's destination and actually properly place people on buses which could then disperse according to end point locations. This computer system can also easily provide the most efficient post-work rides back to where people's cars were parked.

Studies show that many commuters triangulate. They use their commute to include a third stop — dropping off and picking children up from daycare or shopping for food. But most people also do not triangulate their trip all days of the week. In fact, most drivers average twice a week. An efficient and effective public transportation alternative would create a decisive incentive for commuters to consolidate errands to as few days as possible when they would need use of a private vehicle.

This reality is even more pronounced in twinned communities like Amherst and Northampton where there is significant regular traffic between communities. The answer would be a public transportation alternative that linked these two downtowns; for instance, the destinations in each community could include a provision of some kind of shared, membership arrangement of public both bicycles and Zip-like cars that provide for individually differing endpoints. As scheduling was perfected and shared use arrangements brought into line with real needs, this could become a preferred alternative as well.

In both of these examples, of course, once routes and a rider base are established, the routes could then easily be transformed into rail or even light rail alternatives. These capture not only the efficiency of scale by having larger numbers sharing a vehicle but would also then move to a significantly less energy intensive form of transportation.

For many of our New England communities, trolley tracks lie under our roads, encased in asphalt but many of them are otherwise still in the same functional condition as before they were submerged. The primary argument leveled against trolleys is the complex interaction between the road needs of trolleys and those of cars. In some cases it makes more sense to explore trams or a submerged or raised rail alternative. But the primary complaint of road competition lessens significantly if this is quickly successful and the number of cars on the roads drops.

The primary expense at this point may not be the excavation of tracks or the creation of potentially more efficient trolleys but the institution of frequent signal systems. Traffic lights for cars were last quoted to me to cost $50,000 per traffic light. Many municipalities are already rationing the pace at which they are installing traffic lights at additional intersections. Whatever the potential roadblocks (so to speak), light rail is surely one of the answers of the future. It

moves transportation fuel over to electricity which we already have
alternatives to generate and provides another opportunity for local
manufacturing development.

As someone who ran a nationally recognized transportation
service in Marlborough, one of Massachusetts more moderately sized
cities, the key barrier was very clear to us: the accepted assumptions
underpinning expansion of public transportation were flawed. Based
on funding to increase air quality standards, federal government
policy experts had somehow scope-locked on the idea that public
transportation development should focus on getting people out of
SUVs.

Realistically these drivers seem to be among the least likely to be
served by public transportation. Some people drive SUVs for practical reasons like numbers of people (large families) or things they
have to regularly transport. Public transportation is ill-equipped as a
substitute for real capacity SUV drivers. If the goal was to replace the
single person commuter who drives an SUV, that seemed a bizarre
and unrealistic goal to target; our experience was that if they drove
an SUV as personal preference and convenience and made enough
money to afford such a personal preference, they had almost no
incentive to switch.

In contrast, the real driver of public transportation effectiveness is
ridership: put public transportation where the most people need and
will use it. Making it both a popular and effective alternative spells
its success or failure. The logic is to provide it first to those who need
it the most and do it so well that many people use it. In turn, this will
create pressure to expand it for those for whom it becomes a useful
alternative when there is more of it; and so on until it is so accessible
and plentiful that even the SUV drivers find it more convenient. In
New York City, none of us who grew up there considered owning a
car to get around the city given excellent and prolific subways and
buses; we'd use cabs if we needed a private vehicle occasionally.

While smart and efficient development of public transportation
takes a deep understanding of the needs of potential riders, there are
obvious routes where it is most needed. It is the intelligent integration
of different transportation modalities that will in fact make it work.

Now is the time to prioritize public transportation development.
More than ever, people have personal financial incentives to switch

from private transportation to public transport. Our environment is creating urgent pressure. Neglect of our roads and bridges has reached dangerous proportions while one of the most effective types of stimulus spending, infrastructure funds, are available. Simply using that money to rebuild existing car-centered transportation is only going to continue our present transportation failings — financially and environmentally — for the foreseeable future.

Since the computer modeling and programming exists and successful models of different public transportation arrangements are proving their success in municipalities across the world, we can make huge and lasting improvements even while we await technological improvements in alternatives for cars.

A real impact with our actions, large and small...

The list of all possible actions we can take in our daily lives to lessen our negative environmental impact would be very, very long. I offer one list here, not because it is comprehensive but because each of us can do something; each of us can do many things. None of us can do all of these life changes all at once no matter how much we might try to browbeat ourselves with a sense of urgency. So make change, stretch yourself some but take it in reasonable steps. Every change you make will matter but trying to change faster than you can handle will prove unsustainable. Perhaps if there is one lesson in this crisis it is that as a species we must learn the new practice of sustainability in all areas.

> *Whatever you do may seem insignificant but it is most*
> *important that you do it!*   —Mahatma Gandhi

Millions who have benefited from peer support groups to 12-step programs will tell you as you make changes in your life: Find a buddy for support, it can make all the difference. Look for one fellow/sister traveler or more.

This is a long list of a smorgasbord of activities that will make a difference with global warming, peak oil, peak coal, even peak water in New England. It will also save you money:

1. Replace your light bulbs with fluorescents — quick, pretty cheap and almost immediate pay back from decreases in your lighting bill. Beware, most of that technology still uses mercury — so be

294 Main St. $marts
294 Main St. $marts
294 Main St. $marts
294 Main St. $marts

sure to dispose of them properly — although you will find they burn much longer than regular incandescents.

2. Turn everything off when you are not using it — in fact, if you are like me and rarely use your microwave or any other appliance, unplug it except when you are using it.

3. Use phosphorescent night lights.

4. Recycle — get a bin from your municipal government (and the handout with what they accept). Start small, each thing you recycle matters, so keep increasing what you recycle by switching over gradually. Some communities even provide trainings. This saves you and your municipality money and the difference in the environmental impact between production of say plastics from recycled instead of virgin materials is huge.

5. Have a car? Regularly check that your tires have enough air in them and talk to your mechanic. Some even recommend slightly overfilling tires.

6. Regular oil changes (although dealer specifications may be more frequently than necessary) again have a huge impact on the efficiency of your engine.

7. Whenever you can, allow enough time to walk, use public transportation or bike.

8. Weather permitting, always try to line-dry your clothes. Clothes dryers are energy intensive.

9. Have storm windows? Close them as soon as it starts to get cold — even if you leave a few up while you might still want to open a window occasionally in the fall.

10. Weatherize, weatherize, weatherize. Again, everything you do in this area will make a difference — 54 percent of energy use is in our buildings.[59] Easiest — buy some press-in caulking rope and felt stripping for loose windows before it gets too cold in the fall but once the outside air is noticeably colder than in your house. Choose a windy day if you can and walk around your house running your hand a little distance away from the wall around

all windows, doors, molding and corners, outlets (you can buy special outlet inserts), and places where pipes and wires enter.

11. Most utility companies, or if you are income eligible your local community action council, will do an energy audit of your home — and tell you what to spend and how to get your most bang for your buck.

12. If you have access to your basement, you can buy pipe coverings for all your hot water pipes.

13. Old appliances waste huge amounts of money and there are several rebate programs for buying replacement appliances with high Energy Star ratings. Great savings for you and the environment. Especially for appliances like refrigerators that we have to leave on all the time.

14. Replacement windows can make a big difference but it is one of the most expensive retrofits and so takes a long time to pay back in energy costs. In the meantime, putting window plastic over even just your most leaky windows can have a huge impact. I used to put plastic on all but one window per room so I could always easily open one if there was an occasional warm day. If you are really organized and meticulous, you can get plastic window coverings with tracks that you can install and take down and put back up year after year.

15. Check water temperature on your water heater if you can: it should be at 120 degrees but is usually set higher and is a huge user (and waster) of energy. Set it to exactly 120 degrees. I had a friend who actually put a switch on her wall on the first floor that allowed her to turn on the water heater in the basement remotely about a half an hour before showering or bathing or washing dishes! Flash water heaters are available; if you want to make a longer term investment, that is the biggest energy saver.

16. Set-back thermostat. Personally, I had dramatic and huge savings from installing a new thermostat which has a timer you can set for temperature. Many people manage to remember to always turn their thermostat way down when they go out and turn it back up when they come home. A setback thermostat is a

simple replacement of your existing thermostat which allows you to preset temperatures for regular weekly and weekend schedule — if you are always out at work fairly regular hours, you can arrange for the temperature to go down while you sleep but come back up before you have to get up and shower and get dressed, and go back down during work hours!

17. Compost your vegetable waste. Many municipalities still sell cheap self-contained composting units — small enough to fit in the smallest yard. They usually come with a small instruction brochure. They do not have to smell: add yard waste or leaves periodically — charcoal and even sour milk can wipe out even a strong smell. This is usually a third of household waste — and it is the basis of the best soil. Some municipalities even collect compost if you do not have a garden. Keep a bucket by your trash and recycle bin or the kitchen sink which you empty regularly.

18. Have a dishwasher? Change to non-phosphate dishwashing detergent. Phosphates are one of two major municipal (household-source) contributions to water pollution. And while great consumer campaigns in the 1970s led to an end of phosphates in laundry detergent, somehow dishwasher detergents slipped through. Alternatives are on most grocery shelves already: test for the one that satisfies you but they are not appreciably more expensive. You and your municipality paying for increased sewer costs is expensive and as water gets scarcer, the impact of unnecessary phosphates will be clear.

19. Like to garden? Keep a lawn? Get off petroleum products: chemical fertilizer and pesticides. These actually make your soil more water resistant and more likely to erode over time. Organic management already exists and has proven cheaper and less work intensive. The amount of chemicals in your lawn has been shown to be measurable in the body chemistry of especially children and pets. A number of Massachusetts municipalities have shifted away from chemicals; those little yellow chemical flags on your neighborhood school's playing field periodically warning that it is dangerous to especially children to walk on the grass? They should be gone ... So should the danger in your yard. This saves lots of money on chemical products, watering (after a

couple of years, you will do lots less watering) and — as the other major source of phosphates in storm run-off and pollution to local waterways — this will show up in savings in sewage treatment in your municipal sewer bill over time.

20. Do not cut down trees if possible. Plant and nurture trees in as many places as you can.

21. Eat locally grown foods in season where possible.

22. Go more and more vegetarian since not only do animals consume more resources, but they give off methane gas — and the more methane gas the less organic their own food intake. *Methane gas has about 20 times as much greenhouse impact than carbon.*[57]

23. Where possible use non-toxic alternatives for cleaning products.

24. Cutting down regular water use is going to matter more and more. Biggest daily water user? Old toilets. They can be replaced with the ever improving water savers. If not, believe it or not, put a brick in the water tank.

25. Ready to go farther? Heating oil tanks can often use post-consumer vegetable oil. Diesel cars can run on post-consumer vegetable oil. Solar panels get cheaper and cheaper. If ordinances allow, small wind-turbines can be attached to your house or out in your yard.

Maybe it is not about the money: nuclear power

When the Seabrook nuclear plant was being built, the nuclear industry seemed to have a bright future. About 160 nuclear power plants were projected to be built in the next decade.[61]

It was not that the track record of nuclear power plants was so perfect. The accident at the Three Mile Island Nuclear Power Plant occurred in 1979, when Seabrook was barely a year into breaking ground. Three Mile Island was located in the river outside of Philadelphia. But people were worried about their health and possible evacuation as far away as New York City!

One scenario that had worried opponents of nuclear power was the volatility of the nuclear reaction. If the chain reaction that generated enough energy to turn the turbines that created electricity got out of control, one combustion chamber might over-heat and the nuclear reaction continue unabated until it burned itself out. Literally, it could melt its own containment layers and release deadly nuclear radiation with the killing power of a nuclear bomb. A meltdown.

The hot, volatile reaction in a nuclear container is constantly supervised. The chamber's temperature is balanced by water flowing through it and by a set of rods which can be inserted to various depths to moderate the amount of nuclear material able to interact with itself; inserted far enough these rods should interrupt the nuclear interaction. Rigged with a number of fail-safes, the concept is that there are enough protections so that if caught in time, a nuclear reaction can only run away so far.

What happens if human error or mechanical error allows the nuclear reaction to get too hot and the fail-safes do not work? The rods are only able to neutralize the nuclear reaction up to a point — what if it is already so hot that the rods fail even if completely inserted? What if the insertion mechanism itself fails?

What happened at Three Mile Island was that a number of things went wrong at the same time. The rods were inserted, but was it too late? Radiation did escape, but the world waited over a period of days to see if the reaction had been slowed enough so it would stop "burning" before it completely melted its containment or not. If it did burn through completely, there was no magic "solution" or action available to address it.

Unfortunately, we did find out later, when the reactor at the Chernobyl nuclear plant melted down in Ukraine in 1986, that it has long term effects on human health such as deformed children with widespread problems, like holes in their hearts, and a long term devastation of the surrounding countryside.[62]

What many still do not know was that while Three Mile Island was very visible (because of immediate action by activists who had been studying and preparing an anti-nuclear power protest) it was the not first such accident. Years before in a more remote location, another series of errors and/or malfunctions had also allowed a reaction to get beyond human control. Again we in the U.S. have been lucky, there was not a full breach caused before the reaction cooled.

I have heard often from some of the former activists who devoted years of their lives to fighting the construction of the Seabrook Nuclear Power Plant that the organizing failed. Even after years of pointing to dangers, feasibility, and financial problems, the plant was built anyway.

The lesson about successful change that these activists missed must be learned so we can create the broad changes needed to solve today's problems. The measurement of the success of the activism against building Seabrook is that combined with activities in many other places, *Seabrook was the last nuclear power plant commissioned.* Our effectiveness is no more one-dimensional than any of the problems we face.

Because of the profound fear many people have of nuclear reactions, most public attention and visible protest has focused on human health and environmental concerns. What is less frequently pointed out were early concerns cited by activists that nuclear power plants would also be much more expensive to build than the industry had publicized. Since those early protests, when internal industry information was finally made public, in fact some in the industry had also predicted much higher expenses. Indeed, nuclear plants have been much more expensive than original public projections.

So why, then, one might ask, would large industry prioritize nuclear power? Early versions of electric cars, solar and wind energy were developing. Is it possible that with the addition of the resources that got championed for the nuclear power industry, these other cleaner options might have developed more quickly into significant power generation? One has to wonder.

What is clear is that the industry knew that nuclear power was more dangerous to human health and the environment than other forms of power. They knew they had no reliable way to dispose of the waste (still a problem). They knew there would be public resistance. And apparently they knew as well that it was going to be more expensive than other energy sources. Wall Street investors today are shunning underwriting nuclear plants again for the same reason: cost.[63]

Given all these downsides, I have to ask: were there other reasons that mattered more than even profits? One major difference is that unlike the other new energy options, nuclear power required a very large operation which only a large corporation can control. Neither you nor I are going to try to build one in our backyard. Nor are we likely to feel competent — even if we wanted to — to take one over as a community-run power source.

All the alternative renewable energy sources actually lend themselves better to smaller projects, easier to control very locally. In fact, wind and solar power lend themselves better to more residential and community versions. Micro-turbines are making water energy easier in more local and less disruptive forms. Because these are renewable resources, after upfront costs, these are not inherently large money makers — they are instead great money savers if we own them locally and publically or at a community or household level.

Successful electricity production from renewable energy sources meant, after large initial investment, an ever-decreasing production cost and, so, potentially increasing profits. In contrast, nuclear power was clearly not about being an inexpensive source of energy production; why did companies that are supposedly driven by the bottom-line build nuclear power plants?

Getting from Here to There

The policy shifts necessary to drive a social shift to severely limit our human footprint are significant. These policies will not just address global warming but pollution, environmental health impacts, survival of ecosystems, etc. When I started to figure out concrete policy steps, I wondered what such systemic change would require.

I knew that what works early in a process of change may not work later. Sometimes what appears to work a little may actually not work on a larger scale. Most policymakers in this area were thinking of only the next incremental step. Smart policy advocates had a long-term image of where we would likely need and want to end up. I was looking for a more realistic sense of our journey from here to there so that we could avoid pitfalls. We needed to know in advance what might seem like hidden forces that could otherwise stop us dead in our tracks partway down a particular path. I wanted to engage with people who could help think about what dynamic would affect the journey between the next step and the vision.

My ex used to tell of this bridge that folks once tried to build across the Ohio River. In an attempt to speed up the process, they measured carefully and started from both sides of the river, only to find themselves sufficiently off by the time they got near the center of the river that the two sides of the bridge were not going to meet in the middle! Predicting forward in time is even harder than meeting up across physical space. On the other hand, the earlier and more long-term effective our corrective actions are now, the less precious time and resources are wasted.

For instance, in the area of household or small project alternative energy and in terms of large appliance replacement, state policy makers opted to create a grant fund with an initial large state investment. This fund was supposed to pay rebates for alternative energy investment or for the purchase of energy-efficient appliances. Future installments were supposed to come as the funds were needed. Early marketing was, though small, for the general public and not targeted.

How would a program consciously designed to address a wide-spread adoption of new technology be most effective? If you look at how a community or a society picks up a new technology, in most cases there is a predictable curve: an exponential one. This means that if other forces do not derail the process, early acceptance is only by the most adventurous, or the least "risk averse." This is a tiny number early on, almost imperceptible. Eventually the numbers will grow and then take-off, exponentially. (See Figure 5.5.)

Figure 5.5   New technology acceptance curve[64]

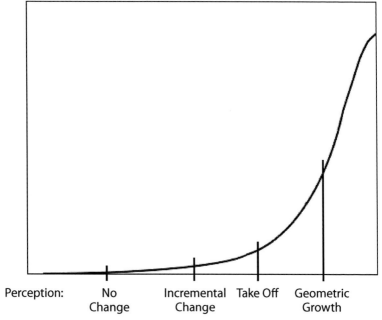

Perception: No   Incremental   Take Off   Geometric
                 Change   Change   Growth

What then are the implications of this for policymaking? First, early marketing should be heavily targeted toward the technologically most adventuresome; broad advertising is a waste of money. Since it is actually the good word of those early risk-takers that will be the most effective next layer of outreach, those "low-hanging fruit" are all that really matter. Why was the state wasting money on general outreach? Why had no one bothered to look at who would be likely to access these funds?

Second, they thought the fund was almost a failure. It was being used very slowly and because they were looking for a steady, linear growth, they were worried. When use started to increase, there was sort of a sense of relief: the incremental climb they thought they wanted. For me, that actually raised concerns: What would happen if interest really started to take off? How many did they have money to serve? How much more money was in the pipeline? The initial investment was tiny compared to the population of Massachusetts, and they seemed to assume that once their money was used up, they would simply see if the legislature would authorize more. Or not.

If we look at the usual curve of acceptance, the assumption of incrementalism meant not only that they misunderstood early movement as no movement but they were going to interpret growth as an infinite slant of the same rate — and miss take-off. They could well have set it up so that just when take-off was about to start the money would run out; instead of take-off the bottom could fall-out, like hitting the gas right before hitting a cement wall. People ready to take-off can just as ficklely give up: waiting for a questionable new round of funding could set back the whole integration of new technology by a significant delay.

Instead, the state should have looked at a revolving loan fund with a small initial investment. While expensive at initial investment, all these technologies are money saving. It was unnecessary to provide a rebate, a permanent public investment, since predictable savings meant repayment would be easy and relatively safe. Since funds would need to grow over time (not be used up) to fuel an exponential growth curve, this was the logical funding mechanism. Over the long term, people would reap the benefits personally after the revolving loan fund was paid back. State government and the public would instead see a successful program self-funding for early stages, likely to be judged as worth an increased investment.

This is just one example of why policy must be based on understanding how change actually happens. I encourage those who are interested in this way of analyzing and understanding change to look up systems theory. The little bit I have learned about thinking in more systemic ways has enabled me to think about how different trends interact with each other and not having to think of everything as a narrow, one thing leads to another process. Just because crime and ice cream eating increase and decrease during the same periods of the year does not mean that ice cream-eating causes crime *or* that crime leads to ice-cream eating. It is that both go up and down with the temperature.

Given the size of the transition required and the limited resources of the government, a really smart, incisive strategy is needed. This type of strategy is going to be both more effective *and cheaper* for the taxpayer. This economy makes that only more crucial. Strategies like revolving loan funds that address multiple problems and are more feasible in a bad economy are the way forward.

A further government incentive for a smart and near-term transition is the increasing importance of those green savings for every single family and household. Remember that mantra I keep repeating? It is restoring the ability of regular people to spend that has to happen to turn our economy around. Here is a behavior change that could help turn our environmental and economic crisis at the same time!

If our state were really smart about its limited funds, we would focus on using them for the purchase and funding of the industries for these new technologies to be built here in our own state. Especially by those whose communities need the jobs the most.

This is one strategy that could start having a positive multiplier effect, the opposite of our present downward spiral where monies are frittered away in an uncoordinated, non-replenishing fashion. Present government emphases lack local multiplier effects of jobs and savings in the communities that need them most; they spend the most tax dollars mostly on out of state technology or on large corporations that send their profits elsewhere.

Stimulus money includes funding for transforming our energy economy and green jobs. If used creatively and as a catalyst, this funding could help us address many of our issues simultaneously, including: global warming, dependence on foreign energy, job creation, the need for economic stimulus at the bottom and our devastating housing crisis.

It turns out that buildings account for 40 percent of energy consumption in the United States and 48 percent of greenhouse gas emissions. In Massachusetts, given our winters, that 40 percent of energy consumption figure rises to 54 percent of our energy consumption.[65] We only need to look at our lovely old houses that tend to leak like a sieve and our annual political struggle for national fuel

assistance monies to know how true this statistic is. Such energy
improvements as sealing, insulation and lighting are the cheapest,
most cost effective means to reduce greenhouse gas emissions. They
create long-term savings; 3.5 percent of the average U.S. resident's
income goes to energy costs. That increases to an average of 14
percent for low-income households.[66]

Existing weatherization programs provide a small percentage
of the retrofitting necessary and have no real advertising. The work
suffers from economies of scale where it is too little work and too
sporadic to provide any significant economic drive. Today, each
survey of a household to assess and prioritize its weatherization
needs costs around $500. Available grants mostly focus on low-
income households and provide up to $5,500 worth of work and
cannot be supplemented in future years. Until stimulus funds, the
number of low-income households that could be retrofitted per year
was a tiny percentage of the need. Most non-low-income households
are not even reached about accessing weatherization information or
options—although many initial steps of energy conservation these
people could afford on their own. Present programs report making
less than 50 percent of recommended weatherization and energy
saving measures. Reaching 60 percent of houses across the income
spectrum would provide a stimulus impact that would dwarf the
value of the stimulus package's tax rebates for households alone.[67]

Most funding is still grants and rebates. This ensures that were we
to move toward achieving the significant public excitement needed
for such a massive scale of retrofit, the government revenue streams
would run out before we even got going.

What if instead we used the green energy revenue streams at the
state and the new ones coming from the federal government in a
coordinated way? Why not set up significant revolving loan funds,
which could then fund a steady stream of work and focus on using
the funds in neighborhoods? The economic impact on the households, the housing quality, and the provision of decent jobs would be
greatest there. This would also access the greatest economic impact
as wages and savings stream into the households in our society
who spend every cent they get, thus generating the most local economic activity and revenue streams for our local, state and federal
governments.

These jobs require relatively short intensive training even for those with little formal education. As this money represents an influx of building trades jobs, these new jobs should be structured to feed into existing unions as apprenticeships — helping to both diversify union membership in the long run and build unions. This will improve the uniform quality of the work, ensure decent wages and working conditions, and strengthen the voice of the full diversity of working people — a key factor in turning around the self-destructive governmental policies of bailouts and giveaways to the largest industry players that continue to undermine our economy.

With wisdom and coordination these funds could be combined with funds tied to rebuilding foreclosed neighborhoods and important public/private policy shifts in foreclosure policies to rebuild green, stable neighborhoods as well.

Are revolving loan funds large enough and affordable?

Suppose green economy stimulus monies get put in a fund created as a wrap-around to existing government weatherization and utility sponsored programs. These revolving loan funds would then be structured to be drawn down for households in lower-income neighborhoods that were not eligible for existing low-income weatherization funds, and, if legal limits can be changed, to supplement weatherization activities beyond the federal cap per household. As rebuilding funds become available as part of the neighborhood stabilization funding to help foreclosed neighborhoods, that funding should be targeted to buildings still occupied. This would not only slow the destabilization of families, our neighborhoods, and degradation of our housing stock, it would lead to the renovation for existing residents to upgrade housing while greening it at the same time. This would significantly expand the funds available to weatherizing the neighborhoods that need it the most and significantly extend the reach of existing funds.

Repayment agreements would be tied to the payback schedule from energy cost savings — so that the household benefits from savings and money is repaid at the same time. The work and savings has to be timed so that money flows back into the fund in a predictable stream, so that work can be done consistently over time without periodic dry spells. Monies could then be opened up for more households.

At the same time, relatively new training programs for green building have just recently been funded and are ramping up at this writing; they can be combined with youth jobs stimulus monies which are funded to provide many new, still undefined opportunities. Existing youth building skills-training and union apprenticeship programs in some municipalities have negotiated mutual arrangements in recent years. These partnerships can provide the vehicle for these new jobs to provide a lasting union membership opportunity. A new skilled, more multi-racial labor force is thus created — providing a significant percentage of the jobs to segments of our society that have been ravaged by 42 percent unemployment rates even before the present economic downturn swept across the entire workforce.[68]

Likewise, this would provide improved health from healthier living circumstances and household savings for the very neighborhoods whose spending stimulates our economy the most. Rather than tying the revolving loan fund repayments to the households which may move out before the repayment period is over, the savings and repayment obligation is tied to the property itself — either through utility bills for the next occupant or as part of municipal water or sewer bills. The proper calculations for timing a realistic repayment has to be balanced with the pace of the work and remaining loan funds.

Existing weatherization models and expertise would need to inform the methods and training needed. Newer techniques need to be incorporated to affordably move us closer to 60 percent or even 80 percent of energy savings retrofits instead of our present below 50 percent completion averages.[69]

Critical to the success of this program is a carefully constructed and informed commitment by numerous community players; their considerable experience is needed to inform the different aspects of the program. A sufficient pot of money has to underwrite the initial loan fund so that it has enough funds to have some money under repayment at any one time and still provide ongoing weatherization work.

Such a program requires many moving parts working together to work successfully on many levels. However, these types of programs greatly extend the reach of our public dollars while addressing many problems at once and, thus, represent the hope for our future.

What if we can reconnect money with actual value?

It turns out that moving from a disposable way of living to a green economy way of living, from a huge profit driven economy to a local sustainable economy, creates jobs — potentially good paying jobs — at the local level.

If we move from expensive, non-renewable fuels from distant places (often hostile, they say, because of U.S. over-reach) we create local jobs. Renewable energy technologies can provide an average four to six times as many jobs as fossil fuel dependent processes when you consider manufacturing, installation, operations and maintenance together.[70]

These benefits require that green technologies manufacture happens here in the U.S. With policy choices that will use a significant amount of our tax-payer dollars, we have a right to require that as much of those dollars get spent here on our jobs as is possible.

For instance, one of the leading wind power contractors in North America (with 27 percent of market share), Mortenson Construction, puts nearly 400 construction workers to work every day across the U.S. This also puts $15 million to $20 million into local economies per 100 megawatts of clean energy per day. If the U.S. keeps with the more stringent carbon reduction goals and really moves to renewable energies, this translates to 18,500 megawatt renewable energy installations per year for 15 years. Studies show that if all components are manufactured in the U.S. this would provide 850,000 full time jobs nationwide. For instance, one of our big white turbines requires 8,000 parts from the towers and blades to software control systems.[71]

When I ran for governor in 2006, the need for more traditional power plants was already being challenged by the realistic math of energy conservation and local renewable energy generation.

In the Northwest United States, the quasi-governmental agency that markets energy from the region's federal dams (providing about 40 percent of electricity for the region), has prioritized conservation in recent years to avoid the expense of building new power plants.[72] It decided in 2007 on a 12 month push to save 52 megawatts through conversation programs — about 1/45th investment out of its annual profits. They actually achieved 58.5 average megawatts — the equivalent of all the power used by a small city! — *one third of that came simply in residential switch over to compact fluorescent light bulbs!*

While predictions of increased energy use are still accepted in many planning circles, the impact of potential savings if enacted will more than cover any projected growth. This means that state spending or enabling of more power plants should be carefully scrutinized if not outright challenged. This is especially true of recent initiatives to permit five biomass plants in the Pioneer Valley. It escapes me why biomass is considered green energy: it is not renewable, it cuts down our forests that are already endangered by climate change and critical for their capacity to sequester carbon. Biomass also pollutes our air, including particulates and, if construction and demolition waste is allowed, mercury and lead![73] We need our government's resources and attention focused on the sustainable future provided by conservation and real renewable energy production instead.

If these renewable energy components are built here in our state, the generation of good paying jobs that provide a *real value* for our dollars, manufacturing base, ongoing and local jobs, and environmental, health and household savings are the real consequence! Win-win-win-win-win-win. Instead we have some political leaders who are figuring out infrastructure deals and tax incentives for huge corporations that take profits elsewhere??? Like the dollars that flow to huge out-of-state banks or huge health insurance companies who charge us more for less services, less jobs, less local investment. And all these policies continue us on this downward economic spiral?

The choices are clear. And now we need to make our elected leaders make them!

Hope and Will

The thing is: it is not hopeless. **With existing technologies, we can already power our nation from indigenous sources of energy; transportation solutions are not far behind.** National studies show that with wind power alone we could provide the electrical energy needed for our nation even with projected energy usage increases for the next couple of decades. Add the savings that weatherizing and greening our buildings can provide and the possibilities are endless. Solar power in our state, placed in simple units on existing houses, could provide those households with 30 percent of their pre-energy conservation household needs.

In Massachusetts, the reality of these figures can be made even more concrete. With weatherization and energy conservation retrofits, we can certainly realize 50 percent, perhaps up to 80 percent savings on home energy use. When building new, it is possible to aim for net-zero energy use — where the building is built with so much energy savings and its own built-in energy sources, that it normally requires no net outside energy sources.

When we add the potential energy savings of increased tree cover or the active energy production of solar panels, even existing, old residences properly weatherized and with energy saving appliances can achieve a zero-net energy rating. Larger buildings with green roofs and taller buildings with wind-electricity generators with newer technologies and again an energy retrofit can also significantly decrease their energy pull.

Even with existing demands, wind turbines alone could provide for Massachusetts' energy needs. If publicly owned — so that financial and environmental savings come back to us, the people of our communities — incentives for wind turbines are enough for residents to support them now. Combined with numerous household sized windmills, we will no longer be confronted by so many windmills along our shore line or mountaintops that they have to be permanently intrusive. Exercising democratic and local rights to our energy choices will only improve our engagement, empowerment, and economic strength as participants in our future.

In total, Massachusetts already has more than enough renewable energy sources. They will have to be properly diversified, tailored to specific areas and meet the needs of different building structures to completely lift our carbon footprint for electricity needs. We can achieve this with no new power plants.

A complete transportation revamp presents some challenges we cannot answer yet. Still, we are already close if we implement cooperative bike systems, Zip-like car share systems, properly implemented and reliable public transportation, greatly increased Corporate Average Fuel Economy (CAFE) standards for our cars (at technological levels already proven and available) and a significant shift to rail travel infrastructures.

Infrastructure stimulus money is going to continue to come for a little while. Like all government spending, we as regular people must become the focus of and return to having a voice in its use. If spent to shift our energy and transportation onto local, people-sized solutions, those of us most in need benefit as we all do: through savings, good job creation, environmental improvements, and in turning our economy and strengthening our democracy.

Government must lead where it has large enough purchasing power to shift a market and sustain Massachusetts-based green-business development. State government must pass enabling legislation to ease household and municipalities development of alternative energy sources, and significantly ratchet up retrofitting and conservation measures, while creating some limits on the most polluting and destructive behaviors. Government must return to being a partner with us, Massachusetts residents, in disseminating examples of success. It must become pro-active in outlining the numerous opportunities for change and working hand-in-hand with our state residents in outreach and education about our options. Every step must be seen as an opportunity for more transparency, greater understanding which will greatly increase civic participation and a realistically-grounded sense that together we can...

Since all of this already exists within our grasp, the problem is not hope, the problem is political will. We know what is already possible. Will we insist that no one — not large corporations, nor some very wealthy who are presently sitting on vast sums of money, nor our presently weak willed government — can put a price tag on our children's future, our children's children's future or even the rest of our own lives? If it is a fundamental ecological shift to monsoon season and flooding for the summer, houses falling into the rising ocean levels on our coast, new health threats to ourselves as well as our trees, our children sent off to foreign lands to try to control dwindling reserves of petroleum, destruction of whole ecosystems to mine ever less productive coal or stripping the remaining rainforest to grow palm oil, or simply the skyrocketing costs of dependence overall on dwindling fossil-fuels, why should we even face such a future when **we simply do not need to?**

Facing the Storm,
Fixing the Ship,
Getting to Safety

When I raised the image of needing to survive this storm on the ship of our Commonwealth, I had to first describe the storm. It has been long in the making. But we have weathered previous storms and can weather this storm as well.

Much of the policy wisdom instituted because of the previous storms has been ignored and our ship is already weakened. For decades when the divide between the front line workers and the captain were not so vast, the ship sailed well. Now, however, there are already rifts in the hull; we have been taking on dangerous amounts of water and too many in-charge have been ignoring them — telling us they have no responsibility or capacity to fix them *and that we cannot and do not need to!*

We need to get out into the deep water quickly, and our ship and its crew's condition are not helping. Those in-charge thought they could ignore the needs for a seaworthy ship, mesmerized by retrofitting it as a fast racing boat just for them and their friends. They were not leading us well then. No matter what tales they tried to distract us with, they ignored the obviously brewing storm. They ignored the warning signs and told us we were bellyaching and nay-saying. They told us we did not need workers in the crow's nests and boiler room even as they were shooting about the storm clouds upon us and the fires in the boiler-room.

Many of these "leaders" are still telling us to ignore what we know and what we are experiencing. They still say the storm was unpredictable, that we need to jettison regular people and belittle the widening rifts in the hull from obvious rocks they refuse to steer the ship away from.

They simply are not leaders, especially not in this weather, not for us, all the regular people. I know we are scared but if they are wrong about our economy, why do we think they are right? Why do we think that they are experts and we are not? We are on the front line. We have always been the skilled labor on the ship. We have always fixed the concrete problems as part of our jobs. Who are we waiting for? Hiding in our cabins or going about our jobs as the ship sinks only ensures that most of us will drown.

Now, some political leaders and opinion leaders are actually fomenting fights among those on the decks over small amounts of money while those in charge party on and the boat continues to take on water.

Rebuilding and Transformation

As we rebuild (or should I say when?), there will be lots of ideological arguments — some legitimate and some consciously trying to protect an ideological perspective. But our statistics and studies of the present and the past show some undeniable facts which I have tried to stick with here. It is time we let the facts get in the way of the good stories out there.

In thinking about overall state policy going forward, clear guide-lines emerge. Our goal must be to assist in an economic transition to sustainability that can simultaneously serve all of us and our environment. Our elected leaders must shift their decisions to re-balance our economy not just the budget of their institutions.

We clearly need to rebuild the economic lives of regular people — if for no other self-serving reason than that it provides the engine of the entire economy. Policies must be enacted as soon as possible to end the impact of foreclosures and change our increasingly expensive and failing systems of health care and criminal punishment. We will have to return to a healthy sustainable economy which we know includes moving back to a tax system that does not prioritize policies that reward money made from money and speculative wealth, but actually scope-lock government on economic activity based on real goods and services. Value must be based on actual labor and materials, income earned not unearned. The economy must be rebalanced making all of our contributions more equally valued.

We are talking about significant retrofitting, moving towards more community friendly neighborhoods, locally driven economies, sustainable and renewable energy, and increasing good jobs. If done right, we can have: renaissance of appropriate manufacturing, locally sustained, which could succeed in the global marketplace; our lives and our communities made livable again; our work and home lives more integrated. These goals cannot be met by policies that exacerbate loss of local control and input, that continue to pull financial resources out of local communities and households to fund large, especially out of state, corporate interests. Solutions cannot be divorced from the full complex of problems that need addressing; each issue cannot be addressed as if in a vacuum.

Economic sustainability and environmental sustainability are intertwined — and experience would tell us that they are intertwined with real democracy where people can politically and economically participate — like Hull and Denmark with their wind turbines. With a political base for regular people in the workplace through real democratic unions and government regained by we-the-people.

The studies and experience also tell us that it is local businesses, locally owned, that provide the new jobs and innovation for our communities — whether pharmaceuticals or electric cars. Union jobs ensure that the interests of all of us are better represented in terms of not just decent wages, sick days and benefits, but better public education and better built buildings, for example. Money that comes into the hands of those who must spend every dime to live creates the greatest, fastest, most reliable and most local stimulus.

More than ever, Massachusetts elected leaders must return to the people, trusting and enabling our ingenuity and fostering again a sense of mutual aid and community. We must draw on the best of our deep roots: when regular Massachusetts colonists, the farmers and craftspeople, built lives based on mutual aid and the upkeep of the common, directly electing their representatives and paid taxes which they continued to track and, when necessary, exert control over.

No overriding of local control as new technologies need to be adopted. Instead, genuine partnering and ultimately, a commitment to having regular people and whole communities benefit and control their future energy resources. Creating funding mechanisms and engagement strategies based in successful models of uptakes of new technologies. With variations in local resources and uses, each household, development, neighborhood and municipality will find a different mix of possible energy solutions, all affordable, putting more money in the pockets of spenders and rejuvenating good jobs.

We cannot dodge the huge scope of the transition ahead of us. Financial planning must be long-term. Financing must also be as renewable as possible, with revolving loan funds and savings plowed back into our communities and further transitional development.

If we continue to not just be fed but eat the ideas that we can reach solutions without seeing connections between our values and other issues, we cannot get there from here. On the other hand, as economic and environmental resources get scarcer, we could re-learn the lessons of reality — that we are interdependent, that real solutions solve many problems simultaneously and most importantly, that we **are** the ones we have been waiting for.

Relatively rapid change

It is important to remember that we are in a period of relatively rapid change as compared to the last 20 years or so. Many of our elected officials are sticking with business as usual. Among other things, this means dealing with one issue at a time and as if they had years to enact any real change.

While periods of such flux can be scary in their pace and seeming uncertainty, it is important to remember that they are also full of opportunity — especially to change things that have been wrong for a long time (or worsening slowly). The obviousness of the need for change is also greater and more obvious to more people *who are ready to be engaged.*

My friend George Friday would say that the issue here is to stay conscious in the chaos. What are our deepest held ideals? How do we find in each other the shared vision and the mutual support to act together in the interest of the greatest good? How to find the courage and the faith (however you interpret that word) to reach for the best we as individuals and a society can be and each day keep putting one foot in front of another towards that end?

In our own history are models of the kind of joint action needed. The balance of listening and engaging our friends and neighbors and acting together to insist on what is right even when the powers that be tell us that we cannot have it. Movements of those out of power have created inclusion and more equality when no one thought it was possible — the end of slavery, women gaining the vote, workers gaining pay and recognition of overtime, the end of segregation … the list goes on and on.

When do we decide to reclaim our democratic birthright, wake from our sleepwalking state to demand what our Constitution guarantees us: we are the "deciders?" As those who settled this state, before any shot was fired (or heard 'round the world) insisted:[74] taxes existed but they were controlled by democratic means through representatives who were held on a very tight leash and told how to vote in the state General Court.

Wall Street cannot be allowed to hold the purse strings and so control the power of our elected representatives. We must re-take our power of democracy and to do that we must come to believe again in Main Street; we are the economic engine of this state and country, yes, and also *we are the ones who have the smarts to solve these crises and run our government as our birthright.* We retain the power of the purse as well as our right to vote — and no one will be allowed to take them from us.

For if we cannot reverse an unhealthy economy now, when will we? If we cannot find the mutual need to impel a transformation of our health care to a universal, affordable model proven across the world instead of our fractured ever more expensive one, then when? If we do not see at this time our mutual benefit of laws that will ensure that working and middle class workers have enough and are treated well enough to once again be the engine of our economy, when will we? As the mounting proof collects that we must take urgent and sweeping action together to avert an environmental catastrophe, if we do not insist and by our very actions ensure a major course change, when will we? As we see the ravages of a representative democracy so entangled with large money that every major policy is being decided against not only the needs but the expressed desires of the majority of the people, when else will we reclaim our democracy?

Real hope is not based in promises, especially promises from the powers that be that they will fix it for us. Lasting hope comes from knowing and experiencing that it has always been people like us, together, who have organized the changes that we needed.

If we believe even part of the vision of a government by and for the people, then we have to start seeing each other and ourselves as the determining forces for our society and our future. Otherwise, we may have betrayed the most fundamental premise of our covenant with each other and the greatest hope for a better future. We must reclaim ourselves as the "deciders," as the government — and reach together for that uniquely American solution: government by and for the people, all the people.

Permissions

Part I: The Storm Brews, the Seas Roughen

"Single unit housing starts 1969–2010," from Barry Ritholz, "Why are people calling a bottom for Real Estate?" *The Big Picture.* <www.ritholtz.com/blog> Aug. 10, 2009. Reprinted with permission of Barry Ritholz.

"Share of family income by quintile 1947–2004," from Jeanette Huezo, Christina Kasica, Dedrick Muhammad and Amaad Rivera, "A Dream Depressed," in *The Silent Depression: State of the Dream 2009* (Boston: United for a Fair Economy 2009), p.13. Reprinted with permission of United for a Fair Economy.

"Real median household income: 1979–2008," by Heidi Shierholz, "New 2008 Poverty, Income Data Reveal Only Tip of the Recession Iceberg." "Real median household income: 1979-2008," by Heidi Shierholz, *New 2008 Poverty, Income Data Reveal Only Tip of the Recession Iceberg* (Washington, DC: Economic Policy Institute, September 10, 2009), p. 4. Reprinted with permission of Economic Policy Institute.

"Consumption share of Gross Domestic Product (GDP)," from Doug Henwood, "Overconsuming Health" *Left Business Observer* #120, August 2009. <www.leftbusinessobserver.com> Reprinted with permission of Doug Henwood.

"Economic benefits of various stimulus provisions," from Ethan Pollack, "A Meaningful Stimulus for Main Street" (Washington, DC: Economic Policy Institute, October, 2008), p.2. Reprinted with permission of Economic Policy Institute.

"Change in real family income by quintile, top 5% 1947–1979," from The Working Group on Extreme Inequality, *Inequality By the Numbers,* (Washington, DC: Institute on Policy Studies, October, 2009), p. 4. Reprinted with permission of The Institute on Policy Studies.

"Change in real family income by quintile, top 5% 1979–2008," from The Working Group on Extreme Inequality, *Inequality By the Numbers* (Washington, DC: Institute on Policy Studies, October 2009), p. 4. Reprinted with permission of The Institute on Policy Studies.

"Historical recessions and timing of job loss and recovery," from Mike Shedlock, "Charting the US Recession Unemployment Crisis." *The Market Oracle.* <www.marketoracle.co.uk/> August 16, 2009. Reprinted with permission of Mike Shedlock.

Part II: Sealing the Holes in the Hull

"Foreclosure rates for Great Depression and 2008," from Amaad Rivera, Jeanette Huezo, Christina Kasica, and Dedrick Muhammad, "A Dream Depressed," in *The Silent Depression: State of the Dream 2009* (Boston: United for a Fair Economy 2009), p. 19. Reprinted with permission of United for a Fair Economy.

"Federal expenditures: home ownership tax loss vs. affordable housing programs," from Western Regional Advocacy Project, *Without Housing: Decades of Federal Housing Cutbacks, Massive Homelessness, and Policy Failures* (San Francisco: Western Regional Advocacy Project, 2006), p. 40. < http://wraphome.org/ > Reprinted with permission of Western Regional Advocacy Project.

"Ratio of home price to rent 1987–2008." © Copyright 2010, Federal Reserve Bank of Boston. Reprinted with permission of the Federal Reserve Bank of Boston.

"Subprime and Alt-A volume quintupled 2001–2006, fell 2007–2008," from Frank E. Nothaft, Chief Economist, Presentation prepared for Milken Institute's Financial Innovations Lab on Housing: Beyond the Crisis (McLean, VA: Freddie Mac, October 7, 2008), p. 29. Reprinted with permission of Frank E. Nohaft.

"Homes-at-risk vs. total lender workouts 2007–2009," from Center for Responsible Lending, "Mortgage Repairs Lag Far Behind Foreclosures." < www.responsiblelending.org> December 4, 2009. Reprinted with permission of Center for Responsible Lending.

"Massachusetts monthly filings of petitions to foreclose Jan 2006–May 2010." Printed with permission of the Warren Group.

"Snapshot 2009 of underwater mortgages by year purchased/refinanced," from Zillow, "Massachusetts Home Prices and Home Values-Local Info. <www.zillow.com> November 2 2009. Reprinted with permission of Zillow.

"Distribution of outstanding mortgages by first month of rate reset," from Addison Wiggin & Ian Mathias, "The Second Wave of the Housing Crisis, Profiting from Carbon Caps, U.S. is "out of money," Lunch with Ron Paul and More!" <www.agorafinancial.com> May 26, 2009. Reprinted with permission of Agora Financial.

"Massachusetts home prices by region 2006–2010," From Zillow, Massachusetts Home Prices and Home Values-Local Info. <www.zillow.com> Reprinted with permission of Zillow.

"Percentage of uninsured in Tennessee 1987–2005," Benjamin Day, *Implementation of Massachusetts Health Reform* (Boston: Mass-Care, 2008), p. 21. Reprinted with permission of Benjamin Day.

"Underinsurance has increased under Massachusetts Reform," from Benjamin Day, *Implementation of Massachusetts Health Reform* (Boston: Mass Care, 2008), p. 13. Reprinted with permission of Benjamin Day.

"Health care expenditure per person by funding source 2004," from Jonathan Cylus and Gerard F. Anderson, *Multinational Comparisons of Health Systems Data: 2006* (Baltimore: Johns Hopkins University, May 2007), p. 14. Reprinted with permission of Jonathan Cylus and Gerard F. Anderson.

"Insurance costs vs. workers` earnings vs. inflation 1999–2008," from Robert Stone, MD, "Healthcare reform: we're still for it, and we're not done yet!" June, 2010. p.6. Reprinted with permission of Robert Stone, MD.

"National health spending per person (U.S. 2000–P.P.P.)," from Catherine Rampell, "U.S. Spending Breaks from the Pack." *Economix* <economix. blogs.nytimes.com> July 8 2009. Reprinted with permission of Catherine Rampell.

"U.S. personal savings rate with and without medical expenses," from Doug Henwood, "Overconsuming Health." *Left Business Observer*, #120, August 2009. <www.leftbusinessobserver.com> Reprinted with permission of Doug Henwood.

"New York cuts crime and incarceration 1997–2007," from The Pew Center on the States, *One in 31: The Long Reach of American Corrections* (Washington, DC: The Pew Charitable Trusts, March 2009), p. 24. Reprinted with permission of The Pew Center on the States.

Part III: Into Deeper Water for Safety

"NYC Homeless Outreach Population Estimate (HOPE) 2005–2009," from The New York City Department of Homeless Services, *Hope 2009: The NYC Street Survey, March 4, 2009.* Reprinted with permission of The New York City Department of Homeless Services.

Part IV: Insuring a Deep-Sea Worthy Vessel

"Growth in annual earnings by wage group, 1979–2007," from Lawrence Mishel, *Waging Inequality in America* (Washington, DC: Economic Policy Institute, 2009), p. 10. Reprinted with permission of Economic Policy Institute.

"Reductions in Massachusetts personal income taxes, declines in sales tax revenues, greater reliance on property tax," from Massachusetts Budget and Policy Center, *Property Taxes: Helping Those Who Need it Most, Policy Brief* (Boston: Massachusetts Budget and Policy Center, May 20 2008), p.1. This work is licensed under the Creative Commons Attribution-NonCommercial 3.0 Unported License. To view a copy of this license, visit <http://creativecommons.org/licenses/by-nc/3.0/> or send a letter to Creative Commons, 171 Second Street, Suite 300, San Francisco, California, 94105, USA. While this work was used in the analysis of issues discussed in *Main St. Smarts*, MBPC has not endorsed the conclusions of the author.

"Distribution of personal income dedicated to state and local taxes in Massachusetts, 2006," from Massachusetts Budget and Policy Center, "Slides on State Taxes," (Boston: Massachusetts Budget and Policy Center, February 2008). This work is licensed under the Creative Commons Attribution-NonCommercial 3.0 Unported License. To view a copy of this license, visit <http://creativecommons.org/licenses/by-nc/3.0/> or send a letter to Creative Commons, 171 Second Street, Suite 300, San Francisco, California, 94105, USA. While this work was used in the analysis of issues discussed in *Main St. Smarts*, MBPC has not endorsed the conclusions of the author.

"Distribution of personal income paid to Massachusetts sales tax, 2006," from Massachusetts Budget and Policy Center, "Slides on State Taxes," (Boston: Massachusetts Budget and Policy Center, February 2008). This work is licensed under the Creative Commons Attribution-NonCommercial 3.0 Unported License. To view a copy of this license, visit <http://creativecommons.org/licenses/by-nc/3.0/> or send a letter to Creative Commons, 171 Second Street, Suite 300, San Francisco, California, 94105, USA. While this work was used in the analysis of issues discussed in *Main St. Smarts*, MBPC has not endorsed the conclusions of the author.

"The Stock Bubble: price surge not based in increased value," from Lawrence Mishel, *Waging Inequality in America* (Washington, DC: Economic Policy Institute, 2009), p. 30. Reprinted with permission of Economic Policy Institute.

"Ratio of CEO to average worker pay, 1965–2005," from Lawrence Mishel, *Waging Inequality in America* (Washington, DC: Economic Policy Institute, 2009), p. 12. Reprinted with permission of Economic Policy Institute.

"Hedge and private equity fund managers," from Mike Prokosch, "Power point presentation on the Economic Crisis, 2008." Reprinted with permission of Mike Prokosch.

"American Profile Poster excerpt." © Copyright 2005, Stephen J. Rose. Printed by permission of Stephen J. Rose.

"Unemployment rates: official, enhanced official and all reported categories," from John Williams, "Alternate Unemployment Charts," in *Shadow Government Statistics*. <www.shadowstats.com> December 7 2009. Reprinted with permission of ShadowStats.

"Job losses in recessions as share of employment," from Bill McBride, "March Employment Report: 162K Jobs Added, 9.7% Unemployment Rate." *CalculatedRISK* <www.CalculatedRiskBlog.com> April 2, 2010. Reprinted with permission of Bill McBride.

"Annual consumer inflation: official (rev.) vs. original formula," from John Williams, "Alternate Inflation Charts," in *Shadow Government Statistics*. <www.shadowstats.com> December 7, 2009. Reprinted with permission of ShadowStats.

"Typical workers' compensation lags productivity growth," from Lawrence Mishel, *Waging Inequality in America* (Washington, DC: Economic Policy Institute, 2009), p. 18. Reprinted with permission of Economic Policy Institute.

"Unions and health insurance," Reprinted with permission of Elaine Bernard.

"Unions and pensions," Reprinted with permission of Elaine Bernard.

"Unions and wages," Reprinted with permission of Elaine Bernard.

"Union membership, 1945–2008," Reprinted with permission of Elaine Bernard.

"U.S. union density 1945–2008 (12.4% in 2008)," Reprinted with permission of Elaine Bernard.

"Unions and public policy," Reprinted with permission of Elaine Bernard.

"The value of the minimum wage, 1939–2006," from Economic Policy Institute, *Briefing Paper #177* (Washington, DC: Economic Policy Institute, 2006). Reprinted with permission of Economic Policy Institute.

"Strong support for Unionization," Reprinted with permission of Elaine Bernard.

Part V: Rebuilding a Better Ship after Storm Damage

"Average commute distance and duration by mode," from Randall Crane, "Is There a Quiet Revolution in Women's Travel? Revisiting the Gender Gap in Commuting." *Journal of the American Planning Association* 3.3 (November, 2007): 8. Reprinted by permission of the publisher, Taylor & Francis Group, www.informaworld.com.

"UCS Massachusetts climate scenarios," from Union of Concerned Scientists, Massachusetts: Confronting Climate Change in the U.S. Northeast (USA: Union of Concerned Scientists, 2007) p. 1. Copyright © Union of Concerned Scientists/Northeast Climate Impacts Assessment, 2007. Reprinted with permission by Union of Concerned Scientists.

"New England carbon dioxide emissions by sector, 2004," by Environment Massachusetts and Clean Water Fund from the Report of the Senate Committee on Pot-Audit and Oversight and the Senate Committee on Global Warming and Climate Change, *The Cost of Inaction: Climate Change in the Commonwealth.* <www.mass.gov/legis/bills/senate/185/st02/st02870.htm> July 2008. Reprinted with permission of Environment Massachusetts and Clean Water Fund.

Endnotes

Introduction

1. "Riding the Rails: Timeline of the Great Depression, 1929–1932," *The American Experience: The 1930s*, PBS, Herbert Hoover, Nov. 1929. <http://www.pbs.org/wgbh/amex/rails/timeline/index.html>
2. Alan Greenspan, "Testimony to Committee of Government Oversight and Reform," U.S. Congress, 23 Oct. 2008. <http://clipsandcomment. com/wp-content/uploads/2008/10/greenspan-testimony-20081023.pdf>

Part I: The Storm Brews, The Seas Roughen

1. Martin Crutsinger and Jeannine Aversa, "Weekly Jobless Claims Drop Below 500,000," *Forbes* 25 Nov. 2009, 30 June 2009. <http://www.forbes. com/feeds/ap/2009/11/25/real-estate-broadcasting-amp-entertainment-us-economy_7158709.html>
2. Drake Bennet, "Paradigm Lost," *Boston Globe [Boston]* 13 Dec. 2009, 21 Dec. 2008. <http://www.boston.com/bostonglobe/ideas/ articles/2008/12/21/paradigm_lost/>
3. Kelly Curran. "New Home Starts Hit Lowest Level Ever," *Housingwire* 18 Dec. 2008, 4 Dec. 2009. <http://www.housingwire.com/2008/12/16/ home-construction-starts-slashed-in-november/>
4. Barry Ritholtz, "Why are People Calling a Bottom for Real Estate?" ritholtz.com, *The Big Picture*, 18 July 2009, 10 Aug. 2009. <http://www. ritholtz.com/blog/2009/07/new-home-starts-2/>
5. Kenneth Gosselin, "Job Growth Outlook Worsens; Region Won't Regain Recession Losses Until 2009, Group Predicts," *Hartford Courant [Hartford]* 12 May 2006 E1.
6. Amaad Rivera, Jeanette Huezo, Christina Kasica, and Dedrick Muhammad, *The State of the Dream 2009: The Silent Depression.* (Boston: United for a Fair Economy, 2009) 13.
7. Heidi Shierholz, "New 2008 Poverty, Income Data Reveal Only Tip of The Recession Iceberg," *(Washington, DC:* Economic Policy Institute, 10 Sep. 2009).
8. Doug Henwood, "Overconsuming Health," *Left Business Observer*: 120, August 2009 <www.leftbusinessobserver.com>
9. Ethan Pollack, "A Meaningful Stimulus for Main Street," *Economic Policy Institute*, 18 June 2009. <http://www.epi.org/economic_snapshots/entry/ webfeatures_snapshots_20081022/>

10. Jesse Van Tol, "Multi-Trillion Dollar Lifeline "Saves" Wall Street, Homeowners Left to Fail," *National Community Reinvestment Coalition,* 14 Sep. 2009, 4 Jan. 2010. <http://www.ncrc.org/index.php?option=com_content&task=view&id=510&Itemid=75>

11. Matthew Jaffe, "23.7 to Fix Financial System?" *Money,* ABC News, 20 July 2009, 13 December 2009. <http://abcnews.go.com/Business/Politics/story?id=8127005&page=1>

12. Paul Krugman, *The Return of Depression Economics and The Crisis of 2008* (New York: W.W. Norton & Company, 2009) 153–154.

13. *Money as Debt,* dir. Paul Grignon, Lifeboat News/Moonfire Studio, Video, Oct. 2007.

14. Grignon.

15. James Lieber, "What Cooked the World's Economy?" *The Village Voice [New York]* 28 Jan. 2009, 30 March 2009. <http://www.villagevoice.com/2009-01-28/news/what-cooked-the-world-s-economy/>

16. Krugman, *Depression Economics* 156.

17. Grignon.

18. Grignon.

19. Paul Jackson, "JP Morgan's Dimon: Prime Mortgages Look 'Terrible,'" *Housing Wire,* 8 Dec 2009. <http://www.housingwire.com/2008/07/17/jp-morgans-dimon-prime-mortgages-look-terrible/>

20. Jamie Dimon, "Dear Fellow Shareholders" J.P. Morgan Chase Bank, New York, United States, 23 March 2009.

21. John Williams, "Inflation, Money Supply, GDP, Unemployment and the Dollar–Alternate Data Series," *Shadow Government Statistics,* 7 Dec. 2009. <http://www.shadowstats.com/alternate_data>

22. Roger G. Altman, "The Great Crash, 2008," *Foreign Affairs* 27 Nov. 2009. <http://www.foreignaffairs.com/articles/63714/roger-c-altman/the-great-crash-2008>

23. Lieber.

24. Krugman, *The Return of Depression Economics* 139–144.

25. Josh Meyer, "FBI expects number of big financial bailout fraud cases to rise," *The Los Angeles Times [Los Angeles]* 11 Feb. 2009. <http://articles.latimes.com/2009/feb/12/nation/na-fraud12>

26. Krugman, *Depression Economics* 158–160.

27. "Derivative," *Wikipedia* 2002, <http://en.wikipedia.org/wiki/Derivative_(finance)>

28. Wikipedia, "Derivative."

29. Chart created for this book using data from James Lieber, "What Cooked the World's Economy?" *The Village Voice [New York]* 28 Jan. 2009, 30 March 2009. <http: www.villagevoice.com/2009-01-28/news/what-cooked-the-world-s-economy/>

30. Lieber.

31. Lieber..

32. Lori Ehrlich, "Swaptions: A train wreck coming down the Pike," *Marblehead Reporter [Marblehead MA]* 11 March 2009, 10 June 2009. <http://www.wickedlocal.com/marblehead/homepage/x1676799421/COLUMN-Swaptions-A-train-wreck-coming-down-the-Pike>

33. Barack Obama, "Inaugural Address," Presidential inaugural address. *Whitehouse.gov*, 21 Jan. 2009. <http://www.whitehouse.gov/blog/inaugural-address/>

34. The Working Group on Extreme Inequality, *Inequality By the Numbers*, (Boston: Institute on Policy Studies, 2009) 4.

35. The Working Group on Extreme Inequality 4.

36. Krugman, *Depression Economics* 138–148.

37. Mike Shedlock, "Charting the US Recession Unemployment Crisis," Marketoracle.co.uk, *Market Oracle*, 6 Aug. 2009, 10 Dec. 2009. <http://www.marketoracle.co.uk/Article12568.html>

38. Shedlock.

39. Tula Connell, "Young Workers: A Lost Decade," *blog.aflcio.org* AFL-CIO, 1 Sep. 2009, 7 Sep. 2009.

40. Chart created for this book with data from Emmanuel Saez and Thomas Piketty, "Income Inequality in the United States, 1913–1998" (with tables and figures updated to 2008 in July 2010), *Quarterly Journal Economics* 118.1 (2003), and from Paul Krugman, "Introducing This Blog: Conscience of a Liberal," *New York Times [New York]* 18 Sep. 2007. <http://krugman.blogs.nytimes.com/2007/09/18/introducing-this-blog/>

41. Chart created for this book with data from Emmanuel Saez and Thomas Piketty, "Income Inequality in the United States, 1913–1998" (with tables and figures updated to 2008 in July 2010), *Quarterly Journal Economics* 118.1 (2003), and from Paul Krugman, "Introducing This Blog: Conscience of a Liberal," *New York Times [New York]* 18 Sep. 2007. <http://krugman.blogs.nytimes.com/2007/09/18/introducing-this-blog/>

Part II: Sealing the Holes in the Hull

1. United States, Office of Federal Housing Enterprise Oversight, *Coast to Coast Home Prices are Down and Families Have Lost Wealth from 2007–2009* (Washington, DC: Congressional Budget Office, April 2008).

2. Peter Goodman, "Reluctance to Spend May Be Legacy of Recession," *New York Times [New York]* 29 Aug. 2009, 8 Dec. 2009. <http://www.nytimes.com/gloginURI=http://www.nytimes.com/2009/08/29/business/economy/29consumer.html>

3. Martin Crutsinger and Jeannine Aversa, "Weekly Jobless Claims Drop Below 500,000," *Forbes* 25 Nov. 2009. <http://www.forbes.com/

feeds/ap/2009/11/25/real-estate-broadcasting-amp-entertainment-us-
economy_7158709.html>

4. Amaad Rivera, Jeanette Huezo, Christina Kasica, and Dedrick
   Muhammad, *The State of the Dream 2009: The Silent Depression.* (Boston:
   United for a Fair Economy, 2009) 19.

5. Western Regional Advocacy Project, *Without Housing: Decades of
   Federal Housing Cutbacks, Massive Homelessness, and Policy Failures*
   (San Francisco: Western Regional Advocacy Project, 2006) 40.

6. Western Regional Advocacy Project.

7. Bernie Sanders, "Billions for Bailouts! Who Pays?" *Huffingtonpost.com.*
   Huffington Post, 19 Sep. 2008. 7 Dec. 2009. <http://www.huffingtonpost.
   com/rep-bernie-sanders/billions-for-bailouts-who_b_127882.html>

8. Krugman, *Depression Economics* 160–164.

9. Eric Stein, "Turmoil in the U.S. Credit Markets: The Genesis of the
   Current Economic Crisis," testimony, Senate Committee on Banking,
   Housing and Urban Affairs, Washington, DC, 2008.

10. Krugman, *Depression Economics* 161–162.

11. Krugman, *Depression Economics* 161–162.

12. Stein.

13. Commonwealth vs. Fremont Investment & Loan and Fremont General
    Corporation, 452mass733, Suffolk County Superior Court, Supreme
    Judicial Court of Massachusetts, 25 Feb. 2008, 6 April 2008. <http://
    masscases.com/cases/sjc/452/452mass733.html>

14. Katalina Bianco, "The Subprime Lending Crisis: Causes and Effects of the
    Mortgage Meltdown," *CCH Incorporated,* May 2008.

15. Paul Willen, *Making Sense of the Subprime Crisis,* (Boston: The Research
    Bureau, 13 Nov. 2008).

16. Willen.

17. Willen.

18. Michael Powell, "Blacks in Memphis Lose Decades of Economic
    Gains," *New York Times [New York]* 7 Dec. 2009, 31 May 2010. <http://
    www.nytimes.com/2010/05/31/business/economy/31memphis.
    html?pagewanted=all>

19. Harvey Pitt, "The Financial Crises: CEOs Discuss Competition and
    Inclusivity in Today's Market," Charting New Pathways to Participation
    & Membership conference, The Charles Hamilton Houston Institute,
    Harvard University, Boston, MA, opening remarks, 17 Oct. 2008.

20. Ed Siefert, "Late-Breaking Letters: Greenspan Could Have Acted to Shut
    Down Sub-Prime Market." *The Orange County Register [Los Angeles]* 14
    Sep. 2007, 7 Dec. 2009. <http://www.ocregister.com/opinion/greenspan-
    59528-real-estate.html>

21. Frank E. Nothaft "Subprime and Alt-A volume Quintupled 2001 to 2006, Then Fell from 2006 to 2008," presentation, 7 Oct. 2008, Milken Institute's Financial Innovations Lab on Housing, Beyond the Crisis, 29.

22. "Mortgage Repairs Lag Far Behind Foreclosures," *Center for Responsible Lending*, 4 Dec. 2009. <http://www.responsiblelending.org/mortgage-lending/research-analysis/mortgage-repairs-lag-far-behind-foreclosures.html>

23. "Mortgage Repairs Lag Far Behind Foreclosures," *Center for Responsible Lending*, 4 Dec. 2009. <http://www.responsiblelending.org/mortgage-lending/research-analysis/mortgage-repairs-lag-far-behind-foreclosures.html>

24. Martha Coakley, "Lenders and Servicers' Promises of Loan Modifications in Massachusetts are Not Matched by Meaningful Actions That Promote Sustainable Loans," testimony, 17 Sep. 2008, U.S. House Financial Services Committee, Washington, DC.

25. Created for this book with data from The Warren Group, "Mass. Foreclosures Jump In October From Prior Month, But Dip From a Year Ago," *Banker and Tradesmen*, 11 Nov. 2009.

26. Rona Fischman, "Ibanez Decision, Round Two," *Boston Globe [Boston]*, 15 Oct. 2009, 12 Dec. 2009. <http://www.boston.com/realestate/news/blogs/renow/2009/10/ibanez_decision.html>

27. "Massachusetts Home Prices and Home Values-Local Info," Zillow, 2 Nov. 2009. <http://zillow.com>

28. "Massachusetts Home Prices and Home Values-Local Info," Zillow, 2 Nov. 2009. <http://www.zillow.com/local-info/MA-home-value/r_26/>

29. Jackson.

30. Addison Wiggin and Ian Mathias, "The Second Wave of the Housing Crisis, Profiting from Carbon Caps, U.S. is "Out of Money," lunch with Ron Paul and more," 5minforecast.agorafinancial.com. *Agora Financial*, 26 May 2009.

31. Amy Goodman, "Facing Foreclosure? Don't Leave. Squat," *San Francisco Chronicle [San Francisco]* 4 Feb. 2009, 12 Dec. 2009. <http://www.sfgate.com/cgi-bin/article.cgi?f=/c/a/2009/02/04/EDK215MNA0.DTL>

32. Janna Tetrault and Ann Verrilli, "Addressing the Foreclosure Crisis: State and Federal Initiatives in Massachusetts," Citizen's Housing and Planning Association/CHAPA Briefing Paper, March 2008, 13 Dec. 2009. <http://www.chapa.org/pdf/StateandFederalForeclosureInitiatives08.pdf>

33. "Mass Foreclosures Spiked in '08," *Boston Business Journal [Boston]* 21 Jan. 2009, 5 Dec. 2009. <http://boston.bizjournals.com/boston/stories/2009/01/19/daily34.html>

34. The Warren Group, "Mass. Foreclosures Jump In October From Prior Month, But Dip From a Year Ago," *Banker and Tradesmen,* 11 Nov. 2009.

35. National Low Income Housing Coalition, *Foreclosure in Massachusetts: Properties, Units, and Tenure,* National Low Income Housing Coalition, Worcester, United States, 9 May 2008.

36. Commonwealth of Massachusetts, Massachusetts Dept of Transitional Assistance, Homeless Family Caseload 2005–2009 (Boston: DTA, 27 Dec. 2009). <www.mass.gov/Ehed/docs/dhcd/hs/homelessnumberchart.pdf>

37. Commonwealth of Massachusetts, Massachusetts Dept of Transitional Assistance, Homeless Family Caseload 2005–2009 (Boston: DTA, 27 Dec. 2009). <www.mass.gov/Ehed/docs/dhcd/hs/homelessnumberchart.pdf>

38. Derek Paulson and Ronald Wilson, "Foreclosures and Crime: A Geographical Perspective," *Geography and Public Safety* 1.3, (2008).

39. Zhenguo Lin, Eric Rosenblatt, and Vincent W. Yao, "Spillover Effects of Foreclosures on Neighborhood Property Values," *Journal of Real Estate Finance and Economics*, 38: 4 (2009) 387–407.

40. Paulson.

41. Zillow.

42. U.S. Office of Federal Housing Enterprise Oversight.

43. Stephanie Armour, "Mortgage Relief Program is Still too Slow, Many Say," *USA Today* 9 Sep. 2009, 4 Oct. 2009. <http://www.usatoday.com/money/economy/housing/2009-09-09-mortgages_N.htm>

44. Stacy Myers, "Feds Look into Mortgage Fraud," *Boston Globe [Boston]* 16 Oct. 2008, 13 Dec. 2009. <http://www.boston.com/realestate/news/blogs/renow/2008/10/feds_look_into.html>

45. Michael Powell, "Bank Accused of Pushing Mortgage Deals on Blacks," *New York Times [New York]* 6 June 2009, 7 Dec. 2009. <http://www.nytimes.com/2009/06/07/us/07baltimore.html>

46. Todd Wallack, "Stricter Rules for Mortgage Brokers keep Hundreds Out," *Boston Globe [Boston]* 9 July 2009, 8 Dec. 2009. <http://www.boston.com/business/articles/2009/07/09/stricter_licensing_rules_cut_hundreds_of_would_be_mortgage_brokers/>

47. Wallack.

48. Powell, *Bank Accused of Pushing Mortgage Deals.*

49. "City Life Vida Urbana," Dec. 2009 <http://www.clvu.org/>

50. Ryan Grim, "Inside IndyMac's Nationalization: A Case Study," *Huffington Post* 24 March 2009, 12 Dec. 2009. <http://www.huffingtonpost.com/2009/03/24/inside-indymacs-nationali_n_178100.html>

51. Community Reinvestment Act, 12 USC 2901, Title VII of Pub. L. 95–128, 91 Stat. 1147, 12 Oct. 1977.

52. David Welna, "Democrats Push to End Insurers' Antitrust Exemption," *Morning Edition,* National Public Radio, 23 Oct. 2009, 27 Dec. 2009. <http://www.npr.org/templates/story/story.php?storyId=114063950>

53. Julianne Pepitone, "Bank Failures Stack Up: Now 106 for 2009," CNN, 29 Oct. 2009, 14 Nov. 2009. <http://money.cnn.com/2009/10/23/news/economy/bank_failure/>

54. Cyrus Sanati, "Merging Banks Soar Past U.S. Deposit Cap," *New York Times [New York]* 17 Oct. 2008, 27 Jan. 2009. <http://dealbook.blogs.nytimes.com/2008/10/17/merging-banks-surge-past-us-deposit-cap/>

55. Jacques Delpla, "Who Should, Who Must, Pay to Save the Banks?" *Truthout* 26 March 2009, 4 Jan. 2010.

56. Van Tol.

57. Dean Baker, "Reverse Bank Robbery," *Guardian UK [London]* 31 Aug. 2009, 4 Dec. 2009. <http://www.truthout.org/090109R>

58. "Where Does All the Bailout and Stimulus Money Come From?" *Newshour*, PBS, 18 March 2009, 4 Dec. 2009. <http://www.pbs.org/newshour/extra/video/blog/2009/03/where_does_all_the_money_come.html>

59. Massachusetts Budget and Policy Center, "Budget Transparency and Balance: The FY 2010 Budget Proposals," (Boston: Massachusetts Budget and Policy, 29 June 2009).

60. Elizabeth Weil, "Grumpy Old Drug Smugglers," *New York Times [New York]* 30 May 2004, Dec. 2009. <http://www.nytimes.com/2004/05/30/magazine/grumpy-old-drug-smugglers.html?pagewanted=all>

61. Jeffrey R. Lewis, *Coordinating Contracting of Prescription Drugs: A Fiscal and Policy Strategy for the Commonwealth of Virginia*," (Washington, DC: Heinz Family Philanthropies, 2003).

62. California Nurse's Association, "California's Real Death Panels: Insurers Deny 21% of Claims," *California Nurse's Association*, 2 Sep. 2009, 12 Dec. 2009. <http://www.calnurses.org/media-center/press-releases/2009/september/california-s-real-death-panels-insurers-deny-21-of-claims.html>

63. Cece Connolly, "U.S. Losing Ground on Preventable Deaths," *The Washington Post [Washington, DC]* 6 Oct. 2009.

64. Goldstein, Amy, "States Cut Medicaid Further," *The Washington Post [Washington, DC]* 26 Dec. 2008, A01.

65. Cathy Schoen, Sara R. Collins, Jennifer L. Kriss, and Michelle M. Doty. "How Many Are Underinsured? Trends Among U.S. Adults, 2003 and 2007," Health affairs.org. *Health Affairs* 27.4 (2008).

66. Benjamin Day, "The Implementation of Massachusetts Health Reform," powerpoint presentation, (Boston: Mass-Care, 2008) 21.

67. Day.

68. Day.

69. Day.

70. Atul Gawande, "The Cost Conundrum: What a Texas Town Can Teach Us About Health Care," *The New Yorker*, June 2009.

71. Gawande.

72. Gawande.

73. Gawande.

74. Gawande.

75. Gawande.

76. Gawande.

77. Gawande.

78. Gawande.

79. Gawande.

80. Gawande.

81. Price Waterhouse Coopers' Health Research Initiative, "Behind the Numbers: Medical Cost Trends for 2010," Price Waterhouse Coopers', June 2009.

82. Aon Consulting, "Employers Face 10.5 Percent Health Care Cost Increases, Says Aon Consulting," Aon Consulting, 25 Aug. 2009, 28 Aug. 2009. <http://aon.mediaroom.com/index.php?s=43&item=1676>

83. Catherine Rampell, "U.S. Health Spending Breaks from the Pack," *New York Times [New York]* 8 July 2009, 7 Aug. 2009. <http://economix.blogs. nytimes.com/2009/07/08/us-health-spending-breaks-from-the-pack/>

84. Rampell.

85. Day.

86. Day.

87. Day.

88. Reed Abelson, "Insured but Bankrupted by Health Crises," *New York Times [New York]* 30 June 2009, 30 June 2009. <http://www.nytimes. com/2009/07/01/business/01meddebt.html?>

89. Jonathan Cylus and Gerard F. Anderson "Multinational Comparisons of Health Systems Data, 2006," (New York: Commonwealth Fund, 2007) 14.

90. Rob Stone, "Healthcare Reform: We're Still for It, and We're Not Done Yet!" June 2010, 6.

91. Stone.

92. Chris Hedges, "This Isn't Reform, It's Robbery." *Truthdig,* 23 Aug. 2009, 25 Aug. 2009. <http://www.truthdig.com/report/item/20090823_this_ isnt_reform_its_robbery/>

93. Rampell.

94. Nicholas Kristoff, "Unhealthy America," *New York Times [New York]* 5 Nov. 2009, A35.

95. Kristoff.

96. Kristoff.

97. Connolly.

98. Taunter, "Unconscionable Math," *Tauntermedia*, 28 July 2009, 8 Aug. 2009. <http://tauntermedia.com/2009/07/28/unconscionable-math/>

99. Hedges.

100. Hedges.

101. Connolly.

102. Mark Hoofnagle, "Are Patients in Universal Healthcare Countries Less Satisfied?" *Science Blogs*, 22 May 2008, 22 May 2009. <http://scienceblogs.com/denialism/2009/05/are_patients_in_universal_heal.php>

103. Hoofnagle.

104. Hoofnagle.

105. Donald Light, "Global Drug Discovery: Europe is Ahead," *Health Affairs* 28.5 (2009) 25 Aug. 2009. <http://content.healthaffairs.org/cgi/content/abstract/hlthaff.28.5.w969v1>

106. Henwood, 120.

107. Kristoff.

108. National Nurses Movement, "A Secret Exposed, Medicare Works Better Than Private Insurance," *Talking Points Memo*, 13 July 2009, 25 Nov. 2009. <http://tpmcafe.talkingpointsmemo.com/talk/blogs/national_nurses_movement/2009/07/a-secret-exposed----medicare-w.php>

109. National Nurses Movement.

110. National Nurses Movement.

111. National Nurses Movement.

112. Jefferson Adams, "Does the Government Actually Run the BEST Healthcare?" *San Francisco Health News Examiner* 10 Aug. 2009, 25 Nov. 2009. <http://www.examiner.com/x-8543-SF-Health-News-Examiner~y2009m8d10-Does-the-government-actually-run-the-best-healthcare>

113. Pew Center on the States, *One in 31: The Long Reach of American Corrections*, (Washington, DC: The Pew Charitable Trust, March 2009).

114. Pew Center on the States.

115. Council of State Governments, Re-entry Policy Council *Report of the Re-Entry Policy Council: Charting the Safe and Successful Return of Prisoners to the Community* (New York: Council of State Governments, January 2005).

116. Commonwealth of Massachusetts, Governor's Commission on Corrections Reform, *Strengthening Public Safety, Increasing Accountability, and Instituting Fiscal Responsibility in the Department of Correction* (Boston: Commonwealth of Massachusetts, 2004).

117. Pew Center on the States.

118. Pew Center on the States.

119. Pew Center on the States.

120. Commonwealth of Massachusetts, Massachusetts Department of Correction, "General Information about the DOC," 12 Dec. 2009.

121. Massachusetts Department of Correction.

122. Commonwealth of Massachusetts, Massachusetts Department of Correction, *Quarterly Report on the Status of Prison Overcrowding, Second Quarter 2009* (Boston: Commonwealth of Massachusetts, August 2009).

123. Council of State Governments.

124. Massachusetts Department of Correction.

125. Governor's Commission on Corrections Reform, *Strengthening Public Safety.*

126. Pew Center on the States.

127. *Criminal Justice Policy Coalition Newsletter* (Criminal Justice Policy Coalition, July 2005) 20 Feb. 2009 <http://www.cjpc.org/JulyNewsletter.htm>

128. Council of State Governments.

129. Claire Kaplan/CEK Strategies, "CORI: Balancing Individual Rights and Public Access," (Boston: Boston Foundation, 2005).

130. Boston Workers Alliance, "An Act to Reform CORI, Restore Opportunity, And Improve Public Safety," *Boston Workers Alliance*, May 2009. <bostonworkersalliance.org/wp-content/.../cori-reform-bill-2009-final.pdf>

131. Boston Workers Alliance, "Remove the Criminal Record Check Box from Initial Job Applications," *Boston Workers' Alliance*, 2009.

132. Pew Center on the States.

133. Pew Center on the States.

134. Pew Center on the States.

135. Pew Center on the States.

136. Pew Center on the States.

137. Pew Center on the States.

138. Sam Wheeler, "Prison Suicide Hearing at MA State House," *Boston Indymedia*, 11 May 2007. <http://boston.indymedia.org/feature/display/199380/index.php>

139. Council of State Governments.

140. Governor's Commission on Corrections Reform, *Strengthening Public Safety.*

141. Counselors and Advocates from Drug and Alcohol Rehabilitation Sector, Personal Communication, Fall 2006.

Part III: Into Deeper Water for Safety

1. Massachusetts Housing and Shelter Alliance, *Home & Healthy for Good: A Statewide Housing First Program Progress Report*, (Boston: Massachusetts Housing and Shelter Alliance, June 2009).

2. Massachusetts Housing and Shelter Alliance.

3. New York City Department of Homeless Services, *Hope 2010: The NYC Street Survey* (New York: New York City Department of Homeless Services, 4 March 2010) 4.

4. United States, Department of Housing and Urban Development, *HomeBase Focuses on Housing Development* (Washington, DC: Research Works, 2009).

5. Massachusetts Senior Action Council, *Home Care For All! Invest in Equal Choice and Community First*, (Massachusetts: Massachusetts Senior Action Council, May 2009). <http://www.massenioraction.org>

6. Massachusetts Senior Action Council.

7. Massachusetts Senior Action Council.

8. Massachusetts Senior Action Council.

9. Massachusetts Law Reform Institute, *Fact Sheet: Food Stamps/SNAP: A Fork-Ready Stimulus, Mass Legal Services*, 30 May 2009. <http://www.masslegalservices.org/node/26545>

10. Massachusetts Law Reform Institute.

11. David Abel, "Childhood Poverty Increasing in Mass," *Boston Globe* [Boston] 17 Sep. 2008, 27 Nov. 2009. <http://www.boston.com/news/local/articles/2008/09/17/childhood_poverty_increasing_in_mass/>

12. The Medical News, "8.3% of Households in Massachusetts Struggle with Food Insecurity," *The Medical News* 20 Nov. 2009, 4 Dec. 2009. <http://www.news-medical.net/news/20091120/8325-of-households-in-Massachusetts-struggle-with-food-insecurity.aspx>

13. Richard Rothstein, "When There's Not Enough Food for Thought," *New York Times* [New York] 1 Aug. 2001.

14. Meaghan Irons, "Economy's Woes Driving More People to Local Food Pantries," *Boston Globe* [Boston] 6 Nov. 2009, 12 Dec. 2009. <http://www.boston.com/news/local/massachusetts/articles/2009/11/06/economys_woes_driving_more_p>

15. Rothstein.

16. Massachusetts Law Reform Institute.

Part IV: Ensuring a Deep-sea Worthy Vessel

1. Lawrence Mishel, *Waging Inequality in America*, (Washington, DC: The Economic Policy Institute, 30 March 2009) 10.

Notes 337

2. Massachusetts Budget and Policy Center, "Property Taxes: Helping Those Who Need it Most," (Boston: Massachusetts Budget and Policy Center, May 2008), 1.

3. Massachusetts Budget and Policy Center, "Property Taxes."

4. Massachusetts Budget and Policy Center, "Slides on State Taxes,"(Boston: Massachusetts Budget and Policy Center, Feb. 2008).

5. Massachusetts Budget and Policy Center, "Slides on State Taxes."

6. Massachusetts Budget and Policy Center, "Slides on State Taxes."

7. Massachusetts Budget and Policy Center, "Slides on State Taxes."

8. Jeff McLynch and James R. St. George, *Gone With the Wind: Massachusetts' Vanishing Corporate Income Tax*, (Boston: Massachusetts Budget and Policy Center, 2003).

9. McLynch and St. George.

10. Robert Tannenwald, "State Business Tax Climate: How Should it Be Measured and How Important Is It," *New England Economic Review*, Federal Reserve bank of Boston, (January/February 1996).

11. Tannenwald.

12. Tannenwald.

13. Tannenwald.

14. Massachusetts Budget and Policy Center, "Slides on State Taxes."

15. Massachusetts Budget and Policy Center, "Property Taxes" 3.

16. Massachusetts Budget and Policy Center, *Facts at a Glance: The Income Tax*, (Boston: Massachusetts Budget and Policy Center, 2 April 2009).

17. Chart created for this book with data from Paul Kivel, *You Call This a Democracy?* (New York: The Apex Press, 2006) 19.

18. Peter R. Orszag and Joseph E. Stiglitz, "Biting the Budget Bullet: Why Raising Taxes Is the Least Painful Way Out of the State's Fiscal Crisis," *Boston Globe [Boston]* 27 April 2003.

19. Larry Beinhart, "TAX CUTS: THEOLOGY, FACTS & TOTALLY F**KED," *Huffington Post* 17 Nov. 2008, 25 July 2009. <http://www.huffingtonpost.com/larry-beinhart/tax-cuts-theology-facts-t_b_144281.html>

20. Tax Policy Center, Urban Institute and Brookings Institution, "Percent of Tax Filers by Marginal Tax Rate," Taxpolicycenter.org, *Tax Policy Center*, 12 Dec. 2009. <http://www.taxpolicycenter.org/taxfacts/displayafact.cfm?Docid=262>

21. Josh Bivens, *Gross domestic income: profit growth swamps labor income*, (Washington, DC: Economic Policy Institute, 2006), 2.

22. Chye-Ching Huang, Jason Levitis, and James R. Horney, "Very Few Small Business Owners Would Face Tax Increases Under President's Budget," *Center on Budget and Policy Priorities*, 28 Feb. 2009, 27 Dec. 2010. <http://www.cbpp.org/cms/index.cfm?fa=view&id=2697>

23. Beinhart.

24. Thom Hartmann, "The Great Tax Con Job," *Huffington Post* 21 July 2009, 25 July 2009. <http://www.huffingtonpost.com/thom-hartmann/the-great-tax-con-job_b_242065.html>

25. Hartmann.

26. Hartmann.

27. Hartmann.

28. Beinhart.

29. Beinhart

30. Created for this book with data from United States Internal Revenue Service, "Statistics of Income Bulletin." *IRS.gov.* Internal Revenue Service, Winter 2002–2003, Publication 1136.

31. Mishel, *Waging Inequality in America* 30.

32. Walter G. Keim, "Prices and Wages," *Journal of the American Statistical Association,* 37.19 (1942).

33. Carl Davis, et al., *Who Pays: A Distributional Analysis of the Tax Systems in All 50 States,* third edition, (Washington, DC: Institute on Taxation and Economic Policy, November 2009).

34. Mishel, *Waging Inequality in America* 12.

35. Sarah Anderson, et. al, *Executive Excess; The Staggering Social Cost of U.S. Business Leadership,* (Boston: United for a Fair Economy, 2008).

36. Mike Prokosch, "Presentation on the Economic Crisis," power point presentation, 2008.

37. Chart created for this book with data from "Banking Compensation," graph, *Reuters Research.* <http://graphics.thomsonreuters.com/099/GLB_EXCMP0909.gif>

38. Alistair Barr and Matt Andrejczak, "Wall Street Pay Changes 'Glacial' Amid Year of Outrage," *MarketWatch* 21 Dec. 2009, 9 Jan. 2010. <http://www.marketwatch.com/story/wall-street-pay-reform-glacial-despite-outrage-2009-12-21>

39. Sarah Anderson, "Can Europe Pop the U.S. CEO Pay Bubble?," *Yes! Magazine* 2 Sep. 2009, 2 Sep. 2009. <http://www.yesmagazine.org/new-economy/can-europe-pop-the-u.s.-ceo-pay-bubble>

40. Chart created for this book with data from Reuters Research.

41. Stephen J. Rose, *Social Stratification in the United States: The American Profile Poster* 2nd edition. (New York: The New Press, 2007).

42. Stephen J. Rose, *American Profile Poster* excerpt. © Copyright 2005, Stephen J. Rose. Printed by permission of the author.

43. Rose, *American Profile Poster* excerpt.

44. Rose, *American Profile Poster* excerpt.

45. Rose, *American Profile Poster* excerpt.

46. Luisa Krull, Matthew Miller, and Tatiana Serafin, "The World's Billionaires," *Forbes Magazine* 11 March 2009, 23 July 2009. <http://www.forbes.com/2009/03/11/worlds-richest-people-billionaires-2009-billionaires_land.html>

47. Robert Reich, "Financing the Common Good," *The American Prospect* 1 Feb. 2008, 17 April 2009. <http://www.prospect.org/cs/articles?\article=financing_the_common_good>

48. David Abel, "Childhood Poverty Increasing in Mass," *Boston Globe [Boston]* 17 Sep. 2008, 27 Nov. 2009. <http://www.boston.com/news/local/articles/2008/09/17/childhood_poverty_increasing_in_mass/>

49. Commonwealth of Massachusetts, *FY 2010 Budget Summary* (Boston: Commonwealth of Massachusetts, 2010). <http://www.mass.gov/bb/gaa/fy2010/app_10/ga_10/hadefault.htm>

50. Randy Albeda, Mary Ann Allard, Mary Ellen Colton, and Carol Cosenza. *In Harm's Way? Domestic Violence, AFDC Receipt and Welfare Reform in Massachusetts.* (Boston, MA: University of Massachusetts Boston Center for Social Policy, 1997).

51. Vicky Lovell, Kevin Miller, and Claudia Williams, *Valuing Good Health in Massachusetts: The Costs and Benefits of Paid Sick Days,"* (Washington, DC: Institute for Women's Policy Research, Feb. 2009).

52. Lovell.

53. Lovell.

54. Lovell.

55. Minnesota Department of Employee Relations, *Minnesota Local Government Pay Equity Compliance Report* (Saint Paul, MN: Minnesota Legislature, Jan. 2009)

56. Carlton Meyer, "America's 20 Percent Unemployment Rate," *Truthout,* 6 April 2009, 24 April 2009. <http://www.truthout.org/041009LA>

57. Meyer.

58. Meyer.

59. Meyer.

60. Union of Minority Neighborhoods homepage 12 Dec. 2009. <http://www.unionofminorityneighborhoods.org/>

61. John Williams, "Alternate Unemployment Charts," *Shadow Government Statistics,* 7 Dec. 2009. <http://www.shadowstats.com>

62. Bill McBride, "March Employment Report: 162K Jobs Added, 9.7% Unemployment Rate," *Calculated Risk,* April 2010, 15 May 2010. <http://assets.theatlantic.com/static/mt/assets/business/job%20losses%20as%20of%20march%2010.png>

63. Williams.

64. Williams.

65. Diana Pearce with Johanna Brooks in partnership with Wider Opportunities for Women, *Self-Sufficiency Standard Report for Massachusetts, Family Economic Self-Sufficiency State Organizing Project,* (Boston: Women's Educational and Industrial Union, 2003).

66. Massachusetts Budget and Policy Center, "Minimum Wage Increase Could Help Close to a Million Low-Wage Workers," (Boston: Massachusetts Budget and Policy Center, 20 March 2006)

67. David Madland and Karla Walter, "Unions Are Good for the American Economy," *Center for America Progress,* 18 Feb. 2009, 23 Feb. 2009. <http://www.americanprogressaction.org/issues/2009/02/efca_factsheets.html>

68. Mishel, *Waging Inequality in America* 18.

69. Martin Crutsinger, "U.S. Productivity Surges in Second Quarter," *Associated Press* 12 Aug. 2009, 13 Aug. 2009. <http://seattletimes.nwsource.com/html/businesstechnology/2009639139_apuseconomy.html>

70. Lawrence Mishel, *Agenda for Shared Prosperity.* (Washington, DC: The Economic Policy Institute, 30 March 2009).

71. Lovell.

72. American Rights at Work, *The Labor Day List: Partnerships that Work,* (Washington, DC: American Rights at Work, 2007).

73. "Lawrence Textile Strike," *Wikipedia,* 2004, 5 Dec. 2009. <http://en.wikipedia.org/wiki/Lawrence_textile_strike>

74. Wikipedia, "Lawrence Textile Strike."

75. Wikipedia, "Lawrence Textile Strike."

76. Wikipedia, "Lawrence Textile Strike."

77. "Trade union," *Wikipedia,* 2001, 30 Aug. 2009. <http://en.wikipedia.org/wiki/Trade_union>

78. Robert Reich, "Why We Need Stronger Unions and How to Get Them," RobertReich, 27 Jan. 2009, 4 Jan. 2010. <http://robertreich.blogspot.com/2009/01/why-we-need-stronger-unions-and-how-to.html>

79. Printed with permission of Elaine Bernard.

80. Printed with permission of Elaine Bernard.

81. Printed with permission of Elaine Bernard.

82. Printed with permission of Elaine Bernard.

83. Mishel, *Agenda for Shared Prosperity.*

84. Bob Cunha and Phyllis Neufield, "Commentary: Unions Urge Transparency in Health Care Talks," *Wicked Local* The Lexington Minuteman 23 April 2009, 4 Jan. 2010. <http://www.wickedlocal.com/lexington/news/opinions/x297232056/Commentary-Unions-urge-transparency-in-health-care-talks>

85. Printed with permission of Elaine Bernard.

86. Printed with permission of Elaine Bernard.
87. Michael Ettlinger, "Securing the Wage Floor: Indexing Would Maintain Minimum Wage's Value, and Provide Predictability to Employers," (Washington, DC: Economic Policy Institute, 12 Oct. 2006).
88. Printed with permission of Elaine Bernard.
89. "Education," *Wikipedia* 14 Dec. 2009 <http://en.wikipedia.org/wiki/Education>
90. Wikipedia, "Education."
91. Thomas Downes, Jeff Abel and Dana Ansel *Incomplete Grade: Massachusetts Education Reform at 15* (Boston: MassINC/Massachusetts Institute for a New Commonwealth, 2009).
92. Downes et al.
93. Downes et al.
94. Jonathan Kozol, "Keynote address," 24th Annual Worcester County Community Breakfast Honoring the Reverend Martin Luther King, Jr., Quinsigamond Community College and the University of Massachusetts Medical School, Quinsigamond Community College Worcester, MA, 19 Jan. 2009, keynote address.
95. Sarah Theule Lubienski and Charles Lubienski "School Sector and Academic Achievement: A Multilevel Analysis of NAEP Mathematics Data," *American Educational Research Journal* 43.4. *(2006)*
96. Lubienski and Lubienski.
97. Louis Kruger "Testimony in Support of House Bill No. 3660: An Act To Improve Assessment And Accountability To Ensure Students Acquire 21st Century Skills," testimony, United States Congress, 23 June 2009.
98. John Hilliard, "Part of MCAS Test May be History," *Daily News Tribune [Boston]* 24 Feb. 2009, 20 Dec. 2009. <http://www.dailynewstribune.com/state/x1749106394/Part-of-MCAS-test-may-be-history>
99. Michael Thompson, "Voter Turnout: Other Nations Overshadow U.S.," *Associated Content* 4 Nov. 2008, 13 Dec. 2009. <http://www.associatedcontent.com/article/1177719/voter_turnout_other_nations_overshadow.html>

Part V: Rebuilding a Better Ship After Storm Damage

1. Daniel Howden, "Deforestation: The Hidden Cause of Global Warming," *The Independent [UK]* 14 May 2007, 14 December 2010. <http://www.independent.co.uk/environment/climate-change/deforestation-the-hidden-cause-of-global-warming-448734.html>
2. Howden.
3. Howden.

4. Maywa Montenegro, "The Big Three: The Numbers Behind Ethanol, Cellulosic Ethanol, and Biodiesel in the U.S.," *Grist Magazine [Seattle]* 4 Dec. 2006.

5. Russell Gold, Ben Casselman and Guy Chazan, "Leaking Oil Well Lacked Safeguard Device," *Wall Street Journal* 28 April 2010, 18 May 2010. <http://online.wsj.com/article/NA_WSJ_PUB: SB10001424052748704423504575212031417936798.html>

6. Ian Urbina, "Despite Moratorium, Drilling Projects Move Ahead" *New York Times* 23 May 2010, 20 August 2010. <http://www.nytimes. com/2010/05/24/us/24moratorium.html?_r=1>

7. Robert Tomsho, "Winds Shift in Energy Debate," *Wall Street Journal* 19 June 2008, July 2010. <http://online.wsj.com/article/ SB121382784900886363.html?mod=special_page_campaign2008_ mostpop>

8. Commonwealth of Massachusetts, Office for Commonwealth Development, *Massachusetts Climate Protection Plan 2004* (Boston: Office for Commonwealth Development, 2004).

9. Paul Chernick, "Commentary: Towns Want 'Muni' Options," *Lexington Minuteman [Lexington, MA]* 17 Sep. 2009, 4 Jan. 2010. <http://mehrco. web.officelive.com/lm_091709.aspx>

10. Illinois Oil and Gas Association., "Petroleum Products in our Daily Lives" *Illinois Oil and Gas Association*, 29 Nov. 2009. <http://www.ioga.com/ Special/PetroProducts.htm>

11. TRIP, *Future Mobility in Massachusetts: Meeting the State's Need for Safe and Efficient Mobility*, (Washington, DC: *TRIP*, June 2008).

12. David Shrank and Tim Lomax, *Performance Measure Summary Boston, MA-NH-RI: Urban Area Report*, (Texas: Central Texas Regional Mobility Authority, 2007).

13. Randall Crane, "Is There a Quiet Revolution in Women's Travel? Revisiting the Gender Gap in Commuting," *Journal of the American Planning Association* 73.3 (September 2007), 8.

14. Alan E. Pisarski, "Commuting in America III: The Third National Report on Commuting Patterns and Trends," TRB.org, *Transportation Research Board of the National Academies*, Nov. 2006, 5 Jan. 2009. <http:// onlinepubs.trb.org/onlinepubs/trnews/trnews247CIAIII.pdf>

15. Jim Motavalli, "The Costs of Owning a Car," *New York Times [New York]* 18 March 2009, 13 Dec. 2009. <http://wheels.blogs.nytimes. com/2009/03/18/the-costs-of-owning-a-car/>

16. Jay Pateakos, "Final Section of Providence Way Project Opens Tuesday," *Herald News [Providence, RI]* 13 Oct. 2009, 4 Nov. 2009. <http://www. heraldnews.com/news/local_news/x593084081/Final-section-of- Providence-Iway-project-opens-Tuesday>

17. Mark Jewell, "Bristol-Myers Squibb to Build Manufacturing Plant at Devens," *Boston Globe [Boston, MA]* 1 June 2006, 27 Dec. 2009. <http://www.boston.com/news/local/massachusetts/articles/2006/06/01/bristol_myers_squibb_to_build_manufacturing_plant_at_devens/>

18. Frannie Carr, "Evergreen Solar to Move Jobs to China," WBUR, Providence, RI, 5 Nov. 2009, 14 Dec. 2010. <http://www.wbur.org/2009/11/05/evergreen-china>

19. "Report: $9M In Stimulus For Gillette Footbridge?" WBZ Television, 7 Nov. 2009, 27 Dec. 2009. <http://wbztv.com/local/gillette.stadium.patriot.2.1298599.html>

20. Peter Medoff and Holly Sklar, *Streets of Hope: The Rise and Fall of an Urban Neighborhood* (Cambridge: South End Press, 1999).

21. "IndieBound FAQ," *IndieBound,* 23 Nov. 2009. <http://www.indiebound.org/indiebound-faq>

22. Civic Economics, *Local Works! Examining the Impact of Local Business on the West Michigan Economy,* (Grand Rapids, MI: Local First, Grand Rapids, 2008).

23. 10percentshift, "Local Shift: Build Local Economies by Purchasing with Purpose," *10% Shift,* 12 March 2009. <http://www.10percentshift.org/design/localshift.php?p=studies>

24. 10percentshift.

25. "Issue 3: Will Casinos Come to Ohio?" WTVG-TV, 3 Nov. 2009, 27 Dec. 2009. <http://abclocal.go.com/wtvg/story?section=news/politics&id=7096141>

26. Carol Costello, "Small Business Owners Make Big Sacrifices," CNN, 25 March 2009, 22 Dec. 2009. <http://amfix.blogs.cnn.com/2009/03/25/small-business-owners-make-big-sacrifices/>

27. Jeff McLynch and James R. St. George, *Gone With the Wind: Massachusetts' Vanishing Corporate Income Tax,* (Boston: Massachusetts Budget and Policy Center, 2003).

28. David Schepp, "Wal-Mart to Pay $40 Million to Settle Labor Lawsuit in Massachusetts," *Daily Finance,* 3 Dec. 2009, 4 Jan. 2010. <http://www.dailyfinance.com/story/wal-mart-pays-40m-to-settle-labor-lawsuit-in-massachusetts/19264429>

29. Commonwealth of Massachusetts, Executive Office of Health and Human Services, Division of Health Care Finance and Policy, *Employers Who Had Fifty or More Employees Using MassHealth, Commonwealth Care, or the Uncompensated Care Pool/Safety Net in FY08* (Boston, MA: Division of Health Care Finance and Policy, April 2009).

30. Al Norman, "Wal-Mart's Self-Dealing Income Tax Scam: North Carolina Court Tosses Out $33.5 Million Case," *Huffington Post* 8 Jan. 2008, 30 March 2009. <http://www.huffingtonpost.com/al-norman/walmarts-selfdealing-inco_b_80524.html>

31. Union of Concerned Scientists, *Massachusetts: Confronting Climate Change in the U.S.*, (Boston: Northeast Climate Impacts Assessment, 2007), 1.

32. Norton Juster, *The Phantom Tollbooth* (Bel Air, CA: Bullseye Books, 1988).

33. United States Department of Energy, Energy Efficiency and Renewable Energy, "Electric Power and Renewable Energy in Massachusetts," *EERE State Activities & Partnerships*, 25 June 2008. *<http://apps1.eere.energy. gov/states/electricity.cfm/state=MA>*

34. Environment Massachusetts and Clean Water Fund from the Report of the Senate Committee on Post-Audit and Oversight and the Senate Committee on Global Warming and Climate Change, *The Cost of Inaction: Climate Change in the Commonwealth.* (Boston: Commonwealth of Massachusetts, July 2008). <www.mass.gov/legis/bills/ senate/185/st02/st02870.htm>

35. Donald Fournier and Eileen Westervelt, *Energy Trends and Their Implications for U.S. Army Installations* (Washington, DC: US Army Corps of Engineers, Sep. 2005).

36. Massachusetts Department of Fish and Game River Advocate, Personal communication, 2007.

37. Bryan Walsh, "Denmark's Wind of Change," *Time Magazine* 25 Feb. 2009, 4 Jan. 2010. <http://www.time.com/time/magazine/ article/0,9171,1881646,00.html>

38. Walsh.

39. Commonwealth of Massachusetts, *Climate Protection Plan 2004.*

40. John Farrell and David Morris, *Energy Self-Reliant States*, Second and expanded edition, (Minneapolis, MN: Institute for Local Self-Reliance/ New Rules Project, May 2010).

41. *Beals and Thomas, Inc.* for Alternatives Unlimited, Inc., *Whitin Mill Complex Green Design Feasibility Study*, (Boston: Massachusetts Technology Collaborative, March 2003).

42. State of Illinois, Chicago Department of Environment, *Data Comparison Between the City Hall Rooftop Garden and the Black Tar Roof of the Cook County Building* (Chicago: Chicago Department of Environment, 2001).

43. "Residential Customers: Energy Facts," *MassSAVE*, 13 Dec. 2009. <http:// www.masssave.com/residential/heating-and-cooling/get-the-facts/ energy-facts/>

44. "Residential Customers: Energy Facts," *MassSAVE*, 13 Dec. 2009. <http:// www.masssave.com/residential/heating-and-cooling/get-the-facts/ energy-facts/>

45. Farrell.

46. United States Department of Agriculture Forest Service, Northeast Area State and Private Forestry, PA and Mid-Atlantic Center for Urban and Community Forestry, "The Value of Trees," Urban and Community Forestry Appreciation Tool Kit *Parks and People*, 13 Dec. 2009. <http://parksandpeople.org/publications/special_reports/TreeBenefits.pdf>

47. United States Department of Agriculture Forest Service et al., "The Value of Trees."

48. *In the Loop!* (Boston, MA: MassRecycle/Massachusetts Recycling Coalition, Jan.–Feb. 2008) No. 3.

49. Commonwealth of Massachusetts, City of Worcester, *Report on Implementation of Climate Action Plan* (Worcester, MA: Office of Economic and Neighborhood Development, City Council of Worcester, Massachusetts, July, 2007).

50. "Technology Quarterly," *The Economist* 9 June 2007.

51. "The State of Waste in Massachusetts," Massachusetts Recycling Coalition.

52. *"In the Loop!* (Boston, MA: MassRecycle/Massachusetts Recycling Coalition, Oct. 2009) No. 7.

53. *In the Loop!* (Boston, MA: MassRecycle/Massachusetts Recycling Coalition, April 2009) No. 6.

54. Commonwealth of Massachusetts, *Climate Protection Plan, 2004.*

55. Safe Car Guide, "New or Used —What's Best for Me?" *Safe Car Guide,* 12 Dec. 2009. <http://www.safecarguide.com/gui/new/idx.htm>

56. Motavalli.

57. Pam Belleck, "Massachusetts Proposal Would Repeal Income Tax," *New York Times [New York]* 28 Sep. 2008, 27 Jan. 2009. <http://www.nytimes.com/2008/09/28/us/28ballot.html?em>

58. Petz Scholtus, "Barcelona's Bike Sharing Program Celebrates its 2-Year Anniversary with its 186,000 Users," *Treehugger,* 19 March 2009. <http://www.treehugger.com/files/2009/03/bicing-barcelona-2-year-anniversary.php>

59. Commonwealth of Massachusetts, *Climate Protection Plan 2004.*

60. Ezra Klein, "The Meat of the Problem," *Washington Post [Washington DC]* 29 July 2009, 4 Sep. 2009. <http://voices.washingtonpost.com/ezra-klein/2009/07/this_weeks_gut_check_column_th.html>

61. Citigroup Global Markets, et al., in response to "Notice of Proposed Rulemaking on Loan Guarantees for Projects that Employ Innovative Technologies (RIN 1901-AB21), 72 Federal Register 27471," Citigroup Global Markets, Inc., Credit Suisse Securites, LLC, Goldman Sachs & Co., Lehman Brothers Inc., Merrill Lynch & Co., and Morgan Stanley & Co. Incorporated, letter, 2 July 2007.

62. *Chernobyl Heart,* dir. Maryann De Leo, HBO Films, 2009.

63. Citigroup, et al.

64. Everett M. Rogers, *Diffusion of Innovations* (Glencoe, IL: Free Press, 1962).

65. Commonwealth of Massachusetts, *Climate Protection Plan 2004*.

66. Stacy Ho and Satya Rhodes-Conway, *A Short Guide to Setting Up a City-Scale Retrofit Program*, (Oakland: Green for All and COWS/ Center On Wisconsin Strategy, June 2009).

67. Ho and Rhodes-Conway.

68. Union of Minority Neighborhoods.

69. Ho and Rhodes-Conway.

70. BlueGreen Alliance, *Clean Energy Economy Report: How to Revitalize America's Middle Class with the Clean Energy Economy*, (Minneapolis: BlueGreen Alliance, 2009).

71. BlueGreen Alliance.

72. Michael Jamison, "Conservation Saved Enough to Power a Small City," *The Missoulian [Missoula, MT]* 20 Jan. 2008, 30 July 2009 <http://www.bluefish.org/bpasaved.htm>

73. Mary Serreze, "Biomass or Biomess?" *Valley Advocate [Northampton, MA]* 30 June 2009, 4 Jan. 2010. <http://www.valleyadvocate.com/article.cfm?aid=9967>

74. Ray Raphael, *The First American Revolution* (New York: The New Press, 2002) 13–14.

Bibliography

Abel, David. "Childhood Poverty Increasing in Mass." *Boston.com.* Boston Globe, 17 Sep. 2008. Web. 27 Nov. 2009.

Abelson, Reed. "Insured but Bankrupted by Health Crises." *NYTimes.com.* New York Times, 30 June 2009. Web. 30 June 2009.

Adams, Jefferson. "Does the Government Actually Run the BEST Healthcare?" *Examiner.com.* San Francisco Health News Examiner, 10 Aug. 2009. Web. 25 Nov. 2009.

Albeda, Randy, Mary Ann Allard, Mary Ellen Colton, and Carol Cosenza. *In Harm's Way? Domestic Violence, AFDC Receipt and Welfare Reform in Massachusetts.* Boston, MA: University of Massachusetts Boston Center for Social Policy, Feb. 1997. Print.

Altman, Roger G. "The Great Crash, 2008." *ForeignAffairs.com.* Foreign Affairs, *Jan./Feb.* 2009. Web. 27 Nov. 2009.

American Rights at Work. *The Labor Day List: Partnerships that Work.* Washington, DC: American Rights at Work, 2007. Print.

Anderson, Sarah. "Can Europe Pop the U.S. CEO Pay Bubble?" *YesMagazine. com.* Yes! Magazine, 2 Sep. 2009. Web. 2 Sep. 2009.

Anderson, Sarah, and John Cavanagh, Chuck Collins, Sam Pizzigati, and Mike Lapham. *Executive Excess.* Boston: United for a Fair Economy, 2008.

Aon Consulting. "Employers Face 10.5 Percent Health Care Cost Increases, Says Aon Consulting." Press Release. *aon.mediaroom.com.* Aon Consulting, 25 Aug. 2009.

Armour, Stephanie. "Mortgage Relief Program is Still too Slow, Many Say." *USAtoday.com.* USA Today, 9 Sep. 2009. Web. 4 Oct. 2009.

Baker, Dean. "Reverse Bank Robbery." *Guardian.co.uk.* The Guardian UK [London], 31 Aug. 2009. Web. 4 Dec. 2009.

Barr, Alistair and Matt Andrejczak. "Wall Street Pay Changes 'Glacial' Amid Year of Outrage." *MarketWatch.com.* MarketWatch, 21 Dec. 2009. Web. 9 Jan. 2010.

Beals and Thomas, Inc. for Alternatives Unlimited, Inc. *Whitin Mill Complex Green Design Feasibility Study.* Boston: Massachusetts Technology Collaborative, March 2003. 12 March 2003. PDF file.

Beinhart, Larry. "TAX CUTS: THEOLOGY, FACTS & TOTALLY F**KED." *Huffingtonpost.com.* Huffington Post, 17 Nov. 2008. Web. 25 July 2009.

Belleck, Pam. "Massachusetts Proposal Would Repeal Income Tax." *NYTimes. com.* New York Times, 28 Sep. 2008 Web. 27 Jan. 2009.

Bender, Bruce. "State Must Act to Control Costs of Top-Heavy Health-Care System." *Telegram.com.* Telegram & Gazette [Worcester], 11 March 2009. Web. 12 March 2009.

Bennet, Drake. "Paradigm Lost." *Boston.com.* Boston Globe, 13 Dec. 2008. Web. 21 Dec. 2009.

Bernard, Elaine. "Re: Union slideshow explanation". Message to the author. 9 July 2009. E-mail.

Bernard, Elaine and Sonte DuCote. "Why Unions Matter." *AFSCME Next Wave Conference.* Chicago, Illinois. 19 June 2009. Presentation.

Bianco, Katalina. "The Subprime Lending Crisis: Causes and Effects of the Mortgage Meltdown." *CCH Incorporated.* CCH Incorporated, May 2008. Web.

Bivens, Josh. *Gross domestic income: profit growth swamps labor income.* Washington, DC: Economic Policy Institute, 2006. Print.

BlueGreen Alliance. *Clean Energy Economy Report: How to Revitalize America's Middle Class with the Clean Energy Economy.* Minneapolis: BlueGreen Alliance, June 2009. Print.

Boston Workers' Alliance. "An Act to Reform CORI, Restore Opportunity, And Improve Public Safety." *Boston Workers' Alliance.* Bostonworkersalliance. org, May 2009. Web.

Boston Workers' Alliance. *Remove the Criminal Record Check Box from Initial Job Applications.* Boston, MA: Boston Workers' Alliance, 2009. PDF file.

California Nurse's Association. "California's Real Death Panels: Insurers Deny 21% of Claims." *Calnurses.org.* California Nurse's Association, 2 Sep. 2009. Web. 12 Dec. 2009.

Center for Economic and Policy Research. *"CEPR Statement on the Increase of the Minimum Wage."* *CEPR.net.* Center for Economic and Policy Research, 20 July 2009. Web. 13 Nov. 2009.

Chernick, Paul. "Commentary: Towns Want 'Muni' Options." *Lexingtonminutemen.com.* Lexington Minuteman [Lexington,MA], 17 Sep. 2009. Web. 4 Jan. 2010.

Chernobyl Heart. Dir. Maryann De Leo. HBO Films, 2009. Film.

Citigroup Global Markets, et al., in response to "Notice of Proposed Rulemaking on Loan Guarantees for Projects that Employ Innovative Technologies (RIN 1901-AB21), 72 Federal Register 27471." Citigroup Global Markets, Inc.; Credit Suisse Securities, LLC; Goldman Sachs & Co.; Lehman Brothers Inc.; Merrill Lynch & Co.; and Morgan Stanley & Co. Incorporated. Letter, 2 July 2007.

City Life Vida Urbana. *CLVU.org.* City Life Vida Urbana, n.d. Web. 14 June 2090

Civic Economics. *Local Works! Examining the Impact of Local Business on the West Michigan Economy.* Grand Rapids, MI; Local First, Grand Rapids, 2008.

Coakley, Martha. "Lenders and Servicers' Promises of Loan Modifications in Massachusetts are Not Matched by Meaningful Actions That

Promote Sustainable Loans." Testimony. U.S. House Financial Services Committee, 17 Sep. 2008. Print.

Commonwealth of Massachusetts, City of Worcester. *Report on Implementation of Climate Action Plan.* Worcester, MA: Office of Economic and Neighborhood Development, July, 2007. Print.

Commonwealth of Massachusetts, Executive Office of Health and Human Services. *Employers Who Had Fifty or More Employees Using MassHealth, Commonwealth Care, or the Uncompensated Care Pool/ Safety Net in FY08.* Boston: Division of Health Care Finance and Policy, April 2009. 4 Jan. 2010. PDF file.

Commonwealth of Massachusetts. *FY 2010 Budget Summary.* 2009. Web. 16 Dec. 2009

Commonwealth of Massachusetts, Governor's Commission on Corrections Reform. *Strengthening Public Safety, Increasing Accountability, and Instituting Fiscal Responsibility in the Department of Correction.* Boston: Commonwealth of Massachusetts, 2004. Print.

Commonwealth of Massachusetts, Massachusetts Department of Correction. "General Information about the DOC." *Massachusetts Department of Correction.* Web. 12 Dec. 2009.

Commonwealth of Massachusetts, Massachusetts Department of Correction. *Quarterly Report on the Status of Prison Overcrowding, Second Quarter 2009.* Boston: Commonwealth of Massachusetts, August 2009. Print.

Commonwealth of Massachusetts, Massachusetts Department of Transitional Assistance. *Homeless Family Caseload 2005–2009. Mass.gov.* Department of Transitional Assistance, 27 Dec. 2009. Web.

Commonwealth of Massachusetts, Office for Commonwealth Development. *Massachusetts Climate Protection Plan.* Boston: Commonwealth of Massachusetts, 2004. Print.

Commonwealth vs. Fremont Investment & Loan and Fremont General Corporation. 452mss733, Suffolk County Superior Court. Supreme Judicial Court of Massachusetts. *WorcesterActivist.org.* 25 Feb. 2008. Web. 6 April 2008.

Community Reinvestment Act. Federal Reserve Records. Pub. L. 95–128. Title VII. 91 Stat. 1147. 12 USC 2901. 12 Oct. 1977. Web. 27 Dec. 2009.

Connell, Tula. "Young Workers: A Lost Decade." *blog.aflcio.org. AFL-CIO,* 1 Sep. 2009. Web. 7 Sep. 2009.

Connolly, Cece. "U.S. Losing Ground on Preventable Deaths." *Washingtonpost. com.* The Washington Post, 6 Oct. 2009. Web. 6 Oct. 2009.

Connor, Steve. "Warning: Oil Supplies are Running Out Fast." *Independent. co.uk.* The Independent [London], 3 Aug. 2009. Web. 4 Aug. 2009.

Costello, Carol. "Small Business Owners Make Big Sacrifices." *CNN.com.* CNN, 25 March 2009. Web. 22 Dec.2009.

Council of State Governments, Re-Entry Policy Council. *Report of the Re-Entry Policy Council: Charting the Safe and Successful Return of Prisoners to the Community.* New York: Council of State Governments, Jan. 2005. Print.

Counselors and Advocates from Drug and Alcohol Rehabilitation Sector. Personal Communications. Fall 2006.

Crane, Randall. "Is There a Quiet Revolution in Women's Travel? Revisiting the Gender Gap in Commuting," *Journal of the American Planning Association.* 73: 3 (2007) 298–316. Print.

Criminal Justice Policy Coalition Newsletter. CJPC.com. Criminal Justice Policy Coalition, July 2005. Web. 20 Feb. 2009.

Crutsinger, Martin. "U.S. Productivity Surges in Second Quarter." *AP.org.* Associated Press, 12 Aug. 2009. Web. 13 Nov. 2009.

Crutsinger, Martin and Jeannine Aversa. "Weekly Jobless Claims Drop Below 500,000." *Forbes.com.* Forbes, 25 Nov. 2009. Web. 30 June 2009.

Cunha, Bob and Phyllis Neufield. "Commentary: Unions Urge Transparency in Health Care Talks." *www.wickedlocal.com.* The Lexington Minuteman [Lexington, MA], 23 April 2009. Web. 4 Jan. 2010.

Curran, Kelly. "New Home Starts Hit Lowest Level Ever." *Housingwire.com.* Housingwire, 18 Dec. 2008. Web. 4 Dec. 2009.

Cylus, Jonathan and Gerard F. Anderson. "Multinational Comparisons of Health Systems Data, 2006." New York: Commonwealth Fund, 2007. Print.

Davis, Carl and Kelly Davis, Matthew Gardner, Robert S. McIntyre, Jeff Lynch and Alla Sapzhnikova. *Who Pays: A Distributional Analysis of the Tax Systems in All 50 States.* Washington, DC: Institute for Taxation and Economic Policy, Nov. 2009. Print.

Day, Benjamin. "Implementation of Massachusetts Health Reform." Boston: Mass-Care, 2008. Print.

Delpla, Jacques. "Who Should, Who Must, Pay to Save the Banks?" *Truthout. com.* Truthout, 26 March 2009. Web. 4 Jan. 2010.

"Derivative." *Wikipedia.* Wikimedia Foundation, 2002. Web. 20 Nov. 2009.

Dimon, Jamie. "Dear Fellow Shareholders." Shareholder letter. J.P. Morgan Chase Bank, New York, NY. 23 March 2009. Print.

Downes, Thomas, Jeff Abel and Dana Ansel. *Incomplete Grade: Massachusetts Education Reform at 15.* Boston: MassINC/Massachusetts Institute for a New Commonwealth, 2009. *Print.*

Eder, Steve. "Study Shows U.S. Bank CEO Pay Dwarfs the Rest of World." *Reuters.com.* Reuters, 23 Sep. 2009. Web. 28 Sep. 2009.

"Education." *Wikipedia.* Wikimedia Foundation, 2001. Web. 14 Dec. 2009.

Ehrlich, Lori. "Swaptions: A train wreck coming down the Pike," *wickedlocal. com.* Marblehead Reporter [Marblehead, MA], 11 March 2009, Web. 10 June 2009.

Environmental League of Massachusetts. *"State of the Environment."* Boston, MA: Environmental League of Massachusetts, 2006. Print.

Environment Massachusetts and Clean Water Fund from the Report of the Senate Committee on Post-Audit and Oversight and the Senate Committee on Global Warming and Climate Change. *The Cost of Inaction: Climate Change in the Commonwealth.* Boston: Commonwealth of Massachusetts, July 2008. Print.

Ettlinger, Michael. "Securing the Wage Floor: Indexing Would Maintain Min Wage Value, Provide Predictability to Employers." *EPI.org. Economic Policy Institute,* 12 Oct. 2006. Web. 7 Dec. 2009.

"Evergreen Solar to Move Jobs to China." Narr. Frannie Carr. WBUR, Providence, 5 Nov. 2009. Audio.

Farrell, John and David Morris. *Energy Self-Reliant States.* Second and expanded edition. Minneapolis, MN: Institute for Local Self-Reliance/ New Rules Project, May 2010. Print.

"FDIC: Number of Troubled Banks Rises to 416." *Marketwatch.* NPR, 27 Aug. 2009. Web. 27 Aug. 2009. MP3 file.

Fischman, Rona. "Ibanez Decision, Round Two." *Boston.com.* Boston Globe [Boston], 15 Oct. 2009. Web. 12 Dec. 2009.

Fountain, Robert. "Single Payer/Medicare for All. V. 1.0." Washington: Institute for Health & Socio-Economic Policy, 2008. Print.

Fournier, Donald and Eileen Westervelt. United States. US Army Corps of Engineers Engineer Research and Development Center. *Energy Trends and Their Implications for U.S. Army Installations. Stinet.dtic.mil.* US Army Corp., Sep. 2005. Web. 25 Nov. 2009.

Gawande, Atul. "The Cost Conundrum: What a Texas Town Can Teach Us About Health Care." *The New Yorker* June 2009. Print.

Gold, Russell, Ben Casselman and Guy Chazan. "Leaking Oil Well Lacked Safeguard Device." *WSJ.com.* Wall Street Journal [New York, NY], 28 April 2010. Web.

Goldstein, Amy. "States Cut Medicaid Further." *WashingtonPost.com.* The Washington Post, 26 Dec. 2008: A01+. Print.

Goodman, Amy. "Facing Foreclosure? Don't Leave. Squat." *SFGate.com.* San Francisco Chronicle, 4 Feb. 2009. Web. 12 Dec. 2009.

Goodman, Peter S. "Reluctance to Spend May Be Legacy of Recession." *NYTimes.com.* New York Times, 29 Aug. 2009. Web. 8 Dec. 2009.

Gosselin, Kenneth. "Job Growth Outlook Worsens; Region Won't Regain Recession Losses Until 2009, Group Predicts." *HartfordCourantcom.* Hartford Courant, 12 May 2006. Web. 12 Dec. 2009.

Gowen, Annie. "Child Poverty Rising, Report Says." *WashingtonPost.com.* Washington Post, 11 July 2009. Web. 13 July 2009.

Green for All and COWS. *A Short Guide to Setting Up a City-Scale Retrofit Program.* Madison: Green for All and COWS, 5 May 2009. Print.

Greenspan, Alan. Testimony to Committee of Government Oversight and Reform." Testimony, U.S. Congress. Washington, DC: Committee of Government Oversight and Reform, 28 Oct. 2008. Web. 7 Dec. 2009.

Greider, William. "Dismantling the Temple." *The Nation.* 20 July 2009. Print.

Grim, Ryan. "Inside IndyMac's Nationalization: A Case Study." *HuffPost.com.* Huffington Post, 24 March 2009. Web. 12 Dec. 2009.

Hartmann, Thom. "The Great Tax Con Job." *HuffPost.com.* Huffington Post, 21 July 2009. Web. 25 July 2009.

"Health Care in Massachusetts: Key Indicators." *Massachusetts Division of Health Care Finance and Policy.* Nov. 2008. Print.

Hedges, Chris. "This Isn't Reform, It's Robbery." *Truthdig.com.* Truthdig, 23 Aug. 2009 Web. 25 Aug. 2009.

Henwood, Doug. "Overconsuming Health." *Left Business Observer,* 120. Aug. 2009. Print.

"High Noon: Geithner v. the American Oligarchs." *Bill Moyers Journal. Narr.* Bill Moyers. PBS, n.d. PBS.org. Web. 30 June 2009.

Hilliard, John. "Part of MCAS Test May be History." *Dailynewstribune.com.* Daily News Tribune [Boston], 24 Feb. 2009. Web. 20 Dec. 2009.

Hoofnagle, Mark. "Are Patients in Universal Healthcare Countries Less Satisfied?" *Scienceblogs.com.* Science Blog, 22 May 2008. Web. 22 May 2009.

Howden, Daniel. "Deforestation: The Hidden Cause of Global Warming." *TheIndependent.co.uk.* The Independent [London], 14 May 2007. Web.

Huang, Chye-Ching, Jason Levitis, and James R. Horney. "*Very Few Small Business Owners Would Face Tax Increases Under President's Budget.*" *CBPP.org.* Center on Budget and Policy Priorities, 28 Feb. 2009. Web. 27 Dec. 2010.

Illinois Oil and Gas Association. *Petroleum Products in our Daily Lives.* Chicago: Illinois Oil and Gas Association, 29 Nov. 2009. PDF file.

IndieBound. "IndieBound FAQ." *IndieBound.org.* IndieBound, 13 Dec. 2009. Web.

In the Loop! Free Newsletter. MassRecycle, the Massachusetts Recycling Coalition Issue. Jan.–Feb. 2008: #3. Print.

In the Loop! Free Newsletter. MassRecycle, the Massachusetts Recycling Coalition Issue. April 2009: #6. Print.

In the Loop! Free Newsletter. MassRecycle, the Massachusetts Recycling Coalition Issue. Oct. 2009: #7. Print.

Internal Revenue Service. "Statistics of Income Bulletin." *IRS.gov.* Internal Revenue Service, Winter 2002–2003, Publication 1136. Web.

Irons, Meaghan. "Economy's Woes Driving More People to Local Food Pantries." *Boston.com.* Boston Globe, 6 Nov. 2009. Web. 12 Dec. 2009.

"Issue 3: Will casinos come to Ohio." ABClocal.go.com/wtvg. WTVG-TV, Toledo, 3 Nov. 2009 Web. 27 Dec. 2009. SWF file.

Jackson, Henry. "Number of Americans on Food Stamps Rises." *AP.org.* Associated Press, 3 Sep. 2009. Web. 5 Sep. 2009.

Jackson, Paul. "JP Morgan's Dimon: Prime Mortgages Look 'Terrible.'" *HousingWire.com.* Housing Wire. Web. 8 Dec. 2009.

Jaffe, Matthew. "23.7 to Fix Financial System?" *Money.* ABC News, 20 July 2009. Web. 13 Dec. 2009.

Jamison, Michael. "BPA: Conservation Saved Enough to Power Small City." *Missoulian.com.* The Missoulian [Missoula, MT], 20 Jan. 2008. Web. 30 July 2009.

Jewell, Mark. "Bristol-Myers Squibb to Build Manufacturing Plant at Devens." *Boston.com.* Boston Globe, 1 June 2006. Web. 27 Dec. 2009.

"JP Morgan Throws 'Toxic' Plan for a Loop."*American Public Media.* Narr. Jeremy Hobson.16 April 2009. Radio.

Juster, Norton. *The Phantom Tollbooth.* New York: Bullseye Books, 1988. Print.

Kaplan, Claire and CEK Strategies. *CORI: Balancing Individual Rights and Public Access.* Boston: Boston Foundation, 2005. Print.

Keim, Walter G. "Prices and Wages." *Journal of the American Statistical Association.* 37.19 (1942). Print.

Kivel, Paul. *You Call This a Democracy?* New York: The Apex Press, 2006. Print.

Klein, Ezra. "The Meat of the Problem." *Washingtonpost.com.* Washington Post, 29 July 2009. Web. 4 Sep. 2009.

Kohl, Rhiana, et. al. "Massachusetts Recidivism Study: A Closer Look at Releases and Returns to Prison." Washington, DC: The Urban Institute, Justice Policy Center, April 2008. Print.

Kozol, Jonathan. "Keynote Address." 24th Annual Worcester County Community Breakfast Honoring the Reverend Martin Luther King, Jr. Quinsigamond Community College and the University of Massachusetts Medical School. Quinsigamond Community College, Worcester, MA. 19 Jan. 2009. Keynote address.

Kristoff, Nicholas. "Unhealthy America." *NYTimes.com.* New York Times, 5 Nov. 2009. Print.

Krugman, Paul. "Introducing This Blog: Conscience of a Liberal." *NYTimes. com.* New York Times, 18 Sep. 2007. Web. 18 Sep. 2007.

Krugman, Paul. *The Return of Depression Economics and The Crisis of 2008.* New York: W.W. Norton & Company, 2009. Print.

Kruger, Louis. "Testimony in Support of House Bill No. 3660: An Act To Improve Assessment And Accountability To Ensure Students Acquire

21ˢᵗ Century Skills." Testimony. Washington, DC: US Congress, 23 June 2009.

Krull, Luisa, Matthew Miller, and Tatiana Serafin. "The World's Billionaires." *Forbes.com.* Forbes Magazine, 11 March 2009. Web.

"Lawrence Textile Strike." *Wikipedia.* Wikimedia Foundation, 2004. Web. 5 Dec. 2009.

Lazar, Kay. "Costs are Keeping Patients from Care." *Boston.com.* Boston *Globe*, 21 June 2009. Print.

Lewis, Jeffrey R. *Coordinating Contracting of Prescription Drugs: A Fiscal and Policy Strategy for the Commonwealth of Virginia.* Washington, DC: Heinz Family Philanthropies, April 2003. Print.

Lieber, James. "What Cooked the World's Economy?" *Villagevoice.com.* The Village Voice [New York], 28 Jan. 2009. Web. 30 March 2009.

Light, Donald. "Global Drug Discovery: Europe is Ahead." *Healthaffairs.org.* Health Affairs 28.5 (2009). Web. 25 Aug. 2009.

Local Shift: Build Local Economies by Purchasing with Purpose. 10% Shift, 12 March 2009. PDF file.

Lovell, Vicky, Kevin Miller, and Claudia Williams. *Valuing Good Health in Massachusetts: The Costs and Benefits of Paid Sick Days.* Washington, DC: Institute for Women's Policy Research, Feb. 2009. Print.

Lubienski, Christopher and Sarah Theule Lubienski. "School Sector and Academic Achievement: A Multilevel Analysis of NAEP Mathematics Data." *American Educational Research Journal* 43.4 (2006). Print.

Madland, David and Karla Walter. *"Unions are Good for the American Economy."* *Americanprogressaction.org.* Center for American Progress, 18 Feb. 2009. Web. 23 Feb. 2009.

"Mass Foreclosures Spiked in '08." *Bizjournals.com.* Boston Business Journal, 21 Jan. 2009. Web. 5 Dec. 2009.

Massachusetts Budget and Policy Center. *Budget Cuts, Taxes, and the Fiscal Crisis.* Boston: Budget and Policy Center, 2003. Print.

Massachusetts Budget and Policy Center. "Budget Transparency and Balance: The FY 2010 Budget Proposals." *Massbudget.org.* Massachusetts Budget and Policy Center, 29 June 2009. Web. 13 Dec. 2009.

Massachusetts Budget and Policy Center. *Facts at a Glance: The Income Tax.* Boston, MA: Massachusetts Budget and Policy Center, 2 April 2009. PDF file.

Massachusetts Budget and Policy Center. *Minimum Wage Increase Could Help Close to a Million Low-Wage Workers.* Boston: Massachusetts Budget and Policy Center, 20 March 2006. PDF file.

Massachusetts Budget and Policy Center. *Property Taxes: Helping Those Who Need it Most.* Policy brief. Boston: Massachusetts Budget and Policy Center, 20 May 2008. PDF file.

Massachusetts Budget and Policy Center. *Slides on State Taxes.* Boston, MA: Mass. Budget and Policy Center. Feb. 2008. Web.

Massachusetts Housing and Shelter Alliance. *Home & Healthy for Good: A Statewide Housing First Program.* Boston: Massachusetts Housing and Shelter Alliance, 2009. Print.

Massachusetts Law Reform Institute. *Fact Sheet: Food Stamps/SNAP: A Fork-Ready Stimulus.* Boston: Mass Legal Services, 19 March 2009. Web. 30 May 2009.

Massachusetts Recycling Coalition. *The State of Waste in Massachusetts.* Boston: Massachusetts Recycling Coalition, n.d. Print.

Massachusetts Senior Action Council. *Home Care For All! Invest in Equal Choice and Community First.* Boston: Massachusetts Senior Action Council, May 2009. Print.

McBride, Bill. "March Employment Report: 162K Jobs Added, 9.7% Unemployment Rate." *Calculatedriskblog.com* Calculated Risk, April 2010. Web. 15 May 2010

McLynch, Jeff and James R. St. George. *Gone With the Wind: Massachusetts' Vanishing Corporate Income Tax.* Boston: Massachusetts Budget and Policy Center, 2003. Print.

Medical News. "8.3% of Households in Massachusetts Struggle with Food Insecurity." *News-Medical.net.* The Medical News, 20 Nov. 2009. Web. 4 Dec. 2009.

Medoff, Peter and Holly Sklar. *Streets of Hope: The Rise and Fall of an Urban Neighborhood.* Cambridge: South End Press, 1999.

Mencimer, Stephanie. "Bigoted Banks 0, Eliot Spitzer 1." *Motherjones.com.* Mother Jones, n.d. Web. 25 Aug. 2009.

Meyer, Carlton. "America's 20 Percent Unemployment Rate." *Truthout.org.* Truthout, 6 April 2009. Web. 24 April 2009.

Meyer, Josh. "FBI Expects Number of Major Financial Bailout Fraud Cases to Rise." *Latimes.com.* Los Angeles Times, 11 Feb. 2009. Web.

Minnesota Department of Employee Relations. *Minnesota Local Government Pay Equity Compliance Report* Saint Paul, MN: Minnesota Legislature, January 2009. Submitted to the Minnesota Legislature, January 2009.

Mishel, Lawrence. *Agenda for Shared Prosperity.* Washington, DC: Economic Policy Institute, 2009. 30 March 2009. Print.

Mishel, Lawrence. *Waging Inequality in America.* Washington, DC: Economic Policy Institute. 30 March 2009. Print.

Mishel, Lawrence and Matthew Walters. *How Unions Help All Workers.* Washington, DC: Economic Policy Institute, 13 Aug. 2003. Print.

Money as Debt. Dir. Paul Grignon. Lifeboat News/Moonfire Studio. Web. 23 Feb. 2009.

Monkerud, Don. "US Income Inequality Continues to Grow." *Cap Times.* The Capital Times, 17 July 2009. Web. 13 Nov. 2009.

Montenegro, Maywa. "The Big Three: The Numbers Behind Ethanol, Cellulosic Ethanol, and Biodiesel in the U.S." *Grist.org.* Grist Magazine [Seattle], 4 Dec. 2006. Web.

Mortgage Repairs Lag Far Behind Foreclosures. Center for Responsible Lending. Web. 4 Dec. 2009.

Motavalli, Jim. "The Costs of Owning a Car." *NYTimes.com.* New York Times, 18 March 2009. Web. 13 Dec. 2009.

Mui, Ylan. "New Coalition Targets Policies of Wal-Mart." *Washingtonpost.com.* Washington Post, 2 Sep. 2009. Web. 13 Nov. 2009.

Myers, Stacy. "Feds Look into Mortgage Fraud." *Boston.com.* Boston Globe, 16 Oct. 2008. Web. 13 Dec. 2009.

Nardin, Rachel. "Massachusetts' Plan: A Failed Model for Health Care Reform." *PNHP.org.* Physicians for a National Health Plan, n.d. Web. 13 March 2009.

National Low Income Housing Coalition. *Foreclosure in Massachusetts: Properties, Units, and Tenure.* National Low Income Housing Coalition, 9 May 2008. Web. 13 Dec. 2009.

National Nurses Movement. "A Secret Exposed, Medicare Works Better Than Private Insurance." *TPMcafe.talkingpointsmemo.com.* Talking Points Memo, 13 July 2009. Web. 25 Nov. 2009.

New York City Department of Homeless Services. *HOPE 2010: The NYC Street Survey.* 2010. Web. 4 March 2010.

Nichols, John. "Single-Payer Health Care Would Stimulate Economy." *Nation. com.* The Nation, 15 Jan. 2009. Web. 25 Nov. 2009.

Norman, Al. "Wal-Mart's Self-Dealing Income Tax Scam North Carolina Court Tosses Out $33.5 Million Case." *HuffingtonPost.com.* Huffington Post, 8 Jan. 2008. Web. 30 March 2009.

Nothaft, Frank E. "Subprime and Alt-A volume quintupled 2001 to 2006, then fell from 2006 to 2008." Presentation. 7 Oct. 2008. *Beyond the Crisis.* Milken Institute's Financial Innovations Lab on Housing. McLean, VA: Freddie Mac. 29. Print.

Obama, Barack. "Inaugural address." Presidential inaugural Address. *Whitehouse.gov.* 21 Jan. 2009. Web. 9 Dec. 2009.

Orszag, Peter and Joseph E. Stiglitz. "Biting the Budget Bullet: Why Raising Taxes Is the Least Painful Way Out of the State's Fiscal Crisis." *Boston. com.* Boston Globe, 27 April 2003. Web.

Orszag, Peter and Joseph E. Stiglitz. *Budget Cuts vs. Tax Increases at the State Level: Is One More Counter-Productive Than the Other During a Recession?* Washington, DC: Center on Budget and Policy Priorities, 2001.

Pateakos, Jay. "Final Section of Providence Way Project Opens Tuesday." *Heraldnews.com.* The Herald News [Providence], 13 Oct. 2009. Web. 4 Nov. 2009.

Paulson, Derek and Ronald Wilson. "Foreclosures and Crime: A Geographical Perspective." *Geography and Public Safety* 1.3 (Oct. 2008). Web. 13 Dec. 2009.

Pearce, Diana with Johanna Brooks in partnership with Wider Opportunities for Women. *Self-Sufficiency Standard Report for Massachusetts.* Boston: Women's Educational and Industrial Union, 2003. 12 Dec. 2009. PDF file.

Pepitone, Julianne. "Bank Failures Stack Up: Now 106 for 2009." *CNN.com.* CNN, 29 Oct. 2009. Web. 14 Nov. 2009.

Petz, Scholtus. "Barcelona's Bike Sharing Program Celebrates its 2-Year Anniversary with its 186,000 Users." *Treehugger.com.* Treehugger, 19 March 2009. Web.

Pew Center on the States. *One in 31: The Long Reach of American Corrections.* Washington, DC: The Pew Charitable Trust, March 2009. Print.

Pisarski, Alan E. "Commuting in America III: The Third National Report on Commuting Patterns and Trends." *TRB.org.* TRB.org, *Transportation Research Board of the National Academies,* Nov. 2006. Web. 5 Jan. 2009.

Pitt, Harvey. "The Financial Crises: CEOs Discuss Competition and Inclusivity in Today's Market," Charting New Pathways to Participation & Membership conference, The Charles Hamilton Houston Institute, Harvard University, Boston, MA, opening remarks, 17 Oct. 2008. Web. Dec. 2009

Pollack, Ethan. *A Meaningful Stimulus for Main Street.* Washington, DC: Economic Policy Institute, 18 June 2009. Print.

Powell, Michael. "Bank Accused of Pushing Mortgage Deals on Blacks." *NYTimes.com.* New York Times, 6 June 2009. Web. 7 Dec. 2009.

Powell, Michael. "Blacks in Memphis Lose Decades of Economic Gains." *NYTimes.com.* New York Times, 7 Dec. 2009. Web. 31 May 2010.

Price Waterhouse Coopers' Health Research Initiative. *Behind the Numbers: Medical Cost Trends 2010.* Washington, DC: Price Waterhouse Coopers', June 2009. Web. 4 Jan. 2010.

Prokosch, Mike. "Presentation on the Economic Crisis." 2008. Power point presentation.

Rampell, Catherine. "U.S. Health Spending Breaks from the Pack." *NYTimes.com.* New York Times, 8 July 2009. Web. 7 Aug. 2009.

Raphael, Ray. *The First American Revolution.* New York: The New Press, 2002. Print.

"Recession's End Won't Stop Job Loss Pain." *CBSNews.com.* CBS News, 27 Oct. 2009. Web. 4 Jan. 2010. Television.

Reich, Robert. "Financing the Common Good." *Prospect.org.* The American Prospect, 1 Feb. 2008. Web. 17 April 2009.

Reich, Robert. "Why We Need Stronger Unions and How to Get Them." *Robertreich.com.* RobertReich, 27 Jan. 2009. Web. 4 Jan. 2010.

"Report: $9M In Stimulus For Gillette Footbridge?" *WBZTV.com.* WBZ Television, 7 Nov. 2009. Web. 27 Dec. 2009.

"Residential Customers: Energy Facts." *MassSAVE.com.* MassSAVE, n.d. Web. 13 Dec. 2009.

Reuters Research. "Banking Compensation." Reuters. *Reuters Research,* n.d. Web. 13 Nov. 2009.

"Riding the Rails: Timeline of the Great Depression, 1929–1932." *The American Experience: The 1930s,* Herbert Hoover, Nov. 1929. *PBS.org.* PBS, n.d. Web. 3 Dec. 2009.

Ritholtz, Barry. "Why are People Calling a Bottom for Real Estate?" *Ritholtz. com.* The Big Picture, *18 July 2009.* Web. 10 Aug. 2009.

Rivera, Amaad, Jeannette Huezo, Christina Kasica, and Dedrick Muhammad. "The Silent Depression: State of the Dream 2009." Boston: United for a Fair Economy, 2009. Print.

Rogers, Everett M. *Diffusion of Innovations.* Glencoe, IL: Free Press, 1962. Print.

Rose, Stephen J. *American Profile Poster* excerpt. © Copyright 2005, Stephen J. Rose. PDF file.

Rose, Stephen J. *Social Stratification in the United States: The American Profile Poster.* Second edition. New York: New Press, 2007. Print.

Rothstein, Richard. "When There's Not Enough Food for Thought," New York Times, 1 Aug. 2001. Print.

Saez, Emmanuel and Thomas Piketty, "Income Inequality in the United States, 1913–1998." Tables and figures updated to 2008 in July 2010. *The Quarterly Journal of Economics* 118.1 (2003)

Saez, Emmanuel. "Striking it Richer: The Evolution of Top Incomes in the United States". *Pathways.* Stanford University, Center for the Study of Poverty and Inequality. Winter 2008.

Safe Car Guide, "New or Used—What's Best for me?" *Safecarguide.com.* Safe Car Guide, n.d. Web. 12 Dec. 2009.

Sanati, Cyrus. "Merging Banks Soar Past U.S. Deposit Cap." *NYTimes.com.* New York Times, 17 Oct. 2008. Web. 27 Jan. 2009.

Sanders, Bernie. "Billions for Bailouts! Who Pays?" *Huffingtonpost.com.* Huffington Post, 19 Sep. 2008. Web. 7 Dec. 2009.

Schepp, David. "Wal-Mart to Pay $40 Million to Settle Labor Lawsuit in Massachusetts." *DailyFinance.com.* Daily Finance, 3 Dec. 2009. Web. 4 Jan. 2010.

Schmitt, John and Nathan Lane. *An International Comparison of Small Business Employment. CEPR.net.* Center for Economic and Policy Research, Aug. 2009. Web.

Schoen, Cathy, Sara R. Collins, Jennifer L. Kriss, and Michelle M. Doty. "How Many Are Underinsured? Trends Among U.S. Adults, 2003 and 2007." *Health Affairs* 27.4 (2008). Print.

Serreze, Mary. "Biomass or Biomess?" *ValleyAdvocate.com.* Valley Advocate [Northampton, MA], 30 June 2009. Web. 4 Jan. 2010.

Shedlock, Mike. "Charting the US Recession Unemployment Crisis." *Marketoracle.co.uk.* Market Oracle, 6 Aug. 2009. Web. 10 Dec. 2009.

Shierholz, Heidi. "New 2008 Poverty, Income Data Reveal Only Tip of The Recession Iceberg." Washington, DC: Economic Policy Institute, 10 Sep. 2009. Print.

Shrank, David and Tim Lomax. *"Performance Measure Summary Boston, MA-NH-RI: Urban Area Report.* Texas: Central Texas Regional Mobility Authority, 2007. Print.

Siefert, Ed. "Late-breaking Letters: Greenspan Could Have Acted to Shut Down Sub-Prime Market." *Ocregister.com.* The Orange County Register, 14 Sep. 2007. Web. 7 Dec. 2009.

Sinclair, Shelly-Ann. "The Costs of Doing Nothing: What's at Stake Without Health Care Reform." Washington,, DC: American Association of Retired Professionals Public Policy Institute, 2008. Print.

Sisko, Andrea, Christopher Truffer, Sheila Smith, Sean Keehan, Jonathan Cylus, John A. Poisal, M. Kent Clemens and Joseph Lizonitz. "Health Spending Projections Through 2018: Recession Effects Add Uncertainty To The Outlook." *Healthaffairs.org.* Health Affairs, 7 Aug. 2009: 28.2.

State of Illinois, Chicago Department of Environment. *Data Comparison Between the City Hall Rooftop Garden and the Black Tar Roof of the Cook County Building.* Chicago: Department of Environment, 2001. Print.

Stein, Eric. "Turmoil in the U.S. Credit Markets: The Genesis of the Current Economic Crisis." Testimony. Senate Committee on Banking, Housing and Urban Affairs, Washington, DC. 2008.

Stone, Rob. "Healthcare Reform: We're Still for It, and We're Not Done Yet!" June 2008. Print.

Tannenwald, Robert. "State Business Tax Climate: How Should it Be Measured and How Important Is It." *New England Economic Review.* Federal Reserve Bank of Boson. (January/February 1996). Web. 4 Nov. 2009.

Taunter. "Unconscionable Math." *Tauntermedia.com.* Taunter Media, 28 July 2009. Web. 8 Aug. 2009.

Tax Policy Center, Urban Institute and Brookings Institution. *Percent of Tax Filers by Marginal Tax Rate. Taxpolicycenter.org.* Tax Policy Center, 12 Dec. 2009. Web.

"Technology Quarterly." *The Economist*. 9 June 2007. Print.

Tetrault, Janna and Ann Verrilli. "Addressing the Foreclosure Crisis: State and Federal Initiatives in Massachusetts." *Chapa.org*. Citizen's Housing and Planning Association/CHAPA, March 2008. Web. 13 Dec. 2009.

Thompson, Michael. "Voter Turnout: Other Nations Overshadow U.S." *AssociatedContent.com*. Associated Content, 4 Nov. 2008. Web. 13 Dec. 2009.

Tomsho, Robert. "Winds Shift in Energy Debate." *WSJ.com*. Wall Street Journal, 19 June 2008. Web. July 2010.

"Trade union." *Wikipedia*. Wikimedia Foundation. 2001. Web. 30 Aug. 2009.

TRIP. *Future Mobility in Massachusetts: Meeting the State's Need for Safe and Efficient Mobility*. Washington, DC: TRIP, June 2008. Print.

Union of Concerned Scientists. *Massachusetts: Confronting Climate Change in the U.S. Northeast*. Boston: Northeast Climate Impacts Assessment, 2007. Print.

Union of Minority Neighborhoods. *www.unionofminorityneighborhoods.org*. Web. 12 Dec. 2009.

United States Department of Agriculture Forest Service, Northeast Area State and Private Forestry, PA and Mid-Atlantic Center for Urban and Community Forestry. "The Value of Trees." *Urban and Community Forestry Appreciation Tool Kit. Parksandpeople.org*. Parks and People Foundation, n.d. Web. 13 Dec. 2009.

United States Department of Energy, Energy Efficiency and Renewable Energy. "Electric Power and Renewable Energy in Massachusetts." *EERE.energy. gov*. EERE State Activities & Partnerships, 25 June 2008. *Web.*

United States Department of Housing and Urban Development. *HomeBase Focuses on Housing Development. HUD Research Works, 27* Nov. 2009. Web.

United States Office of Federal Housing Enterprise Oversight. *Coast to Coast Home Prices are Down and Families Have Lost Wealth from 2007–2009. CBO.gov. Congressional Budget Office*, April 2008.

Urbina, Ian. "Despite Moratorium, Drilling Projects Move Ahead." *NYTimes. com*. New York Times, 23 May 2010. Web. 20 Aug 2010.

Van Tol, Jesse. "Multi-Trillion Dollar Lifeline "Saves" Wall Street, Homeowners Left to Fail." *NCRC.org*. National Community Reinvestment Coalition, 14 Sep. 2009. Web. 4 Jan. 2010.

Wallack, Todd. "Stricter Rules for Mortgage Brokers Keep Hundreds Out." *Boston.com*. Boston Globe, 9 July 2009. Web. 8 Dec. 2009.

Walsh, Bryan. "Denmark's Wind of Change." *Time.com*. Time Magazine, 25 Feb. 2009. Web. 4 Jan. 2010.

The Warren Group. *"Mass. Foreclosures Jump In October From Prior Month, But Dip From a Year Ago." Thewarrengroup.com.* The Warren Group, 11 Nov. 2009. Web. 13 Dec. 2009.

Weil, Elizabeth. "Grumpy Old Drug Smugglers." *NYTimes.com.* New York Times, 30 May 2004. Web.

Welna, David. "Democrats Push to End Insurers' Antitrust Exemption." *Morning Edition.* National Public Radio. 23 Oct. 2009. Web. 27 Dec. 2009.

Western Regional Advocacy Project. *Without Housing: Decades of Federal Housing Cutbacks, Massive Homelessness, and Policy Failures.* San Francisco: Western Regional Advocacy Project, 2006. Print.

Wheeler, Sam. "Prison Suicide Hearing at MA State House." *Boston.indymedia. org.* Boston Indymedia, 11 May 2007. Audio report.

"Where Does All the Bailout and Stimulus Money Come From?" *PBS Newshour. PBS.* 18 March 2009. Web. 4 Dec. 2009.

Wiggin, Addison and Ian Mathias. "The Second Wave of the Housing Crisis, Profiting from Carbon Caps, U.S. is "Out of Money," lunch with Ron Paul and more." *5minforecast.agorafinancial.com. Agora Financial.* 26 May 2009. Web.

Willen, Paul. *Making Sense of the Subprime Crisis.* Boston, *The Research Bureau,* 13 Nov. 2008. Print.

Williams, John. "Alternate Unemployment Charts," *Shadowstats.com.* Shadow Government Statistics, n.d. Web. 7 Dec. 2009.

Williams, John. *Inflation, Money Supply, GDP, Unemployment and the Dollar – Alternate Data Series.* Shadow Government Statistics, n.d. Web. 7 Dec. 2009.

The Working Group on Extreme Inequality. *Inequality By the Numbers.* Boston, MA: Institute on Policy Studies, The Program on Inequality and the Common Good, Oct. 2009.

Zhenguo Lin, Eric Rosenblatt, and Vincent W. Yao, "Spillover Effects of Foreclosures on Neighborhood Property Values," *Journal of Real Estate Finance and Economics,* 38: 4 (2009). Web. 13 Dec. 2009.

Zillow. "Massachusetts Home Prices and Home Values-Local Info." *Zillow.com.* Zillow, n.d. Web. 2 Nov. 2009.

Index